JEAN-PIERRE MELVILLE

'An American in Paris'

Ginette Vincendeau

First published in 2003 by the British Film Institute
21 Stephen Street, London W1T 1LN

Reprinted 2006

The British Film Institute promotes greater understanding of, and access to, film and moving image culture in the UK.

Cover design by Barefoot
Cover images: (front) Jean-Pierre Melville in the 1960s; (back) *Le Doulos* (1963); *Le Samouraï* (1967); *Léon Morin, prêtre* (1961); *Le Deuxième souffle* (1966)

Set by Fakenham Photosetting Limited, Fakenham, Norfolk NR21 8NN
Printed in the UK by St Edmundsbury Press, Bury St Edmunds, Suffolk

British Library Cataloguing-in-Publication Data
A catalogue record for this book is available from the British Library

ISBN 0 85170 949 4 (pbk)
ISBN 0 85170 950 8 (hbk)

Contents

Acknowledgments

I want to thank first of all people who in different ways shared their views on Melville with me: Olivier Bohler, who let me read his impressive thesis (which I hope will soon be published); Colin McArthur, whose early work on Melville and more recently on *Le Samouraï* was an inspiration; and Rick Menello, with whom I had a lively internet exchange. I am also endebted to several groups of students at the University of Warwick; as well as bringing their own insights, they often helped me clarify my thoughts.

I am very grateful to Monsieur Jacques Nataf, who talked to me about his time with Melville in the Free French army, and to Véronique and Michel Bourdis-Gispalou and Monsieur Michel Bourdis, who helped me track him down.

Jean-Louis Vincendeau, Peter Graham and Geneviève Sellier, as usual, were a precious source of essential video recordings. For their help in providing video and other material, thanks also to Dudley Andrew, Anne Boston, Annette Caulkin, Klaus Davidowicz, Renée and Jonathan Fenby, Susan Hayward, David Horrocks, Simon Horrocks, Carol Jenks, Sylvie Lindeperg, Laurent Marie, Michel Marie, Silke Panse and Ulrike Sieglohr.

The writing of this book was supported by a term of leave from the University of Warwick and a term from the AHRB. Charlotte Brunsdon and Ed Gallafent were supportive heads of department, enabling me to obtain study leave and benefit from research assistance. Other colleagues deserve thanks, in particular José Arroyo, Jon Burrows, Erica Carter, Richard Dyer and V. F. Perkins. Special thanks to Tracey Bale and Richard Perkins, who were extremely patient and helpful with my endless requests for more videos and books.

For research assistance, many thanks go to Theodora Hadjiandreou, Min Lee, Barbara Lehin, Valerie Orpen, Nick Potamitis and Leila Wimmer. In Paris, Pierre Chaintreuil and Thérèse Duhin kindly let me consult the censorship files on Melville's films at the Centre National de la Cinématographie, and Régis Robert and the staff at the Bibliothèque du Film (BIFI) archives were also helpful in providing access to Melville's scripts.

Jim Cook, Alastair Phillips and Tom Brown read parts of the manuscript of this book and gave invaluable feedback. Part of the work now in Chapter 6 was developed for a chapter in Alex Hughes and James Williams' book *Gender and French Cinema* (Oxford and New York: Berg, 2001), and discussed at Phil Powrie's conference on masculinity (University of Newcastle, July 2001), as well as at research seminars at the University of Kent, East Anglia and Essex.

At the BFI, sincere thanks to Andrew Lockett for being such a supportive and patient editor, and to Sophia Contento for her diligent work with illustrations. For their support and interest in Melville, thanks to Geoff Andrew, Philip Kemp and Hilary Smith at the NFT, London, and Geraldine d'Amico, Julien Plante and Vincent Mellili at the Institut Français, London.

Finally, none of this would have been possible without Simon Caulkin's editorial, intellectual, emotional, technological and gastronomic support.

NOTE TO THE READER

References throughout the book are as complete as possible. However, a number of daily and weekly press references do not indicate a page number. This is because they were obtained from the database at BIFI (Bibliothèque du Film) in which the scanning of articles has deleted page numbers. Readers wishing to consult the full articles are directed to the BIFI Library (100, rue du Fg Saint-Antoine, 75012 Paris) which offers fast and convenient on-line access to the material. The Bibliothèque Nationale de France holds full issues of the papers but is more difficult to access.

All translations from the French are mine, unless reference is given to a published English version.

Brief accounts of film plots can be found within the chapters at the beginning of each film analysis. A more detailed version of plot summaries is available in the filmography at the end of the book.

Introduction: Jean-Pierre Melville, 'An American in Paris'

Jean-Pierre Melville (1917–73) made thirteen feature films between 1947 and 1972, most of them ranking among the best in post-war French cinema. As a young man, he directed a poetic adaptation of Cocteau's classic *Les Enfants terribles* (1950). His thrillers *Bob le flambeur* (1956), *Le Doulos* (1963) and *Le Samouraï* (1967) among others, with their cool noir style, are defining instances of the French *policier*. In a different mode, *Le Silence de la mer* (1947–9) and *L'Armée des ombres* (1969) are revered classics of Resistance cinema. A supreme master of style, Melville was a 'film-maker's film-maker', as this comment from *L'Express* confirms: 'Each time Jean-Pierre Melville releases a new film, all filmmakers, including those who hate him, book a seat to see "how it's done".'[1] The brilliance of Melville's work alone would be reason enough to write a book about him.

While many of his films were highly successful at the box-office, Melville's critical reputation suffered spectacular ups and downs, ranging from being credited as 'father of the New Wave' to disparagement and oblivion for decades. Yet recently, his critical currency has dramatically risen again, both in France and internationally. Prominent figures like Quentin Tarantino and John Woo have paid tribute to his influence. In 1999, Jim Jarmusch's *Ghost Dog, The Way of the Samurai* was in homage to *Le Samouraï*, and in the spring of 2003, Neil Jordan brought out a remake of *Bob le flambeur* (*The Good Thief*). This roller-coaster critical fate is another reason for delving into Melville's films, and assessing the critical debates they provoked.

One positive effect of Melville's renewed reputation is that his films have become more widely seen. *Le Samouraï* was reissued in the UK in 1996, to great acclaim. After decades of patchy availability, all Melville's films can now be viewed on video, some on film and, increasingly, on DVD (as a final piece in the puzzle, the internet delivered to me Melville's rare 1946 short *24 heures de la vie d'un clown*). This easier availability makes an exhaustive study possible.

This book is a critical study of Melville's films, the first in the English language. A film-maker with an exceptional degree of control over his work (he owned his own studio), Melville is a clear case of an auteur who created a unique film universe. The sub-title of this book, 'An American in Paris', is an ironic comment on Melville's well-known Americanophilia and the deployment of the Hollywood gangster iconography in his movies. While I refute the cliché that Melville 'copied' American cinema, my project is to place his films within a transnational film culture.

A LOOK, A NAME, AN ATTITUDE

The photograph which illustrates the cover of this book concentrates the complex and fascinating identities of Jean-Pierre Melville the man and Jean-Pierre Melville the authorial voice, as well as the themes that run through this book.

Melville, wearing a Stetson hat, ostensibly reads an issue of the journal *Arts*. Large letters on the cover spell out 'Melville accuses Truffaut'. What does this image tell us? That Melville liked dressing in a way which proclaimed, as if in quotation marks, an 'American-ness' derived from the Western. Many other photos and André S. Labarthe's documentary[2] show him wearing the Stetson, often with dark glasses and a trench-coat – so we are also in a film noir – while roaming the streets of Paris in a huge, open-top American car (although he owned other flashy, but less cinematic cars, such as a Rolls-Royce). Melville's 'American-ness' is the identity most frequently attached to his films, but his dress sense tells us that he could put it on and take it off as he wished.

Melville's American-ness is also, of course, displayed in his name. Jean-Pierre Grumbach adopted the name Melville as both a *nom de guerre* (he took it, he says, when he joined the Resistance) and a *nom de plume*, because of his admiration for the novelist Herman Melville. That a young, highly cultured Parisian would choose the name of an American novelist as a pseudonym in the early 1940s is not in itself surprising, given the prestige American literature held among French intellectuals. We may speculate on personal similarities with Herman Melville, by all accounts like Jean-Pierre a brilliant maverick and solitary character. But is it a coincidence that he took a name that sounds French? 'Melville' turns out to be a Norman name (derived from a village called Malville in Normandy), which emigrated to Scotland in the twelfth century, and then on to the United States.[3] Thus if Melville was canny in taking up an American name that sounds French – 'Hawthorne' or 'Faulkner' could have been awkward – there is a pleasing historical parallel between the transatlantic journey of his adopted name and the transnational identity of his cinema.

Finally, the photograph tells us that, apart from a mischievous sense of self-dramatisation, Melville was a cinephile who was involved in a critical dialogue with the New Wave, represented by its most prominent figure François Truffaut. If we turn to the inside of the magazine, we find a piece in which, under the guise of reviewing Truffaut's book on Hitchcock, Melville talks, with regret, about their split after a period of friendship. At the time of the article (December 1966), Truffaut's box-office currency was down after *Fahrenheit 451*, but Melville's very much up: a month earlier he had released his greatest hit so far, *Le Deuxième souffle*. The picture thus also concentrates Melville's dual identity on the film scene, as a successful mainstream film-maker and someone ready to enter the fray of critical debates in an arts journal.

WRITING ABOUT MELVILLE

Despite Melville's flamboyant personality, this book does not attempt a biography, partly because of the paucity of available sources and partly because Melville was someone whose life was largely subsumed by his films.

A cinephile, Melville occasionally wrote critical pieces on his own and others' film-making. He was also interviewed at length. In fact the only book about him previously available in English is the series of interviews – on the Hitchcock/Truffaut model – by critic Rui Nogueira, first published in 1971, and a precious source of information. Also of note is Colin McArthur's very useful chapter on Melville in his seminal book *Underworld USA* (1972) and more recent work on *Le Samouraï* (2000). Unsurprisingly there have been a few more books on Melville in French. Jean Wagner wrote a pioneering study, though one limited by its admiring tone and time-scale, as it was published in 1963. Twenty years later came Jacques Zimmer and Chantal de Béchade's *Jean-Pierre Melville*, a useful journalistic précis rather than an in-depth analysis, and later still Denitza Bantcheva's more original account, *Jean-Pierre Melville: de l'oeuvre à l'homme* (1996). Bantcheva's study contains interesting insights though she tends to refrain from detailed textual analysis and, like Wagner, is reluctant to take a critical view. More recently, Olivier Bohler generously allowed me to read his outstanding PhD thesis, the most detailed and insightful study so far. I have read all these with great interest and I hope I do them justice in the course of this book (more references are contained in the bibliography). There have also been numerous interviews with, and articles about, Melville and his films (most of these in French), in publications ranging from *Cahiers du cinéma* and other specialist film journals, to the French daily and weekly press. A pleasing, though poignant by-product of this research was to renew acquaintance with the exceptionally high quality of film reviews in the 1950s and 60s press, remarkable in itself and remarkably better than what often passes for film reviewing today.

In adding my voice to those who have been fascinated by Melville's work, and to Melville's own comments, I cannot claim total originality. I do however bring my own perspective, as outlined below and, while hugely admiring Melville's work, try to break from the reverential tone of much writing on him.

The book is divided into six chapters. Chapter 1 is an account of Melville's life, career and overall critical trajectory. Chapters 2 to 6 carve out his films in blocks of two or three, an approach which made more sense than a strict film-by-film chronology, though we start at the beginning and end on the last thriller. Chapter 2 looks at Melville's short *24 heures de la vie d'un clown*, his adaptation of Cocteau's *Les Enfants terribles* and the melodrama *Quand tu liras cette lettre* (1953). I argue that these films are '*exercices de style*' with which Melville explores various forms in order to find his stylistic bearings. Chapter 3, 'Melville's War', looks at his three films about the Resistance: *Le Silence de la mer*, *Léon Morin, prêtre* (1961) and *L'Armée des ombres*. Bringing these films – made across the whole of Melville's career – together allows for an overview of Melville's evolving style as well as changing attitude to World War II. Chapters 4, 5 and 6 look at the great body of Melville's thrillers. Chapter 4 explores three films that I see as located 'between the New Wave and America': *Bob le flambeur*, *Deux hommes dans Manhattan* (1959) and *L'Ainé des Ferchaux* (1963). Chapter 5 examines Melville's two films which are actual adaptations of the Série Noire, *Le Doulos* and *Le Deuxième souffle* (1966). Chapter 6 is about the 'Delon Trilogy': *Le Samouraï*, *Le Cercle rouge* (1970) and *Un flic* (1971). The Conclusion attempts a synthesising view of the Melvillian style.

Cutting across Melville's body of work are four approaches which reverberate through the book in ever-increasing concentric circles: film style, popular French cinema, national/transnational film-making, identity/gender.

Film style

My first level of concern is to provide a close and detailed account of Melville's style. Framing, camera movements, lighting, the use of location shooting and of studio sets, and other aspects of *mise en scène* are scrutinised, in an attempt to pin down Melville's original 'style', its evolution across time and its relationship to contemporary films, where relevant comparisons can be made. This textual approach is not a simple formalist exercise; I aim to articulate it with a contextual approach, within the areas defined below.

Popular French cinema

As evinced by his box-office record (which I indicate in an appendix and comment on at various points in the book), Melville, for a significant part of his career, mastered the codes of popular French cinema. At the same time, the startling originality of his *mise en scène* and prevailing pessimism placed him apart from the mainstream. This duality, which could be rephrased as that of classicism vs modernism, classicism vs 'mannerism', constitutes a crucial aspect of his work. In order to gauge Melville's specificity in this respect, throughout the book I place his work in relation to other French films of the period. Here I consider two important aspects which embed Melville further in popular French film culture. First is the literature on which many of his films are based, both high (Vercors, Cocteau) and popular (Simenon, the Série Noire). Second are film stars. From *Léon Morin, prêtre* in 1961, Melville worked with stars of the calibre of Jean-Paul Belmondo, Lino Ventura, Charles Vanel, Yves Montand and Alain Delon – stars who, beyond their box-office appeal, had a significant impact on the meaning of the films.

National/transnational identity

A view of Melville's films cannot remain solely within the French film industry, but must consider his place within a wider French culture, and an international context. Melville's French-ness was deeply marked by World War II, both as a soldier, and as someone who lived and worked in post-war France, and I trace this legacy especially in Chapter 3 but also throughout all his work. Melville was also an international figure, deeply marked by America in his cultural references and practice. His thrillers (like his person) celebrated the cars, guns and attire of the American gangster, even though he was at pains to point out, tongue in cheek: 'My cinema is specifically French. When I read the opposite, I am amazed. I look in my films for what is American about them and I cannot find anything.'[4] Rather than a crude division of 'French' and 'American' (or other cultural references), I try to see how, at different moments of his career, Melville engaged with the transnational culture of his time, in which, nevertheless, a (largely imaginary and definitely cinematic) 'America' looms large.

Identity/gender

It would be hard to miss the masculine – not to say masculinist – focus of Melville's work, especially the post-*Léon Morin, prêtre* films. But this obviousness has somehow inhibited analysis. Throughout the book I consider masculinity in Melville's films, and more generally bring a gender perspective to all aspects of his films, for example, his portrayal of his war films' heroines. Here my approach, I hope, usefully bridges a gap between Anglo-American and French studies of Melville. In the Anglo-American context, writers such as Steve Neale and Stella Bruzzi have considered aspects of Melville's films (notably *Le Samouraï*) in gender terms. Their important insights, however, have been limited by their restricted focus. In the French context, writers have ignored gender or denied its importance in the name of a 'defence' of Melville (as if analysing gender in the films boiled down to accusing Melville of misogyny[5]).

Writing this book, watching Melville's films again and again, each time brought renewed pleasure, discoveries and comfort, especially after seeing some particularly nasty, needlessly sexual or just ugly contemporary film. However bleak, Melville's work is always beautiful, stylish and profound, in a surprisingly modern way. I hope this journey through his films will bring some light to those familiar with his work, and inspire those who are not to discover this brilliant and wonderful film-maker.

NOTES

1. *L'Express*, 15 September 1969.
2. André S. Labarthe, *Jean-Pierre Melville: Portrait en 9 poses* (1970).
3. 'Melville', in Patrick Hanks and Flavia Hodges (eds), *A Dictionary of First Names* (Oxford: Oxford University Press, 1990).
4. In François Guérif, 'Jean-Pierre Melville', *Les Cahiers de la cinémathèque*, no. 25, Spring–Summer 1978, p. 96.
5. See Jacques Zimmer and Chantal de Béchade, *Jean-Pierre Melville* (Paris: Edilig, 1983), p. 33 and Denitza Bantcheva, *Jean-Pierre Melville: de l'oeuvre à l'homme* (Troyes: Librairie Bleue, 1996), p. 51. This issue is discussed further in Chapter 1.

1

From Film Lover to Film-maker: The Life and Career of Jean-Pierre Melville

The details of Jean-Pierre Melville's life are sketchy and ambiguous – he deliberately cultivated mystery, and the meagre sources that exist are mostly interviews, with all the possibilities for biases, exaggeration and contradiction that such encounters contain. Since this book is a study of Melville's films, not a biography, this may not matter. It is also the case that to a remarkable degree, Melville was someone whose life *was* his work. The man who hated holidays, about whom Volker Schloendorff (his assistant on *Léon Morin, prêtre* and *Le Doulos*) reflected, 'He had an almost religious passion for the cinema. Everything related to it,'[1] this man coined the word 'opocentric' – 'opo' from opus – about himself and confirmed, 'Nothing matters except my profession and therefore my work.'[2] Indeed when, on 2 August 1973, at the age of fifty-five, Melville collapsed from a heart attack in the PLM St-Jacques restaurant in Paris in the arms of writer and film-maker Philippe Labro, he was discussing difficulties with his latest script (Labro subsequently wrote a moving tribute to Melville).[3]

Yet film-makers are not just concepts: they are also human beings whose background, personal life and choices inflect their work. This is why, despite the reservations expressed above, I begin with a brief account of Melville's life and career before moving on to his films. The task is not easy. The Melville archives at the Bibliothèque du Film (BIFI) in Paris contain mostly scripts – including the unpublished *Un flic* (unrelated to the 1972 film of the same name) – and I was able to glean a few facts in the censorship files kept at the Centre National de la Cinématographie (CNC) as well as from meeting a wartime army colleague. Reputedly, other archives perished when his studio burnt down in 1967. The gaps in documentation leave plenty of room for speculation about all kinds of matters, from his part in the Resistance to his personal relationships. My task is not to elucidate these, but to present the information as clearly as possible insofar as it helps throw light on the films.

RÉSISTANT, CINEPHILE, 'OPOCENTRIC'

Melville was born Jean-Pierre Grumbach on 20 October 1917 (as already mentioned, he adopted the name Melville in honour of the American novelist). His ancestors were Eastern European Jews who had settled in Belfort, in Alsace, in the 1840s. Several generations of Grumbachs were butchers in the old part of the city. They were a close-knit, extended family: Melville's parents were first cousins. His father, a businessman, moved to Paris where Jean-Pierre was born. He grew up in rue d'Antin in the ninth *arrondissement* in central Paris, in a cultured, bourgeois-Bohemian environment, and a family with socialist leanings. Although he would later move to the right, Melville declared that he was 'a Communist from the age of 16, in 1933, until 25 August 1939. After that I stopped being a Communist. I am not religious either.'[4] Melville's family was sufficiently unconventional to give young Jean-Pierre a Pathé Baby camera in 1924 for his seventh birthday, and soon after a projector which delighted him even more since it enabled him to view recent releases on 9.5mm. According to Jean Wagner, starting in February 1925 he shot a number of films during his youth; by 1939 he had totalled the equivalent of thirty features in various non-theatrical formats.[5] Melville had one sister, Janine, and an older brother Jacques, a high-ranking civil servant who was killed during the war (Jacques' son Rémy Grumbach is a television director; the film-maker Michel Drach was also a cousin).[6]

Although Melville's centre of gravity was Paris, he retained links with the extended family in Belfort. A formative experience was seeing his first film there, in a brasserie.[7] Much later he called the production company formed to produce *Deux hommes dans Manhattan* 'Belfort Films'. Belfort repaid the compliment. On 26 November 1987, a street in the city centre was renamed 'Rue Jean-Pierre Melville' by Jean-Pierre Chevènement, Belfort's mayor and then (socialist) government minister. On the day of the inauguration Chevènement joked that a grim and forlorn suburban street might have been more in keeping with the setting of Melville's films, but that the city wanted to honour him with a major artery.

Melville went to school at the Lycée Condorcet near Gare St Lazare in central Paris, a well-regarded *lycée* for middle-class children. He reports not being particularly academic and being more interested in the youthful shenanigans of the 'Gare Saint-Lazare gang', 'a real gang of hooligans'[8] made up of pupils from Condorcet, a gang perhaps not unlike that seen at the beginning of *Les Enfants terribles*. Melville dates from this period a taste for slang and low-life characters – however, if some testimonies speak of his acquaintance with real gangsters, others have disputed his knowledge of the underworld.[9]

In any case, a bigger adventure was around the corner. Melville started his military service in the 'Spahis' (colonial cavalry) at the age of twenty in 1937.[10] He was still a conscript when the war began. In September 1940, his regiment got caught in Belgium. He was evacuated to England via Dunkirk and repatriated to France. On his return he moved to Castres in the South, where his family had relocated, and spent the period to 1942 there, joining the Resistance networks 'Libération' and 'Combat' under the name Cartier, and later Melville.[11] After the Allied landing in North Africa in November 1942, 'Cartier-Melville' tried to reach London via Algiers. His ship was stopped and he was jailed in Spain for two months (his brother Jacques died tragically while attempting to get to Spain). At some point in 1942–3 Melville spent some time in London, where he says he worked as a sub-agent for the BCRA.[12] He reached Tunisia in autumn 1943, where he joined the First Regiment of Colonial Artillery of the Free French. At first assigned as a colonel's chauffeur, he took part in the Italian and French liberation campaigns. On 11 March 1944 he was crossing the Garigliano below Mount Cassino. On 15 August of the same year he landed in Provence and in September he was in Lyon. His regiment was awarded the Croix de la Libération on 24 September 1945.[13]

These are the facts, as far as they can be ascertained, of Melville's war and his involvement with the Resistance. While he unarguably belonged to the First Regiment of Colonial Artillery, as confirmed to me by one of his former co-soldiers, it has proved more difficult to trace his London activities. Dates are hazy and testimonies contradictory. This does not signify that the claims he makes are false or incorrect, since by definition records of underground movements are scanty. Two things in any case are certain. On the one hand, there is no doubting Melville's bravery in joining the Free French, however modest his part and however much he played it down, claiming that 'being in the Resistance if you're a Jew is infinitely less heroic than if you're not'.[14] The second, and to us today particularly important, certainty is the deep impact the experience left on his work. Melville acknowledged the trauma the war and German occupation left on his generation. After seeing Marcel Ophuls' documentary *Le Chagrin et la pitié* (1969–71), he recalled: 'The first feeling we experienced was *shame*. [. . .] Grief, of course. But above all, shame.'[15] But he was also able to rework this trauma creatively through his films. 'Melville' after all was the name he took as a *Résistant*. A number of his later film collaborators, such as Jean-Marie Robain, Nicole Stéphane and Pierre Grasset were wartime contacts. It was while in the Resistance that he read both Vercors' *Le Silence de la mer*[16] and Joseph Kessel's *L'Armée des ombres* – books which he adapted respectively in 1947–9 and 1969, and which have stood the test of time as two great French classics.

After being demobilised between October and November 1945, Melville returned to Paris. There he encountered a young woman called Florence, whom he had met briefly in 1939. They remained together from that moment until the end of his life. They married in 1952 and Florence was to act variously throughout Melville's career as adviser, production manager and studio administrator. Although her name appears only occasionally on the credits, she was an important, if discreet, presence. Melville set about doing various jobs such as, allegedly, travelling salesman,[17] while planning his first film, *24 heures de la vie d'un clown*. This short, amateurish film completed in 1946 is about a famous clown, Béby. As such it is a tribute to one of Melville's passions, the circus. It is also an indication of his pressing desire to become a film-maker – on his own terms – without serving an apprenticeship, the usual way to get into the profession at the time.

Apart from his interest in cinema and the circus, as well as the music hall (to which an uncle took him regularly),[18] Melville was passionate about more 'legitimate' culture. As an adolescent he had discovered French and American literature, in particular three writers who 'left their mark on my adolescence: Poe, London, and of course Melville' [. . .] I discovered Melville, long before Jean Giono's translation of *Moby Dick*, by reading in English *Pierre: or the Ambiguities*, a book which left its mark on me for ever.'[19] Melville thus spoke English at an early stage; he certainly became fluent, as we can hear in *Deux hommes dans Manhattan* in which he plays the lead, and, for instance, in a 1961 radio interview with Gideon Bachmann.[20] Melville moved in the fashionable milieu of post-war left-bank Paris, and was familiar with such figures as Jean Cocteau and Juliette Gréco. The latter, whom he would cast in *Quand tu liras cette lettre* in 1954, was

> a good friend from the Saint-Germain days of '47, '48 and '49. At that time, I remember, I often went to the Club Saint-Germain where they had a band with fabulous musicians. It was there I had some marvellous times with Django Reinhardt. [. . .] Saint-Germain became something else after 1950, but before then . . . it was marvellous.[21]

Cocteau, American literature, St-Germain-des-Prés chanteuses and jazz – all these ingredients place Melville within the intellectual and cultural milieu which would some years later produce the New Wave. His 'schooling' in the Parisian left-bank culture also clearly left a mark on his beliefs: 'I'm wary of any political credo, and I have no religious beliefs whatsoever. So what I have left is morality and . . . conscience,'[22] an 'existentialist philosophy' that can, as we will see, be traced in many of his films.

But clearly the crucial intellectual influence on Melville was the cinema, and especially American cinema. In the 1920s, thanks to his Pathé Baby projector, 'every week I was able to see four or five new films, either two, three or four-reelers. It was *l'amour fou*, completely. The basis of my cinematographic culture.' Then, with the coming of sound, 'the mania had really begun: my days began at 9 a.m. in a cinema (the Paramount), and ended the same way at 3 a.m. the next morning. The pull was stronger than anything else.'[23] Melville's film education, in its voracity and Americanophilia, also anticipated that of the future New Wave critics – one reason why he was such a model for Godard, Truffaut and Chabrol. Consumed by his love for the cinema, he would learn 'even the credits by heart'.[24] Jacques Nataf, Melville's friend in the Free French army, reports that already then he talked of nothing but the cinema.[25] At the Liberation, his cinephilia and familiarity with the film milieu would lead him to make his own film but also to appear in a few others.

While he was making *Le Silence de la mer* and *Les Enfants terribles* (in which he can be seen in a brief cameo), Melville appeared in two films by the now forgotten journalist-turned-director Jacques Loew. Melville appears in the short *Les Drames du bois de Boulogne* (1948), jokingly titled to evoke Bresson's *Les Dames du bois de Boulogne* (1945). It is a comic fantasy with voiceover commentary by Gérard Philipe and a cast of well-known actors (Blanchette Brunoy, Maurice Baquet), and Melville as 'guest star'.[26] Melville also appeared in Loew's only feature made in 1951 but never released in Paris and thus usually not referenced, including in his own filmography. The film was variously titled *Quatre sans millions!*, *Cri du coeur* or *Si ça vous chante*. Part set in the Cannes Film Festival, it features Melville 'perorating among an assembly of cinephiles'; for Beylie and d'Hugues the film 'looks a bit like a "New Wave" comedy *avant la lettre*'.[27]

Once awakened, Melville's love of films never waned. He watched them everywhere: characteristically he met Volker Schloendorff 'at the Ciné-Club du Lycée Montaigne. Bertrand Tavernier had dragged me there to see that monstrosity called *Johnny Guitar.*'[28] Later he always made sure he had his own viewing facilities. In 1957 while his studio was hired out, he missed having his own projection room so much that he built a new one: 'I rented [it] out to other people but could use it myself in the evenings to run through any films I wanted to see.'[29] Apart from having very strong likes and dislikes, Melville also indulged in that great cinephile passion, making lists. In October 1961 *Cahiers du cinéma* published his list of 'sixty-three' (actually sixty-four) pre-war American film-makers (see Appendix 3). The list is Melville's tribute to 'a kind of film-making that inspired my vocation'.[30] Long, inclusive and eclectic – directors of women's films and comedies are cheek-by-jowl with those of Westerns and gangster films – rather than representing a trend or genre, the list pays tribute to the era and mode of film-making that he worshipped, classical Hollywood cinema of the 1930s. Melville's declaration in the same issue of *Cahiers* that one day he hoped to sell his studio and go to the USA to shoot not just American films 'but pre-war American films'[31] gives away the nostalgic dimension of his cinephilia. So did his signature Ray-Bans and hats: Trilbys and from 1963 Stetsons (many have pointed out that the hats also conveniently concealed his baldness). In 1949, writing his 'manifesto' in *L'Écran français*,[32] he identified Frank Lloyd's *Cavalcade* (1933) as the epitome of classical Hollywood cinema. Since the film is based on a Noel Coward play and features mostly British actors, this would seem an odd choice were it not for the film's dynamic, unstagy, 'American' camerawork and editing (with hindsight too, the film's topic of loss, grief and the impact of war must have chimed with his own concerns). Even when Melville moved on to post-war Hollywood films, such as favourites like John Huston's *The Asphalt Jungle* (1950) and Robert Wise's *Odds Against Tomorrow* (1959), these remained in the classical mould. Although Melville anticipated *Cahiers' mise en scène* criticism by about ten years, he did not share the *Cahiers* critics' taste for baroque melodrama, such as *Johnny Guitar*.

MELVILLE'S BRILLIANT CAREER

After his short (which found a distributor and made a modest amount of money), Melville started his career proper with a bang. Not only by making a strikingly original and successful feature, *Le Silence de la mer*, but doing so against the wishes of the book's author and outside the film industry. Barred by the communist-backed Film Technicians' Union from obtaining the essential professional card in 1945, he was 'forced to become a producer to give myself the task of making my film'.[33] Not that this was very advantageous in the immediate post-war since he 'had no right to coupons for film stock'.[34] Problems did not stop there. Melville was fined FF 50,000 by the CNC;[35] it was also rumoured that he had made a film 'with Rothschild money' because star and co-backer Nicole Stéphane was a Rothschild.[36] His perseverance and independent stance would, however, remain a model for later generations. He produced or co-produced his own films for the rest of his career.

The success of *Le Silence de la mer* established Melville's name even though at the time it was overshadowed by that of the author, Vercors. The *succès d'estime* of his next film, *Les Enfants terribles* (based on Cocteau and also a relatively small-scale production), confirmed Melville's reputation as an innovative and distinctive film-maker, although here again he was outshone by a famous author. His dream, however, was to attain total

Melville at the premiere of *Le Silence de la mer* (1949). (left to right) Nicole Stéphane, Melville, Jean-Marie Robain, Howard Vernon

independence and this he achieved by the unusual step of setting up his own studio, made possible by the FF 2 million he earned from directing his next film, the more 'commercial' *Quand tu liras cette lettre*.[37] Built in a disused factory at 25bis rue Jenner, in what was then a semi-industrial thirteenth *arrondissement* in south-east Paris, Melville's studio was in a street whose bleakness would not have been out of place in *Le Doulos* or *Le Samouraï*. As Schloendorff reports, 'The studio wasn't especially large [...] but it was large enough nonetheless to house two sound stages, one small wardrobe room, two cutting rooms, and a screening room.'[38] Labro adds a description of Melville's office above the studio, which can also be glimpsed in André S. Labarthe's documentary *Portrait en 9 poses* – an office 'bigger than the salon of a transatlantic ship, with his books, records, a samurai sword, a few weapons, two armchairs, souvenirs and, on his immense desk, photographs, newspapers, magazines, telephones'.[39] Above was Melville's flat where he lived with his wife and cats (commemorated in a small and apparently typically troublesome role in *Le Cercle rouge*).

The rue Jenner studio made Melville, like Méliès and Pagnol before him, an exceptionally independent figure in French cinema, even though financially it was 'the worst deal I ever did, a folly',[40] as many testimonies confirm. Daniel Cauchy, one of the leading actors in *Bob le flambeur*, Melville's next film and the first properly shot in the rue Jenner studio, recalls how lack of money made the shoot long and hazardous. Melville supported himself by letting the studio to television,[41] and he allowed friends to use it (it is there that Jacques Becker 'entirely re-shot *Le Trou*').[42] As proudly announced on the credits, the interiors of *Bob le flambeur*, *Deux hommes dans Manhattan*, *L'Aîné des Fer-*

chaux, Le Doulos and *Le Deuxième souffle*, and part of *Le Samouraï* were shot there. Sadly, the studio burnt down in 1967 half-way through shooting the latter film – a blow to Melville's spirit and a financial one too, as Florence had failed to renew the insurance policy.[43] Melville had plans to reconstruct the studio but although he was able to rebuild some editing facilities, they came to nothing. Nor did Melville become a producer of other people's films, after a couple of inconclusive attempts.[44]

Accounts of Melville's career usually split it in two: a first phase, from *Le Silence de la mer* to *Deux hommes dans Manhattan*, of small-scale, critically acclaimed but sparsely watched auteur works, and a second phase, starting with *Léon Morin, prêtre*, of big-budget genre films, popular at the box office but which gradually caused him to fall out of favour with critics. In fact, in terms of both box-office and critical reception, the reality is more complicated. Repeated assertions about the commercial failure of his early films are contradicted by the figures. Both *Le Silence de la mer* and *Quand tu liras cette lettre* achieved ticket sales of more than a million, an excellent score in the French context (500,000 is considered a significant threshold by the compilers of CNC box-office statistics).[45] *Les Enfants terribles* and *Bob le flambeur* reached the smaller but still respectable score of 719,844 and 716,920 tickets; more significantly, because of their small budget, they were profitable. Only *Deux hommes dans Manhattan* with 308,000 tickets can be called a flop. Its failure prompted him to move on to films made on larger budgets and with stars. From *Léon Morin, prêtre*, Melville's films would repeatedly achieve high box-office takings, even a so-called 'failure' like *L'Armée des ombres* (as I discuss in Chapter 3). Thus, though chequered, even the first half of Melville's career was not exactly that of a marginal film-maker. Yet it is this image which has endured. This misapprehension is partly based on Melville's own declarations. No doubt the figure of the *auteur maudit*, of the embattled – and occasionally impecunious – film-maker possesses a romantic aura. But it also fits with Melville's obstinate, not to say plain difficult, nature, a fact that he had the grace to recognise:

> I often say – which isn't true – that I have always been rejected by the profession. Actually, it is I who have always rejected the profession. I have always had offers to make films which I have always refused. I have never been forced into unemployment. I was impossible to deal with, there's no doubt about that, and quarrelled with all the producers.[46]

Actually he quarrelled with just about everyone.

Obstinate, proud and authoritarian in person, Melville frequently argued and fell out with his collaborators, beginning with writers such as Vercors, Cocteau and José Giovanni.[47] Relationships with stars could also be stormy, in particular with Jean-Paul Belmondo, Charles Vanel and Lino Ventura. According to one of Ventura's biographers, 'it was war between them during the shoot [of *L'Armée des ombres*]. Lino swore he would never again have anything to do with Melville!'[48] Of his major stars, apparently only Alain Delon did not fall out with the director, until, that is, the release of *Un flic*, their last collaboration and Melville's last film.[49] Melville was also involved in several highly public 'settlings of scores' – for instance with Truffaut (through the journal *Arts*, as discussed in the introduction), and with Claude Lelouch on television.[50] Labro reports that in the 1960s Melville was good value on television and therefore was often invited to appear. At the same time, Melville's all-absorbing love of film, his 'opocentrism' and demanding attitude to his work made him tyrannical to the point of eccentricity and unfairness on set. He would summon cast and crew in the middle of the night; as editor Françoise Bonnot said, 'You were not supposed to have a private life. You had to work at night and at the weekend!'[51] Melville was fanatical about the smallest detail, down to the width of the brim of a hat,[52] suffered no contradiction and disapproved of affairs on set because they were a distraction.[53] Cauchy reports receiving a lawyer's writ for supposed lateness, immediately followed by an apology – not an unusual occurrence, as in most cases the fights ended in reconciliation. Melville may have been tyrannical and difficult, but he was also immensely cultured and witty, not to mention talented, an influential and imposing figure with the aura of a 'master' or *padrino*, as Labro puts it.[54] He could be very generous with his friends and collaborators and in return elicited fierce loyalties. He formed particularly strong bonds with young male colleagues, such as Labro and Schloendorff, whom he treated like symbolic sons. The latter said, 'During filming [of *Le Doulos*] Melville did not have to shout. He behaved like a benevolent though extremely authoritarian boss. [. . .] In any case it was love between us. We all loved him so much, just as he was.'[55] As Yves Montand summed it up on Melville's death: 'He was not an easy man but you had to respect him.'[56]

Melville's perfectionism and obstinately independent stance came at a price which is directly reflected in his filmography: 'just' thirteen features in twenty-four years. His career was punctuated by drawn-out shoots, false starts and periods of inactivity. Two years elapsed between the making and release of *Le Silence de la mer*, four years passed between *Enfants* and *Lettre*. The shooting of *Bob* took eighteen months, and there was a three-year gap between *Bob* and *Deux hommes dans Manhattan*. Melville's rhythm speeded up in the early 1960s, with three films in two years (*Léon Morin, prêtre*, *Le Doulos* and *L'Ainé des Ferchaux*), although there was another three-year pause between *Le Doulos* and *Le Deuxième souffle* because of setbacks in the making of the latter film ('1964 to 1966 were years in the wilderness for me').[57] In 1967–8, following *Le Samouraï* and the destruction of his studio, Melville was involved in a feud with the Hakim brothers who failed to honour his contract to make *La Chienne*: 'They made me lose a whole year immediately following the fire at my studios, which was a terrible blow in a lot of ways.'[58] Similarly, Melville's career is littered with unrealised or cancelled projects, a fate no doubt shared by many film-makers, although he seems to have had more than the usual share. The list below does not claim to be exhaustive, but apart from its anecdotal value, it gives a fascinating glimpse of the different directions Melville's work might have taken.

1946: an adaptation of Proust's *Swann's Way*[59]

1949: *Un brin de bruyère* (with Howard Vernon)[60]

Late 1940s: *Le Journal d'un curé de campagne* (Melville wanted to do it after *Le Silence de la mer*, but was delayed by *Enfants* – he abandoned the project when he found Bresson was doing it)[61]

1952: *Le Bourgeois gentilhomme*, *La Flêche et le flambeau*[62]

1954: *Du rififi chez les hommes*[63]

1957: a spy story with Pierre Grasset[64]

1958: a thriller set in Cannes during the film festival, for which Melville had begun building a set[65]

1958: *L'A.F.P. nous communique*, a story about a French politician who dies of a coronary in his mistress's flat – the story evolved, significantly modified, into *Deux hommes dans Manhattan*[66]

Early 1960s: *Trois chambres à Manhattan*, a Georges Simenon novel which Melville wanted to shoot with Jeanne Moreau; it was eventually filmed by Marcel Carné with Annie Girardot.[67]

1962: *Les Dons Juan*, for Georges de Beauregard, based on a Mérimée story, *Les Âmes du purgatoire*, with Belmondo and Anthony Perkins. The project fell through because Belmondo demanded too much money.

Other scripts by such writers as Monique Lange, Michel Mardore and France Roche were reportedly burnt with Melville's studio in 1967[68]

1968: *La Chienne* (see above)

1969: *Papillon*, with 'no stars'[69]

1973: *Contre-enquête*, a thriller starring Yves Montand which was about to be shot when Melville died

Although there were mishaps and obstacles along the way, Melville's general trajectory was a rising curve. After his beleaguered beginnings his star rose steadily. At the release of *L'Armée des ombres* in 1969 he agreed with radio interviewer Jacques Chancel that 'his name on the poster was sufficient to attract an audience'.[70] During the last years of his career, Melville achieved massive popular success with *Le Cercle rouge*, a film singled out by Pathé News for an item on a typical 'major French film production', and which broke his own box-office record, with more than four million spectators. Melville had become a member of the French film establishment, teaching at the IDHEC film school and sitting on the Censorship Commission.[71] His last film *Un flic* (1972) had a mixed reception and was perceived, including by Melville, as a 'failure'. Yet it sold 2.8 million tickets, which can only be a disappointment in relation to the stratospheric success of the preceding film. Objectively speaking, Melville's career was thus a success story. By contrast, critical reception of his work during his lifetime took a dramatically different path.

Briefly, the reception of Melville's films while he was alive can be divided into three phases (more details for each film will be found in the relevant chapters). The first phase, from *Le Silence de la mer* to *Quand tu liras cette lettre*, sees Melville somewhat overshadowed by three well-known writers (Vercors, Cocteau and Deval), although immediately singled out by perceptive critics. André Bazin, for instance, praised *Le Silence de la mer* for the novelty and authenticity of Melville's adaptation,[72] while a survey by *Cahiers du cinéma* in 1957 viewed Melville as one of the white hopes of French cinema.[73] During the second phase, from *Bob* to *Le Doulos*, the reception of Melville's films is coloured by their relation to the New Wave and the director's recognition as an auteur.

Originality, independence, small budgets, the use of location shooting and the innovative photography of Henri Decae are all adduced to designate Melville as one of the fathers of the New Wave, a distinction he enthusiastically claims. As he said to *Combat* in 1961, 'The new cinema is: natural location, non-synchronised shooting, fast film stock, small crew and . . . Henri Decae.'[74] He even traced his innovation further back: 'What the new filmmakers are doing, I wanted to do it in 1937. Alas, I could only do it in 1947, with *Le Silence de la mer*.'[75] Reviews in the late 1950s and early 1960s routinely make reference to Melville as 'a particularly original *auteur* within French cinema'.[76] A number of substantial interviews, from the same period, appear in a range of publications, by writers who emerge as Melville's champions: in particular Jean Wagner, Henry Chapier, Bertrand Tavernier and Claude Beylie (the latter two in *Cahiers du cinéma*), who consolidate his auteur status. During that period, Melville's closeness to the New Wave and especially the *Cahiers* group (*Positif* was less enthusiastic) translated for a while into professional and personal friendships with Chabrol, Truffaut and especially Godard.[77] Melville was one of the founder members, with Truffaut and Godard, of the Association des Créateurs Indépendants du Cinéma Français (ACI), an ephemeral association of independent filmmakers created in 1959. Then Godard, as is well known, cast Melville as 'Parvulesco', a comically pretentious writer modelled on Nabokov according to Melville, though it later emerged that both Godard and Melville were friendly with an extreme right-wing Romanian writer called Parvulesco, whom Melville apparently resembled, who had emigrated to Spain.[78] Chabrol also cast Melville in a brief cameo in *Landru* (1963). In that film Melville plays Mandel, secretary to statesman Clémenceau, whose character is played by the writer Raymond Queneau (according to the New Wave tradition of casting 'real people' which Melville had himself practised: casting not only himself but Cocteau in cameos in *Les Enfants terribles*, and the director of the Deauville casino in his own role in *Bob le flambeur*, as well as taking the lead in *Deux hommes dans Manhattan*). *Landru*'s colour photography gives us a rare glimpse of Melville's pale blue eyes.

The closeness with the New Wave was short-lived, however – on both sides. *Léon Morin, prêtre*, which signalled Melville's move to mainstream cinema and the use of stars, also heralded the third phase of Melville's critical reception during his lifetime. Even though most reviews of *Léon Morin, prêtre* were excellent, this film in retrospect initiated the deep split that would characterise this third phase. On the one hand, his films received abundant and largely enthusiastic reviews in the mainstream press, generating lively debate – *Léon Morin, prêtre*, *L'Aîné des Ferchaux* and *L'Armée des ombres* for their contents; *Le Doulos*, *Le Deuxième souffle*, *Le Samouraï* and *Le Cercle rouge* for their use of the gangster genre and their extreme foregrounding of a minimalist style. Even when doubts were raised about the 'emptiness' of his increasingly bleak universe from *Le Doulos* onwards, Melville was always saluted as a supreme artist and true auteur whose rigorous style expressed a coherent vision (the generally abusive reception of *Un flic*, discussed in Chapter 6, is in a category of its own). By contrast, during this third phase, he was the subject of vitriolic attacks from the cinephile press (*Cahiers du cinéma*, *Positif* and *Jeune cinéma*) – attacks he had in part provoked with declarations such as, 'That's it. Now I am going to make commercial films.'[79] The estrangement was gradual, especially while Beylie, a Melville fan, was still writing for *Cahiers du cinéma*. However, from the mid-1960s and *Le Deuxième souffle* on, full-blown hostility prevailed, culminating in a famous *Cahiers* article by Jean-Louis Comolli and Jean Narboni, published in October 1969, entitled 'Cinema/Ideology/Criticism'. There, Melville is placed, along with Gérard Oury and Claude Lelouch (two film-makers he would never previously have been bracketed with), in category (a): 'The first and largest category comprises those films which are imbued through and through with the dominant ideology in pure and unadulterated form, and give no indication that their makers were even aware of the fact.'[80]

Such hostility came about as the result of dramatically divergent agendas in the highly politicised climate which followed the events of May 1968. Melville's Resistance epic *L'Armée des ombres*, released just before the above article, was instantly (and wrongly) perceived as a 'Gaullist film'. Meanwhile *Cahiers* was in its most fiercely political phase. The politics of Melville's films were also confused with his own – he would candidly say: 'I am an extreme individualist, and to tell you the truth I don't wish to be either Right or Left. But I certainly live as a man of the Right. I'm a Right-wing anarchist.'[81] He was nevertheless a friend of left-wing icons such as Simone Signoret and Yves Montand. But the divergence between Melville and *Cahiers* went deeper. In this political phase, *Cahiers* was rejecting aesthetic approaches, cinephilia, almost the cinema itself[82] – in other words everything Melville held dearest as he was making his most stylish, even *mannerist*, thrillers, veritable odes to film-making. The flaunting of *mise en scène* which had made him a pioneer in the 1950s now made him *passé*. Melville's frequent pronouncements against the *avance sur recettes*, the lifeline of small-budget auteur films – he thought film-makers should fend for themselves – also did not endear him to cinephiles. At the same time, his strongly individual artist stance fell foul of *Cahiers*' anti-auteurist position at that time. Hence his relegation to the critical purgatory of 'commercial cinema' which made the normally perceptive critic Serge Daney say, of Melville's masterpiece *Le Samouraï*, that Melville might as well make commercials about 'a style in raincoats'.[83] When he died in 1973, Melville was hailed in the mainstream press with a flurry of obituaries celebrating him as a stylish and original director. Typical was Henry Chapier, who spoke of his 'highly recognisable style, his Asiatically slow pace, the elegance of his framings, the perfectionism of his mise-en-scène and the constant though restrained nostalgia of his images'.[84] But there were no major celebrations or retrospectives in the specialist press.

The 1970s were posthumous wilderness years for Melville, although he continued to elicit a minor though passionate cult, now partly fuelled by the difficulties in seeing his work, both in France and abroad. Rui Nogueira's book of interviews had appeared in 1971 and Colin McArthur's *Underworld USA*, which contains a chapter on Melville, in 1972; there were a few isolated cinematic tributes like Walter Hill's *The Driver* (1978). Melville's neglect after 1973, however, was less noticeable in a cinematic climate dominated by politics and sex, themes he had turned his back on (and the ubiquity of which he deplored while a member of the Censorship Commission). His return to critical favour began, modestly enough, in the 1980s. The National Film Theatre (NFT) in

London staged a retrospective in March 1983 and the same year Zimmer and de Béchade's book was published. But the comeback proper only gathered full momentum in the late 1980s and especially the 90s. The studio-based, controlled aesthetics of the *cinéma du look* could be seen within the Melville legacy. Internationally, the rise of 'cool' gangster and neo-noir films – the stylised violence of Tarantino and John Woo – suddenly highlighted Melville's pioneer status. One may venture also that his thrillers fitted the increased masculinisation of late-twentieth-century popular culture. Melville's revival was also spurred by shifts in French film criticism. Political theorising gave way to a triumphant return to aesthetic, even formalist approaches, and the rebirth of the auteur. There was a retrospective in Florence in 1994, and Delon paid tribute to Melville at the 1995 César ceremony. A retrospective at the Cinémathèque Française and a belated special issue of *Cahiers du cinéma*, both in November 1996, put the final seal of approval on a director whose work was now fully recognised as supremely aesthetic and coherent, in short an auteur.

REWRITING THE SELF: MELVILLE AS AUTEUR

It is not hard to make a case for Melville as an auteur in terms of decision-making, since he controlled his work to an unusual degree. Even as a young unknown working with famous and strong-willed writers such as Vercors and Cocteau, he fought tooth and nail to keep control of adaptation and film-making. As the multiple presence of his name on credits attests, he was implicated in many different capacities (studio head, producer, scriptwriter, dialogue, director, actor and sometimes editor and set designer). He declared, 'I am used to supervising everything in my films; I would like to do everything myself: I deal with sets, I dream of writing the music myself,'[85] believing that 'a director must be an artisan. He must be capable of doing everything.'[86] This was not just bragging. His technical expertise, learnt 'on the job', and highly professional standards were widely respected in the industry. Among others François Périer (the Inspector of *Le Samouraï*) testified that Melville was always highly prepared and economical, knew exactly what he wanted and shot few takes.[87] This is why, despite his difficult character and obsessive need to control every aspect of film-making, Melville also enjoyed long partnerships with many actors and crew, creating something of a 'troupe' and, at any rate, a sense of continuity: Grasset, Stéphane, Belmondo, Delon, Ventura, and non-professional actors such as his secretary Monique Hennessy (who appears in *Deux hommes dans Manhattan*, *Léon Morin, prêtre* and *Le Doulos*), and jazz conductor Jerry Mengo in *Deux hommes dans Manhattan* and *L'Ainé des Ferchaux*; all appeared in several roles. Melville was also faithful to key technicians, such as editor Monique Bonnot (on six films), but most prominently director of photography Henri Decae. Discovered by Melville in *Le Silence de la mer* and employed on six other films, Decae said, 'we began together, so to speak, we understood each other very well from the beginning, and we adapted to each other'.[88]

As for thematic and stylistic consistencies, Melville believed that 'the essential thing is that there must be an intrinsic resemblance between the first film and the last'.[89] In order to avoid preconceived homogeneity, the danger of any auteur study, my film

Melville on the set of *Un flic* (1972)

analyses attempt to explore not only 'resemblances' but also discontinuities. I am keen in this book also to consider the contribution of Melville's collaborators, whether writers, cinematographers or stars. Can the main themes in Melville's work be traced back to the man without unduly 'psychologising' him or reverting to an 'intentionalist' mode? Melville was ambivalent about such an enterprise. On the one hand he vehemently told Nogueira: 'You're on the wrong track again. You musn't try to interweave what I do in my films with what I am in life.'[90] On the other hand, when Nogueira suggested that 'The line from the Book of Bushido with which you open [*Le Samouraï*] – "There is no greater solitude than that of the Samurai, unless perhaps it be that of the tiger in the jungle" – might apply equally well to your situation as an independent film-maker outside the industry. . .,' Melville replied enthusiastically: 'Absolutely!'[91] – unsurprisingly perhaps, since this so-called quote from the Book of Bushido was his own invention. Melville's work and life, however, offer some obvious homologies which are worth teasing out before moving on to the films themselves in the rest of the book.

Melville's experience of the war, Resistance and German occupation provided the backbone for his work. His first film, *Le Silence de la mer*, and one of his last, *L'Armée des ombres*, faithfully adapt classics of Resistance literature. *Léon Morin, prêtre*, about a transgressive relationship between a communist woman and a Catholic priest, also takes its place in this thematic axis, forming part of a 'war trilogy' which I examine in Chapter 3. But the war is also a structuring absence throughout Melville's career in subtle ways. Not only does it underpin his unmade 1956 script of *Un flic* (a story of black-market crime during the German occupation) and provide the dénouement of *Deux hommes dans Manhattan*, when the missing French diplomat in New York turns out to have been a Resistance hero: in a more diffuse but fundamental sense the war represented a break with the past for Melville, both in life and film. It engendered a nostalgia which permeates all his work: nostalgia for an idealised golden era of 'honourable' gangsterdom evoked in all the gangster films from *Bob le flambeur*, nostalgia for an equally idealised era of classical film-making throughout his career, a nostalgic fantasy of pre-war America as his 'white whale'.[92] Melville's films can be seen, over more than two decades and across genres, as harking back to this phantasmatic, and nevertheless for him very real, pre-war era (it is noticeable that concurrently he mostly ignored contemporary wars in Indo-China and Algeria).

A self-confessed loner, Melville lived a fairly eccentric life. A journalist in 1969 put it like this:

> For a long time the author of *Le Samouraï* lived in the heart of the 13th arrondissement in a strangely lonely flat on the first floor of [his] studio. But he also had a pied-à-terre in a Passy hotel. One day I was told that he was staying at the Orly Hilton to write the subject of his next film. But when I phoned, he had already moved on somewhere else. Later he gave me a number you will find in no phone book. It was that of his provincial retreat. This is how I entered Melvillian clandestinity.[93]

His widow Florence, and many friends and collaborators have confirmed how, as well as maintaining a country house in Tilly, the Melvilles moved frequently and Jean-Pierre loved plush Parisian hotels such as the Raphael and Suffren Hilton.[94] In respect of his personal image, however, Melville was Janus-faced: a loner and misanthropist who cultivated his 'secret' myth, he also flaunted a highly recognisable, not to say exhibitionist, image: the Stetson and dark glasses, the huge American cars. Part of the Melvillian idiosyncrasy was a well-documented penchant for being a 'creature of the night', as he told *Cahiers du cinéma* among others.[95] This love of solitude and the night was not just a personal quirk; it extended to his working method: 'You really create a film in the editing room, in the silence and night';[96] 'For me, paradise consists in writing the script all alone at home and then in editing it. But I hate the shoot. All this time wasted in useless talk!'[97]

From the man to the film-maker to the character, the leap is tempting; a dominant theme in Melville's films is that of the essential loneliness of his characters, from the crossed lovers of *Le Silence de la mer* to the lone hitman of *Le Samouraï*. Although it is often said that Melville's films are about loyalty and male friendship, they are more accurately about betrayal, the impossibility of bonding, loneliness. While this places Melville's work well within major preoccupations of post-war modernist culture, from existentialist literature to the Theatre of the Absurd, it would be difficult to deny the personal dimension of this concern, however cultivated or intermittent it was (others, for example, evoke a gregarious *bon vivant*). As Volker Schloendorff put it, Melville's films offer a '*mise en scène*' of his own preoccupations and personality:

> Like the priest in *Léon Morin, prêtre*, the gangsters of *Le Doulos* are men without women. And here the link with Melville the man is obvious. With his quasi-obsessional description of solitary heroes, Melville was talking about himself. I would say that he sublimated in his films his own behaviour and psychology with his fears and frustrations. In life, Jean-Pierre loved staging himself with a lot of mystery.[98]

In drawing attention to the gender dimension of Melville's personality and films, Schloendorff raises another key issue. Even largely gender-blind French film critics have not failed to notice the extremely masculine, even macho, stance of both Melville's own image and that of his characters. Can Melville be called a misogynist? Former IDHEC student Dominique Crèvecoeur (now a producer) reports a classic tale of 1960s sexism. Melville had assigned a class an exercise on *L'Armée des ombres*. Giving the assessed work back, 'He called the authors of the most interesting essays. He named me in third position. I stood up. He said "Where is Dominique Crèvecoeur?" I answered "here" putting my hand up. When he saw I was a woman [the name can be masculine or feminine in French] he put the file straight back and moved on to the next person. A murmur went through the room [. . .] I understood a) that my work was among the best and b) that nobody called Béatrice or Jacqueline would have been deemed worthy of attention.'[99] Indeed this is the same Melville who said, in 1968: 'I think that a film artist [*créateur de*

'To become eternal and then die': Melville as 'Parvulesco' in Jean-Luc Godard's *À bout de souffle* (1960)

cinéma] must be a gentleman – this is true, because there are no lady film artists.'[100] Moving to the films, feminist critic Françoise Audé is right when she says: 'Violence among men exists in Jean-Pierre Melville's cinema. But when it is directed against women, its style changes, it becomes violence over them, the power to humiliate, the will to crush. That, too, was the "great" Melville.'[101] These are rare critical positions. Commentators have usually ignored the issue or defended Melville against 'accusations' of sexism. For example, Zimmer and de Béchade write: 'Generally accused of misogyny, Melville has given us, 20 years apart, two of the most beautiful portraits of women that the cinema has offered in a genre reputed exclusively masculine.'[102] And for Bantcheva, 'Some have spoken of misogyny and puritanism in Melville; I would argue that although the film-maker occasionally shows women as humiliated, or leaves off-screen the erotic scenes the audience wants, this is not enough to draw general conclusions.'[103] Rather than defend or condemn, it is more useful, I believe, to consider Melville's films as permeated by a masculine code, which is often referred to as a 'moral code' but needs to be seen in its gender dimension. Along with everyday misogyny and evident difficulties in representing women even in 'women's films' like *Le Silence de la mer* and *Léon Morin, prêtre*, Melville's films also offer a fascinating and disturbing vision of masculinity that is bleakly sexist and hardly triumphalist. Whereas Audé's remark is particularly true of *Le Doulos*, Melville's men are more often, as Schloendorff says, without women. They are solitary, melancholy and vulnerable. In their 'homosocial' world, significant emotions flow only between men. Some, especially *L'Aîné des Ferchaux* and *Un flic*, take this further to a 'homophilic' level while self-consciously reinforcing heterosexuality. For instance, in *L'Aîné des Ferchaux*, Belmondo's macho stance and liaison with the stripper, played by Michèle Mercier, offsets the troubled homoerotic atmosphere between his character and the old man played by Charles Vanel. If there is occasionally a whiff of similar ambivalence in testimonies about Melville, as the Schloendorff quote above implies, others emphasise a strong heterosexual penchant[104] – for example, Godard, who in a startlingly casual aside, mentions that 'With him I could talk about women, in a feeble way, but still he found me girls if I needed them, it was not taboo for him, and that influenced me.'[105] But Melville's private life is not so much in question here as the fact that his masculinist view found such an echo. It is striking that the more 'male' Melville's films are, the more popular they were at the box office, culminating with *Le Cercle rouge* which virtually eliminates women from the screen. In terms of Melville's life and work, Cauchy nicely summed up the issue: Melville, he says, 'liked women a lot but loved men's stories'.[106]

A final thematic link needs to be made between Melville's life and his films – that of his love of America. As in the case of the war, this has several dimensions. It would be absurd to dispute the connection between the man in the Stetson hat who, like Bob, drove round Paris in a convertible American car, who called himself 'Melville' and who loved Sinatra,[107] and the iconography of films like *Le Doulos*, *Le Samouraï* and *Le Cercle rouge*. Melville knew America well and visited several times, always by boat.[108] As we know, his cinephilia was mainly concerned with American cinema, although he was familiar with other national cinemas. But it is equally absurd, in view of the rich, international, cultural texture of his films, to talk of 'copies'. This book is as concerned with Melville's connections with his French contemporaries as it is with his tributes to Hollywood. In any case, the link between Melville's love of American cinema and his own films is also more subtle, informing not just the contents of his work but his entire approach to the cinema. Melville may have said in the early 1960s that he would like to move to America; by the end of the decade he had changed his tune: 'I would be incapable of it. Is it prudence? Here I am in a privileged position, there I would one among so many talented people. They don't need me ... I prefer to make French films in France.'[109] Although it has been argued, for instance by Jean-Marie Frodon, that Melville used (American) genre cinema as a 'cover' to participate in its demise,[110] I agree, rather, with Jacques Doniol-Valcroze that Melville was a truly French film-maker who adopted classical Hollywood's 'golden rules': 'a cinema of entertainment, stars, spectacle, almost always sexual modesty, the simplicity and universality of the message. [A cinema which] takes place in a non-realist universe, which does not exist outside the screen, which is a pure invention.'[111] Thus Melville's avowed ambition to 'fill cinemas'[112] was not, as *Cahiers* saw it, 'selling out', but a celebration and commitment to the ideal of a truly popular cinema which was also compatible with artistic ambition. At the same time it is an ideal which fits post-modern notions of 'double address', which explains the durability of Melville's appeal. He said, 'I would like my films to be, let's say like a *mille-feuilles* cake: two very different, pleasing substances, pastry and cream. Only the real gourmets will taste the pastry, those with less fine taste only the cream. That is the case for *Le Doulos*. It is a gangster action film. But the spectator with finer taste will see in it, I hope, something more profound, more interesting, than a gangster adventure.'[113] The (very French?) gastronomic image is not surprising from someone who was a gourmet (Labro reports that Melville, who disliked his corpulence, would regularly try to diet, but had the appetite of an 'ogre'); it is also a perfect metaphor for Melville's layered aesthetics – an ambitious auteur with a truly popular outlook, a lover of American cinema who made deeply French movies.

NOTES

1. Volker Schloendorff, *Les Nouvelles*, 17–23 November 1983.
2. Rui Nogueira (ed.), *Melville on Melville* (London: Secker and Warburg and BFI, 1971), p. 151.
3. Philippe Labro, 'Jean-Pierre Melville ou s'avancer masqué', in *Je connais des gens de toutes sortes* (Paris: Gallimard, 2002), pp. 115–36. Melville died technically of an 'aneurysmal rupture' but he also had a weak heart. According to Florence Welsh, his widow, Melville's father, grandfather and great grandfather all died of a heart attack at same age; in Denitza Bantcheva, *Jean-Pierre Melville: de l'oeuvre à l'homme* (Troyes: Librairie Bleue, 1996), p. 170.
4. Claude Beylie, 'Le point de vue du réalisateur' [*Léon Morin, prêtre*], *Télérama*, no. 612, 8 October 1961. Melville is alluding to the Nazi–Soviet pact. Though he frequently repeated this anecdote about turning away from communism, at other times he said he never was a communist.

5. Jean Wagner, *Jean-Pierre Melville* (Paris: Seghers, 1963), p. 16.
6. Jean-Pierre Chevènement, Speech for the inauguration of the rue Jean-Pierre Melville, Belfort, 26 November 1987 (unpublished document, CNC archives), pp. 1–3.
7. Jacques Chancel, 'Radioscopie', *France-Inter*, September 1969.
8. Nogueira, *Melville on Melville*, p. 92.
9. In a report on the ninth 'France Cinema' retrospective in Florence, May 1994, in *Libération*, Mrs Gabin (Florence Moncorgé) claims that 'Melville knew nothing about the underground'.
10. Chevènement, Inaugural speech, p. 3.
11. *L'Aurore*, 15 September 1969.
12. Bureau Central de Renseignement et d'Action (BCRA), an organisation which was part of the Resistance, under the supervision of André Dewavrin who appears as Colonel Passy in *L'Armée des ombres*.
13. On 22 March 1945, the 1er Régiment d'Afrique des Forces Françaises Libres (First African Regiment of the Free French) became the 1er Régiment d'Artillerie Coloniale (RAC [First Regiment of Colonial Artillery]). On 24 September 1945, in Chelles, Seine-et-Marne, the regiment received the Croix de la Libération from General de Gaulle.
14. 'Jean-Pierre Melville talks to Rui Nogueira about *Le Chagrin et la pitié*', *Sight and Sound*, vol. 40, no. 4, Autumn 1971, pp. 181–2.
15. Ibid., p. 207.
16. Melville claims to have read *Le Silence de la mer* in an English translation entitled *Put Out the Light* in August 1943 (Nogueira, *Melville on Melville*, p. 22), though the Cyril Connolly translation came out in 1944 (Melville of course may have read a manuscript). Georges Sadoul in *Les Lettres françaises*, 5 May 1949, claims Melville read it 'on the banks of the Loire', while other sources say he read it in London.
17. *L'Humanité*, 3 August 1973.
18. Eric Breitbart, 'An Interview with Jean-Pierre Melville', *Film Culture*, no. 35, Winter 1964–5, pp. 15–19.
19. Nogueira, *Melville on Melville*, p. 18.
20. Interview with Gideon Bachmann recorded during the 1961 Venice Film Festival, reproduced on the DVD of *Bob le flambeur* (Criterion edition, 2001).
21. Nogueira, *Melville on Melville*, p. 49.
22. Ibid., p. 160.
23. Ibid., p. 13; Chevènement, Inaugural speech, pp. 2–3.
24. Nogueira, *Melville on Melville*, p. 20.
25. Conversation with the author, Paris, 8 July 2002.
26. Claude Beylie and Philippe d'Hugues, *Les Oubliés du cinéma français* (Paris: Éditions du Cerf, 1999), p. 109.
27. Ibid., p. 111.
28. Nogueira, *Melville on Melville*, p. 89.
29. Ibid., pp. 166.
30. Ibid., p. 95.
31. Claude Beylie and Bertrand Tavernier, 'Entretien avec Jean-Pierre Melville', *Cahiers du cinéma*, no. 124, October 1961, p. 21.

32. Jean-Pierre Melville, 'Il n'y a plus à chercher, il faut oser', *L'Écran français*, 3 May 1949, p. 3.
33. *Combat*, 16 April 1949.
34. Nogueira, *Melville on Melville*, p. 23.
35. Ibid., p. 35.
36. Ibid., p. 34.
37. Beylie and Tavernier, 'Entretien avec Jean-Pierre Melville', p. 10.
38. Volker Schloendorff, 'Hommage to a Master', *Time Out*, no. 654, 4–10 March 1983, p. 27.
39. Labro, 'Jean-Pierre Melville ou s'avancer masqué', p. 115.
40. Chancel, 'Radioscopie'.
41. Schloendorff, 'Hommage to a Master', p. 27.
42. Nogueira, *Melville on Melville*, p. 77.
43. Bantcheva, *Jean-Pierre Melville*, p. 167. Here again, there are contradictory statements: Auguste Le Breton claims Melville after the fire 'did not lack money, as he was covered by the insurance'. Auguste Le Breton, *Monsieur Rififi* (Paris: Hachette, 1976), p. 194.
44. Nogueira, *Melville on Melville*, p. 80.
45. See the criteria used by the CNC box-office statistics in *Ciné-Passions, 7e art et industrie de 1945 à 2000* (Paris: Éditions Dixit/CNC, 2000).
46. Nogueira, *Melville on Melville*, p. 64.
47. *Libération*, May 1994 (exact date missing) – report on ninth French Film Festival in Florence which organised a Melville retrospective. A number of critics and friends of Melville were invited, including Claude Beylie, José Giovanni and Florence Welsh, who all spoke about Melville.
48. Gilles Durieux, *Lino Ventura* (Paris: Flammarion, 2001), p. 262.
49. The exact details of their quarrel are unclear. See Bernard Violet, *Les Mystères Delon* (Paris: Flammarion, 2000), pp. 307–8.
50. Melville accused Claude Lelouch of having paid film critic Michel Cournot (who had criticised *Le Samouraï*) to be lenient towards Lelouch's latest film. In *Paris-Jour*, 27 November 1967.
51. Françoise Bonnot, in Bantcheva, *Jean-Pierre Melville*, p. 215.
52. Pierre Grasset, in Bantcheva, *Jean-Pierre Melville*, p. 211.
53. Philippe Lemaire, in Bantcheva, *Jean-Pierre Melville*, p. 193.
54. Labro, 'Jean-Pierre Melville ou s'avancer masqué', pp. 128–9.
55. Schloendorff, *Les Nouvelles*, 17–23 November 1983.
56. Yves Montand, *Les Dernières nouvelles d'Alsace*, 3 August 1973.
57. Nogueira, *Melville on Melville*, p. 112.
58. Ibid., p. 156.
59. Breitbart, 'An Interview with Jean-Pierre Melville', p. 19.
60. *France-Hebdo*, 15 February 1949.
61. Jean Collet, *Télérama*, no. 699, 9 June 1963.
62. *Image et son*, no. 57–8, November–December 1952, pp. 27–8.
63. Melville's name and an early budget estimate for *Rififi* are indicated in the *Rififi* production archive (CN0658 B450 [455]f).

64. Nogueira, *Melville on Melville*, pp. 65–6.
65. Ibid., p. 67.
66. Ibid.
67. Marcel Ophuls, 'A propos du "Chagrin et la pitié"', *Positif*, no. 469, March 2000, pp. 57–8.
68. Nogueira, *Melville on Melville*, p. 91.
69. Guy Teisseire, *L'Aurore*, 15 September 1969.
70. Chancel, 'Radioscopie'.
71. The French Censorship Commission is composed of a mixture of government officials and film personnel.
72. André Bazin, '*Le Silence de la mer*', *Le Parisien libéré*, 27 April 1949.
73. 'Bilan du cinéma français', *Cahiers du cinéma*, no. 71, May 1957.
74. Jean-Pierre Melville, *Combat*, 23 September 1961.
75. 'Jean-Pierre Melville: La nouvelle Vague? Je l'ai inventée en 1937', *Arts*, no. 866, 25 April 1962.
76. *France nouvelle*, 20 February 1963.
77. Florence Welsh says that 'They came to the studio: Godard, Truffaut, Chabrol', in Bantcheva, *Jean-Pierre Melville*, p. 175.
78. The connections between Parvulesco and Godard are fascinatingly revealed in Hélène Liogier, '1960: Vue d'Espagne, la nouvelle vague est fasciste', *1895 (AFRHC)*, no. 26, December 1998, pp. 127–53. Michel Marmin quotes Parvulesco as saying, 'Like John Buchan, like Fritz Lang [. . .] Melville belongs to the great race of those obsessed with absolute power.' *Magazine Hebdo*, 24 October 1983.
79. Jacques Doniol-Valcroze, 'La marque Melville', *L'Express*, 13 August 1973.
80. Jean-Louis Comolli and Jean Narboni, 'Cinema/Ideology/Criticism', *Cahiers du cinéma*, no. 216, October 1969, in Nick Browne (ed.), *Cahiers du cinéma 1969–1972, The Politics of Representation* (London: Routledge/BFI, 1990), pp. 61–2.
81. Nogueira, *Melville on Melville*, p. 159.
82. See Browne, *Cahiers du cinéma 1969–1972*; and Bérénice Reynaud's brilliant introduction to David Wilson (ed.), *Cahiers du cinéma, Volume 4, 1973–1978: History, Ideology, Cultural Struggle* (London: Routledge, 2000), pp. 1–44, for an account (in English) of the evolution of *Cahiers* over this turbulent period.
83. Serge Daney and Jean-Pierre Oudard, 'Work, Reading, Pleasure', *Cahiers du cinéma*, July 1970, in Browne (ed.), *Cahiers du cinéma 1969–1972*, p. 117.
84. Henry Chapier, *Combat*, 3 August 1973.
85. Jean-Pierre Melville, *Les Lettres françaises*, 7 February 1963.
86. 'Jean-Pierre Melville: La nouvelle Vague?'.
87. Interview with François Périer, in Bantcheva, *Jean-Pierre Melville*, p. 203.
88. Henri Decae, in Sharon A. Russell (ed.), *Semiotics and Lighting: A Study of Six Modern French Cameramen* (Ann Arbor, MI: UMI Research Press, 1978), p. 114.
89. Nogueira, *Melville on Melville*, p. 8.
90. Ibid., p. 118.
91. Ibid., p. 129.
92. Breitbart, 'An Interview with Jean-Pierre Melville', p. 19.
93. Teisseire, *L'Aurore*, 15 September 1969.

94. Florence Welsh, in Bantcheva, *Jean-Pierre Melville*, p. 177.
95. Beylie and Tavernier, 'Entretien avec Jean-Pierre Melville', p. 6.
96. Jean-Pierre Melville, *Télérama*, no. 670, 18 November 1962, p. 58.
97. Jean-Pierre Melville, *Paris-Presse*, 24–5 August 1969.
98. Schloendorff, *Les Nouvelles*, 17–23 November 1983.
99. Dominique Crèvecoeur, 'Entretien avec Dominique Crèvecoeur', in Françoise Puaux (ed.), 'Le machisme à l'écran', *CinémAction*, no. 99, 2001.
100. Patrick Bureau, 'Chroniques Melvilliennes – I', *Cinéma 68*, no. 128, August–September 1968, p. 42.
101. Françoise Audé, *Ciné-modèles, Cinéma d'elles, Situations des femmes dans le cinéma français 1956–1979* (Lausanne: L'Age d'homme, 1981), p. 63.
102. Jacques Zimmer and Chantal de Béchade, *Jean-Pierre Melville* (Paris: Edilig, 1983), p. 33.
103. Bantcheva, *Jean-Pierre Melville*, p. 51.
104. Jacques Nataf (interview with the author) and Daniel Cauchy (*Bob le flambeur*, Criterion DVD interview) confirm Melville's heterosexuality.
105. *Godard par Godard, Les Années Cahiers (1950 à 1959)* (Paris: Éditions de L'Étoile/Flammarion, 1989), p. 27.
106. Daniel Cauchy (*Bob le flambeur*, Criterion DVD interview).
107. Chancel, 'Radioscopie'.
108. Bantcheva, *Jean-Pierre Melville*, p. 173.
109. François Guérif, 'Jean-Pierre Melville', *Les Cahiers de la cinémathèque*, no. 25, Spring–Summer 1978, p. 97.
110. Jean-Marie Frodon, '*L'Armée des ombres*, le monument piégé d'un résistant', *Cahiers du cinéma*, no. 507, November 1996, p. 70.
111. Doniol-Valcroze, 'La marque Melville'.
112. Nogueira, *Melville on Melville*, p. 167.
113. Melville, *Télérama*, no. 670, 18 November 1962, p. 58.

2

Stylistic Exercises: *24 heures de la vie d'un clown* (1946), *Les Enfants terribles* (1950), *Quand tu liras cette lettre* (1953)

Jean-Pierre Melville began his career in the cinema with a short film few people have seen and which he vehemently disowned. Of the film, *24 heures de la vie d'un clown*, he told *Cahiers du cinéma*, 'When you say nobody has seen the film, I am delighted and I hope nobody will ever see it.'[1] After this false start, his 'real' debut was much more spectacular – *Le Silence de la mer* became an instant classic. Given the independent nature of its production and its innovative *mise en scène*, I could legitimately have started this chapter with *Le Silence de la mer*. However, because it is a film about the Resistance, a subject of peculiar and recurring significance in the director's life and films, I analyse it alongside the two other films Melville made on the topic, *Léon Morin, prêtre* and *L'Armée des ombres*, in Chapter 3.

With this slight disruption to chronology, therefore, I begin my analysis of Melville's films with a brief discussion of his short *24 heures de la vie d'un clown*, and with an account of the two films he made after *Le Silence de la mer* – *Les Enfants terribles* and *Quand tu liras cette lettre*. I call them 'stylistic exercises' to emphasise their disparate and experimental nature, and the fact that they stand apart from his later films, although sharing many thematic and aesthetic connections with them. The seventeen-minute-long *24 heures* is a semi-documentary on a famous clown, Béby. *Les Enfants terribles*, as an adaptation of Jean Cocteau's most famous novel, is dominated by the writer's personality and voice, yet it is also close to Melville's own concerns. *Lettre*, on the other hand, is a melodrama based on a script by the playwright Jacques Deval, made in the dominant 'Tradition of Quality' of the day. In many respects it is the least typical film in Melville's oeuvre (and certainly the most ignored critically). André Bazin disliked the film in 1953, but aptly called it a 'stylistic exercise'. Indeed, what clearly links all these three disparate works is the use Melville made of them to build up a repertoire of stylistic strategies that would serve as building blocks for his more overtly coherent style subsequently.

24 HEURES DE LA VIE D'UN CLOWN: ALREADY MONTMARTRE

This seventeen-minute-long semi-documentary follows, as its title indicates, twenty-four hours in the life of a clown called Béby (presumably a pun on 'baby'), who works at the Médrano circus in Montmartre. We start just before midnight as Béby's act with his partner, Maïss, is coming to an end. We follow Béby home, see him eat dinner prepared by his wife, look at books and photographs and retire to bed. In the morning he ablutes in the local public baths and amuses patrons at his local café. Later he and Maïss observe real-life incidents in the street and rework them into their act, which we see on stage. The film ends just before midnight.

It is hard to see why Melville should be so dismissive of this short. Admittedly different from his later work, *24 heures* is an original and, as co-producer Pierre Braunberger says, charming movie.[2] For a first film by someone with no formal training it is extremely accomplished. To a large degree, the film's charm derives from its Parisian location shooting, which Melville mobilises in two dovetailing ways. Although the incidents we see are in most cases staged for the film, the locations (the circus, Béby's flat, the streets and cafés), and of course Béby himself, have obvious documentary value. But *24 heures* functions also as a poetic homage to silent cinema as well as to Sacha Guitry's *Le Roman d'un tricheur* (1936). Most of *24 heures* is shot without synchronised sound. Scenes such as the encounters with Béby's wife, the public baths and street incidents are organised like mini-comic gags, and the era of early cinema is further evoked by the bitter-sweet piano music. At the same time, Melville's voiceover, which comments on the action and draws attention to particular moments or objects, functions like Guitry's in *Le Roman d'un tricheur* (like Guitry, Orson Welles and Jean Cocteau – all noted for their voiceovers – Melville has a very distinctive delivery which is already recognisable in *24 heures*, although sounding touchingly young). His employment of it here may be seen as a trial run for the use of the same device in *Le Silence de la mer* and *Les Enfants terribles*, with the voices of Jean-Marie Robain and Cocteau respectively, and in *Bob le flambeur* and *Deux hommes dans Manhattan*, in both of which he used his own voice again. Only at the end of *24 heures*, when we see the circus act, is there synchronised dialogue. Delaying it until the end of the film cleverly provides an element of surprise and gives more relief to Béby's voice. We discover, for instance, that he has a pronounced Southern accent.

24 heures is obviously a tribute to the circus, which Melville credited as one of his great loves and formative influences. The commentary reveals that Béby's family is from Castres in south-west France, the town where Melville's family relocated during the war. It is thus possible that Melville knew the clown personally. In any case, though largely forgotten today, Béby enjoyed some renown in the 1930s and 40s and, oddly enough, attracted the attention of two other eminent film-makers. Jean Vigo's project of a film with Béby entitled *Clown par amour* was never made because of his untimely death. Robert Bresson, on the other hand, did make *Affaires publiques* in 1934, a surreal comic fantasy co-starring Dalio, which is briefly alluded to in *24 heures* when Béby looks at photographs of himself and other circus and music-hall personalities. There is another intriguing parallel between Melville and Bresson's film portrayals of Béby, which is that both subsequently tried hard to erase them from their filmographies:[3] it seems poor Béby is the eternal repressed!

It is of course tempting to look at *24 heures* for evidence of Melville's subsequent work. Apart from its bow to popular entertainment, which later transferred to cinematic homage, and the play with the voiceover, are other future Melvillian themes or motifs in evidence?

Well, yes. Although the commentary pays tribute to a vibrant popular spectacle (and Maïss' glowing costume), the dominant mood is melancholy. This is partly due to the 'sad clown' effect, and partly to Béby's personal circumstances, which are clearly less than grand: his small flat; his solitary wife waiting for him every evening; his grumble about 'spaghetti for the last fifty years'; and the fact that he has to go to the public baths to wash. But there is a more pervasive sense of an ending era. Béby is old, as poignantly recalled by his perusal of his books and photographs, many of which refer to deceased former colleagues (Aubert, Mistinguett and Raimu). In 1970, when asked by André S. Labarthe in his documentary *Jean-Pierre Melville: Portrait en 9 poses* about the increasingly nostalgic tone of his late films, Melville replied that the nostalgia had been there right from *Le Silence de la mer*. But *24 heures* shows that it was present even earlier. With the nostalgia comes the self-consciousness. The film is about a clown but it is about a clown self-consciously living the life of a clown, reminiscing about his past career, looking at mementoes of it, rehearsing and incorporating new material into his act in front of our eyes. This is also expressed in the two rhyming scenes in the dressing room, when Béby and Maïss remove and later apply their make-up in front of a large mirror, itself duplicated in a smaller mirror on the dressing table. We will have many opportunities to note the importance of mirrors, as well as the ritualistic repetition of gestures, in later Melville films.

Another Melvillian theme that will resurface is that of the male couple. Béby and Maïss are shown each to have his own family: we see Béby's wife and Maïss' daughter, but their presence weighs little compared to the male couple. While this is to be expected in professional terms (they *are* the act), *24 heures* deliberately presents the Béby couple through a series of mysogynist comic vignettes: Béby grumbling at his dinner; the matronly wife chiding him for looking at a pretty young woman; the insistence on his sleeping and saying his prayers, not with his wife but with his dog! As the 'Auguste' to Maïss' white clown, Béby is small and slightly disabled by his former career as an acrobat. There is something undoubtedly moving in his rolling gait and winsome facial expressions. The film thus solicits our sympathy for a hen-pecked figure who finds escape and approval in work.

Most *visually* evocative of the Melville to come, however, are the two short moments that bracket the film. The film begins and ends with views of Montmartre (Pigalle) at night, a glamorous noir vision with neon lights which irresistibly evokes *Bob le flambeur*, especially as a mysterious man, whose face is hidden by his trilby and the darkness – Melville? – looks at his watch. The love of popular spectacle is also a love of Montmartre and Pigalle, which will reappear gloriously in 1956 in *Bob le flambeur*. Before then, however, Melville will make three features, including *Les Enfants terribles*, to which I now turn, and *Quand tu liras cette lettre*.

LES ENFANTS TERRIBLES: IN COCTEAU'S ORBIT

Closely following the successful release of *Le Silence de la mer* (see Chapter 3), *Les Enfants terribles*, despite the controversy surrounding it, consolidated Melville's place on the critical map. As with Vercors and *Le Silence de la mer*, collaborating with Cocteau was not easy. Working with such an illustrious writer was a double bind – raising the profile of the young Melville, yet threatening to submerge his identity. Asked why he had not wanted at that point to make a film based on his own script, Melville said: 'The fact of having been chosen by Cocteau flattered me, no doubt, and I quickly got sucked into it.'[4] This presumably answers another, puzzling, question about the Melville–Cocteau partnership: how did Melville, with his strong Resistance background, and who had just made *Le Silence de la mer*, come to agree to work with a well-known collaborator? Although on occasion attacked by fascist writers such as Lucien Rebatet for making 'typical invert's theatre',[5] Cocteau had spent the war working within the collaborationist *tout Paris*. His film *L'Eternel retour* premiered in Vichy, and Cocteau wrote a poem to the glory of German sculptor Arno Breker for the opening of his Paris exhibition in May 1942.

In any event, the poet-film-maker (who had just finished *Orphée*) wanted a greater role in the film-making process than Melville was prepared to concede. Ironically, though, it was Melville who insisted on absolute fidelity. As he said: 'I condemned him to a total respect for the dialogue in the novel. Every time he tried to change something, I'd say, "If you're going to write a new *Enfants terribles*, I'm no longer interested in filming it" '[6] – although, as we will see, a few changes to the novel were made. Cocteau imposed his views in two instances, which Melville resented but was obliged to accept: the casting of Edouard Dermithe (Cocteau's protégé) as Paul, and the setting of the story in the present day as opposed to the time of its writing (1929), as Melville would have liked.

Les Enfants terribles is the story of the incestuous relationship between sister and brother, Elisabeth (Nicole Stéphane) and Paul (Edouard Dermithe), both at an indeterminate age between adolescence and young adulthood. Paul, a pupil at the Lycée Condorcet in Paris, falls ill when hit by a snowball containing a stone thrown by fellow pupil Dargelos (Renée Cosima), with whom he is infatuated. The sickly Paul begins a reclusive existence with his sister Elisabeth and their sick mother in their flat in rue du Rocher. The 'children' turn their cluttered bedroom into a 'theatre' where they play ritualistic games witnessed by their friend Gérard (Jacques Bernard) who loves Paul and later Elisabeth. After their mother dies, Gérard's wealthy uncle takes them to the seaside. Back in Paris Elisabeth finds a job as a haute couture model. There she meets Agathe, who makes a strong impression on Paul because of her uncanny resemblance to Dargelos (Agathe is actually played by the same actress, Renée Cosima). To Paul's annoyance, Elisabeth marries a rich American, Michael (Mel Martin), who dies in a car crash immediately after the wedding. Elisabeth, Paul, Agathe and Gérard move into Michael's huge Parisian town house, where they recreate their old room in a vast gallery. When Paul and Agathe separately confess their love for each other to Elisabeth, she deviously engineers a marriage between Agathe and Gérard. Paul's health worsens when the newlyweds leave on their honeymoon. They come back bearing a (black) ball of poisonous substance sent by Dargelos. Later the distraught Paul takes the poison and dies, while Elisabeth shoots herself.

Even before it came out *Les Enfants terribles* commanded much critical attention. On-set conflicts between Melville and Cocteau were the talk of the town and, in order to scotch the (partly self-fuelled) rumours that it was *his* film, Cocteau told *France-Soir*, 'Although I worked with Melville hand in hand, the film is his, not mine.'[7] Melville for his part stated on numerous occasions that Cocteau left him alone after he asserted himself on day one of shooting, ejecting Cocteau who had 'inadvertently' said 'cut' from the set.[8] Cocteau reportedly directed one day of shooting, of scenes at the 'seaside' (in fact shot in a small town north of Paris, as is plainly evident). Still, this did not stop reviewers trying to apportion the relative inputs of the two men and, inevitably, in this game Melville was overshadowed by Cocteau.

On its release the film violently divided critical opinion, while box-office sales were average (its total of 719,844 tickets was significantly fewer than for *Le Silence de la mer*). Jacques Siclier noted that 'its career was mostly in film clubs'.[9] From the left-wing *Combat* to the Catholic *La Croix*, Melville was deemed to have made an excellent adaptation of a canonical book, retaining its 'spirit'[10] and 'making a very good job of a difficult task'.[11] On the other hand his camera movements were felt by some to be excessive and Cocteau's voiceover overbearing. In several cases *Les Enfants terribles* was compared unfavourably to *Le Silence de la mer*. Actors' performances, however, united all critics, then and later: Nicole Stéphane's Elisabeth was universally lauded while Dermithe's Paul was comprehensively condemned.

The fiercest attacks, though, were directed at the film's contents, and therefore at Cocteau. *L'Écran français*, the leading specialist film journal of the Liberation, which had championed *Le Silence de la mer*, trashed the film, calling it a 'grotesque story' with a 'pseudo-poetic commentary crammed with wilfully obscure terms'.[12] *L'Aube* condemned it for wallowing in the 'moral indigence of bourgeois bohemian youth' while *Franc-Tireur*[13] described the bedroom as 'a dustbin in which lie, pell-mell, human detritus'. Homosexual and incestuous undertones were not picked up as such. This could be because they were toned down from the novel. Reportedly, a shot showing Elisabeth and Paul in a passionate embrace was cut,[14] although there is no trace of this in the Censorship Commission files, a fact which suggests self-censorship in anticipation of what would be acceptable to the audience. Instead, surrealism was the overt focus of attack. Whether favourable or unfavourable to the film, reviewers in such publications as *Le Monde* hated 'the hideous apparatus of Surrealism, the mustachioed statues, the artificial flowers and the convoluted objects dear to the creator of *Le Sang d'un poète*'.[15] It is conceivable that these attacks may have been disguised homophobia since there were also veiled references to Dermithe's 'effeminate' looks.

Two years after the film's release, Noël Burch wrote a detailed textual analysis of it that can hardly be bettered.[16] Burch exhaustively examines the complex camerawork, the role of music, the substitution of visual for verbal poetry and the use of objects. Burch's originality was to claim full authorship of the film for Melville: '*Les Enfants terribles* may be a great film because of Cocteau's novel, but it is that, especially in spite of, and beyond, the novel.'[17] For Burch, Melville was, 'with Bresson, Franju and Tati, the only French filmmaker who was capable of making a film which is art, like a string quartet, a poem or a painting, independently of any intellectual or literary content'.[18] Burch thus perceived at the time the shift historians such as Kristin Thompson and David Bordwell later would chart: '*Les Enfants terribles* exemplifies the rethinking of the relation between film and other arts that was taking place in postwar modernism.'[19]

It is worth noting that the re-release of *Les Enfants terribles* in the mid-1970s also attracted both violent attacks (being seen as indulgently bourgeois in the post-May 1968 context) and high acclaim. One writer who did praise *Les Enfants* was Truffaut, who wrote in 1974:

> When this Cocteau–Melville film appeared in 1950, it wasn't like anything else being done in French cinema at the time. [. . .] There is no need to carefully distinguish what is Melville's and what is Cocteau's in this four-handed concerto; the former's calm strength is well served by the latter's spirited writing. The two artists worked together like Bach and Vivaldi. Jean Cocteau's best novel became Jean-Pierre Melville's best film.[20]

The last sentence is often cited – it appears on the film's VHS jacket. Yet Truffaut had not always thought so, contrary to what is often asserted. In 1953, in a harsh review of *Quand tu liras cette lettre* (discussed later), he dismissed Melville's contribution to both *Le Silence de la mer* and *Les Enfants terribles*, attributing their qualities solely to the writers. Reasons for this change of mind are unclear. Truffaut and the *Cahiers du cinéma* group were close to Cocteau, and their friendship possibly made them reluctant to accept Melville's contribution (Jacques Rivette's 1964 review of *Les Enfants* in *Cahiers* astonishingly makes absolutely no refence to Melville).[21] However, in 1953 Truffaut was writing from the standpoint of *Quand tu liras cette lettre*, a film he evidently disliked. He came round to Melville after he started making his own films, and the two were friends in the early 1960s (see Chapter 4).

Les Enfants, unlike many Melville films, has attracted a fair amount of scholarly writing, but, in a replay of its reception at the time, this has tended to be mostly from a literary point of view, addressed to Cocteau rather than Melville. Exceptions include Burch, already mentioned. More recently gay and feminist approaches to the film have renewed its critical currency, as will be discussed, though here too the focus tends to be on Cocteau.

Adapting Cocteau: poetry, theatre and cinema

Melville's efforts to assert himself, as distinct from Cocteau, can be seen right from the credit sequence in which their names alternate: Melville's appears four times and Cocteau's three. As befits cinematic conventions, Melville has the last word as 'Producer and Director'.

The credits of *Les Enfants* are superimposed over an extraordinary image: a woman (Elisabeth) stands guard over what looks like a body, laid on a table and covered with a cloth. The tableau is set outdoors, on top of a hill, and a strange, tall pyramid stands erect on the other side of the table from her. Later this image is revealed to be from Elisabeth's dream about Paul's (and her own) death. The table is a billiard table, the strange object a stand with billiard cues. The slanted composition, the incongruity of a table outdoors, the contrast between joyful classical music and the macabre image, all condense many of the stylistic and thematic motifs of the film. We have, in a nutshell, Elisabeth's deadliness, surreal fantasy, the rhythmic beauty of baroque music echoing that of Henri

Decae's black-and-white photography. The opening scene after the credits, which shows a snowball fight in a courtyard, is a clear allusion to the similar scene at the end of Cocteau's own 1931 film *Le Sang d'un poète*. Its function is to anchor the film in Cocteau's literary and filmic universe, especially as his voice, mingling with the music, comments on the boys' snowball fight, the arrogance of Dargelos, the boys' sadistic games and Paul's wounding.

In *Le Sang d'un poète* Dargelos actually kills another boy with a snowball, and we see him bleeding profusely from the mouth while he utters disturbing sounds of both agony and ecstasy. The camera lingers on the boy's mouth, and later a woman and a man play cards on a table stuck over his body, while groups of strange, formally dressed, characters look on from balconies; the dead boy is 'rescued' by a black angel. *Les Enfants* replays this scene in a similar setting, but in a more 'realist' manner (the setting, Cité Monthier, was familiar to Melville who also went to Lycée Condorcet – see Chapter 1). Most of the *outré* surrealist imagery has vanished, although the scene remains oddly oneiric and a-temporal, partly because of the old-fashioned boys' clothes. Here Melville covertly had his way in ignoring Cocteau's wish to update clothes, as he says with a smirk in Labarthe's documentary. Despite the enclosed theatrical set of the school yard and Cité Monthier (shot in the rue Jenner studio), Melville stylistically asserts himself with an extremely mobile camera which tracks with the children as they deliriously run out of the school, and then takes us into the thick of the flying snowballs.

Les Enfants terribles was not the easiest book to adapt for the cinema. For, although several scholars have pointed out the cinematic qualities inherent in the novel, there were obvious pitfalls, including the task of representing a universe half-way between reality and fantasy and characters who are neither children nor adults. Nicole Stéphane is extraordinary as Elisabeth, with her unusual beauty – her chiselled face, sculpted blond hair and pale eyes – and her ability to pass effortlessly from understatement to hysteria. Dermithe's choice was notoriously controversial. Cocteau wanted to launch his new protégé on a film career, as he had done with Jean Marais. This did not happen. Yet Dermithe hardly deserves the abuse he has received. I would agree with Cameron Tolton that 'it is difficult to say whether his performance itself is amateurishly wooden or deliberately equivocal',[22] and would add that even his 'wooden' performance is put to good use by Melville who thereby adds to the character's theatricality. Dermithe is definitely too large compared to the other boys, but as soon as he moves into the flat his looks, which match Stéphane's, visually stress both their androgynous appeal and their incestuous bond. An extended visual metaphor shows them throughout the film in mirroring positions, either in profile or side by side. Similarly, Melville's decision to use a woman (Cosima), for the dual role of Dargelos and Agathe, has been considered inspired by some and a betrayal of Dargelos' homoerotic appeal by others.[23]

As with *Silence*, Melville in *Les Enfants terribles* explores a new type of literary adaptation that departs significantly from the dominant 'Tradition of Quality' of the time (discussed in greater detail in Chapter 3). His innovation, like Robert Bresson's in *Le Journal d'un curé de campagne* (1951), is to give equal weight to the literary and the filmic. Where Vercors' house stood for the writer's presence in *Silence*, Cocteau's voice performs this function in *Les Enfants*. As Turk says, it is both an instrument of omniscience, as it 'objectively' provides a commentary on the action, and a poetic device in itself.[24] An example of Michel Chion's '*texte-roi*',[25] the voice takes on an almost concrete quality: it is like another character and a Greek chorus. Like Vercors' house too, it also adds documentary value and charm to the film, especially given Cocteau's inimitable diction.

Melville's decision to resist Cocteau's idea of a jazz song and to replace it with music from the baroque (Bach and Vivaldi) was inspired. The glorious music, like Cocteau's voice, weaves in and out of the soundtrack from the beginning to the end of the film, imparting a lyrical feeling to moments of intensity, elation, fantasy and dream. It accompanies Paul's sleep-walking, the friends' flight after Gérard's theft at the seaside, Paul dragging his bedclothes to recreate 'the bedroom' in Michael's house (a surrealist image *par excellence*, evoking the dragging pianos of *Un chien andalou* [1928]). The music also has a sinister, hypnotic function when it seemingly drives Elisabeth along, like an automaton, on her deadly machinations between Paul and Agathe. As Cocteau's voice tells us that 'the spirit of the bedroom was possessing her', a complex equivalent is thus established between characters, setting and music. Bach and Vivaldi's relentless rhythm gives these scenes a fateful quality, to which Melville appears to choreograph both characters' movements and editing. One such music-led moment is the celebrated scene in which Paul, Elisabeth, Agathe, Michael and Gérard ascend a grand staircase in Michael's house. The moment is given portentous weight through *mise en scène*: seen from an extreme high angle (the camera was placed on a lift to imitate a crane shot[26]), they indeed appear to walk to the rhythm of the music. The angle reveals the grand space and the black-and-white tiled floor, like a giant chessboard, emphasising both the idea of a game and of fate. The music here acts as a bridge between the old room and the new space.

Other devices – such as the unusual camera angles, rhythmic editing and expressionist lighting – illustrate Melville's dual strategy (with the help of Decae), to transform a theatrical space into a cinematic one, while retaining the 'theatricality' of Cocteau's universe. Making the most of limited means, Melville inventively used theatrical equipment (some scenes were shot in the Théâtre Pigalle). With trick photography he shows the room sliding away – literally and metaphorically – from behind Gérard. Gérard's distant gaze acknowledges the off-screen space, 'breaking the fourth wall', as does Elisabeth's fixed gaze when she discovers the resemblance between Agathe/Dargelos and all the photographs on Paul's wall, and the camera denies us a reverse angle.[27]

The self-conscious theatricality of *Les Enfants* – like the snowball fight – cues the spectator into Cocteau's universe, here his own *Les Parents terribles* (1948). Both films share the idea of characters elevating theatrical games to the level of a lifestyle. The theme of theatricality pervades *Les Enfants* on many levels: the enclosed settings (the room, Michael's house); the 'props' (in particular the mustachioed statue); Paul and Elisabeth's conversations; Elisabeth's manipulations; and the actors' performance style. Elisabeth and Paul at various times self-consciously declaim their 'text' to each other and to Gérard and Agathe (Gérard in particular frequently occupies the position of the spectator in the text), pacing up and down the width of the room, arms stretched, fingers pointed in 'theatrical' gestures, as the camera pans to follow them with fluid long takes. At other times Paul and Elisabeth address the camera directly or through a mirror. The extreme mobility of Melville and Decae's camera throughout the film thus creates a dynamic cinematic space, while still being put to the service of Cocteau's theatricality.

Les Enfants terribles: mirrors and mirrorings – Elisabeth (Nicole Stéphane) and the moustachioed bust

Agathe (Renée Cosima) and Elisabeth surround Paul (Edouard Dermithe) in a *mise en abyme* of their sexual dynamic

Elisabeth looks at herself before the dreadful ending

Elisabeth and Paul as mirror images

For Richard Dyer, such theatricality relates to gay aesthetics: 'It may well be that the ability to hold together a passionate belief in something with a concomitant recognition of its artificiality is a defining feature of much gay culture [. . .]. Thus "poetry" is both cult and cultivation.'[28] But it is also possible to relate the theatricality of *Les Enfants* to the cinematic self-consciousness of Melville's later work. This duality coalesces around the use of mirrors. Dyer points out that 'Aestheticism in Cocteau is often realised through the image of the mirror. Mirrors aestheticise because they frame sections of reality and render them on a shimmering, one-dimensional surface: they make reality into beautiful pictures,' and again links this to gay aesthetics, as 'mirrors (in Cocteau) connect narcissism and homoeroticism'.[29] Mirrors will play a key role in Melville's work for both similar and different reasons. For Melville, mirrors are always a formal cinematic feature, a way to dynamically increase space and self-consciously play on the medium; they are also a device with which to explore narcissism and issues of identity – from *Bob le flambeur* to *Un flic*, and perhaps most famously in *Le Samouraï*. As he said, 'There is a moment of truth in all my films. A man before a mirror means a stock-taking.'[30] The most significant moments in *Les Enfants* to occur in front of a mirror involve Elisabeth, and indeed they are moments of stock-taking. She looks at herself while washing her hands towards the end of the film. This scene, Turk convincingly argues, connects her to Lady Macbeth, symbolically referring to her crime to come, especially as Cocteau's voiceover adds a sentence from *Macbeth* that was not in the novel ('All the perfumes of Arabia will not sweeten this little hand').[31] Just before the end of the film, Elisabeth presses her hands to her head, addressing the mirror/camera in a hallucinating manner, announcing the dread of the ending to come. But equally interesting is the scene in which Elisabeth, in mourning for Michael, and Agathe sit on either side of the mirror of a dressing table, framing Paul reflected in the centre of it, in a powerful *mise en abyme* of their sado-masochistic three-way relationship.

Les Enfants terribles: androgyny and misogyny

On several occasions later in his career Melville has referred to his penchant for ambiguous situations as 'my *Enfants terribles* side', linking this to Herman Melville's *Pierre, or The Ambiguities*, also a story of incest. Even in its toned down way, *Les Enfants* remains explicit about incest. Paul and Elisabeth live a relationship of physical contiguity, like twins in the womb-like space of the room, as Cocteau's voice puts it, 'like two members of the same body'. As they fight, make up, are jealous of each other's partners, they act out one of the great Melvillian themes, that of 'underground' relationships with alter egos and impossible loves. The death-drive of the characters also strikes a familiar note to those acquainted with Melville's subsequent work. Elisabeth and Paul's motto written on the mirror – 'suicide is a mortal sin' – anticipates the end of their story (both commit suicide), and many subsequent Melville films. The connection is most explicit with *Le Doulos*, *Le Deuxième souffle*, *Le Samouraï*, *L'Armée des ombres* and *Le Cercle rouge* in which the fateful message is written both literally (on pre- or post-credit texts) and metaphorically in the characters' position or behaviour. Thus *Les Enfants* can be seen as a powerful thematic matrix for Melville's subsequent work. At the same time it also remains closely tied to Cocteau's universe. Al La Valley, for example, considers the linking of sex with violence and death in Cocteau's work to be a covert 'Discourse of ritual sex, sado-masochism and taboo sexuality – the sleazy hotel corridor of *Blood of a Poet*, the labyrinthine world of male brothels and sleazy hotels in *The White Book*, Paul and Lisa's [sic] famous disordered room in *Les Enfants terribles*.'[32] In his meticulous reading of the book-to-film adaptation of *Les Enfants*, Turk points to the reduction of the homoerotic appeal of Agathe/Dargelos, and of the way the film's ending modifies the book's. In the novel, Paul briefly outlives Elisabeth and enjoys a final blissful vision of Dargelos. In the film Paul dies first after a 'vision' of the boys which does *not* include Dargelos (contrary to what Turk says). The last, morbidly triumphant shot is of Elisabeth shooting herself and thereby collapsing the screens under her, as the camera soars magnificently above the space, accompanied by the glorious music. By returning Paul's vision simply to childhood rather than Dargelos, and giving Elisabeth 'the last word' visually, the film arguably 'de-queers' the novel, as we would say today.

This last shot of Elisabeth's 'triumphant' suicide is an arresting image of her ambivalent power. In both Cocteau's and Melville's work, she is possibly the strongest female character, but one whose power is deadly. As Roxanne Chee argues in her analysis of the gaze in the film, *Les Enfants* does not 'fetishise' Elisabeth in a traditional way, focusing rather on Paul's body. One cannot, however, agree with her that 'Elisabeth's androgynous

Les Enfants terribles: the last shot – Elisabeth (Nicole Stéphane) has killed herself after Paul's death

face complete with thick unplucked eyebows, square jaw and chin, and Roman profile are more suited to a man than a movie star. Rather than a Hollywood construction of glamorous "to-be-looked-at-ness", Elisabeth is a case of to-be-looked-at-*mess*'[33] (her emphasis). Apart from the fact that Stéphane's jaw is not square but very pointed and her features extremely fine, her svelte figure is enhanced by the Dior outfits in a visual contrast with the amorphous dressing-gowns. She is, however, as Chee and all scholars on the film have discussed, symbolically linked to the female plaster bust with a moustache, a symbol of androgyny, a mocking of the feminine (as in Duchamp's iconoclastic Mona Lisa) and an image of phallic power.

Despite the emphasis on androgyny and the mirroring of brother and sister, *Les Enfants* systematically presents an imbalance between the two. On the one hand the male homoerotic gaze that pervades the film has no female equivalent (the possibilities offered by the Dior models are not exploited, beyond a shot which visually doubles Elisabeth's gestures with those of the 'masculine' looking model played by Annabel Buffet). On the other hand, the film consistently foregrounds Elisabeth as the dominant partner. Where Paul is petulant, she is vicious. Throughout the film she towers over him, dominates his sickly frame as he lies 'embalmed' in bed (when he walks it is often in a sleep-walking trance), and she is endowed with an active, piercing, 'castrating' gaze; at Dior, Agathe teaches her to stare contemptuously at female customers. There is no doubt that, as

Burch and Sellier also argue, she is a 'deadly figure'.[34] As if it was necessary, Cocteau's voice reinforces the point, commenting on her as a black widow, a 'nocturnal spider' weaving her deadly web. The choice of Dior is one interesting way in which Melville did update the 'great couture house' of the novel and the costumes themselves and thereby contributed to the gender imbalance. Dior's New Look fashions in the immediate post-war offered a return to extravagant lengths of fabric after wartime austerity. His tailored suits, as worn by Elisabeth (and lovingly detailed in the production files)[35] both celebrate the female body and constrict it within sharp lines and strict fabrics; by contrast Agathe tends to wear dresses in softer fabrics, like velvet. The simultaneous representation of women in contemporary dress and men in nostalgic or timeless garb is a feature which will recur in Melville's films. Notably his gangsters adopt the anachronistic pre-war Hollywood gangster clothes, while women are seen in 1950s or 60s outfits.

Turk provides a final twist on Elisabeth with his comparison between her and Lady Macbeth. His impressively learned analysis convincingly argues that, like Lady Macbeth, Elisabeth is 'the more masculine component in her symbiotic, androgynous relationship with her feminized brother'. However, was it necessary to enlist Freud in order to add that 'with the chance for healthy procreation precluded, she too experiences the impotence and barrenness that Freud diagnosed in Lady Macbeth'?[36] So, not only a schemer and a murderer, but barren too! Power in women does come at a price. In this respect the murderous virgin of *Les Enfants* will become the deadly nun of *Quand tu liras cette lettre*.

By 1950 then, Melville was a well-established young independent film-maker with two substantial films under his belt and his own studio. The rue Jenner studio was unfinished but he had still been able to film parts of *Les Enfants* there: for instance, the scene with Paul and Gérard in the taxi, which he fondly recalls in *Jean-Pierre Melville: Portrait en 9 poses*. Given his fairly conflictual experience with two domineering literary figures, one might have expected him at that point to switch to his own script. However, he made a different move, working with yet another writer, though in a very different register. With *Quand tu liras cette lettre*, Melville moved from two sombre dramas, each with a high literary pedigree, to an over-the-top melodrama that included a defrocked nun, a gigolo, a rape, a sabotaged car and the male lead dying under a moving train.

QUAND TU LIRAS CETTE LETTRE: MELODRAMA ON THE CÔTE D'AZUR

Among Melville's films, *Quand tu liras cette lettre* is always presented as a 'commercial' project, a perception that stems partly from his own declaration that he had only signed the contract to direct it to earn quick money, in order to complete the furbishing of the rue Jenner studios.[37] Melville also frequently asserted that *Lettre* was meant to prove to the industry that he was not an 'amateur':

> So I had to make a very conventional, very sensible film; a film within the system and not outside it. And that is why, from a very good script, admirably written by Jacques Deval, I made a film which could just as well have been made by any French director of the period.[38]

Perhaps *Lettre* could have been made by any French director of the time, but it certainly does not look like anything anyone else would have made. Also, Melville's characterisation of *Lettre* as a 'sensible film' is, to say the least, open to question. Jacques Deval, who wrote the screenplay, was not a nobody, but he moved in very different spheres from Vercors and Cocteau. A highly successful boulevard playwright, he had also worked as a film director and dialogue-writer. Several of his plays were adapted to the cinema, notably the comedy *Club de femmes* (now reclaimed as a cult lesbian film) which he directed in 1936, and which was remade in 1956. Theatre historians see his work as marked by both brilliance and eclecticism,[39] his plays ranging from comedy to psychological drama. In fact this eclecticism is at the very centre of *Lettre*, where there are abrupt and sometimes bizarre changes of tone.

The story, set in Cannes, concerns two sisters, Thérèse (Juliette Gréco), a novice in a convent, and the younger Denise (Irène Galter). On the sudden death of their parents, Thérèse reluctantly renounces her vocation to run the family stationery shop and support Denise. Meanwhile, the attractive but louche Max (Philippe Lemaire), a young mechanic and boxer at the Riviera Dancing club, seduces a rich older woman, Irène (Yvonne Sanson), with the help of Carlton Hotel groom Biquet (Daniel Cauchy). Max and Denise's paths cross, and later Max, who has become Irène's chauffeur and lover, brutally rapes Denise as she delivers stationery. She tries to commit suicide, leaving a letter for her sister, but is rescued in time. Max doctors Irène's car, which Biquet wants to borrow, in order to stop Biquet blackmailing him. However, Irène unexpectedly takes the car and it is she who is seriously injured. Max is cleared by the judge, even though Irène's jewels have disappeared (in fact stolen by Biquet). Thérèse obliges Max to marry Denise to atone for the rape. He agrees but falls in love with her instead. He steals Denise's dowry to join Biquet in Tangiers, and hoping Thérèse will join him, he asks her to meet him the following day in Marseille. Thérèse, however, ostensibly decides to go on a retreat. Max waits for her at a railway station, but accidentally falls under the train in which she is sitting, bound for the convent (as discussed later, the ending is highly ambiguous; it is possible to interpret it as Thérèse having decided to join Max).

Melville achieved his aim of joining the mainstream with *Quand tu liras cette lettre*, which was a success, with box-office sales of over a million tickets. The appeal of Deval, of the sensational topic and of the two leads, Philippe Lemaire and Juliette Gréco, was sufficient for *Lettre* to be serialised in the popular weekly *Mon Film*.[40] Critical reception, however, was generally hostile. There was dismay at the fact that the auteur of *Le Silence de la mer* and *Les Enfants terribles* could 'lower' himself by making a melodrama characterised by excess, bad taste and improbable coincidences – a film reminiscent of 'bad theatre'.[41] The 'impossible love story' between an ex-nun and a gigolo was too much to take – it is a good thing, then, that Melville deleted a final plot twist from the script: originally the fatal train which crushes Max, bearing a grim-looking Thérèse, *also* carried Irène in a wheelchair.[42] As it is, in the released film, Irène, equally improbably simply vanishes from the screen after her car crash. For Gilles Martain in *Rivarol*, 'We reach the height of the grotesque'.[43] Jacques Doniol-Valcroze saluted the director of *Silence* and *Enfants* but thought 'the film seemed to

Quand tu liras cette lettre: 'novelisation' in the popular weekly *Mon Film* (10 February 1954)

have been put together like a cooking recipe'.[44] The most vitriolic criticism came – what a surprise – from François Truffaut (writing as Robert Lachenay) in *Cahiers du cinéma*: 'J. P. Melville is not an *auteur*, nor even a good maker of bad films.' For Truffaut *Lettre* only achieved a 'permanent compromise between a "tone" which aims to be high and only succeeds in being grotesque'.[45] It is therefore deeply ironic that at the time of writing the only available VHS of this film appears under Truffaut's label in the 'Films de ma vie' series.

There were a few exceptions to this hostility, such as *Combat*, in which R.-M. Arlaud wrote that 'Jean-Pierre Melville confirms his class.'[46] Lemaire's performance as the alluringly disreputable Max was a rallying point. Gréco was more controversial, hailed by some as 'a real new talent',[47] harshly criticised by others for her 'wooden' acting, and derided as the erstwhile 'dark muse of a fake existentialism'.[48] The deliberate irony of her casting, against the grain of her image as Saint-Germain-des-Prés iconoclastic *chanteuse*, does not seem to have been perceived. In this respect, though, Gréco anticipated the casting of New Wave idol Jean-Paul Belmondo as a priest in *Léon Morin, prêtre* (see Chapter 3).

One of the writers who perceived the irony but did not appreciate it was André Bazin, who wrote that the film left the 'unpleasant impression that the authors make fun of their subject and only use it as a springboard for a stylistic exercise'.[49] Pointing to 'elaborate lighting' and 'artful framings', Bazin indicted the film's 'snobbish' take on melodrama, a position consonant with his assault on the 'cultural chic' of such popular films as *Caroline Chérie* (1951).[50] The disparagement of *Caroline Chérie* and *Lettre* can be seen too as a wider critical contempt at the time for melodrama and other 'women's genres'. Similarly, Truffaut's acerbic review of *Lettre* prefigured his incendiary indictment of mainstream French cinema in his 1954 article, 'A Certain Tendency of the French Cinema', an attack on the mere illustrators of scriptwriters like Deval (as discussed further in Chapter 3). Since for Bazin and Truffaut the hallmarks of the true film auteur were realism and personal vision, a stylistically ostentatious melodrama written by an 'old hand' of boulevard theatre was not going to go down well. But, however insightful Bazin and Truffaut's views may have been about French cinema in general, here was a case where their polemic blinded them to some of this film's qualities.

Stylistic exercises

As will be gathered from the above descriptions, *Lettre* does not deal in subtlety in plot terms. Its melodramatic polarisation of characters and milieus is extreme: the world of Thérèse, both as pious nun and industrious shopkeeper (not forgetting grandparents who are peasants from the Provence hinterland) is pitted against the rich, the idle and the cosmopolitan world of Côte d'Azur grand hotels and louche cabarets. The meeting of the two worlds, through Max picking up Denise in the street, is arbitrary. The two worlds are echoed on the soundtrack by a rather mechanical alternation of dissonant harpsichord music (like a distorted version of the music of *Les Enfants*) and birds screeching for the sisters, and a sleazy accordion tune for Max. However, while *Lettre* may be uneven, some of the 'stylistic exercises' it contains deserve a second look.

One noteworthy aspect, compared to contemporary mainstream French cinema, is the extensive location shooting in Henri Alekan's stunning black-and-white photography. Melville and Alekan clearly enjoyed themselves with the opportunities offered by location photography: for instance, the magnificent wide pan over the bay of Cannes which opens and closes the film, the slanted camera angles that depict the convent, the experiments with noir photography both outdoors and indoors – as *Le Monde* said, 'astonishing views of Cannes in the fog and the rain'.[51] One such outdoor scene is the one in which Thérèse threatens Max in the park. Despite the implausibility of the narrative situation (Thérèse blackmailing Max with a gun), the rain adds a fresh, poetic quality to the image of their encounter not often seen in the films of the time. Some shots call attention to themselves in a flamboyant way: for example, the 'calligraphy' of the scenes through lace curtains in Thérèse and Denise's home (a favourite of Melville's, as seen in *Les Enfants* and *Léon Morin, prêtre*); the depth of field in the scene where Thérèse opens Venetian blinds at the back of the room, while a chair in focus in the foreground elongates the depth of the already deep room. Particularly remarkable is a scene on the beach in which Thérèse, having pursued Max ostensibly to retrieve the money he has stolen, is finally seen to fall for his charm. Hit by a pebble Max has thrown at her (shades of Dargelos' snowball?), Thérèse falters and he holds her in his arms on the moonlit beach, with the sea in the background. The shot is held for an unusual two minutes and twenty-three seconds. Although Therese's sudden change of heart about Max seems badly motivated, the shot pictorially has a poetic charge which overrides nar-

Quand tu liras cette lettre: dominating female, weak male – Max (Philippe Lemaire) and Thérèse (Juliette Gréco)

rative inconsistency. At that point too, Gréco's hair, which had hitherto been tightly pulled back, suddenly falls loose on her shoulders and she is finally her 'real' self, in the more familiar Gréco image.

If the shot jars so much, it is also because it comes after some indoor scenes in the women's home, which look stilted and drab. There is, however, one indoor space which offers Melville the opportunity to explore stylistic complexity in a way which anticipates his later films – that is the Riviera Dancing club. This space contrasts strongly to the sisters' mundane home and stationery shop. The first scene in the Riviera Dancing club is a model of the Melvillian discreet virtuosity which will increasingly characterise his work. The first shot is a stunning one-minute twenty-second take. We start close on the feet of a male tap-dancer (Mel Martin). The camera then pulls back to reveal four female dancers rehearsing with him on the raised stage; behind them we see two boxers practising with their trainer. The camera then pans right to reveal two other boxers (one of them Max) also practising. The dancers are now out of shot (to the left) but a mirror on the right behind the boxers and the pianist keeps them in the frame. A further pan back reveals a young hotel groom (Biquet) entering the club. With a three-step pan we have almost come 360 degrees around the room We cut to the barman (the truculent Robert Dalban) who is watching the dance practice, which we can also see in a mirror behind him. As Biquet and Max sit at a table, the dancers are again in view behind them.

Throughout the three-minute sequence, the dancers have been almost constantly kept in view either directly or indirectly and, more discretely in the background, a cleaning lady making her progress round the room also stresses the dynamic representation of space. Thus the various layers of activity that make up the mixed social milieu of the club are concentrated in spatial layers. When a young woman arrives, the scene switches to a celebration of Max as sexual predator. First he and then Biquet stare at the pretty young woman who walks on exaggerated high heels. Max, however, asserts the right to follow her up to her dressing room where she is rehearsing a nude dancing act with a balloon which hides her breasts. Max enters the room and in an astonishingly aggressive (if humorous) gesture, punctures the balloon with his cigarette. The camera just cuts to a record getting stuck. The combination of the woman's ostentatious walk and the presentation of Max as a cynical but sympathetic character produces the beginning of a discourse on women 'deserving' sexual harassment. As Denise was seen in the previous scene showing off her legs to a shocked Thérèse, the sequence prefigures her connection to this sexual narrative and her forthcoming rape.

Another kind of 'stylistic exercise' takes place in the final scene at the railway station, Les Arcs, which alternates between the buffet in which Max is having a celebratory meal (he thinks Thérèse is joining him) and the train in which she is sitting. Next to her is an old woman (Yvonne de Bray), who talks away to a friend, while Thérèse grimly stares ahead. Melville cast Yvonne de Bray as a tribute to her role as the mother in Cocteau's *Les Parents terribles*. But her speech, shot in one long take – one minute fifty-eight seconds – is also part of a more diffuse tribute to *Brief Encounter* (1946): the station and its role in the romantic intrigue; the banter in the buffet (Champagne and pineapple with Kirsch replacing tea and Banbury cakes); and the violent contrast between the distraught heroine and the talkative neighbour. *Brief Encounter* was one of the films Melville had cited as part of his 1949 'manifesto' (see Chapter 3), and generally an important point of reference for French film critics of the time, as a novel way of depicting interiority. Beyond the cinephilic nod, Melville cannot be said, however, to emulate the British film's foregrounding of its heroine's desire – for one thing the crucial voiceover is missing. If *Lettre* is the closest among Melville's films to a 'woman's film' (together with *Léon Morin, prêtre*), it casts its representation of women in a very French mould.

The sadistic nun

After the (modest) debate it provoked at the time, *Lettre* went into a long tunnel of critical oblivion. It resurfaces with Noël Burch and Geneviève Sellier's 1996 analysis of gender in French cinema. Burch and Sellier's feminist analysis places *Lettre* within a wider gender pattern in post-war French cinema. For them the couple formed by the two sisters is a transposition of the 'demonic' mother–daughter couples prevailing in the French cinema of the time (the archetype of which can be found in Yves Allégret's 1950 *Manèges*), and who illustrate the peculiar misogynist formation of the time – woman as both passive and evil: 'the two sisters separated by a substantial age difference (Juliette Gréco/Irène Galter), one dark, the other blonde, one strong, the other weak, two sides of the same trap in which Philippe Lemaire will be caught.'[52]

Burch and Sellier's analysis of the representation of women as symptomatic of a historical 'settling of scores' is enormously productive (it is discussed further in Chapter 3). Yet it is worth taking a closer look at *Lettre* because its many ambiguities and ironies make it a less straightforwardly misogynist text than such a reading assumes, if only in relation to the ending. For Burch and Sellier, as the train leaves the station, Max 'is crushed under a train, as he was going to join the tamed shrew, who now ends up alone'.[53] For others, by contrast, Thérèse was clearly going to the convent and Max was deluded. The film here clearly plays with the spectator by wilfully withdrawing crucial information and denying Thérèse subjectivity (unlike Laura in *Brief Encounter*). Thérèse says she is going to the convent to her sister, but she may have been lying, or may have changed her mind later. This may, in fact, be the point of Yvonne de Bray's speech which, on the surface, appears to be about unreliable men (and therefore Max), and yet could equally apply to Thérèse. Her complete impassivity on the train, as she (like other passengers) is oblivious to the accident, could equally mean that she is going to the convent, or is distraught at Max's failure to join her on the train. The condensed version of *Lettre* in *Mon Film* states that she was going to the convent, but the images and sounds at our disposal are not so clear-cut (and nor is the script). Nor is her final prayer as we see her in the convent (and the only example of her voiceover), in which she asks forgiveness for denying Max to Denise. In this respect *Lettre*, despite its emphatic melodramatic form, prefigures the impassivity of future Melvillian characters, and Melville's ambiguous withdrawal of information.

Not all representations of women in *Lettre* are so ambivalent. The film abounds in female caricatures – Irène, the object of derision as the mature sexual woman (Sanson, here used as a relatively minor character, was a star of 1950s Italian melodrama); the rapacious neighbour who comes to steal the dead mother's pots and pans; Thérèse's own punitive black widow look, hair scraped back; Denise the 'perverse' little sister; Lola, the dancer, ready to drop her clothes for Max at any time. What is more unusual for the period is the representation of female desire, albeit in a gauche and stereotypical way. This is most evident in a steamy montage of three 'desiring' women: Denise in bed rubbing her body with the scarf Max has touched, Thérèse putting on her nightdress, Irène in bed at the Carlton. All three are linked aurally by the accordion musical theme associated with Max, the *mise en scène* here giving the women what the narrative denies them.

What is surprising in the critical reception of the film is how little is made of the rape. At the time it was mostly seen as evidence of the film's 'bad taste', and it reveals prevailing attitudes, illustrated by a cynical aside in a contemporary review in the left-wing *Combat*, disparaging the character of Denise as 'a little sister who does not even deserve to be raped'.[54] Later it has been simply ignored, and is even made surprisingly light of by Burch and Sellier who write: 'A villain having raped the naïve young lady, the older one, veritable feminine Statue of the Commander, blackmails him so that he marries her sister.'[55] *Lettre* does not offer a progressive social commentary on rape, yet its sheer presence is noteworthy. It is not exploited for titillation (the camera cuts away quickly) but it shows enough of the brutality. The fact that Max is also portrayed sympathetically

Quand tu liras cette lettre: ambiguous sisterly love – Denise (Irène Galter), left, and Thérèse (Juliette Gréco)

is symptomatic of the dominant gender pattern outlined by Burch and Sellier, but the simultaneous emphasis on female sexuality and its repression reflects contradictory impulses which cannot all be put down to misogyny. What is clearly of interest to Melville too is the sisters' ambiguous relationship. Thérèse's feelings for her sister are visually expressed in an oddly sensual way: while repressing her sexuality, she strokes her hair, embraces her, smoothes the skirt on her legs. The scenes where she mortifies her flesh by slamming a drawer shut on her hand and where she literally 'burns' in front of Max (her dress gets caught in a bonfire) present an almost Buñuelian sado-masochistic nun, underscored by the gap between Gréco's persona and the character of Thérèse. Thus while fitting within dominant gender patterns of the time, *Lettre* also leaves open the possibility of a particular type of female spectatorial pleasure unusual in the cinema of the time and in Melville's own films.

Quand tu liras cette lettre signalled the end of the first era of Melville's film-making, in which he adapted well-established figures of the French literary and theatrical establishment, presenting stories set in a provincial village (*Le Silence de la mer*), a fantasy theatrical world (*Les Enfants*) and the socially mixed world of the Côte d'Azur (*Lettre*). His next two films, *Bob le flambeur* and *Deux hommes dans Manhattan*, switch to urban crime stories and celebrations of Paris and New York, which would place him within both a more transnational cultural milieu and the orbit of the New Wave.

NOTES

1. Claude Beylie and Bertrand Tavernier, 'Entretien avec Jean-Pierre Melville', *Cahiers du cinéma*, no. 124, October 1961, p. 3.
2. Pierre Braunberger, *Cinémamémoire* (Paris: Centre Georges Pompidou, 1987), p. 141.
3. See Claude Beylie and Philippe d'Hugues, *Les oubliés du cinéma français* (Paris: Éditions du Cerf, 1999), pp. 141–6.
4. Beylie and Tavernier, 'Jean-Pierre Melville', p. 7. There are, however, conflicting statements about who approached whom. Melville, in various contexts, has said Cocteau phoned him after seeing *Le Silence de la mer*, while some press articles, such as *France-Soir* of 29 March 1950, reported Melville got permission to adapt the novel from Cocteau, after the latter had turned down Claude Autant-Lara and John Ford.
5. Gilles Ragache and Jean-Robert Ragache, *La Vie quotidienne des écrivains et des artistes sous l'Occupation, 1940–44* (Paris: Hachette, 1988), p. 236.
6. Rui Nogueira (ed.), *Melville on Melville* (London: Secker and Warburg and BFI, 1971), p. 55.
7. Jean Cocteau, *France-Soir*, 4 May 1950.
8. André S. Labarthe, *Jean-Pierre Melville: Portrait en 9 poses* (1970); Nogueira, *Melville on Melville*, p. 40.
9. Jacques Siclier, *Le Monde*, 11 April 1975.
10. *Combat*, 30 March 1950.
11. *La Métropole*, 13 October 1950.
12. Suzanne Rodrigue, *L'Écran français*, 3 April 1950.
13. *Franc-Tireur*, 1 April 1950.
14. Nicole Stéphane, interview in *The Village Voice*, quoted in Edward Baron Turk, 'The Film Adaptation of Cocteau's *Les Enfants terribles*', *Cinema Journal*, vol. 19, no. 2, Spring 1980, p. 40.
15. *Le Monde*, 1 April 1950.
16. Noël Burch, '*Les Enfants terribles*', *Fiche filmographique IDHEC*, no. 94, 1 January 1952.
17. Ibid., p. 29.
18. Ibid.
19. Kristin Thompson and David Bordwell, *Film History, An Introduction* (New York: McGraw-Hill, Inc., 1994), pp. 444–5.
20. François Truffaut, *The Films in My Life* (London: Allen Lane, 1980), p. 223.
21. Jacques Rivette, 'Les Enfants terribles', *Cahiers du cinéma*, vol. 26, no. 152, February 1964, pp. 12–14.
22. C. D. E. Tolton (ed.), *The Cinema of Jean Cocteau* (New York/Ottawa/Toronto: Legas, 1999), p. 17.
23. For Bantcheva, the dual casting of Renée Cosima 'enriches the meaning of the story'; in Denitza Bantcheva, *Jean-Pierre Melville: de l'oeuvre à l'homme* (Troyes: Librairie Bleue, 1996), p. 29. Edward Baron Turk advances the opposite view (Turk, 'The Film Adaptation of Cocteau's *Les Enfants terribles*', p. 29).
24. Turk's analysis of Cocteau's voiceover is excellent, see Turk, 'The Film Adaptation of Cocteau's *Les Enfants terribles*', pp. 32–3.
25 Michel Chion, *La Parole au cinéma, La toile trouée* (Paris: Cahiers du cinéma, 1998), p. 94.
26. Nogueira, *Melville on Melville*, p. 44.

27. For Melville this was a tribute to the scene in *The Magnificent Ambersons* where Joseph Cotton and Anne Baxter walk in a 'cotton tree garden' which is never seen, though actually Melville's close-up on the character's face and refusal of reverse angle are more extreme. Ibid., p. 43.
28. Richard Dyer, *Now You See It, Studies on Lesbian and Gay Film* (London and New York: Routledge, 1990), p. 66.
29. Ibid, pp. 66–7.
30. Nogueira, *Melville on Melville*, p. 55.
31. Turk, 'The Film Adaptation of Cocteau's *Les Enfants terribles*', p. 33.
32. Quoted in Dyer, *Now You See It*, p. 72.
33 Roxanne Chee, 'Melville's Version of *Les Enfants terribles*: What's in a Look?', in Tolton, *The Cinema of Jean Cocteau*, p. 164.
34. Noël Burch and Geneviève Sellier, *La Drôle de guerre des sexes du cinéma français 1930–1956* (Paris: Nathan, 1996), p. 325.
35. *Les Enfants terribles* – files held at the Bibliothèque du Film (BIFI), Paris. Ref: PINOTEAU07 B3.
36. Turk, 'The Film Adaptation of Cocteau's *Les Enfants terribles*', p. 38.
37. Beylie and Tavernier, 'Entretien avec Jean-Pierre Melville', p. 10.
38. Nogueira, *Melville on Melville*, pp. 48–9.
39. Jacqueline de Jomaron (ed.), *Le Théâtre en France, 2. De la Révolution à nos jours* (Paris: Armand Colin, 1992), p. 357.
40. *Mon Film*, no. 390, 10 February 1954.
41. *France-Soir*, 17 November 1953.
42. *Quand tu liras cette lettre* – script held at the Bibliothèque du Film (BIFI), Paris. Ref: SCEN2251 B676, p. 196.
43. Gilles Martain, *Rivarol*, 4 November 1953.
44. Jacques Doniol-Valcroce, *L'Observateur d'aujourd'hui*, 26 November 1953.
45. Robert Lachenay [Truffaut], *Cahiers du cinéma*, no. 29, December 1953, pp. 59–60.
46. R.-M. Arlaud, *Combat*, 17 November 1953. See also: *Les Lettres françaises*, 19 November 1953; *Le Figaro*, 14 November 1953; and *Comoedia*, 18 November 1953.
47. *Le Figaro*, 14 November 1953.
48. Ibid.
49. André Bazin, *Radio-cinéma-télévision*, 29 November 1953.
50. Dudley Andrew, *André Bazin* (New York: Colombia University Press, 1978), p. 204.
51. *Le Monde*, 20 November 1953.
52. Burch and Sellier, *La Drôle de guerre des sexes du cinéma français*, p. 229.
53. Ibid.
54. Arlaud, *Combat*, 17 November 1953.
55. Burch and Sellier, *La Drôle de guerre des sexes du cinéma français*, p. 229.

3

Melville's War: *Le Silence de la mer* (1947–9), *Léon Morin, prêtre* (1961), *L'Armée des ombres* (1969)

It seems to me that all over the world, cinema has reached its definitive though imperfect form as a 'monument', whose keystones are action and movement.

So do we have to stick for ever to the rules, followed a thousand times, which, year in year out, produced five good films? Can we not try something new? Can we not learn from the lessons of the past and try to renew this art form? [. . .] It is the war which, by providing us with topics, allows us to attempt such an evolution. [. . .] The war is also the hidden ringmaster behind the three characters of *Le Silence de la mer*.

Jean-Pierre Melville[1]

Under the impetus of de Gaulle, France had, at the end of the war, the historical and political ambition to belong fully to the circle of victors. The Resistance, therefore, even when underground, needed to appear as the detachment of a regular, perfectly organised army, and the life of the French, even when full of conflict and ambiguities, needed to appear as a contribution to victory. These conditions were not favourable to a renewal of the cinematographic image, which found itself constrained within the framework of a traditional action-image, at the service of a properly French 'dream'. The result of this was that the cinema in France was only able to break with its tradition rather belatedly and by a reflexive or intellectual detour which was that of the New Wave.

Gilles Deleuze[2]

Melville's remarks above, taken from his first published article in *L'Écran français*, show extraordinary prescience about film history. Deleuze, who ignores Melville in his two-volume work on cinema, would have done well to look at *Le Silence de la mer*, a groundbreaking film which heralded the changes he was calling for and which influenced, among others, the film-makers of the New Wave. But where Melville and Deleuze converged is on the importance of World War II for European and French cinema. The centrality of the Occupation and Resistance to Melville's life and cinema as well as French society runs through this chapter, which brings together three films spanning almost the whole of his career – films linked by their historical topic but which also at different points in Melville's career raised different aesthetic questions about literary adaptation, *mise en scène* and Melville's place in French cinema.

The war and the Resistance played a crucial part in Melville's life, as we saw in Chapter 1. He did his national service in 1937 before joining Resistance networks in France and de Gaulle's Free French army, fighting liberation battles from Africa to France via Italy. The importance of *Le Silence de la mer*, *Léon Morin, prêtre* and *L'Armée des ombres* as 'war films', however, is not only a function of Melville's *private* experience, but of how they explore and rework the *public* 'myth' of the Resistance. André Bazin remarked that 'in France Resistance immediately entered the realm of legend',[3] and this legend, or myth, as Sylvie Lindeperg puts it, was 'crystallised during the period of the Liberation and then subjected to successive transformations'.[4]

THE SEARCH FOR AUTHENTICITY

Melville's three war films are all based on autobiographical books by writers with impeccable Resistance credentials. *Le Silence de la mer*, 'probably the single most famous Resistance story',[5] was a 1942 clandestine publication by 'Vercors' (his real name was Jean Bruller), whose stature as a *Résistant* and co-founder of the underground press Éditions de Minuit was considerable if at times controversial, as we will see. Béatrix Beck's *Léon Morin, prêtre* (1952) forms part of a series of novels featuring a central female character, Barny, who, as the widow of a communist Jew, is a thinly disguised version of the author. Her vision of France under the Occupation was effectively approved by the award of the Goncourt prize to *Léon Morin, prêtre* in 1952. Kessel's credentials were if anything loftier still. A World War I hero and prize-winning novelist and journalist, he was co-author (with his nephew Maurice Druon) of *Le Chant des partisans*, the anthem of the Resistance composed in May 1943 in London, where he also wrote *L'Armée des ombres* in the same year. In 1964 he was elected to the Académie Française.

All three source books, written during or shortly after the war, belong to the first phase of works on the Resistance in which personal experience was paramount as a guarantee of authenticity. While Beck uses the more intimate first person, Vercors and Kessel claimed a direct link to a consensual ideal of the Resistance as expression of national unity and identity. Vercors declared that *Silence* 'is not a book like any other. [. . .] It does not belong to me alone. It belongs to [French people] more than it does to me.'[6] Kessel begins *L'Armée des ombres* thus: 'There is no propaganda in this book and there is no fiction. No detail has been forced and none has been invented.'[7] In presenting their works as the quasi-spontaneous emanation of a people united in resistance, Vercors and Kessel worked within what Henry Rousso calls the 'Gaullist resistancialist myth', which 'celebrated people in resistance, a people symbolized exclusively by the "man of June Eighteenth" (de Gaulle)',[8] and played down internal ideological conflicts – what he terms the 'Franco-French war'[9] – as well as other aspects of World War II such as the Holocaust. Melville used these texts as sources of authenticity, but also, in adapting them in ways which served his own purposes, as screens between him and the events and ideology of the time.[10]

LE SILENCE DE LA MER

Le Silence de la mer (henceforth *Silence*) depicts a war of attrition: the decision of an elderly Frenchman (Jean-Marie Robain) simply called 'the uncle' in the film and his niece (Nicole Stéphane) to 'resist' the German officer Werner von Ebrennac (Howard Vernon) billeted with them, by refusing to speak to him. Night after night, von Ebrennac, a cultured Francophile and believer in a greater union between France and Germany, talks to them by the fireside. Mutual respect and affection build up, but uncle and niece never relent. During a trip to Paris von Ebrennac discovers the brutal truth about the Nazis. The shock prompts him to volunteer for the Eastern front (see filmography for a detailed synopsis).

The highly unusual circumstances of the making of *Silence* have become legendary. Melville read Vercors' book in English (presumably *Put Out the Light*, Cyril Connolly's translation) in London in 1943. Hearing that the stage and film star Louis Jouvet wanted to film an adaptation – in the book, the uncle remarks on '[von Ebrennac's] startling likeliness to the actor Louis Jouvet'[11] – Melville says he manoeuvred Resistance friend Jean Pierre-Bloch to stop Jouvet's project. At that stage his sole credit was one independent short, *24 heures de la vie d'un clown* (discussed in Chapter 2). Melville encountered fierce bureaucratic and political opposition to this project from the ranks of the French film industry. He lacked the necessary professional membership card, and the cheap production and small crew contravened the rules of the then strongly unionised profession. Additionally, Vercors refused to give his approval. Melville went ahead with no adaptation rights, no union card and a small amount of film stock acquired on the black market (he did, however, receive help from the head of GTC Laboratories, who advanced money for processing the film).[12] He won over Vercors by promising that if he and other 'eminent *Résistants*' disapproved of the finished product, the movie would be destroyed. Vercors gave in and offered the use of his house, but kept a close watch over the adaptation.[13] Correspondence between the two men, widely reported in the press, attests that Melville found Vercors' close surveillance hard to take: 'If only I'd had a free hand . . . But Vercors intended his novel to be followed to the letter and he maintained this intransigent attitude till the end.'[14]

The scenes showing von Ebrennac in Paris were shot on location, including those at the Kommandantur, for which Melville used 'the office which had actually served the purpose, so as to have the view of the Opéra from the window'.[15] But the bulk of the shooting took place at Vercors' home in Villiers-sur-Morin, east of Paris, over several months during 1947 and 1948. Director of photography Henri Decae helped edit the film in precarious conditions, watching rushes projected on a sheet in Melville's hotel bedroom.[16] When completed, *Silence* was shown to the 'jury' of Resistance members on 29 November 1948. With one exception, they enthusiastically endorsed the film. Vercors' U-turn made little impression on the industry: at the film's premiere the projection box had to be cordoned off to prevent the print being seized.[17] Melville also allegedly received personal threats.[18] *Silence* was finally released in April 1949 in Paris' two largest cinemas (the Gaumont Palace and the Rex), with an enormous publicity campaign, largely built on Vercors' name. The two cinemas were hung with paintings of the house, a model of which also featured in a window display at the department store Les Galeries Lafayette. The film was seen by more than 1.3 million spectators, a substantial success even by the standards of the bigger audience of the time.

Le Silence de la mer: for the promotion of the film, a model of Vercors' house was displayed in a window at the Galeries Lafayette department store

Vercors' attitude hitherto may have lacked generosity but, as André Bazin elegantly put it, if '[Vercors'] outlandish reservations complicated Melville's task, they also provided him with such enormous publicity that the film was in danger of being destroyed by it'.[19] Melville's innovative *mise en scène*, however, saw to it that he was hailed by critics as a new artistic presence. Melville was well placed to emerge as a fresh voice since his record was untainted, unlike film-makers such as Carné, Clouzot, Guitry and Autant-Lara who had worked under the Vichy regime and all had to pay for it in various ways. Melville's 'symbolic capital' as a member of the Resistance was thus enhanced by his lack of association with the wartime film industry. He could put it to the service of both Vercors as a Resistance writer and his own film-making agenda.

Resistance in *Le Silence de la mer*

The immediate post-Liberation period in France saw the emergence of the cinematic Resistance myth in a flurry of documentary and fiction films, of which the most famous are three 1946 films: *La Bataille du rail*, *Jéricho* and *Le Père tranquille*, contemporary with Italian films such as *Roma, città aperta* (1945) and *Paisà* (1946). In line with the exaltation of the historical moment, these films depict France as a country unified in resistance against the German occupier, through the spectacular action of dynamic young Frenchmen (*Bataille*, *Jéricho*) or the undercover work of deceptively placid old ones (*Le Père tranquille*). Soon though, as the hopes of a new dawn gave way to political disillusion, government instability and social malaise, the struggles of the partisans faded from memories, or at least from screens. Films shifted from a Manichean depiction in which all but a few truly evil figures (such as Pierre Brasseur's hysterical collaborator in *Jéricho*) supported the patriotic struggle against the German arch-enemy, to the blurred moral and political universe of the Occupation and its aftermath. Already in Carné's bitter *Les Portes de la nuit* (1946), a certain amount of Franco-French settling of scores was appearing. In Clouzot's even darker *Manon* (1949), the young Free French Fighter (FFI) played by Philippe Lemaire abandons the fight to follow Manon and becomes compromised with the collaborationist milieu of his brother-in-law (Serge Reggiani, reprising his role in *Les Portes de la nuit*). By 1950, René Clément's *Jeux interdits* portrays the Occupation as a burden to be endured by a population of grasping and cowardly peasants; only two children embody positive values, and they are tragically separated at the end. How does *Silence* fit within this shifting ideological terrain?

Early European Resistance films deployed plenty of action, but, as Bazin noted, if 'The Resistance constitutes a common [European] mythology', French films were different in that they did not generally portray atrocities like torture.[20] The minimalism of *Silence*, in which resistance is personal, small-scale, 'passive' and ... silent, both fits within a French pattern (no atrocities) and stretches it by pushing the lack of action to the limit. Like the book, the film raises the question of whether the uncle and niece's silence is admirable in its dignity, or if it is, as the uncle says at one point, 'absurd'. Does it place the characters on the side of the *attentistes* (those who just waited for the war to end), or does it reflect an inescapable reality? I would agree with Anne Simonin who rebuts the charge of *attentisme* by pointing out that through their silence the characters strike a position.[21] They stand for those who endured and waited, but marked their distance from the occupier. *Les Lettres françaises* was typical in its approval of the film: 'In this obstinate and implacable silence was incarnated the immense dignity of France.'[22] Pierre Sorlin, who argues that 'Resistance meant mostly silent hope, persistence, waiting',[23] later praised Bresson's *Un condamné à mort s'est échappé* (1956) as 'the definitive film on [the Resistance]' largely for its silence.

Why would silence be so important a symbol of the Resistance? Vercors' notion of the silence 'of the sea' was meant to evoke the 'submerged life of hidden and conflicting feelings, desires and thoughts',[24] a poetic notion (and title) which Melville appropriates in his *mise en scène*. Silence had other symbolic connotations: under torture it was the measure of heroism, and it may be seen as the only response to the horrors of the Nazi victory and occupation of France. In terms of Resistance it was also a useful concept; in hiding divisions and compromises it dispensed characters – and therefore book and film – from articulating a precise political position, ensuring the longevity and universal appeal of both. Although, novel and paradoxically even more so film, are in thrall to the word. Vercors resisted through writing and *Silence* is a tribute to the spoken and written word.

Writing as resistance

With the words 'Pierre Braunberger presents Vercors' famous book', *Silence* begins with a night-time scene which is not in the book. At a street corner, a man glimpsed only in silhouette waits silently to the right of the screen as another approaches, his steps echoing in the empty street. The second man carries a suitcase which he sets down at the feet of the standing man, before walking away. Neither speaks. The first man picks up the suitcase and opens it. The camera in close-up shows a folded shirt. Under the shirt are two bundles of newspapers, *Libération* and *Combat* – clandestine newspapers but also, not coincidentally, Resistance networks Melville claims to have worked for. From beneath the newspapers the man's hand brings out the book *Le Silence de la mer*, with the words 'Vercors' and 'Les Éditions de Minuit' clearly visible. The man's hand opens the book, and music swells over the words 'To the memory of Saint-Pol-Roux, assassinated poet'.[25] After a fade, the credits continue, as if written in the same book. Pages turn (now with no hand visible), showing the names of the actors, director of photography, etc., ending with Melville's name (the end of the film likewise shows Vercors' last sentence and a note about the book's underground publication).

I am tempted to see the opening of Melville's first feature as premonitory. Décor, lighting and action combine the two major strands of his future work, the thriller and the war film. The two men in the prologue clearly signify the 'army in the shadows', but equally they could be two gangsters doing a 'drop'. The contents of the suitcase, however, and the solemn music triggered by the opening of the book confirm the cult of 'Vercors' famous book'. Arguably, too, the meeting of two anonymous men dramatises the adaptation: the writer brings his 'baggage' to the film-maker who will translate it into a different medium.

Vercors' *Le Silence de la mer* was published on 20 February 1942, the first book from the clandestine Éditions de Minuit. At the time, Vercors' identity remained a secret, though speculation was rife that he was André Gide or François Mauriac or some such celebrity. As Anne Simonin explains, during the war 'It was crucial to let people believe that behind Vercors hid a great French writer, in order to impose the myth of France's fighting genius.' After the war, on the contrary, his identity as a *new* writer was equally crucial, to prove what 'a [creative] matrix the Resistance had been'.[26] The book, a novella, was immediately smuggled out of France, reprinted, translated into several languages and serialised in the London-based Gaullist periodical *La Marseillaise*. Initially meant for a small elite, it became a popular success, attributable in equal measure to its literary power, its underground publication and its advocacy of non-violent resistance. Vercors wanted *Silence* to be a cautionary tale for those who were still 'deluding themselves'[27] that collaboration could lead to the renewal of France. Initially well received, the book was later attacked, in particular by the communists, because non-armed resistance was then associated with Gaullism, but especially for its praise of the 'good German'. Given that Melville was then unknown, the popular success of the film points to Vercors' renewed currency. Clearly the polemics around the book had sufficiently died down for it to stand as symbolic of the whole Resistance. By chance too, the writer's chosen Resistance name (picked at the beginning of the war) happened to be that of the most heroic maquis during the 1943–4 Liberation campaign. The clandestine publication and topic of *Silence* signified writing – and reading – as an act of Resistance and an early model for the committed literature that Jean-Paul Sartre would theorise after the war.

Besides celebrating the book's own history, the opening scene of the film visualises the importance of *the word* as a Resistance weapon, introducing the theme of reverence for literature that runs throughout the film. Most of the action is set in Vercors' own library which anchors von Ebrennac's monologues in the concrete world of culture that is both his as a fictional character and Vercors' in real life. Uncle and niece remain silent, but their books 'speak' for them. The way Vercors has von Ebrennac ecstatically praising French literature and rhapsodising about the glory of French culture – first through shots of book covers and then through his visit to the great Parisian monuments – is not without chauvinistic overtones, which, understandable as they are in the Resistance context, no doubt contributed also to the success of both book and film.

The uncle's voiceover also has a distinctly literary flavour which was commented upon by reviewers, both positively and negatively. Its literariness stems from the verbatim use of passages from the book, and the way Robain's declamatory voiceover 'answers' von Ebrennac's monologues, couched in slightly accented but literate French (also faithfully transposed from the book, including original errors). This intense verbalisation transposes the 'literature of persuasion', committed to speaking the truth of the Occupation.[28] Yet in other ways, *Silence* is far from the didacticism of much literature and film about the Occupation. Melville uses purely cinematic means to adapt Vercors' book, starting with his representation of the German officer.

Werner von Ebrennac: the 'good German'

Vercors' von Ebrennac was loosely based on a German officer who had occupied his house, and on the writer and officer Ernst Jünger, based in Paris during the war.[29] In showing a humane, cultured German in *Silence*, Melville was following the book, but he was also countering representations of 'bad' (cruel, sadistic) Germans in such films as *La Bataille du rail*, *Le Père tranquille* and *Jéricho*, many of whom were played by Howard Vernon who, understandably, hesitated before accepting the part of von Ebrennac.[30]

If Vernon's von Ebrennac irresistibly evokes Eric von Stroheim's von Rauffenstein in Renoir's 1938 *La Grande illusion* – both are gallant, aristocratic and Francophile officers who happen to be on the 'wrong' side – the screen representation of the German officer had become a complex issue in the post-war context. *La Grande illusion*, much celebrated before the war, was harshly criticised in 1946 for the relationship between the French soldier (Jean Gabin) and the German woman (Dita Parlo); two years later, films such as *Retour à la vie* (1948), showing Franco-German relations in a more positive light, were well received. With changing polarities attendant on the building of Europe and the Cold War, the German was – again – becoming more 'acceptable'. And yet the issue was still sensitive. Towards the end of the war, the communist writer Ilya Ehrenbourg had railed against *Silence*, a 'book which celebrates the moral and physical beauty of a Boche'.[31] Such controversies explain why Vercors asked Melville to make a small but significant change: as von Ebrennac is about to leave for the front, the uncle shows him a quote from Anatole France which amounts to a call for rebellion: 'It is a noble thing for a soldier to disobey a criminal order.'[32] As the German officer hesitates but ultimately leaves, the spectator recalls the words at the beginning of the film which had triggered the flashback narration: 'And thus he left. Thus he bowed down, like the others ... like all the others, like the whole country.'[33] By making this addition Vercors countered accusations of French passivity (the uncle takes a risk) and undermined the German's goodness (von Ebrennac still chooses to go and fight for Germany). Furthermore, as Lindeperg points out, the text that was added before the beginning of *Silence* ('This film does not claim to solve the problem of relations between France and Germany, a problem which will exist for as long as the barbarous Nazi crimes, perpetrated with the complicity of the German people, remain in people's memory ...') was intended to show that the film, despite its flattering portrayal of the German officer, did not exonerate German responsibility.[34] It also introduced the 'good' German/'bad' Nazi dichotomy which structures the representation of the officer.

Book and film multiply the signs of von Ebrennac's sensitivity. His bad leg signals his vulnerability, as do his tears as he relays the shock of discovering the Nazi grand plan. He is highly cultured (a musician who plays Bach and wants to compose 'humane' music) and disinterested (his refusal to join the Nazis hindered his career). Vulnerability, sensitivity and culture allied to youth build up a portrait close to what Richard Dyer has called the 'sad young man', a figure usually, though not necessarily, read as gay.[35] Von Ebrennac's slightly effeminate manner, enhanced by Vernon's slender figure and fine features, nevertheless can be adduced to his portrayal of a 'good German'. By contrast, a first hint of German brutality comes in the flashback of his fiancée pulling the legs off a mosquito, a prelude to his encounter with the SS officers he meets in Paris. There, Nazi perversity is indicated by the contrast between the refined décor of the Kommandantur which, like the uncle's library, contains books, pictures and musical instruments, and the horror of the revelations it yields. The sweet love ballad sung by an SS officer to other SS officers acts as a *mise en abyme* of this shocking dichotomy. A similar scene occurs in *Roma, città aperta*, where SS officers play Chopin and sip wine while prisoners are being tortured. The music-loving sadistic Nazi was emerging as an enduring stereotype, although Melville's contrasts are more subtle.

Rather than tortured prisoners, the film offers the more subdued (in the form of a report), but more horrific, revelation of Treblinka. This is another notable addition to Vercors' book – doubly anachronistic, since not only is the report dated 21 March 1941, whereas Treblinka did not open until July 1942, but at the time the camps were not on French film-makers' agenda. As Pierre Colombat says, 'The history of French cinema during and after the Liberation shows a very similar lack of concern, embarrassment, ignorance or rejection about the destiny of the Jews.'[36] Melville's own Jewishness may have a bearing on his mention of Treblinka, although the report makes no reference to Jews (neither would Resnais' *Nuit et brouillard* in 1956). Nor does it allude to French responsibility: Treblinka is strictly connected to Nazi crimes – as von Ebrennac reads about the camp in shock, a tracking shot ends on a close-up of Hitler. (The script of *Silence* makes mention of a 'despicably obsequious' collaborator in the Kommandantur scene, but the character does not appear in the finished film.[37]) Melville added another scene to the book in which von Ebrennac sees a 'No Jews' sign on a café door. But the

Le Silence de la mer: von Ebrennac (Howard Vernon) sees a sign saying 'forbidden to Jews' in a French café

sign is half cut by the frame and the moment extremely brief. Nevertheless, the sensitivity of the topic is illustrated by the fact that, according to Nicole Stéphane, the passage about Treblinka, spoken in German, was not sub-titled in early releases of the film.[38]

Whether 'good' or 'bad', the German officers on-screen share a common iconography handed down in film history by the likes of von Rauffenstein and *Casablanca*'s (1942) Major von Strasser. German officers are normally tall, slender and elegant (von Stroheim is not slim but he wears a corset). Melville enhances Vernon's height with frequent low-angle shots of him towering above his seated French hosts. Vernon's gaunt face and piercing stare owe a lot to Veidt in Hollywood and in German cinema (his Cesare in *Caligari* [1919]). This connection is exploited by Melville in von Ebrennac's strikingly theatrical entry into the film.

Von Ebrennac arrives on a dark night, as the pair are sitting by the fire. Over the clock ticking, uneven steps are heard, then a dog barking, then sharp knocks at the door. The niece gets up to open the door, the music rises to a crescendo, then stops abruptly as the door opens. As von Ebrennac emerges out of the darkness, excessively bright lighting delineates the chiselled contours of Vernon's face and his unusually large eyes – dark irises surrounded by a lot of white, evoking a monstrous doll. While Melville's von Ebrennac is in many respects close to Vercors', the literary protagonist is blond and has pale, 'golden' eyes, whereas Melville's creation is darker. Inside the house the lighting on his face becomes more naturalistic, but still his piercing, unblinking eyes evoke the horror film, as do his uneven steps (unsurprisingly, Vernon's subsequent career was in horror film). The German invasion of France comes in the form of this 'alien' entering a quiet home. Although throughout he will systematically be presented as a civilised, humane figure, he never entirely loses his ghostly persona, enhanced by the film's 'expressionist' lighting, presenting him lit by the fire from underneath, or seen through the flames. At the local Kommandantur, von Ebrennac first appears to the uncle (and the spectator) as a reflection in a mirror. His playing of Bach's 'inhuman' music, his quoting from *Macbeth* continue the theme. In the streets of Paris, as he visits the great monuments, his way of gliding into the shot gives him an eerie quality. At the end of his last scene with the niece, his face disappears into the darkness just as he came out of it at the beginning. Von Ebrennac thus is dual: a rational, urbane literary protagonist overlaid with a dark, ghostly figure which is largely Melville's creation. In this respect, and in his death-driven trajectory, von Ebrennac prefigures other 'ghostly' figures in Melville's cinema.

Woman as *Résistante*

The war and liberation had a massive impact on relationships between the sexes, an impact registered by screen representations. For Noël Burch and Geneviève Sellier, Resistance films such as *Le Diable au corps* (1946) and *Le Silence de la mer* are 'completely on the side of misogyny' in their domination by a male narrator-hero.[39] However, they also see *Silence* as part of a minority 'feminist' trend.[40] This contradictory view reflects the complexity of the niece, a silent yet memorable figure, especially as played by the unusually beautiful Nicole Stéphane, a former *Résistante* and co-financer of the film.[41] By virtue of her extended screen presence, the niece is indeed an exception in French Resistance cinema which, in comparison with other national cinemas, utterly marginalised women – think of *Went the Day Well?* (1942), *Roma, città aperta* and *Odette* (1950) (significantly Françoise Rosay portrays a *Résistante* from Brittany in a British film, *Johnny Frenchman*, an Ealing production of 1945). Yet her silence belongs to a wider cultural history which denies female subjectivity by constructing it through male discourse. Against her uncle and von Ebrennac's flow of words, surrounded with the implied words of all the male writers in the library, the niece has altogether four words to say, all of them about, or to, the German officer: 'he is leaving', and 'adieu'. An earlier brief scene shot from outside the house shows uncle and niece talking and laughing, but their conversation is indistinct.

Throughout the film, virtually always sitting by the fire, the niece is engaged in female tasks such as darning, knitting and serving her uncle's coffee, while he, in a cliché of bookish, a-sexual masculinity, puffs on his pipe. We could read her sewing as a metaphor for the home front. The heroine of *Odette*, later an undercover liaison agent who is tortured by the Nazis, is first glimpsed at home, sewing. Sewing also echoes the real women who, at great risk, stitched books for Éditions de Minuit in Parisian cellars. Besides this domestic imagery, the film encourages us to read the niece on the level of myth (Ariadne whose thread leads Theseus to the Minotaur in the Labyrinth and back) and fairy tale. Von Ebrennac's rendering of Beauty and the Beast expresses his desire for his 'distant princess'.[42] Ideology and sexuality merge as his voice tries to penetrate her consciousness while he also aims to convince his hosts of his views on France and Germany in a

Le Silence de la mer: the uncle (Jean-Marie Robain) and his niece (Nicole Stéphane)

relentlessly gendered language full of references to marriage and motherhood. The niece is the angel of the hearth, the live version of the angel on the wall that von Ebrennac gazes at on his arrival. Within the library, a space of (masculine) culture, the fireplace and she by association are the warm (feminine) heart of the home and the country, a flame to which the German officer is attracted like a moth.

The niece is mostly immobile, her head surrounded by a halo of light. She is usually seen in profile (only at the end do we see her full face), her hair lifted away from her face, equating her with emblematic figures on medals. Her serious – proud? – pose is that of a statue, first seen against the wall as a caryatid when von Ebrennac arrives, prefiguring the statue of Marianne discarded against a wall in the local Kommandantur. With her halo of light, her white scarf decorated with Cocteau motifs and her visual association with snow,[43] the niece is an icon of virginal purity. In this she is explicitly contrasted to the sadistic German fiancée and implicitly with the *femmes tondues* – the women who would later have their heads shaven for sleeping with the enemy – scapegoats for the (male) shame of the 1940 debacle. On one or two occasions the uncle wavers in his determination to remain silent – a feeling presented as good sense, yet one which could be seen as an indictment of masculine weakness (Jean-Marie Robain is made up as a doddery, emasculated old man, a feature criticised by many reviewers who pointed to his – unwitting? – resemblance to Marshal Pétain). In each case, with just a withering look, the niece intimates that this is out of the question.

Written in 1942, filmed in 1947 and released in 1949, *Silence* in its genesis charts a period of massive change for women, from antiquated Vichy patriarchy to resistance, to political emancipation and participation in 1946, to the publication of Simone de

Beauvoir's *The Second Sex* in 1949, the year *Silence* was released. This trajectory of emancipation was, however, quickly undermined by various forms of patriarchal backlash on the one hand and by the intellectual dominance of humanism which tended to efface gender on the other.[44] In this context femininity could only be asserted allegorically: the untainted, uncompromising young woman who sits by the fireside is a vision of a France both youthful and maternal ('She must offer her breast in a maternal gesture', says von Ebrennac). The alliteration between 'mer' (sea) and 'mère' (mother), as in 'mère patrie' (motherland), together with the visual rhyme with Marianne, suggests such a reading. If the niece is the antithesis of post-war cinema harpies such as the heroine of *Manon* (products of a patriarchal backlash in Burch and Sellier's scheme), her relation to feminism is ambivalent at best. Her moral superiority and stronger patriotic resolve are at the price of repressing her attraction to von Ebrennac, and of being turned into a statue.[45]

Within the shifting terrain of cinematic representations of the Occupation in the late 1940s, *Silence* thus occupies a complex position. Resistance is no longer a celebration of heroic action, as in *La Bataille du rail*, but literary, passive and symbolic. Yet the symbolism and silence of the film erase conflicts and impose a high moral tone, not to mention nationalistic sentiment, already out of sync with the seedy portrayals of the Occupation offered by such films as *Les Portes de la nuit*, *Manon* and *Jeux interdits*. And there is another difference. Whereas these three films belonged to the mainstream 'Tradition of Quality', Melville's *Silence* was, on the other hand, aesthetically highly original and innovative.

Forging a new film aesthetics

On 3 May 1949, shortly after the release of *Silence*, Melville published what amounted to an aesthetic manifesto in *L'Écran français*, part of which is quoted at the beginning of this chapter. In terms which uncannily prefigure Gilles Deleuze's division between the 'movement-image' and the 'time-image',[46] Melville praised classical Hollywood cinema, citing Frank Lloyd's 1933 epic *Cavalcade* as the '*film-type*' of a cinema whose 'keystones are action and movement' (even though it is based on a Noel Coward play). Judging that such cinema had reached perfection, he welcomed the change, linked to the shock of the war, towards more introspective film. Echoing post-war debates in *L'Écran français*, he judged *Brief Encounter* a 'pure masterpiece' and lauded neo-realist experiments. Melville ended the short piece on a critique of the kind of films that advertise 'legs, behinds and breasts' (although, he wryly notes, these are generally less visible on-screen than on cinema awnings) and advocated a search for new directions. If these are left vague, Melville gives enough clues: interiority rather than 'action and movement', small-scale rather than spectacular, a noir cinema (he also cites *Une si jolie petite plage* [1948], his only French reference). Much later, in his 1971 interview with Rui Nogueira, Melville confirmed that at the time of *Silence* he had tried to make 'an anti-cinematographic film' and to 'attempt a language composed entirely of images and sounds, and from which movement and action would be more or less banished'.[47] Yet he also said that he wanted to 'be classical and not try to revolutionize the cinema'.[48] Rather than a contradiction, these statements encapsulate Melville's ability to make innovative cinema within a classical mould, a duality perceived by critics in 1949 and which would continue through his career. The *France-Hebdo* reviewer, among others, noted his amazement at 'a highly distinguished film, devoid of the action and movement normally associated with cinema',[49] a film which moreover did very well at the box office. In what ways does *Silence* fulfil Melville's call for a new cinema? To ask the question differently, in what ways is it a precursor of the New Wave? Apart from its novel production method, *Silence* must be recognised as a radically new kind of literary adaptation and for its original use of cinematography and sound.

A new kind of literary adaptation

As we saw, Vercors' tight control ensured that *Silence* was highly faithful to its source. Yet Melville's film was a complete departure from the dominant aesthetics of 'quality' post-war literary adaptation which Truffaut would attack in 1954,[50] and especially from the work of scriptwriting team Jean Aurenche and Pierre Bost. Characterised by high-profile productions, the adaptations of well-known plays and novels such as *Le Diable au corps* and *La Symphonie pastorale* (both 1946) were designed to display the text as part of an atmosphere of cultural quality constructed through studio sets, expensive costumes and stars. What Truffaut, following Bazin, deplored particularly were the so-called transfers, that is to say the transformation of passages of text deemed unfilmable. In Bazin's much-quoted phrase, Aurenche and Bost were the 'Viollet-le-duc of cinematographic adaptation'[51] (a reference to the nineteenth-century restorer of medieval cathedrals). Bazin coined this phrase in an article on Bresson's *Le Journal d'un curé de campagne*, the antithesis of the Aurenche–Bost style. But if Bresson is to be celebrated for the 'austerity'[52] of his adaptation of Bernanos and the feat of remaining faithful to the book while inscribing his own voice as an auteur, so must Melville. In his review of *Silence* Bazin praised the film precisely for its novel approach to literary adaptation. In terms that echoed his then current concern for an 'impure cinema', he judged that *Silence* successfully meets the challenge Melville had set himself: to follow the novel word for word, aiming at total fidelity. I am not one of those who believe, a little hastily I think, that cinema must tell everything visually and that words may not parallel images.

For Bazin, in *Silence*, 'far from duplicating each other, words and images are orchestrated in intriguing counterpoints. At times they reinforce each other, as in an echo chamber. At other times they do duplicate each other and destroy their effect through redundancy.' But 'these awkward moments', which he attributes to Vercors' heavy hand and Melville's inexperience, 'are however of no importance in view of the essential point: perfect sincerity and the right tone'.[53] Despite such praise, Bazin later set the tone of the Melville–Bresson unequal comparison. Though he recognised in his *Journal* essay that 'Melville has the merit, with *Le Silence de la mer*, of having first dared set the text against the image',[54] he then proceeded to write on Bresson but more or less ignore Melville, imitated by many in this respect, much to Melville's irritation.[55]

Silence follows Vercors closely in plot and dialogue. With the writer's consent Melville

made a few discreet but significant additions: the pre-credit sequence, the Anatole France quote, the niece walking the dog, the revelation of Treblinka. In one other important respect, though – von Ebrennac's visit to Paris – Melville departs from the book. Vercors' *Silence* is in two parts, on either side of the Paris visit, signalled by a quote from *Othello* ('Put out that light'). Melville splits the visit in two. The first part, introduced by von Ebrennac's elated declaration of the imminent marriage between France and Germany, shows him admiring Parisian monuments, ending on Notre Dame. The second part, which picks him up again at Notre Dame, comes after the uncle's visit to the Kommandantur and von Ebrennac's second highly dramatic entrance to the library. With these two flashbacks, Melville does more than simply illustrate the visit. First, he fleshes out the officer's desire to inspect the cultural marvels of Paris, signalled earlier by book covers (anticipating similar scenes in many Godard films). Second, he subtly shifts the narrative point of view as von Ebrennac focalises an increasingly painful vision of Paris under the occupation after the Nazi revelations – German street signs, closed shops, etc. This shift is reinforced by two contrasting moments which bookend the flashbacks. On his departure von Ebrennac is standing at the station, oblivious and smiling in front of a poster warning the population (presumably of reprisals). On his return, he turns towards the wall and reads, horrified, the names of hostages who have been shot. From being observed, he has become, temporarily, the subjective point of identification for the audience.

Like Bresson's *Journal*, Melville's *mise en scène* is both self-consciously literary and highly cinematic. Vercors' text is faithfully reproduced (Georges Sadoul talks of a 'passionate adaptation'[56]) but instead of being spoken in the classical manner by the great theatrical stars in the 'Tradition of Quality', the materiality of the text is foregrounded self-consciously through the uncle's voiceover and von Ebrennac's monologues over the stark images. As Bazin says, image and text 'confront' each other, rather than being smoothly blended. Shooting the film in the writer's own home, Melville also combined in one stroke of genius respect for the literary with the authenticity of location.

The looks and sounds of silence

Melville's use of Vercors' house was both highly symbolic and a triumph of practical inventiveness on the part of both himself and his director of photography, Henri Decae. As *Combat* reported, 'The room in which half the film takes place measures barely 8m25 by 4m25, with a ceiling 2m50 high.'[57] After the prologue, the film opens with outdoor wintry views of the village and the park outside the house, documenting von Ebrennac's arrival. The film then moves into the wood-panelled library, covered in shelves of books and ancient maps. The encounters between the three characters follow a routine: uncle and niece sit by the fire, von Ebrennac stands. They are initially filmed in static medium shots, frequently from high or low angles that highlight their actual and symbolic positions and show them boxed in by the cluttered room and its low ceiling. Camera movement is discreetly introduced. For instance, by the time von Ebrennac talks about Beauty and the Beast (about two-thirds in), the camera pans round to follow him, ending on a slight track up close to his face, something that would become a favourite Decae shot.[58] Gradually increased movement and relatively wider views echo the greater intimacy between the characters.

The claustrophobia of the library scenes is subtly balanced by a few outdoor scenes – the uncle at the Kommandantur, the niece walking in the snow, von Ebrennac's visit to Paris – which emphasise space. For instance, von Ebrennac in Paris is placed in front of monuments shot from a low angle, thus with a lot of sky in the background. Yet outdoor space is also filled with German presence, evoked by Melville with great economy: compared to the decorated 'quality' adaptations, a few shots of Vernon in German uniform, a handful of Nazi soldiers in a room, a few military caps on a table, a Nazi flag outside the Kommandantur, a poster with the name of hostages are sufficient to give a vivid sense of the period. To be sure Melville worked on a low budget, yet his minimalism should not be ascribed to financial constraints alone – it is a constant throughout his career, even when he had access to large budgets.

That minimalism was part of Melville's aesthetic programme was evident in his 'manifesto' in *L'Écran français*. It was also clear in his choice of cinematographer. In Henri Decae, then a newcomer, Melville found someone willing to work outside the industry and the aesthetic norms of the period, and in difficult conditions. *Silence* was Decae's first feature as director of photography (previously a photographer and editor, he would also help Melville edit *Silence*). Some technically advanced effects in the film have been noted: the depth of field in the breakfast sequence created by trick photography – a tribute to *Citizen Kane* (1941) according to Melville (steaming pans in the foreground, uncle and niece at table behind and, further back, von Ebrennac in the doorway, are all in focus)[59] – the lateral tracking shots between uncle and niece at table which foreshadow Godard, and the many ostentatious wipes. Yet the most memorable and influential aspects of *Silence* reside not in these flashy effects but in the simplicity of Decae's outdoor location photography and the dramatic noir images in the library. Melville's ability to combine realist photography with high expressionism shows the eclecticism of his aesthetic references as well as his distance from contemporary films. It is instructive to contrast *Silence* with Yves Allégret's *Une si jolie petite plage* (which Melville admired). The film is also set in a small village. Its studio-shot opening at night under torrential rain is highly melodramatic, contrasting sharply with the tranquil vistas of *Silence* with their limpid wintry light. Henri Alekan, who had shot *La Bataille du rail* in neo-realist style, filmed *Plage* in pure 'Tradition-of-Quality' noir style, with complex camera movements and dramatic but polished visual contrast. Yet the visual contrasts never impair visibility and the lighting always serves the star, enhancing Gérard Philipe's chiselled cheekbones. By contrast many scenes in the library in *Silence* feature whole areas of the frame in near darkness; characters' faces are sometimes obscured or in complete shadow against a back light, for instance as von Ebrennac plays the harmonium. The darkness of the film may be symbolic of the 'dark years' of the Occupation. It is also daring: like Godard with *À bout de souffle* (in 1960), Melville had to impose his requirements on a horrified lab: 'They were scared, because at that time they had never done [real] *noir* in France.'[60] Melville and Decae's images thus foreshadow the New Wave in two ways: in the use of location shooting for both outdoor and indoor scenes (the mainstream films of the time which used outdoor locations switched to sets for indoor scenes, for instance Carné's *La Marie du port* [1949]), and in the drive towards more 'natural' lighting for indoor scenes, sometimes to the detriment of visibility. Throughout *Silence*, pools of light are created by accentuating light sources such as the two globe lamps and the fire, and they are used at times for 'expressionistic' purposes: most strikingly in von Ebrennac's first appearance (discussed earlier) or when firelight flickers over the whole room. Predominantly though, lighting is deployed in a way which connotes authenticity. As was said later about *À bout de souffle*, 'the grain, the shallow depth of field, the bursts of light, underwrite a feeling of reality'.[61]

Melville and Decae's images were so striking that the communist daily *Ce soir* thought that the film was 'the epitome of cinematographic art, going back to the subtle effects of silent cinema',[62] and many commentators have emphasised the quality of *silence* in the film. Yet, paradoxically, the soundtrack of *Silence* is particularly 'noisy'. Its most conventional aspect is the music, an orchestral score heard virtually throughout the film. At times subdued and at times bombastic or strident, the music functions as traditional mood setting. Instrumentalisation, pitch and volume change according to dramatic need, underlining particular moments (the letter announcing the billeting of the German officer, von Ebrennac's arrival), and the melody incorporates fragments of German military music or French revolutionary song, for instance over the bust of Marianne in the Kommandantur. The background music only stops completely when von Ebrennac takes over by playing Bach on the harmonium. Melville's use of conventional 'film music' is thus significantly different from Bresson's in *Journal* and *Condamné*, where a film score in the former and a Mozart mass in the latter are used very sparingly.

While few commented on the music in *Silence*, the voiceover was controversial. Sadoul among others criticised what he saw as excessive wordiness. Arguing that Vercors' text was already 'cinematic', he pointed to the scene where von Ebrennac returns from Paris and, on the verge of revealing his fateful discovery, betrays his agitation through his involuntary hand movements. Sadoul said: 'Why does the voice-over, now turned wordy commentator, recite a text describing an action perfectly expressed by the images?'[63] Actually, the scene shows a more subtle use of the voiceover than Sadoul credits. The uncle's voice does begin to speak Vercors' lines over an image of the agitated hand, but soon stops; Melville illustrates a large chunk of text which continues to describe von Ebrennac's hand movements but also his eyes and general demeanour by purely visual means. Here image and voiceover perfectly complement each other. At other times the voiceover anticipates events, sometimes in sync, sometimes trailing behind. Sadoul's idea of redundancy needs to be challenged also on a more general level. The voiceover in *Silence* works on several levels. First, it gives us the uncle's inner thoughts – as in *Brief Encounter*. Second, in its emphasis and persistence it is an example of what Michel Chion calls the '*texte-roi*' (another, as we saw, was in *Les Enfants terribles*), where 'the sound of the words has the value of a text in itself'.[64] If, as Chion argues, this kind of voiceover usually represents the author's voice, here it is ostensibly

Vercors' in its textuality (quoting passages from the book), but in a more subtle way it is also that of Melville, who cites *Le Roman d'un tricheur* as a formative text.[65] Chion argues that the powerful voiceover must be contained because 'it tends to negate the autonomy of the visual'.[66] But Melville's use of it preserves that autonomy. Rather than the redundancy signalled by Sadoul, voiceover and image track 'sign' the dual authorship of the film.

The voiceover also plays the classic role of putting the story in the past, yet here it adds another layer of 'pastness' as the outcome of the war, the Eastern front and the camps were known to the spectators of 1949, unlike the characters in the film and the original readers of the book. Finally, the voiceover establishes a complicity with the audience which underlines von Ebrennac's status as an outsider – we hear it but he does not. Via the book but also purely on an aural level, it constructs a French community of resistance.

With all this noise on the soundtrack, why then has *Silence* been perceived as so silent? The paradoxical reason, I believe, is Melville's use of sounds. As opposed to music, voiceover and monologues, we hear very few sounds in *Silence*. But as with Bresson, their sparseness and clarity gives them added weight. From time to time we hear footsteps, a train whistling, gunfire (just once). Melville uses the sound of a dog barking very effectively. The dog, associated with the niece, barks a few times, always outside the house, connoting the isolation of the house; it has a sinister ring to it when von Ebrennac first arrives. But it is the ticking of the clock which is most effective. At times the grandfather clock in the library ticks very loudly, at others in a more subdued fashion. It stops altogether as he is about to go to Paris, and is loud again when he returns. It is a fairly constant, and insistent, leitmotiv. An aural emblem of old-fashioned domesticity, it can be understood as the suspended, 'waiting' time of the nation during the Occupation. That *Silence* takes place in suspended time is signalled by the niece's interrupted music on the harmonium. The clock's slow, ponderous rhythm fills the space and echoes the dramatic simplicity of the images, economically indicating the dreadful, drawn-out dark years of the Occupation. The clock does not figure in the book, but Melville brilliantly and paradoxically uses it as a way of creating silence.

The innovative aesthetics of *Silence*, advanced in both literary and cinematic terms, enabled it to find an original place in the canon of early post-war Resistance films, midway between the didactics of *La Bataille du rail* or *Odette* and the emotional melodrama of *Roma, città aperta*. Subsequently Melville's career took him to a variety of different projects. *Les Enfants terribles* and *Quand tu liras cette lettre*, two distinct 'stylistic exercises' which I examined in Chapter 2, have little to do with the Occupation. The war indeed reappears as the 'hidden ringmaster' in *Bob le flambeur* and *Deux hommes dans Manhattan*, but these two films, being predominantly concerned with issues of genre, the city and Franco-American hybridity, are analysed separately in Chapter 4. With *Léon Morin, prêtre*, however, Melville returned explicitly to the war, and accordingly it is to this film that I now turn.

LÉON MORIN, PRÊTRE

Set in a small town in the Alps during and at the end of the war, *Léon Morin, prêtre* is the story of Barny (Emmanuele[67] Riva), the widow of a communist and mother of young daughter, France, who works in a relocated school. A communist herself, she provokes a young Catholic priest, Léon Morin (Jean-Paul Belmondo), with an anticlerical remark. His unexpectedly sympathetic response attracts Barny to both the priest and religion. She re-converts to Catholicism. Morin nurtures the relationship, befriends Barny's daugher and encourages other attractive women to visit him. Against the background of the Occupation and then Liberation, Barny's desire for Morin grows to the point that she tries to seduce him. He rejects her. They meet once more before he leaves to take up another ministry.

Between *Silence* and *Léon Morin*, Melville's career had had its ups and downs. *Quand tu liras cette lettre* had done well commercially but not critically, *Bob le flambeur* and *Deux hommes dans Manhattan* rather the opposite. *Deux hommes dans Manhattan* marked the low point in terms of box office of all his films. After that, he 'had had enough of being an *auteur maudit* known only to a handful of crazy film-buffs'.[68] His attempts at being a producer had not worked out, and as 'Georges de Beauregard and Carlo Ponti wanted me to make a film for them, I finally decided to adapt *Léon Morin, prêtre*'.[69] With its big-shot producer, large budget and stars, and its popular success – more than 1.7 million people saw it in France, which made it Melville's biggest success so far – *Léon Morin* was a turning point, marking Melville's move to mainstream film-making, a position he would occupy to the end of his career.

When *Léon Morin* was released on 22 September 1961, the reputation of Béatrix Beck's Goncourt-winning novel, the film's stars and its potentially 'scabrous' topic all conspired to make it something of an event. A Catholic consultant, Father Lepoutre, was on hand to assist Melville with advice, and the then powerful Centrale Catholique duly gave it its seal of approval, as did the Censorship Commission. Melville's relationship with Beck was a lot easier than with Vercors. Although present at the rushes she did not take part in the adaptation and declared herself very happy with the film and its cast.[70] *Léon Morin* narrowly missed being part of the French selection at Venice that year, but was shown out of competition and was awarded the Venice City prize. Given the film's subject matter, French critics predictably split in their reactions along ideological lines. The film was highly praised by the Catholic daily *La Croix* and the right-wing *Le Figaro* ('an honest, moving and beautiful film – like the novel which it reproduces so faithfully'[71]) and harshly criticised by left-wing papers like *L'Humanité* and *Combat* ('recalls Bresson, but more vulgar and more insistent'[72]). The majority of critics, however, hailed the quality of Melville's film-making: as *Le Canard enchaîné*'s Michel Duran put it: 'It won't make me go to Mass, but I like this film.'[73] Belmondo and Riva's performances received ecstatic praise.

By contrast with its high-profile reception in 1961, *Léon Morin* has since occupied an awkward place in Melville's oeuvre. Here is a Catholic film by an atheist Jew, a Melville film with a central female protagonist, a film that stars Belmondo as a priest. Yet despite some fading of the novel's historical detail, as we shall see, the key background and structuring element of *Léon Morin* remains the war, which is why I examine it here as a 'war film'. I then look at the representation of its two central characters in relation to gender and religion, before moving on to the *mise en scène* of Melville's first foray into mainstream classicism.

From book to film: *Léon Morin, prêtre* as a 'war film'

A great deal had happened in the fifteen years since *Silence*. It was a period which scholars such as Joseph Daniel, Henry Rousso and Sylvie Lindeperg[74] see in terms of a 'submergence' of the topic, as the need for national unity overcame the traumatic divisions of the Occupation – symbolised by the amnesty laws passed between January 1951 and August 1953. Concurrently, the rise of the European Community, the French defeat in Indo-China in 1954 and the beginning of the Algerian war shifted the figure of the enemy from the German to the colonial 'other'. But, while there is an observable retreat of films celebrating the Resistance, the phenomenon is not uniform. Films about the Occupation and Resistance *were* made, and there was even a mini-revival when de Gaulle came to power in 1958. Most adopted either an oblique avant-garde approach, as in *Hiroshima, mon amour* (1959), or a comic one. From the bitterly ironic *La Traversée de Paris* (1956) to the feel-good comedies of *La Vache et le prisonnier* (1958, starring Fernandel) and *Babette s'en va-t-en-guerre* (1959, with Brigitte Bardot), or Renoir's gentle prisoner-of-war satire *Le Caporal épinglé* (1962), the Resistance itself, the Resistantialist myth and the compromises of the Occupation were mocked, even though the tone was far from the trenchant critique of *Le Chagrin et la pitié* (1969–71).

Beck's 'very autobiographical'[75] novel, and the 1952 Goncourt prize with which it was crowned, certainly belies the disappearance of the topic during that period. Beck, like her fictional creation Barny married in 1936 to a Jew who died in 1940, had a half-Jewish daughter who had to be sent away to relatives in Grenoble. Melville praised the book as 'the most accurate picture I have read of the life of French people under the Occupation'.[76] Indeed, although its heart is the relationship between Barny and Morin, Beck's novel is richly textured in historical detail about everyday life under Italian and German occupations, resistance activities and instances of collaboration, fascism and anti-Semitism. Melville's adaptation of the book arguably fits the 'submergence'/oblique approach. He reduced the historical background substantially, largely a result of the cuts he made in his very long[77] original version which, as the shooting script[78] shows, was closer to the book.

Léon Morin, the film, retains the background of the Italian and German Occupation and references to Resistance activities, especially by the church: an old priest baptises Jewish children; Morin helps *Résistants* and shelters Jews. Book and film present an honourable institution on the side of the Resistance, with only a brief mention of the Bishop's disapproval of Morin (we are a long way from Costa-Gavras' 2002 *Amen*). Such activities, however, are off-screen, discussed or heard in voiceover and even music (after the baptisms, as the camera shows the hills where the *Résistants* are going to hide, we hear the tune of the 'Chant des partisans'), or in the case of hostages taken by German soldiers, reflected in a shop window. Many scenes about the everyday context, for

Léon Morin, prêtre: a small town under the German Occupation. A German raid reflected in a window as a German soldier watches

instance the persistent hunger, are absent from the final version. Melville also significantly reduced the Jewish strand of the narrative. In the novel Barny hides a Jewish couple and their child; in the released film this remains as a baffling moment when she takes a little boy to the country on her bicycle. Nazi atrocities are equally off-screen, 'deportations' left vague in relation to Jewishness. More strikingly, the German presence is unthreatening – a 'very nice Boche' befriends France, an armed sentry (cameo by Volker Schloendorff) stops Barny but lets her go, a child mocks a German colonel (cameo and nod to *Silence* by Howard Vernon). Conversely, the most threatening foreign presence is that of two GIs who help Barny at the Liberation, one of whom seriously harasses her. In the novel the scene is a near rape – perhaps Melville's Americanophilia made him tone it down. If Nazi/anti-Semitic deeds are left out, reprisals against collaborators at the Liberation – young *miliciens* executed, a collaborationist couple who meet an 'accident', Jewish property stolen, etc. – are also deleted.

In view of the fact, however, that Melville kept the lengthy discussions about theology between Morin and Barny, we may ponder his choice of cuts, especially as they create incoherences in the narration (the abrupt baptism scene, the boy taken to the country, characters' disappearance). Melville's decision makes commercial sense in that the final version tightens the script and keeps the two stars in the frame. But equally, the suppression of inglorious internecine French divisions fitted the *zeitgeist* and arguably made the film more palatable to censorship. And yet, remarkably, some uncomfortable issues are still there. Melville retained several of the explicit discussions of collaboration and anti-Semitism between Barny and her colleagues, especially her Pétainist and anti-Semitic friend Christine (as I shall discuss later there is an interesting gender aspect to this). Meanwhile the role of state and church in relation to collaboration and the Holocaust remains unexposed, partly because such concerns are not articulated as such in the book, and partly because it would have been censored: famously, in 1956 Alain Resnais had to remove one shot of a French gendarme at the Pithiviers camp in his documentary *Nuit et brouillard*. Whatever the reason in this particular case, while several Czech, Hungarian and German fiction films of the 1950s and 60s were about these countries' implication in the Holocaust, in France the topic would only emerge in the 1970s.[79] Tellingly, in *Léon Morin*, a graffiti on a wall indicating that a shop is closed is accompanied by the word 'Jude', as if written by a German hand.

The retreat from realistic depictions of the Occupation in the late 1950s/early 60s may be one reason why Melville never shot his original script entitled *Un flic* (nothing to do with the 1972 thriller of the same title). The 1956 *Un flic*, of which a manuscript still exists,[80] fascinatingly brings together the thriller and the war film in a story of collaboration and crime around the black market. Melville must have felt that the moment was not right for a story of bitter fraternal French divisions. A few years later *Léon Morin* enabled a revisiting of the period in which these divisions could at least be addressed, even if they are marginalised and filtered through individual ethical concerns. Melville recognised that the released print of *Léon Morin* was a less potent war film than his original 'great fresco of the Occupation'.[81] *Léon Morin* is nevertheless a rare document about the period. It also shows strong thematic continuity with *Silence*: a tribute to the Resistance (albeit oblique) set in a village/small town, a strong-willed *Résistante*, the necessity of moral choice, and a transgressive love story.

Desire, religion and gender in *Léon Morin, prêtre*

Two New Wave stars

The casting of two famous New Wave actors – Emmanuele Riva and Jean-Paul Belmondo – as the protagonists of *Léon Morin* stirred much interest in 1961 and contributed to the popular success of the film. While the relationship between Melville and the New Wave had already entered a difficult phase (see Chapter 4), Riva and Belmondo anchored *Léon Morin* in the New Wave canon in the public perception at the time, despite its stylistic hybridity. Riva was (and would be forever) associated with her role as 'Elle' in *Hiroshima, mon amour*, in which she plays a French actress who goes to Hiroshima to act in a documentary about the bomb; her affair with a Japanese man helps her recall a traumatic relationship with a German soldier in Nevers during the war. Riva, together with Jeanne Moreau, embodied a new femininity: sexy in a 'realistic', less glamorous, and intellectual way (compared with sex symbols like Brigitte Bardot), related to the sensitivity and modernity of the New Wave films.[82] Melville was struck by Riva's talent and, apparently, resemblance to Beck. He used her screen persona to the full: her 'new woman' image as well as her dual association, born of *Hiroshima*, with war and sexual transgression. His extensive use of voiceover also showcased Riva's famous voice, a unique blend of cultured and halting elocution, lyrical yet fragile tones. The very first images of Riva with 1940s hairstyle and clothing riding a bicycle in *Léon Morin* thus place her in the *Hiroshima* lineage. Later, when the two old ladies who looked after her daughter say jubilantly that they have come to watch the parade of women with their heads shaven, again *Hiroshima* comes to mind. Reviewer Jean Collet echoed many others when he said 'she seems never to have left Nevers'.[83] Even some musical passages by Martial Solal evoke Giovanni Fusco's avant-garde score for Resnais' film.

Melville says he had waited for a suitable actor for Morin since the publication of the book in 1952. He found him in Jean-Paul Belmondo, the overnight sensation of *À bout de souffle*, who set a new pattern for modern French masculinity: cynical, athletic and nonchalant, unconventionally sexy.[84] The success of *À bout de souffle* launched Belmondo on a prolific career (nine films in less than two years between *À bout de souffle* and *Léon Morin*) and his currency was high in 1961. Melville's use of Belmondo is complex. A priest was, to say the least, against type compared to the thrillers and comedies Belmondo was used to; indeed he took some convincing before accepting the part.[85] However, Melville was right, it is precisely the contrast between his *À bout de souffle* star persona and his identity as priest which creates Morin's sexual and emotional charge. A survey conducted by the Catholic publication *Les Amis du film* indicated that Morin had been dubbed a 'New Wave priest – a priest with a direct, honest and virile attitude, a kind of comrade.'[86]

Together, Riva and Belmondo lent modernity, sex-appeal and 'New Waveness' to a story that would otherwise have appeared dusty and old-fashioned, with its theological discussions set in a drab small town. Even the distinguished Catholic novelist François Mauriac was moved to comment on the quality of Belmondo and Riva's performances in *Le Figaro littéraire.*[87]

Léon Morin, prêtre: a Melvillian woman's film?

Based on an autobiographical book by a woman, *Léon Morin* is unusually female-centred for Melville, leading the trade paper *Le Film français* to assume the film would 'especially touch women'.[88] The film's visual and oral construction of Barny is markedly different from that of other Melville heroines. Notwithstanding some strong female performances – the niece in *Silence*, the sisters in *Quand tu liras cette lettre*, Mathilde in *Armée* – the women in the thrillers are variants on male stereotypes of women ranging from idealisation (*Silence*, *Armée*) to demonisation (*Quand tu liras cette lettre*, *Le Doulos*). Elisabeth in *Les Enfants terribles* is extraordinary but ultimately dominated by her love for her brother and Cocteau's voice. By contrast, Barny's voiceover narration and visual focalisation of the story foreground her subjectivity throughout the film (including scenes she cannot have witnessed), with classic point-of-view shots and subjective shots (her gaze at Morin's threadbare cassock or at his neck in church, the visualisation of her erotic dream) and sound focalisation: for instance, Morin's voice is distorted, as if heard through her strained state of mind, just before she attempts to seduce him. Does this mean we can agree with Françoise Audé that 'the confrontation between Emmanuele Riva and Jean-Paul Belmondo is that of equal contestants'?[89] Unfortunately not.

Well served by Riva's powerful and subtle performance, Barny is brave, resourceful and intelligent. She dominates a gallery of less-developed and flawed female characters: Christine (collaborationist, vain), Marion and Arlette (vulgar flirts). Unlike them she is indeed Morin's intellectual equal. But Riva's star persona, 'dragged' from *Hiroshima*, also constructs a tragic, even neurotic victim of war and love. Like Elle, she slides from competent professional to woman consumed by passion. Unsurprisingly, her desire for Morin is a source of anguish. Her (re)conversion fares no better, presented as, on the one hand, inauthentic – she desires Morin rather than faith (for Melville, inelegantly, Barny converts 'in order to get laid'[90]) – and, on the other, as dictated by greater forces which rob her of agency: 'I don't want to, but I'm forced. It is not a decision, I have no choice; it is in spite of myself.' Interestingly, one reviewer who noticed the undermining of Barny's subjectivity said approvingly: 'From a subjective novel [Melville] made an objective film. A novel about a crisis has become a film about a case study.'[91] The end of the film shows Barny bereft of both Morin and faith, her abject solitude visualised by her staggering along the pavement, clinging to the walls; no more voiceover. Barny's relation to Morin is thus fundamentally unbalanced, and she frequently apologises to him. As suggested by the film's title, he remains Priest, she is Woman.

Although this unequal characterisation originates in the book, Melville made adjustments which, in addition to the unequal weight of the two stars, further contradict the notion of 'equal contestants'. Beck's novel documents a female community's wartime struggle, while the film focuses on the heterosexual couple (Barny's attraction for Sabine and Christine is acknowledged by book and film but remains marginal). Although Melville took from the book Barny's blunt reference to 'making love with a piece of wood', Beck gives a more sympathetic sense of women's desire exacerbated by the historical context of men's absence. Melville deleted a bawdy song which in the book points to the absurdity of Catholic sexual repression, thus legitimising Barny's desire. Beck's Barny has two dreams: an erotic one followed by one in which she rides through the universe. Melville kept only the erotic dream. For Beck, female desire is empowering (even if only in fantasy), in the film it leads only to grief and frustration. Finally, in a key moment in the novel Barny asks Morin, who at that point is chopping wood for her, if he would marry her if he was a Protestant. First he jokes that 'of course'. When asked by Barny to be serious, he pauses, answers 'yes', picks up the axe and gives a mighty blow before storming out of the room. The film here follows the book but for one crucial omission: Morin strikes the blow but remains silent before leaving. Beck's heroine is ultimately frustrated, but Morin has revealed his feelings. By contrast Melville's Morin divulges nothing.[92] In a story where confession is crucial, his single word admission in the novel establishes a symbolic equality. In the film his refusal to speak prepares the spectator for Barny's eventual rejection and humiliation. True, his violent blow with the axe symbolically signifies his frustration as well as the limit she must not overstep, as later his vivid recoiling when she grabs his arm in her bid for seduction betrays that he is not indifferent, yet he remains in control and immediately orders her to confess in church. In this respect Barny's voiceover becomes a double-edged weapon, verbalising her agonising desire and doubt, while his thoughts remain a blank. Contemporary reactions are revealing of how this gender imbalance found wide approval. The reviewer for *La Croix*, the only one to notice the missing 'yes', said approvingly: 'This too is an improvement on the book: ambiguity means refusal.'[93] The left-wing *Libération* thought Barny's conversion a typical displacement of sexual privation: 'All priests know that four-fifths of their female flock – adolescents, widows or spinsters, jilted women – frequently find in religious fervour an exaltation born of their sexual frustration.'[94] It appears that neither the film nor the critics thought of asking the same about the character more likely to be sexually frustrated, the priest. At the same time *Léon Morin* is remarkable for the way it constructs its male protagonist as an object of desire.

A film about a beautiful priest

Melville, an atheist Jew, repeatedly stated that *Léon Morin* was not about religion. This may seem strange given the lengthy theological discussions between Morin and Barny and details such as a pointed shot of the star of David on the ceiling of Morin's church (Melville is also reported to have immersed himself in religious books in preparing for the film). But mostly one can agree with the assessment of Catholic critic Amédée Ayfre who praised Melville for having 'gone beyond the usual stereotypes [of priests in films]',[95] but found Morin 'too human'. Like many others, Ayfre compared *Léon Morin* to Bresson's *Le Journal d'un curé de campagne* and found that *Léon Morin* lacked transcendence: 'We stay all the time on men's earth.'[96] Indeed Melville's Morin is neither the militant priest in the community of for instance *Monsieur Vincent* (1947, a biopic of St Vincent de Paul), nor the other-wordly, alienated hero of Bresson's *Journal*.[97] And while Morin's feelings towards women are impenetrable, he is certainly sexually desirable. As Melville said, 'The main idea was to show this amorous priest who likes to excite girls but doesn't sleep with them. Léon Morin is Don Juan.'[98] In this respect, Morin is thematically linked to many other Melvillian heroes who combine an aura of virile masculinity with a-sexuality (see especially chapters 5 and 6).

As a taboo to be broken, the celibacy of Catholic priests has long offered a ready-made plot – for example, *Francesco giullare di Dio* (1950), *I Confess* (1953), *The Singer not the Song* (1961), *La moglie del prete* (1970), *La Faute de l'abbé Mouret* (1970), *Camila* (1984), *Priest* (1994). The way *Léon Morin* specifically deals with the theme reflects both Melville's interests and early 1960s mores. An important predecessor to Melville's film is Hitchcock's *I Confess* (starring Montgomery Clift). As appears typical of this 'genre', both *Léon Morin* and *I Confess* feature a very good-looking star as the sexually taboo priest whose youth and handsomeness are enhanced by the austere black cassock, lack of rivals and contrast with older and/or uglier men. Even Claude Laydu, the sick hero of *Journal*, follows this pattern, with his angelic face. The priest's beauty and remoteness are also a weapon. As V. F. Perkins says, Clift as Morgan is 'impossibly attractive and frustratingly distant'. Perkins also points out that 'There is a potent anomaly in putting a Method actor of such intense inner turbulence into a role whose interior world is to remain hidden and whose motives the film will not expose.'[99] Although Belmondo always distanced himself from method acting, preferring a more spontaneous approach, a similar effect is achieved in *Léon Morin*. Like Morgan with the woman who loves him (Anne

Baxter), Morin manipulates Barny by combining his attractiveness with opacity. His clerical authority gives him license to make Barny confess – including her desire for him – while he withholds his feelings, even when directly questioned. The church as institution thus reinforces traditional gender definitions, where masculinity is defined by emotional control and femininity by excess.

Melville may not have made a 'religious film', but the investment of sexuality solely in women recalls the Judeo-Christian myth of Eve as temptress: Morin tells Barny she's 'impure' and her revelation that she 'makes love with a piece of wood' sounds desperate and shocking, as is her declaration that '[her] mind feels like a brothel'. In the earlier *I Confess*, the woman's desire is contained by marriage (and Hollywood mores). In *Journal*, centred on the hero's spiritual odyssey, women's sexuality is 'redeemed' according to religious mythology: Seraphita, the young temptress, becomes a Mary Magdalene, wiping the priest's brow. Barely a decade after *Léon Morin*, Franju's *Mouret* celebrated *and* criticised the myth of woman as sexual temptress in a lurid combination of Zola's anticlericalism with post-1968 permissiveness. Later still, Maria-Luisa Bemberg's *Camila* adopted the heroine's point of view in depicting Camila's triple challenge to family, church and state. *Léon Morin*, in 1961, occupies a transitional place. Morin has none of the religious transcendence of Bresson's hero. Compared to *I Confess*, *Léon Morin* acknowledges more openly the sexual allure of the Catholic priest. But Morin's control, and arguably humiliation, of Barny and other women perfectly overlaps with his institutional role. As the town women's *directeur de conscience*, Morin judges their actions and remarks on their looks in ways which would now be construed as sexual harassment. It also overlaps with the patriarchal family – when he visits Barny at home, he takes the symbolic place of her dead husband. Where feminist director Bemberg uses the sexual transgression inherent in the topic to criticise the patriarchal Catholic church, *Léon Morin* identifies with its gendered power structure. The enthusiastic reception of the film, including by the Catholic press, tells us that it was in harmony with a period when the Catholic church was still a powerful force in French society. *Léon Morin*'s construction of masculinity also takes us back to the French context of the war.

By contrast to Bresson's weak, child-like hero[100] and to Bemberg's and Franju's 'feminised' priests, Morin is unambiguously virile. Although Belmondo's movements are subdued compared to his other roles at the time, there is, despite the cassock, a powerful sense of his energy and athleticism. In a town full of women and old men, it is left to Morin to represent virility. Morin, however, is not just a priest: he hides Jews and protects resisters against public opinion and the Bishop's disapproval. On the other hand Barny's transgression is purely sexual: her relationship with Morin dominates all other aspects of her life, and the Liberation of the town coincides with the 'liberation' of her sexual desire. Morin's patriotic rebellion recalls the bold young Resistance fighters who symbolically atoned for the humiliating French defeat in 1940.[101] Indeed Melville has described Morin as 'a bit like a FFI [Free French Fighter] from 1942'.[102] Is this why he replaced the prayer Morin recites to France in the book with the 'paratrooper's prayer' written by Legionnaire André Zirnheld, a former theology student who joined the Free

Léon Morin, prêtre: Barny (Emmanuele Riva) and the 'beautiful priest' (Jean-Paul Belmondo) discussing theology

Confession

Morin in noir lighting

Barny's erotic dream

French army in North Africa and died in 1942? The reference to the paratrooper who died in North Africa may well also have reminded French spectators of 1961 (towards the end of the Algerian war) of other French soldiers dying in the sand.

Underneath the story of a priest and a woman, *Léon Morin* continues to register the shock waves of the war on French identity, in particular in terms of gender. Morin is virtually the only man in the film (the other one is the old Jewish teacher who goes into hiding). He is also the one who concentrates all Resistance actions – it is telling in this respect that the brief view of the *maquisards* is in the church, when they come to the children's baptism. Opposite him, given that Barny's Resistance activities have more or less vanished from the film, it is left to the female population of the town to embody collaboration (sexual and otherwise), fascism and anti-Semitism.

Melville's new classicism

Thematically, *Léon Morin* pursues Melville's interest in the German Occupation and Resistance, relating it back to *Silence*. But stylistically it marks a major turning point in his oeuvre. After the personal essays of *Bob le flambeur* and *Deux hommes dans Manhattan*, *Léon Morin* is both a return to literary adaptation and a move forward into mainstream cinema. For the first time Melville had a large budget and a major star, and he broadcast loudly his new approach. Among other things, he told *Cahiers du cinéma*:

> This is a cautious film, polished and perfect, comfortable morally and technically [...] I made it for the producer and the mass audience. I've had enough of being an *auteur maudit*, a maverick who can't be trusted. With *Morin* they'll be gobsmacked.[103]

They were: although later, when *Cahiers* and other cinephile publications turned against mainstream cinema, he would pay for these statements with decades of critical oblivion. At the time, though, he was also keen to stress that his new approach to film was part of an aesthetic plan in which 'commercial cinema', sincerity and personal style merged. As he put it to *Combat*:

> There is no question for me to stop having a style – since people are kind enough to recognise that I have one – but why should I not put my way of conceiving a story, of developing an adaptation, of directing a film, to the service of a cinema that is intelligent without being intellectual, efficient without being basely commercial?[104]

As he also pointed out, his topic was not entirely without risk, as 'a film about a priest at a time when box-office records are broken by films such as *Les Liaisons dangereuses* and *La dolce vita*'.[105]

Compared to his reverential versions of Vercors and Cocteau, Melville's adaptation of Beck's novel is a more traditionally restructured script in which he dispersed some of the early background scenes throughout the film and cut others (some scenes in the script were shot but were further cut as mentioned earlier). He introduces Morin much earlier than in the novel, while keeping Barny's conversion as the half-way point of the story – adaptation in the classic mould worthy of Aurenche and Bost. However, at the same time, as in *Silence* and *Les Enfants terribles*, instead of playing down the wordiness of the source book, he kept the long discussions between Barny and Morin and foregrounded the text through Barny's voiceover. This verbosity, resented by some critics at the time, tipped the film into the camp of literary cinema. Yet *Léon Morin* was also a great popular success. The stars and topic helped, as did, then, the reputation of the book (today it is remembered because of the film). But the documentary quality of the photography and the naturalistic performances also rebalanced the film. Even more than in *Silence*, Melville achieved in *Léon Morin* a brilliant synthesis of literariness with the dynamic qualities of popular cinema. He also succeeded in fashioning a hybrid of classical and New Wave French cinema, which explains his inclusion in the 'Films de ma vie' New Wave video series.

Camerawork and editing are a compendium of 'old' and 'new'. The film starts with a series of elliptical scenes (several in just one long take), notations in the life of the small town in Decae's subdued black-and-white photography, a clear filiation to the New Wave cinematography, as is, in parts, Martial Solal's music – for instance, its modernist tone over the credits, the jaunty tune over the scene of the women on bicycles taking the children to be baptised, or the jazz-like harmonica. As the film moves on to studio shots of Barny at work and encounters with Morin, classic *découpage* prevails with shot/counter-shot editing and apparently more static camerawork, and a more classic film score. A leitmotiv of contemporary reviews was that the camera in *Léon Morin* did not move, but a close examination shows that in fact it is quite fluid, though in a discreet way. As in *Deux hommes dans Manhattan* several complex scenes with crane shots and reframings exemplify Melville's 'quietly virtuoso' full exploitation of the possibilities of studio film-making; as he said, 'I had my dolly, my Mitchell, not at all the "hand-held Caméflex" kind of thing'.[106] The staircase leading to Morin's flat is unusually wide, allowing for crane shots to follow Barny's ascent or descent. Inside Morin's lodgings deceptively simple scenes involve long mobile takes and the complex choreography of the characters across the space. For instance, Barny's second visit to Morin is composed of two symmetrical takes of over two minutes each, separated by a few brief takes. In such scenes, the fluidity of the camerawork provides a corrective to the potentially static encounters. When movement is difficult, for instance in the confessional scenes, Melville and Decae inventively play with camera angles, including several 'impossible' ones, for instance from behind the wall of the confessional box.

They also make full use of the 'expressionist' possibilities offered by lighting through the confessional grille. As in earlier films such as *Deux hommes*, Melville is not afraid of juxtaposing naturalistic outdoor photography, darkly contrasted expressionist images and high-key studio lighting. Interestingly, the differentiated lighting pattern follows the gendered logic of American film noir: namely, flat high-key lighting is applied to Barny at home and to the female environment of the school's office, and contrasted noir photography tends to be applied to Morin. *Mise en scène* thus confirms the difficulties the film has with constructing female subjectivity – the overt subject is Barny but the real interest is Morin, represented as an opaque, darkly mysterious character through dramatic lighting, while women bathe in the light of the everyday. On the occasion when Barny visits Morin during the day, incredibly bright sunlight floods in from the window for the only time in the film, confirming that Morin benefits from the extremes of dark and light. The *mise en scène* fully exploits the contrasts between his black cassock and bare white walls with their few spare icons (a cross, a Picasso Madonna), while the women's homes are swathed in 'busy' patterned wallpaper. The dual lighting pattern is most evident in the dream sequence: Morin's footsteps are heard almost as in a horror film before he appears as a shadow through a patterned glass door, and 'his' lighting invades Barny's space. But it is also true of the scenes in his flat where his desk lamp becomes an important visual signifier, creating a pool of light which reflects on characters' faces, especially his own. Low-angle shots, not used elsewhere, imbue him with authority. Morin's privileged visual treatment culminates in the last scene, and is enhanced by sound effects. As Barny visits him for the last time, she finds the place almost abandoned. The room stripped bare, a door banging loudly and exaggerated wind on the soundtrack poetically illustrate Morin's image of 'breaking his moorings'. As they part, the camera follows her staggering downstairs and along the street. Here Beck's novel ended. But Melville returns to Morin at the top of the stairs, shot from a low angle, back lighting creating a halo effect. The film ends on Morin's 'sainthood' rather than Barny's pain.

Melville's classicism in *Léon Morin* is a skilful integration of innovative New Wave-style naturalistic photography and long takes with studio-based classical camerawork and highy contrasted 'expressionist' lighting, a blend of modernist, elliptical montage with mainstream shot counter-shot *découpage*. The stylistic factor that ensured coherence over this variety, across *Léon Morin* and across Melville's oeuvre, is its sobriety – pared down décors and austere black-and-white photography served the economy with which Melville recreated the period: a Nazi flag over Barny's head, the sound effects of the Germans and then the Allies entering town, a reflection in a shop window. Melville's understated yet intense *mise en scène* would find fuller expression in his next film, *Le Doulos*, and be refined to an extraordinary degree in the films that followed. One of these is *L'Armée des ombres*, Melville's next and last film on the war, in which Occupation and Resistance return to occupy centre stage.

L'ARMÉE DES OMBRES

Based on Joseph Kessel's popular 1943 novel, *Armée* is the story of a group of resisters headed by Philippe Gerbier (Lino Ventura), an engineer before the war. After internment in a French camp and escape from the Kommandantur in Paris, Gerbier rejoins his comrades Félix (Paul Crauchet), Le Bison (Christian Barbier) and Le Masque (Claude Mann) in Marseille to execute a traitor, Dounat (Alain Libolt). The group of resisters also includes Mathilde (Simone Signoret) and Jean-François Jardie (Jean-Pierre Cassel), whose older brother Luc (Paul Meurisse) is, unbeknown to him, the head of the network. Gerbier and Luc meet General de Gaulle in London. Félix is arrested and Mathilde plans his escape, but he is too damaged by torture to be moved. Jean-François gets himself arrested to reach Félix but is also too late. Gerbier is arrested; Mathilde helps him escape from a Gestapo 'shooting gallery' and hide in an isolated house. Mathilde is arrested. Fearing that the Germans will make her talk by threatening her daughter (whose photograph she has kept), Gerbier and his comrades gun her down. A text unfolds, announcing that Gerbier, Le Masque, Le Bison and Jardie all die later in action or under torture.

Bad timing

Released on 12 September 1969, *Armée* completed Melville's triptych about the Occupation and Resistance: 'Now I have said everything about the war', he told *Paris-Presse*.[107] Although in colour, unlike *Silence* and *Léon Morin*, *Armée* is an exceptionally dark film, a twilight vision of the Resistance, supported by powerfully restrained performances, especially by Lino Ventura in the lead. Today *Armée* is Melville's best-known and highest-rated war film, but it was not always so. The film's critical reception was split and box office considered disappointing. However, if popular success did not quite match up to expectations created by the film's high budget of FF 8,175,000, starry cast and famous source novel, its so-called 'failure', reiterated by most commentators, has been greatly exaggerated. The film actually sold 1.4 million tickets – a more than respectable figure. Like *Silence* and *Léon Morin*, *Armée* needs to be understood in relation to Melville's own past, to the book on which it is based and to the moment of its making and release. In respect of the latter, it suffered from spectacular bad timing.

Melville had thought of adapting *Armée* ever since the release of Kessel's book in 1943. He said: 'This is a film I have wanted to make for 25½ years, exactly since I read Joseph Kessel's book, that is to say in July–August 1943, in London, at the same time as *Le Silence de la mer*.'[108] The scale of the project, other film offers and Lino Ventura's unavailability delayed him until the late 1960s.[109] When Melville started the film in early 1969 de Gaulle was still in power, but by the time it came out the General had retired from politics after a vote of no confidence in the referendum which followed the events of May 1968. Sarcastically dubbed 'the first and greatest example of Gaullist film art'[110] by *Cahiers du cinéma*, *Armée* appeared (to some) out of date, a last stand against the tide of history. These reactions make sense in the post-1968 context. Georges Pompidou, de Gaulle's successor, was leading France into a new age, and attitudes to the war were about to take a U-turn. From serious historiography to literature and the movies, new voices were exploding the Resistantialist myth which, for Rousso, had 'reach[ed] its apogee between the end of the Algerian war and May 1968'.[111] Soon the four-hour long documentary *Le Chagrin et la pitié*, shot during 1967 and 1968 but not released until 1971, would put the final nail in the coffin of the old-style Resistance myth by documenting a nation not only split between collaborationists and resisters, but largely composed of uncommitted or indifferent *attentistes*; in 1974 Louis Malle's *Lacombe Lucien* illustrated this in fictional form. Mentalities were changing fast, and it would seem that, as Rousso puts it, *Armée* 'arrived on the scene too late'.[112]

The background I have just sketched out needs modifying. There is no gainsaying the changes brought by May 1968, the impact of a new generation of writers, the ground-breaking nature of Stanley Hoffman's (and later Robert O. Paxton's) historical accounts of the Occupation,[113] or the importance of *Le Chagrin et la pitié*. Yet if it is true that the colonial wars and then May 1968 partly obliterated World War II from French memories, the topic by no means disappeared. We saw how in 1961 *Léon Morin* featured discussions of French collaboration and anti-Semitism. But other films such as *La Traversée de Paris*, *La Vache et le prisonnier* and *Le Passage du Rhin* (1960), all incidentally very popular, hardly presented a heroic picture of the French – in *Vache*, Fernandel plays a cowardly and incompetent prisoner, in *Traversée* the only resister, a woman, is keener on black-market pork than politics; the pro-European *Le Passage du Rhin* blurs the resistance/collaboration dichotomy. It is also true that the 1960s comedies – such as *La Grande vadrouille* (1966) and *La Vie de château* (1965) – are less trenchant and that several films, including *Armée* again, focused on the Resistance. To call Melville's film 'Gaullist film art' as *Cahiers* did, is, apart from the calculated insult, a gross simplification. As we will see, that title would be better suited to René Clément's bombastic *Paris brûle-t-il?* (1966), or even Chabrol's Manichean *La Ligne de démarcation* (1965). With *Armée* Melville certainly produced a deeply felt tribute to the Resistance and de Gaulle (Kessel's book in itself was a guarantee of that), but, unlike Clément's, it was also a profoundly ambivalent one. Its pessimistic narrative and bleak minimalist style turn it into a reflection on solitude and on the tragic futility of war, life and death. No wonder contemporary reactions were split.

Melville, Kessel and the Resistance

Like *Silence* and to some extent *Léon Morin*, *Armée* the book is the work of a high-profile Resistance member, with whom Melville stressed a personal connection. He told Nogueira:

> As the story proceeds, my personal recollections are mingled with Kessel's, because we lived the same war. [. . .] The Gerbier of the concentration camp is my friend Pierre-Bloch, General de Gaulle's former Minister. The Gerbier who escapes from the Gestapo Headquarters at the Hôtel Majestic in Paris is Rivière, the Gaullist deputy. As a matter of fact it was Rivière himself who described this escape to me in London.[114]

Resistance hero Jean Moulin is also a model for Gerbier and Luc Jardie, who 'died revealing only one name, his own' as Moulin had done. The release of the film was surrounded by accounts of Melville's Resistance past in the papers. This was in contrast with his more discreet public image of 1949. Apart from the fact that Melville by then was an altogether more public person, the era was one of commemoration, and the release of the film roughly coincided with the twenty-fifth anniversary of the liberation of Paris.

Although Kessel, unlike Vercors, appears not to have exerted control over the adaptation of his book, Melville arranged a screening of *Armée* for the twenty-two 'great *Resistants*', as he had done for *Silence*. Since this time he did not need their approval, the gesture must be seen as part respect and part quest for authenticity, for a book which itself claimed to stem directly from the true spirit of the Resistance. After the showing Melville said: 'I could see how moved they were. They were all Gerbiers, Jardies, Félixes.'[115]

But for all this recourse to authenticity, Melville's attitude to his source and to 'real life' was highly ambivalent. He repeatedly claimed that there was only one unspecified 'two-minute' scene in the film which related to his own past, and he made many changes to the book. For him, *L'Armée des ombres* was

> *the* book about the Resistance: the greatest and the most comprehensive of all the documents about this tragic period in the history of humanity. Nevertheless, I had no intention of making a film about the Resistance. So with one exception – the German Occupation – I excluded all realism.[116]

As the last sentence betrays (how can the German Occupation be just an 'exception'?), in *Armée* more than in the previous two films, Melville plays a game of hide and seek, both grounding his film in the historical reality of the Occupation and elevating it to a more abstract level.

From book to film

Kessel and Melville's *Armée* plunge reader and viewer alike into the intense internal world of the Resistance. Germans and French collaborators are not absent: German soldiers parade on the Champs-Elysées and are glimpsed in hotels and prisons; an internment camp is run by a French official under a portrait of Pétain; two *bon vivant* gendarmes stop at a farm to buy black-market food; members of the (French) *milice* arrest Gerbier. Nevertheless book and film concentrate on the Resistance, from a very specific angle. This is not the Resistance of spectacular action – the sabotaged train of *Jéricho* or the storming of the Préfecture de police in *Paris brûle-t-il?* In *Armée* as in *Silence*, Resistance is a moral and intellectual concept. Kessel, like Vercors, resisted through his writing, through his intellect. Kessel's Gerbier eulogises about Jardie's writing: 'It is because of this book that I wanted to know him. He has been my spiritual leader for a long time.'[117] Melville's Gerbier reverentially looks at the covers of books written by 'Luc Jardie' (the titles are those of books by real-life philosopher Jean Cavaillès, a professor at the Sorbonne and Resistance hero who was shot by the Gestapo in 1944). As the Germans prepare to shoot at him, his main thoughts, in voiceover, are that they are breaking his *spirit*.

To the extent that it involves action at all, for Kessel and Melville Resistance is a shadowy clandestine world where 'work' consists of liaisons and quiet executions, of the internal relationships of the group. Marcel Martin's complaint in *Les Lettres françaises* that 'These obscure and heroic fighters spend their time liquidating traitors and evacuating their friends: did they really do nothing else?'[118] was, in its hostile way, spot on. While Melville defended the veracity of such details as Dounat's execution,[119] his and Kessel's low-key representation is more 'realistic' than spectacular heroics. At the same time, the dark, morbid tone of the film is set within an overall aesthetic project and is indicative of a different take on the war, compared to the poetic *Silence* and the more humanist *Léon Morin*.

While Melville adopted Kessel's concept of the Resistance, his adaptation significantly altered the novel. He kept the basic sequence of events – Gerbier's escape, Dounat's execution, the submarine, London, the shooting gallery, Gerbier going into hiding and the killing of Mathilde – but drastically edited and redistributed the large section of anecdotes entitled 'Philippe Gerbier's notes' which dominates the second half of the book. Although some commentators criticised the film's fractured, episodic narrative, Melville turned Kessel's uneven patchwork of anecdote into a structured narrative which culminates half-way through in London (*Armée* was sometimes shown in two parts, the first one ending with the London sequence, the second beginning with Gerbier being parachuted into France). Some episodes were inflated, in particular the attempt to extract Félix from the Gestapo jail (from one paragraph to fifteen minutes), while others were reduced. We need not review all the alterations, but two must be singled out: Kessel's Gerbier survives, Melville's hero dies; in the film, unlike in the novel, brothers Jean-François and Luc Jardie never realise that they are both in the Resistance. These and other aspects of the film point to a radically different vision, characterised by pessimism and abstraction.

Kessel's account, written in 1943, is tragic but hopeful. It ends with Gerbier travelling to London after liquidating Mathilde and returning to France 'in good health and calm. He was able to half-smile again.'[120] Melville's choice of Lino Ventura already signals a more sombre character. Of Gerbier's death in his film, he said 'the film must resemble one of life's truths. And the truth is that man is always defeated.'[121] While Gerbier in the book successfully escapes from the internment camp, Melville has him taken away by the Gestapo just before his carefully worked out escape plan with the young communist Derain can be implemented. Similarly, Mathilde's elaborate plan to get Félix out of jail fails in the film where in the book it succeeds. Some models for the characters – most famously Jean Moulin – did die as a result of their Resistance activities, many were atrociously tortured, but many survived, such as 'Colonel Passy', who appears as himself in the film, as well as Lucie Aubrac and Dominique Desanti, models for Mathilde. Melville's 1969 film ends with a bleak roll-call of the main protagonists' deaths under torture or in combat. The difference reflects the disillusions of the post-Liberation period and symbolically inscribes atrocities only revealed after the war. A sense of futility, morbidity and the absurd pervade the film and give it its uniquely disturbing feel. Human endeavour is negated by the arbitrariness of fate – as in Douglas Sirk's *A Time to Love and a Time to Die* (1958), an anti-Nazi war film set in the rubble of a German city in which the main character shockingly dies at the end, a film which Melville particularly admired.

As in *Léon Morin*, Melville also deleted much social and political background. The book contains explicit details about torture and radio work; it discusses the complex role of the communists, the special plight of the Jews and the evolution of Gestapo policies. But Melville 'didn't want to make a picturesque film about war'.[122] Nor did he want to explore the psychology of characters such as Dounat, which the book renders at length. Instead, as we shall see in more detail below, he appropriated the Resistance through a process of narrative abstraction and *mise en scène* minimalism, in line with the austere late thrillers with which the film belongs chronologically (*Armée* was made between *Le Samouraï* and *Le Cercle rouge*, which are discussed together in Chapter 6). Compared to his own earlier war films, he also steeped the film in a singularly dark and pessimistic vision.

The opening

The one-minute, single-take opening sequence showing the Wehrmacht marching down the Champs-Elysées is one of only two shots Melville claimed he was 'proud of'.[123] Notwithstanding Melvillian exaggeration, it was an exploit:

> It was a crazy idea to want to shoot this German parade on the Champs-Elysées. Even today I can't quite believe I did it. No one managed it before me, not even Vincente Minnelli for *The Four Horsemen of the Apocalypse*, because actors in German uniform had traditionally been banned from the Champs-Elysées ever since the First World War.[124]

The soldiers file first left to right in the distance; as they arrive in front of the Arc de Triomphe they turn abruptly ninety degrees to the right towards the camera. The vision of German soldiers advancing towards the spectator to the sound of military music and marching feet (Melville used the 'inimitable' sound of real German soldiers but employed dancers to act the goosestep), shot from a static camera, is an aggressively powerful opening. It is therefore a surprise to find that Melville had initially placed it at the end of the film. The script states that 'this last scene must give both a feeling of terrible truth and unreality, like a nightmare'.[125] Evidence suggests the film was briefly released that way, probably to press screenings: the *Cinémonde* review, discussing Mathilde's killing at the end of the film, mentions the 'fateful Wehrmacht music' rising at that point, which of course does not happen in the final version.[126] Shifting the scene to the beginning makes sense chronologically since the Germans entered Paris on 14 June 1940 and the action of the film begins on 20 October 1942.[127] As Mathilde is shot down in view of the Arc de Triomphe at the end, the film is thus bookended with a bitter-ironic reflection on an 'arch of triumph' presiding over, respectively, military humiliation and murder.

The evocative and tone-setting force of this opening is also related to the way it is shot. In this respect it is useful to compare *Armée* to Minnelli's *The Four Horsemen of the Apocalypse* (1961) and other films such as Autant-Lara's *La Traversée de Paris* which feature the same event. Minnelli's parade, though it is, as Melville claims, 'fake' (the Arc de Triomphe is superimposed at the end of a Versailles avenue[128]), is 'realistically' placed in time with leafy green trees, and Minnelli intercuts shots of the soldiers with (studio) shots of the crowd watching, including heroes Glenn Ford and Ingrid Thulin, thus integrating the historical moment into the diegesis. In *La Traversée de Paris* (as do later *Le Caporal épinglé* and *Paris brûle-t-il?*), Autant-Lara uses black-and-white archive footage of the parade,[129] which shows vast crowds watching, while editing and music also connect the parade to the fiction that follows. The ubiquity of this scene in films about the Occupation points to its symbolic weight in representing the bitter trauma of the French defeat; after all the Champs-Elysées is the most prestigious thoroughfare in Paris, the Arc de Triomphe the most spectacular representation of Republican grandeur. By comparison with the other films, Melville also hammers the point in, but his starkly realistic yet detached shot performs a more ambivalent function. His German soldiers marching directly at the spectator must have packed a punch for the 1969 audience. As

Olivier Bohler argues, it is like history coming straight at the spectator.[130] Yet, with its bare trees and emptiness, the scene looks extra-diegetic, its historicity blurred. In contrast to the exuberant parade in the archive footage (presumably shot by German cameramen), Melville's parade with its military march, unusually, played in a minor key, announces the 'funereal' tone of the whole film. By contrast the London sequence in the middle of the film goes out of its way to present itself as a document and it contains the only joyful moments in the film.

The London visit

In both novel and film, the London visit occupies a distinct position and deploys a different mode of address to the rest of the text(s). Kessel's London scene takes place after Gerbier's two escapes, Dounat's execution and the boarding of the submarine – tough masculine situations in bleak, dark locations. The London scene transports us to a pink candle-lit salon in Belgrave Square, where an elderly aristocratic English hostess welcomes French *Résistants* to a lavish dinner. Great contrast is established, then, in the book, with poverty-stricken France (no mention of English wartime privations or rich French profiteers), enhanced by a stylistic switch from third- to first-person narration. The unnamed narrator, 'a friend of Gerbier's', happens to sit next to 'Saint-Luc' (Luc Jardie), the head of the network as the reader already knows. It is in this scene that Mathilde's activities are first discussed, emphasising the notion that the Resistance encompasses the social spectrum from working-class housewife to rich aristocrat. Given that Kessel wrote his book in London, the switch to first-person narration can also be taken as authorial signature.

Though his sequence is different in virtually every way, Melville signals how special London is with his own internal structural and *mise en scène* changes. The sequence is expanded in length, recentred in the overall film and shot in a lyrical and fluid style that contrasts to the minimalism of the rest of the movie, a lyricism also enhanced by music. At the end of the previous sequence, strings swell as the submarine submerges, and the continuation of the tune provides an oral bridge to Luc and Gerbier driving round London in an open-top car. Melville's topography is no class-bound Belgravia, but a historic and cinematic city. Gerbier and Luc visit carefully signposted Free French landmarks (Wigmore House, Frognal, Carlton Gardens) and the emblems of victorious Britain: Nelson's column, Westminster Abbey, the Houses of Parliament and the highly symbolic Big Ben – one shot pauses as Gerbier and Luc gaze at the chiming clock. As the men sweep through the city accompanied by a tracking camera, low-angle shots point at the top of façades and monuments and at the sky. While this must have been motivated by the need to avoid showing 1969 shops and clothing, this style creates a mood of elation and freedom. By contrast, the inserted scene of Félix's arrest and the two scenes surrounding the London sequence (the boarding of the submarine and Gerbier's parachute jump) are all dark and claustrophobic.

Besides the landmarks described above, Gerbier makes three other momentous visits. The first is the much-decried encounter with 'de Gaulle' for Luc's decoration. This very brief scene (less than a minute) shows Luc and Gerbier and real-life Resistance hero

'Colonel Passy' waiting in a room at 99A Frognal, one of de Gaulle's London residences. At the sound of a door opening the men look awe-struck. A low-angle medium shot shows de Gaulle (look-alike actor Adrien Cayla-Legrand) entering the room. A reverse-angle shot follows the General, whose right shoulder is left of frame, as he moves towards Luc and Passy. The latter produces the medal which de Gaulle pins on Luc's jacket. The relative position of Luc's upturned head and de Gaulle's shoulder, as well as the camera's slightly low angle, suggests a gigantic de Gaulle towering above the other men, surely beyond verisimilitude. Melville's play with space and the distance at which the General is held by the camera cannot be accounted for only by the need to blur the features of the actor who is *not* de Gaulle. The representation of the General is clearly imbued with respect, but it is also humorous (a dimension which seems to have escaped most commentators) as well as a commentary on his elevated mythical status in 1942. The same mixture of respect, humour and myth informs the next sequence (and second visit), when Luc and Gerbier go to see *Gone With the Wind* (1939), which they contemplate with apparently the same awe as they did de Gaulle. History and cinema here merge for Melville, who was fond of pointing out that

> when Gerbier and Jardie are crossing Leicester Square with the Ritz Cinema behind them advertising *Gone With the Wind*, I was thinking of what Pierre Brossolette said to me in the same circumstances: 'The day the French can see that film and read the *Canard Enchaîné* again, the war will be over.'[131]

The point is not simply that Gerbier and Luc are combining Resistance work with American cinema, but that American cinema *is* Resistance, in the context of the German ban of American films in the occupied territories.

This theme is pursued in the next scene, Gerbier's third visit, and the longest in the London sequence. Since it lasts exactly the specified time, there is a strong suggestion that this may be the '2½-minute scene' Melville mentions as the only 'personal' one in the film. Significantly, another shift in *mise en scène* takes place. As Gerbier walks through London at night under an air raid, the set and yellow lighting construct a dream-like blitz, making no attempt to disguise its studio sets and models. Gerbier hears muffled music and enters a YMCA/YWCA club where young people in uniform dance to Glenn Miller's 'In the mood'. In the club the camera picks up picturesque details (a man in a kilt kisses a woman in trousers) in a series of counter-shots to Gerbier's astonished gaze. While Gerbier and Melville admire British courage in the face of adversity (couples keep dancing as bombs fall), the emblematic music, like *Gone With the Wind*, suggests also American culture as resistance to oppression.

The mood of elation is short-lived, though, as the scene shifts to Félix's arrest in Lyon and the beginning of his interrogation by the Gestapo. We return to Gerbier who, over a shot of a Free French Cross of Lorraine at Carlton Gardens, announces his immediate return to France. He goes back to his plush room in the Park Lane Hotel and to another level of meaning. In a symmetrical moment to the beginning of the sequence, he folds the smart suit, shirt and tie he was supplied with to attend the decoration ceremony. The sartorial care, well in excess of narrative requirement, points to the symbolism of this masculine narcissistic ritual, linking the film to Melville's thrillers. As Félix in Lyon is bundled into a Gestapo car, his bowler hat rolls to the ground, where it is picked up by the camera. Gerbier's gesture in leaving his hat in the London hotel room is motivated by practicality (he could hardly wear it for a parachute drop), but it acquires its symbolic importance as a poetic rhyme with Félix, prefiguring both men's deaths.

Minimalism and abstraction: *L'Armée des ombres* as a gangster film

Félix and Gerbier's hats also point outwards – to *Le Doulos*, in which the camera similarly lights on Silien's hat ('doulos') rolling on the floor as he collapses, as well as to Melville's other thrillers, all of which make play of male sartorial ritual. This iconography, together with *Armée*'s thematics and *mise en scène*, led many critics to think, like Jacques Doniol-Valcroze, that 'this Resistance epic was, in the end, a sublime thriller'.[132] Although Melville thought such readings 'absolutely idiotic',[133] the connections between *Armée* and his gangster films are evident.

As discussed in Chapters 4 and 5, the post-war thriller can be read both as oblique representation of the war and as manifestation of its legacy: the emphasis on underground activities and armed struggle, the importance of loyalty and betrayal, the blurred and often corrupt moral universe in which both sides uncannily echo each other. The mimicking of police methods by the gangsters in the thrillers finds a strong reversed echo in *Armée*, where the Resistance adopts the weapons and tactics of the German and French police: for instance, in order to capture Dounat, Félix and his friends pose as members of the police; the vision of Dounat tied to his chair rhymes with later images of Félix and Jean-François tied to a chair after being tortured by the Gestapo. Gerbier escapes from the Hôtel Majestic by plunging a knife in a German guard's neck, the deed seen in unforgiving close-up.[134] Mathilde only escapes torture at German hands by being killed by her friends.

Dounat and Mathilde's killings feature in Kessel's novel, but the minimalism of Melville's direction recalls his thrillers, especially from *Le Doulos* onwards. As mentioned earlier, Kessel's description of Dounat's assassination provides the reader with the young traitor's thoughts. Equally, in a later scene, Gerbier's co-prisoners, while awaiting the death squad, each in turn evoke their Resistance past. Melville by contrast withdraws any insight into Dounat's motives or feelings, and films the prisoners passing a cigarette packet round in near-total silence. Melville's argument that 'To explain [Dounat's motives] would have been to detract from the idea of what a betrayal means,'[135] is of a piece with the unsigned quote (by the playwright Georges Courteline) which opens the film. Melville wants his war film, like his thrillers, to reach beyond the generic realm, into a 'universal' (masculine) moral code and a tragic mode; by contrast, *Paris brûle-t-il?* operates in a melodramatic mode, for instance staging Leslie Caron's discovery that her husband was in the Resistance. Melville's tragic mode and abstraction ensured the more durable impact and exportability of his films; the classic status of *Armée* as a war film (like *Silence*) is thus paradoxically linked in part to its erasure of detail, while a film like *Paris brûle-t-il?*, which laboriously recreates a gallery of real characters and events, remains a curiosity of the 1960s.

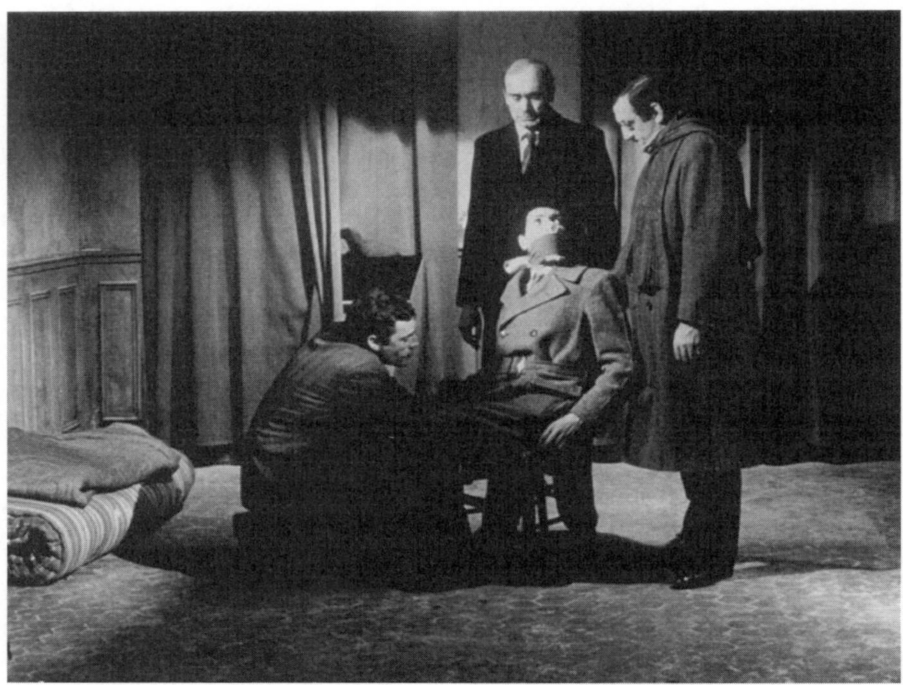

L'Armée des ombres: the *Résistants* prepare for the grim task of killing traitor Dounat (Alain Libolt, seated) – (left to right) Le Masque (Claude Mann), Félix (Paul Crauchet), Gerbier (Lino Ventura)

Armée blatantly exploits similarities with the gangster film in its iconography and the direction of very Melvillian action set pieces, with their suspenseful slow rhythm, meticulous detailing and technical mastery. *Armée* was made in between *Le Samouraï* and *Le Cercle rouge*, and it bears many stylistic similarities with these two films, especially the latter. The Gestapo officers who come to retrieve Gerbier from the Vichy camp look like gangsters, decked out in trench-coats, wide-brimmed hats and guns; as they are shot in menacing silhouette, their identity is all the more blurred and their iconic status enhanced. Ventura's star persona – laconic, tough, brooding – ensured continuity from *Le Deuxième souffle* and the numerous thrillers he made in the 1950s and 60s. The same car, the classic black Citroën *traction avant*, serves ubiquitously for *Résistants*, French police and Gestapo, as it did for *flics* and gangsters until *Le Deuxième souffle* (a small detail – the unlocking of the gates in the Lyon jail makes exactly the same clicking noise as the security locks in the Place Vendôme shop in *Le Cercle rouge* – connects *Armée* also forward to Melville's later thrillers).

Gerbier's escape from the Gestapo's Hôtel Majestic in Paris and concealment at a barber's (a superb cameo by Serge Reggiani),[136] like his escape from the German shooting gallery, are tense, thrilling scenes. But the most thrilling set piece is the attempt to rescue Félix from the Lyon Gestapo jail by Mathilde (dressed as a nurse), and Le Masque and Le Bison in stolen German uniforms. The operation, a classic heist, succeeds inso-

L'Armée des ombres: the *Résistants* plan Félix's rescue in Lyon – (left to right) Le Masque (Claude Mann), Mathilde (Simone Signoret), Gerbier (Lino Ventura), Jean-François (Jean-Pierre Cassel)

far as they are not unmasked by the Germans, but fails as Félix is too badly hurt to be moved – a perfect Melvillian configuration of brilliant but tragic futility. A series of long takes[137] describes the arrival of the van, the lengthy wait before the Germans open the gates and the van's progress around the jail's large inner courtyard. Dialogue is kept to a minimum, there is no music, the only noise on the soundtrack is that of the engine and muted German voices. As in *Le Deuxième souffle* and *Le Cercle rouge*, the perpetrators of the heist, like true 'professionals', maintain total silence among themselves. As the van leaves the jail without Félix and moves out of Gestapo reach, a few increasingly closer shots show us grief and disappointment etched on the three characters' faces and the hint of a tear on Signoret's cheek, and still they do not speak. Suspense arises from the contradictory pull of the agonisingly slow pace – for instance, as the three protagonists wait interminably for the gates to open – and silence, with the mounting sense of danger created by the trap-like configuration of the double gates and inner courtyard and the suspicion shown by the 'real' German soldiers until the end. This scene is a perfect example of the way Melville eschews emphasis but builds up tension. The visual style of the film also echoes the thrillers: the distressed walls of the semi-derelict houses that open and close the film (the house where Dounat is killed and Gerbier's hide-away) resemble Gilbert's house in *Le Doulos* and Costello's rooms in *Le Samouraï*. In their minimalist way, like the walls of the prison cells, they are as 'expressionist' as the décors of

The Cabinet of Dr Caligari (1920), as is the striking use of colour. Throughout *Armée*, blue-greys dominate, occasionally relieved by muted yellows. The only vibrancy occurs in the London outdoor shots and the vivid blue and red of Mathilde's van in the attempted escape sequence.

For Jean-Marie Frodon, this scene acts as a metaphor for the film's undermining of genre conventions: 'Under the "cover" of maker of popular gangster movies, [Melville's] work aims to undermine not only the genre he appears to illustrate brilliantly, but the aesthetic, economic and sociological apparatus he epitomises: classical cinema.'[138] Frodon's piece, like the rest of the November 1996 *Cahiers du cinéma* special dossier, aims to re-claim Melville as auteur after the long disparagement and neglect of his work since the mid-1960s ... especially in *Cahiers*. Given *Cahiers*' continuing auteurist stance, however, this reappraisal needs to position Melville's recourse to popular genre as only a cover for his 'true' concerns. For this reason, Frodon (whose analysis of the 'funereal' quality of the film is acute) overstates his case. I would turn his argument upside down: the Lyon jail scene, and indeed the rest of the film, are a magisterial demonstration of Melville's mastery of genre cinema. In the Lyon jail scene he transforms a few lines from Kessel's novel into an edge-of-seat action sequence as if to say, 'this is what the cinema can do!', exactly as he had done in *Le Deuxième souffle* with the bullion robbery. For if Melville works within a pared-down *mise en scène* (the long, slow, 'empty' takes, the silence) often compared to Bresson's asceticism, a comparison to Bresson precisely shows his use of genre cinema codes. For instance, when the protagonist of *Un condamné à mort s'est échappé* escapes from the Gestapo jail, Bresson also uses long takes, pared-down *mise en scène* and silence, but he violates elementary conventions of genre cinema by leaving the killing of the German guard completely off-screen. Where Bresson flouts the rules of classical cinema, Melville deploys them to his own purpose.

Mathilde: femininity as the weakest link

Armée's construction of gender is another important connection to the gangster genre – both in the treatment of Mathilde and in the film's definition of masculinity. *Armée* focuses on a virtually all-male group. This is not immediately obvious because, as a star with charisma, popular following and a committed left-wing image, Signoret endows Mathilde with a significance far in excess of her screen time and narrative importance. She figures on most illustrations for the film, and her performance is always singled out by reviewers along with that of Ventura, Meurisse and Cassel. For example, *Cinémonde* reviewed the film in these terms: 'The immediate attraction in a film like this is the quartet of actors [Ventura, Meurisse, Cassel, Signoret] who lead the cast.'[139] Yet, if she is strong iconically and symbolically, she is weak narratively. Although this is also a feature of Kessel's novel, Melville made changes to her character which emphasise further the masculinist stance of the film.

Generically, the fact that *Armée* is both a Resistance film and a thriller militates against significant female characters. We have already mentioned how the contribution of women to the Resistance has been marginalised in the cinema. In *Armée*, despite numerous notations about women's Resistance work in the novel, and real-life *Résistantes* as inspiration, the character of Mathilde is significantly reduced.[140] In Melville's thrillers, women are also peripheral or absent, a point which I make throughout this book, especially in chapters 5 and 6. The closest to Mathilde is Manouche in *Le Deuxième souffle* (who was initially to be played by Signoret – see Chapter 5). Both are shown as a-sexual mature women, idealised mother figures who are ultimately ineffectual (Manouche) or dangerous (Mathilde). In *Armée*, Signoret's tough ageing looks, tightly permed short hair and boxy, unflattering clothes construct a sexless but almost masculine image. This dovetails with Melville's deletion of much of the book's quite detailed characterisation of Mathilde as a hard-pressed working-class mother of seven. Instead, we see Signoret adopting several feminine disguises. One, as Mathilde steals a nurse's uniform in a German hospital, is that of a 'black widow' swathed in black veils, a sinister figure in the brightly lit hospital and a clear harbinger of death. The other is that of a prostitute, reminiscent of the star's younger self in *Dédée d'Anvers* (1948), a brief erotic vision which serves to offset Mathilde's sexless identity.

Despite the erasure of her sexuality, and despite her courage and brilliance as an agent, celebrated by the male characters and graphically illustrated during the attempted raid to free Félix, Mathilde's femininity makes her the weakest link: against Gerbier's express advice she keeps a picture of her daughter, providing a point of vulnerability that leads to her death and possibly that of others. In this context, two changes made by Melville to Kessel's story suddenly make more sense: the fact that Jean-François and Luc never know of each other's Resistance activity on the one hand, and Jean-François' anonymous

L'Armée des ombres: the *Résistants* as gangsters – Le Bison (Christian Barbier) aims at Mathilde with Gerbier (Lino Ventura) in back of car

sacrifice on the other. Both modifications reveal Melville's extreme gender polarisation. Femininity, associated with connectedness, spells danger. The other betrayer, Dounat, is 'feminised' through his youth and soft good looks. Masculinity by contrast is self-contained almost to the point of 'autism', a feature of Melville's thrillers that I go into especially in Chapter 6. Thus Luc and Jean-François do not 'need' to communicate. In appearance and name Gerbier, Le Masque and Le Bison fit the traditional hard-man pattern, perfectly epitomised by Ventura – tough, physical, unsmiling with a performance style to match. Gentler images, such as that of Jean-François helping a young woman with a child, or Luc in his old jacket and woolly hat, turn out to be put on for Resistance work. It may be objected that these ultra-masculine figures also end up in death. Yes, but theirs is noble and heroic: staying silent under torture, self-sacrifice, stoically giving away one's last cigarette while waiting for the Gestapo death squad. By contrast, Dounat's and Mathilde's are ignoble: Dounat is throttled with a tea-towel, Mathilde collapses ignominiously – pitifully? – on the pavement within sight of the Arc de Triomphe – no chance of heroism here. Even the threat hanging over her daughter (to be sent to a brothel on the Eastern front) is sordid. Mathilde's death concludes the trajectory of women in Melville's three war films on a shocking note which in its own way signals a wider loss of idealism. The niece in *Silence* was a pure, exalted emblem of the Resistance spirit; Barny in *Léon Morin* was a compromised figure (because of her desire for the priest) whose Resistance work was largely suppressed by the film; but with Mathilde, femininity has become a weakness and a threat. It is a measure of Signoret's talent that against all these odds she still emerges as a moving and memorable figure, as powerful as anything in the film – including the men.

A 'funereal' monument to the Resistance

Within its historical framework *Armée* generates the pervasive morbid ethos which characterises Melville's late thrillers. With the exception of Jean-François, the film's protagonists are middle-aged, a long way from the heroic young *Résistants* of *La Bataille du rail* or *Paris brûle-t-il?*. *Armée*'s opening quote, 'Bad memories, you are welcome ... you are my distant youth ...', points to a homology between the fifty-two-year-old Melville and his protagonists. But Melville speaks also for a generation suddenly rendered old by the shock of May 1968, displaced by those who had 'never heard of Hitler', as in the title of Bertrand Blier's 1963 documentary. As he put it, 'Out of a sublime documentary about the Resistance, I have created a retrospective reverie; a nostalgic pilgrimage back to a period which profoundly marked my generation.'[141] Choice of actors, desolate décors, subdued colour scheme and plangent score construct and underline this melancholy message.

In its sombre form and contents, *Armée* is an anti-*Paris brûle-t-il?*. From the pre-credit text celebrating the epic struggle of the people of Paris to the triumphant ending, Clément's film is a classic upbeat action movie (co-scripted by F. F. Coppola). Its depiction of the liberation of Paris ends with archive footage of de Gaulle in the midst of delirious crowds on the Champs-Elysées. Melville by contrast places a theatrically mythical de Gaulle half-way through his film and then stages the demise and death of all his protagonists. As in Billy Wilder's *Sunset Boulevard* (1950), Gerbier's voiceover takes on the status of the dead speaking to us; like Cavaillès' books, it reaches from beyond the grave. A low-key, melancholy ode to the Resistance, *Armée* is a film about sacrifice rather than exploit, in which effort, though for an unimpeachable cause, is rewarded by death. Rather than the hymn to the Gaullist myth that it was accused of being, *Armée* is a passionate but lucid portrayal of the end of the Resistantialist myth. It may have felt badly timed in 1969, but today it appears amazingly clear-sighted.

CONCLUSION: MELVILLE'S WAR

In *Armée*, the death-driven trajectory of Melvillian characters finds its apotheosis and historical justification. The romantic vision of *Silence* in the immediate post-war gave way to a sceptical humanism in *Léon Morin* in the early 1960s and in turn to a deep melancholy in *Armée* in 1969. Across this increasingly pessimistic trajectory, the three films share structural narrative elements. All three are tense but slow moving, episodic and cyclical rather than goal-oriented. They are punctuated by subdued, sombre rituals and repetitions: the German officer's entrances and exits in *Silence*, Barny's visits to Morin, clandestine meetings in *Armée*. The link between melancholy and rituals is also in evidence in the late thrillers, as we shall see in Chapter 6. But I would also like to put a historical slant to these features, borrowing from Mikhail Bakhtin's concept of the 'chronotope', which he defines as the 'intrinsic connectedness of temporal and spatial relationships that are artistically expressed in literature'.[142] Representations of the German occupation of France in literature and film constitute one such 'chronotope', the conjunction of a disconnected tranche of time (the German occupation as a 'parenthesis') and claustrophobic space: the village and house in *Silence*, the small town in *Léon Morin*, the enclosed locations of *Armée* – the spatio-temporal expression of a memory and/or experience both oppressive and compulsive. Melville's playing down of the temporal and geographical markers in the three films indicates the readability of the chronotope for the audience with only minimal indications (dates are indicated but fleetingly and not at all systematically; spaces are generic in *Silence* and *Léon Morin*; *Armée* zigzags between Paris, Lyon and Marseille; precise locations, such as the Arc de Triomphe, tend to be emblematic).

A reversed mirror image of Paris in *Silence*, Gaullist London in *Armée* remains a moment of bliss, precisely located, yet also bathed in myth: de Gaulle's awesome stature, *Gone With the Wind*, British courage. Melville's rendering of the Occupation chronotope is gendered; at the time of *Léon Morin*'s release in 1962, he said:

> All the men who were in the war, as I was, talk about it as 'the best years of their lives', to use a film title. Horror is not the only thing in the war. In war you achieve greatness, you are strong, you are pure, you are simpler. You achieve an amazing detachment. You don't fear death any more. You love danger.[143]

The masculinist overtones of this statement hardly need stressing, and it is interesting that many years before Klaus Theweleit's groundbreaking study of *Male Fantasies*, Melvillian masculinity is so explicitly tied to the male comradeship of the war.[144] But his is a uniquely nostalgic version of this 'male fantasy', celebrating it at the same time as he proclaims it dead.

Melville's career itself shows a compulsion to return to the Occupation and Resistance. His personal history, engaging with the *zeitgeist*, produced three fundamentally different films about them. In the late 1940s, *Silence* was an emblematic 'peace film',[145] ostensibly warning of the danger of Nazism yet giving so much space to von Ebrennac's arguments for harmony between the two nations; in 1962 *Léon Morin* was, even in attenuated form, an Occupation film; it took until 1969 and *Armée* for the Resistance proper to appear – in however minimalist a fashion. At the same time at these three different points of his career and life, Melville searched for, and found, imaginative solutions to the different aesthetic questions that interested him at each period. *Silence* was a breakthrough in literary adaptation and a prototype of early modern cinema in its depiction of interiority and rule-bending noir photography, in all these respects anticipating the New Wave; *Léon Morin* created Melville's special niche in French cinema for the rest of his career with a unique classical–New Wave hybrid; in *Armée* Melville showed that he could still reach a mass audience with a deeply pessimistic account of the Resistance couched in the austere yet suspenseful *mise en scène* of his late thrillers. In each of these films Melville responded to his own need for aesthetic renewal while addressing the most traumatic moment in twentieth-century French (and European) society.

NOTES

1. Jean-Pierre Melville, 'Il n'y a plus à chercher, il faut oser', *L'Écran français*, no. 201, 3 May 1949.
2. Gilles Deleuze, *Cinema 1, The Movement-Image*, translated by Hugh Tomlinson and Barbara Habberjam (Minneapolis: University of Minnesota Press, 1986), p. 211. First published in France 1983.
3. André Bazin, *Esprit*, January 1948, pp. 61–2.
4. Sylvie Lindeperg, *Les Écrans de l'ombre: la Seconde Guerre mondiale dans le cinéma français* (Paris: CNRS Histoire, 1997), p. 8.
5. Margaret Atack, *Literature and the French Resistance: Cultural Politics and Narrative Forms* (Manchester: Manchester University Press, 1989), p. 63.
6. Vercors, *L'Écran français*, no. 180, 7 December 1948.
7. Joseph Kessel, *L'Armée des ombres* (Paris: Librairie Plon, 1963), p. 5.
8. Henry Rousso, *The Vichy Syndrome: History and Memory in France since 1944,* translated by Arthur Goldhammer (London: Harvard University Press, 1991), p. 18. Originally published in French as *Le Syndrome de Vichy* (Paris: Éditions du Seuil, 1990).
9. Ibid., p. 4 and passim.
10. Lindeperg points out that in 1949, when presenting *Le Silence de la mer* Melville made his own Resistance past secondary to his identity as a film-maker, whereas for the release of *L'Armée des ombres* in 1969 the opposite was true. She ascribes this to the fact that in 1949 Melville's aim was to fight for his place within the film industry; as she puts it, he translated his Resistance 'symbolic capital' into professional capital. Lindeperg, *Les Écrans de l'ombre*, p. 298.
11. Vercors, *Le Silence de la mer* (Paris: Éditions Albin Michel, 1951), p. 64. First published by Les Éditions de Minuit, 1942.

12. Rui Nogueira (ed.), *Melville on Melville* (London: Secker and Warburg and BFI, 1971), p. 22.
13. The script of *Le Silence de la mer* deposited in the Bibliothèque du Film (BIFI) archive in Paris (ref. CJ1360 B176) bears the mention 'Mr Vercors' copy'.
14. Correspondence Jean-Pierre Melville/Vercors, *Combat*, 16 April 1949.
15. Nogueira, *Melville on Melville*, p. 30.
16. Ibid., p. 34.
17. Claude Beylie and Bertrand Tavernier, 'Entretien avec Jean-Pierre Melville', *Cahiers du cinéma*, no. 124, October 1961, p. 2.
18. François Chalais, *Le Figaro*, 4 November 1987.
19. André Bazin, '*Le Silence de la mer*', *Le Parisien libéré*, 27 April 1949.
20. André Bazin, *Le Cinéma de l'occupation et de la résistance* (Paris: Union Générale d'éditions, 1975), pp. 167–8.
21. Anne Simonin, *Les Éditions de Minuit 1942–1955, Le Devoir d'insoumission* (Paris: IMEC, 1994), p. 94.
22. *Les Lettres françaises*, 26 April 1949.
23. Pierre Sorlin, *European Cinemas, European Societies, 1939–1990* (London: Routledge, 1991), p. 76.
24. Vercors, *Le Silence de la mer*, p. 48.
25. Saint-Pol-Roux (1861–1940), a poet and precursor of surrealism who died in October 1940, shortly after German soldiers raped and beat up his daughter and destroyed many of his manuscripts.
26. Simonin, *Les Éditions de Minuit*, p. 95.
27. Ibid., p. 149.
28. Atack, *Literature and the French Resistance*, p. 159.
29. Ernst Jünger, an enlightened German officer and writer based in Paris during the war, published *Jardins et routes* in 1941. He was considered 'dangerous' by Vercors because he presented an ideal of moderate German-ness.
30. Vernon claimed that 'It was because of *Le Silence de la mer* that I never had a successful career', in *Le Quotidien de Paris*, 5 November 1987. Vernon's subsequent career was in off-beat horror movies, in particular with Spanish director Jesus Franco.
31. Simonin, *Les Éditions de Minuit*, p. 95; in May 1999, John Nangle commented that 'the Nazi is so refined Melville might be accused of humanizing a demon', in *Classic Images*, May 1999, p. 42.
32. Melville used a page of *L'Humanité* on which 'Anatole France's phrase was published at the time of the Marty and Tillon affair'; Nogueira, *Melville on Melville*, p. 29. The script bears a typed indication of an extract from Jules Vallès' *L'Insurgé*, changed by hand to Anatole France.
33. The uncle's reflection (though not the Anatole France quote) appears in a slightly modified version in editions that came out after the film was made, but placed after von Ebrennac announces his decision to go to the front; Vercors, *Le Silence de la mer*, p. 75. The statement, however, appears at the beginning of the story on the script, clearly a later addition as it is in Melville's handwriting opposite the typed page.
34. Lindeperg, *Les Écrans de l'ombre*, p. 272.

35. Richard Dyer, 'Coming out as Going in: The Image of the Homosexual as a Sad Young Man', in *The Culture of Queers* (London and New York: Routledge, 2002), pp. 116–36.
36. André Pierre Colombat, *The Holocaust in French Film* (Metuchen, NJ, and London: Scarecrow Press, 1993), p. 13.
37. *Le Silence de la mer* – script held at the Bibliothèque du film (BIFI), Paris. Ref. CJ1360 B176, p. 44.
38. Nicole Stéphane, *Le Matin*, 14–15 November 1987.
39. Noël Burch and Geneviève Sellier, *La Drôle de guerre des sexes du cinéma français 1930–1956* (Paris: Nathan, 1996), p. 224.
40. Ibid., p. 238.
41. Nicole Stéphane later became a film-maker and producer; among other films she produced Jean-Paul Rappeneau's *La Vie de château* (1965) and Volker Schloendorff's *Un amour de Swann* (1984).
42. We may note here that Melville's choice of subjects with couples, as opposed to his male thrillers, always emphasises the theme of 'impossible love': the brother and sister in *Les Enfants terribles*; the woman and the priest in *Léon Morin, prêtre*; the nun and the cad in *Quand tu liras cette lettre*.
43. The niece and von Ebrennac don't actually meet in the same image in the film, as opposed to the famous production still, used on the cover of the video. This scene, which is a Melville addition, balances out the scene at the Kommandantur where the uncle meets von Ebrennac.
44. See Claire Gorrara, 'Reviewing Gender and the Resistance: The Case of Lucie Aubrac'; and Michael Kelly, 'The Reconstruction of Masculinity at the Liberation'; both in H. R. Kedward and Nancy Wood (eds), *The Liberation of France, Image and Event* (London: Berg, 1995), pp. 143–53 and 117–28.
45. Sylvie Lindeperg reports Nicole Stéphane's irritation with the passivity of the character. Lindeperg, *Les Écrans de l'ombre*, p. 262.
46. Deleuze, *Cinema 1*; Gilles Deleuze, *Cinema 2, The Time-Image* (London: Athlone Press, 1989).
47. Nogueira, *Melville on Melville*, p. 27.
48. Ibid., p. 32.
49. *France-Hebdo*, 3–9 May 1949.
50. François Truffaut, 'A Certain Tendency of the French Cinema', in Bill Nichols (ed.), *Movies and Methods*, vol. I (Berkeley, CA: University of California Press, 1976); originally published in *Cahiers du cinéma*, no. 31, January 1954.
51. André Bazin, '*Le Journal d'un curé de campagne* and the Stylistics of Robert Bresson', in *What is Cinema?*, translated by Hugh Gray (Berkeley, CA: University of California Press, 1967), p. 143.
52. Keith Reader, 'The Sacrament of Writing; Robert Bresson's *Le Journal d'un curé de campage*', in Susan Hayward and Ginette Vincendeau (eds), *French Film, Texts and Contexts*, 2nd edition (London and New York: Routledge, 2000), p. 137.
53. André Bazin, *Le Parisien libéré*, 27 April 1949.
54. Bazin, '*Le Journal d'un curé de campagne* and the Stylistics of Robert Bresson', p. 138; my phrasing is a retranslation of the original as I find the published translation confusing ('having set text over against image') – though the original is slightly ambiguous.
55. Nogueira, *Melville on Melville*, p. 27.

56. Georges Sadoul, *Les Lettres françaises*, 5 May 1949.
57. *Combat*, 16 April 1949.
58. Sharon A. Russell, *Semiotics and Lighting: A Study of Six Modern French Cameramen* (Ann Arbor, MI: UMI Research Press, 1978), p. 115.
59. As a result of a mistake by Decae, one pan has two handles; Nogueira, *Melville on Melville*, p. 31.
60. Beylie and Tavernier, 'Entretien avec Jean-Pierre Melville', p. 6.
61. Charlie Van Damme, *Lumière actrice* (Paris: Femis, 1987), p. 109.
62. *Ce soir*, 24 April 1949.
63. *Les Lettres françaises*, 5 May 1949.
64. Michel Chion, *La Toile trouée – la parole au cinéma* (Paris: Cahiers du cinéma, 1998), p. 94.
65. Melville said, 'I always liked the voice-over and the commentator in the cinema. The first time I saw a film with a commentary was of course *Le Roman d'un tricheur* – I thought it was an extraordinary mode of cinematic expression.' Beylie and Tavernier, 'Entretien avec Jean-Pierre Melville', p. 14.
66. Chion, *La Toile trouée – la parole au cinéma*, p. 94.
67. Frequently (mis)spelt as 'Emmanuelle'.
68. Nogueira, *Melville on Melville*, p. 79.
69. Ibid., p. 80.
70. Interview with Béatrix Beck, *Les Nouvelles littéraires*, 2 February 1961.
71. Claude Mauriac, *Le Figaro*, 30 September 1961.
72. Pierre Marcabru, *Combat*, 25 September 1961; though an earlier issue of *Combat* carried a positive assessment by Henry Chapier (4 September 1961).
73. *Le Canard enchaîné*, 27 September 1961.
74. Lindeperg, *Les Écrans de l'ombre*; Rousso, *The Vichy Syndrome*; Joseph Daniel, *Guerre et cinéma, grandes illusions et petits soldats 1895–1971* (Paris: Armand Colin, 1972).
75. Béatrix Beck, in *Les hommes-livres, Les femmes-livres*, documentary directed by Gérard Mordillat (Jérôme Prieur, producer), INA, 1991, Ref: Bnf Tolbiac IKM002337.3.
76. Claude Beylie, 'Le point de vue du réalisateur', *Télérama*, no. 612, 8 October 1961.
77. The original running time was 193 minutes; Nogueira, *Melville on Melville*, p. 86. It would appear that the version released in 1961, variously credited between 125 and 130 minutes, was further cut as a few scenes mentioned in 1961 reviews do not appear in the video prints.
78. *Le Silence de la mer* – script held at BIFI, Paris. Ref. CJ1360 B176.
79. With films such as *Les Guichets du Louvre* and *Les Violons du bal* in 1974, *M. Klein* in 1976. Colombat mentions *L'Enclos* (Armand Gatti, 1961) and Frédéric Rossif's *Le Temps du ghetto* (also 1961). But he points out that the first film, set in a camp, centres on the psychological problems of two individuals, while the Rossif film was entirely set outside France. Colombat, *The Holocaust in French Film*, p. 29.
80. *Le Silence de la mer* – script held at BIFI.
81. Nogueira, *Melville on Melville*, p. 86.
82. Ginette Vincendeau, 'Jeanne Moreau and the Actresses of the New Wave: New Wave, New Stars', in *Stars and Stardom in French Cinema* (London and New York: Continuum, 2000), pp. 110–35.

83. Jean Collet, 'Une cathédrale tout en verre', *Télérama*, no. 612, 8 October 1961, p. 50.
84. Ginette Vincendeau, 'Jean-Paul Belmondo and Alain Delon: One Smiles, the Other Doesn't', Vincendeau, *Stars and Stardom in French Cinema*, pp. 158–95.
85. Jean-Paul Belmondo, 'Interview fleuve', *Première*, no. 217, April 1995, p. 67.
86. *Le Soir de Bruxelles*, 16 March 1962.
87. François Mauriac, *Le Figaro littéraire*, 29 September 1961.
88. *Le Film français*, no. 905, 6 October 1961.
89. Françoise Audé, *Ciné-modèles, Cinéma d'elles, Situation des femmes dans le cinéma français, 1956–1979* (Lausanne: L'Age d'homme, 1981), p. 63.
90. Nogueira, *Melville on Melville*, p. 84.
91. Collet, 'Une cathédrale tout en verre', p. 4.
92. In the script, he does say 'yes'. Bibliothèque du Film (BIFI), Paris. Ref. SCEN1526 B450.
93. Jean Rochereau, *La Croix*, 3 October 1961.
94. *Libération*, 27 September 1961.
95. Amédée Ayfre, 'Léon Morin, prêtre', in *Conversion aux images? Les Images et Dieu, Les Images et l'homme* (Paris: Les Éditions du Cerf, 1964), p. 118.
96. Ibid., p. 120.
97. Reader, 'The Sacrament of Writing', pp. 80–99.
98. Nogueira, *Melville on Melville*, p. 84.
99. V. F. Perkins, 'I Confess, Photographs of People Speaking', *CineAction*, no. 52, 2000, p. 38.
100. Burch and Sellier, *La Drôle de guerre des sexes du cinéma français*, pp. 284–9.
101. Ibid., pp. 221–4.
102. Jean Collet, Interview with Melville, *Télérama*, no. 670, 18 November 1962, p. 58.
103. Beylie and Tavernier, 'Entretien avec Jean-Pierre Melville', p. 20.
104. Interview with Melville in *Combat*, 23 September 1961.
105. Beylie, *Télérama*, no. 612, 8 October 1961.
106. Beylie and Tavernier, 'Entretien avec Jean-Pierre Melville', p. 20.
107. Jean-Pierre Melville, *Paris-Presse* 24–5 August 1969.
108. *Technique/L'Exploitation cinématographique*, no. 304, February 1969. The exact circumstances of Melville's discovery of Kessel's book seem hazy. Melville has repeated this point in several interviews, though in others mention is made that he had read the book in Algiers in 1943 (*Télé 7 jours*, 25 October 1969). Furthermore, Kessel's book is dated 'September 1943' at the end of the published text. Did Melville read a manuscript or is his memory playing tricks?
109. Jacques Chancel, 'Radioscopie', *France-Inter*, September 1969.
110. Jean-Louis Comolli, *Cahiers du cinéma*, no. 216, October 1969, p. 63.
111. Rousso, *The Vichy Syndrome*, pp. 302–3.
112. Ibid., p. 232.
113. Robert O. Paxton, *Vichy France: Old Guard and New Order, 1940–1944* (New York: Knopf, 1972); Stanley Hoffman, *Essais sur la France: Déclin ou renouveau* (Paris: Éditions du Seuil, 1974).

114. Nogueira, *Melville on Melville*, p. 146.
115. Ibid., p. 142.
116. Ibid., p. 141.
117. Kessel, *L'Armée des ombres*, p. 173.
118. Marcel Martin, *Les Lettres françaises*, 17 September 1969.
119. Jean-Pierre Melville, *L'Aurore*, 15 September 1969: 'This story was not invented and today a Parisian street bears the name of the man who committed this atrocious but necessary murder.'
120. Kessel, *L'Armée des ombres*, p. 253.
121. Quoted by Bertrand Ferriot, *Télérama*, 28 September 1969.
122. Nogueira, *Melville on Melville*, p. 146.
123. Ibid., p. 143.
124. Ibid.
125. The censorship file contains a letter in which Melville's producer asked for permission to move the sequence from the end to the beginning and the unpublished script shows that the sequence indeed was planned at the end. The date of this letter – 16 September – is puzzling since the film had been released on 12 September; I found no evidence as to the placement of the sequence in the first release print, which could mean that the letter simply confirmed the final editing.
126. *Cinémonde*, no. 1802, 23 September 1969, pp. 10–11.
127. The date is that of Melville's twenty-fifth birthday and, according to him, the day American films were banned in France for the duration of the war (*L'Aurore*, 15 September 1969).
128. Vincente Minnelli, *I Remember It Well* (New York: Doubleday, 1974), p. 343.
129. *L'Avant-scène du cinéma*, no. 66, *La Traversée de Paris*, January 1967, p. 7.
130. Olivier Bohler, 'Jean-Pierre Melville', unpublished thesis, p. 260.
131. Nogueira, *Melville on Melville*, p. 146.
132. Jacques Doniol-Valcroze, *L'Express*, 13 August 1973.
133. Nogueira, *Melville on Melville*, p. 142.
134. The two shots of Gerbier's knife going into the German guard's neck are missing from UK broadcast recordings.
135. Nogueira, *Melville on Melville*, p. 147.
136. William Kidd indicates that the barber's episode, though in Kessel's book, is also close to an episode in Vercors' *Les Armes de la nuit*, published in 1951; William Kidd, 'Vercors – Writing the Unspeakable: From *Le Silence de la mer* (1942) to *La Puissance du jour* (1951)', in Helmut Peitsch, Charles Burdett and Claire Gorrara (eds), *European Memories of the Second World War* (New York and Oxford: Berghahn Books, 1999), p. 48.
137. The ten-minute sequence contains just over fifty takes, thus the average shot length (ASL) is of shots of over one minute long each. However, as there are a few clusters of very short takes, many takes are nearer two minutes.
138. Jean-Marie Frodon, '*L'Armée des ombres*, le monument piégé d'un résistant', *Cahiers du cinéma*, no. 507, November 1996, p. 70.
139. *Cinémonde*, no. 1802, 23 September 1969, pp. 10–11.
140. Both Lucie Aubrac and Dominique Desanti have been cited as models. Signoret also mentioned that a woman called Maud Begon worked as make-up assistant on the film: 'We

had a "real Mathilde" on the set. Maud Begon clocked up nineteen months in jail between fortress and camps.' Simone Signoret, *La Nostalgie n'est plus ce qu'elle etait* (Paris: Seuil, 1976), p. 365.

141. Nogueira, *Melville on Melville*, p. 140.
142. Mikhail M. Bakhtin, 'Forms of Time and of the Chronotope in the Novel: Notes toward a Historical Poetics', in *The Dialogic Imagination: Four Essays by M. M. Bakhtin* (Austin: University of Texas Press, 1981), p. 84.
143. Jean-Pierre Melville, in Jean Collet, 'Entretien avec Jean-Pierre Melville', *Télérama*, no. 670, 18 November 1962, p. 58.
144. Klaus Theweleit, *Male Fantasies* (Cambridge: Polity Press, vol. 1: 1987; vol. 2: 1989). Volume 1, page 60: 'In countless different forms, then, the activities of these men in postwar Germany – their own part in the struggle against the revolution – are brought into association with the word "love".'
145. F. Laurent, *Image et son*, no. 57–8, November–December 1952, p. 28.

4

Between the New Wave and America: *Bob le flambeur* (1956), *Deux hommes dans Manhattan* (1959), *L'Ainé des Ferchaux* (1963)

Bob le flambeur inaugurates Melville's series of great gangster films. It has now attained cult status, and 2003 has seen the release of Neil Jordan's remake *The Good Thief*.[1] In 1956, however, it was greeted with a mixture of enthusiasm and bafflement, a reflection of its novelty. Rather than bracketing *Bob* with Melville's 'mature' gangster films – *Le Doulos*, *Le Deuxième souffle*, *Le Samouraï*, *Le Cercle rouge* and *Un flic* (analysed in chapters 5 and 6) – I examine it here with two films which are closer to it in style and spirit: *Deux hommes dans Manhattan*, the film that chronologically followed *Bob*, and *L'Ainé des Ferchaux*, which was made several years later, after *Léon Morin, prêtre* and *Le Doulos*.

After three literary adaptations, *Bob*, *Deux hommes* and *Ferchaux* were personal projects which 'mean[t] a great deal'[2] to Melville: *Bob* and *Deux hommes* are original scripts, *Ferchaux* an idiosyncratic interpretation of Georges Simenon's novel. All three are *policiers* in a loose sense, which need to be seen as part of the revival of the genre in post-war French cinema (especially *Bob*, with its dialogues written by Série Noire star author Auguste Le Breton), but which also significantly depart from it. Whereas the 1950s gangster films are mostly studio-bound, *Bob*, *Deux hommes* and *Ferchaux* are not only closely tied to real locations, they are veritable 'love letters' to places of great significance to Melville: respectively, Paris, New York and America. Indeed *Bob*, *Deux hommes* and *Ferchaux* engage in a more *explicit* Franco-American dialogue than any other films in Melville's oeuvre. *Bob* sets the iconic American gangster on the realistically filmed streets of Paris, while *Deux hommes* and *Ferchaux*, in a reverse angle, take French characters to the streets of New York and the highways of America. In their foregrounding of specific locations, these films are, as Melville put in *Bob*'s trailer, 'atmospheric films'. Last but not least, all three films belong to the period when Melville was prominently within the orbit of the New Wave, whether as model (*Bob*), ambivalently viewed practitioner (*Deux hommes*) or distant epigone (*Ferchaux*). Thus, while I begin by placing *Bob* within the generic context of the Série Noire and the *policier*, the chapter addresses the three films as three transitional works in Melville's career between the 'stylistic exercises' of the early period and the mature genre cinema of the mid- and late 1960s, and between the New Wave and America.

BOB LE FLAMBEUR: POETRY AND THE *POLICIER*

Following adaptations of three 'very French' literary authors in *Le Silence de la mer*, *Les Enfants terribles* and *Quand tu liras cette lettre*, *Bob* marked Melville's switch to a dialogue with American cinema through the *policier*. *Bob* reverberates with a celebration of the American gangster iconography, but it is couched in the French slang of Série Noire author Auguste Le Breton: 'At that time, after *Rififi* and *La Chnouf*, Auguste Le Breton was a star.'[3] Although Melville later rejected Le Breton's style of dialogue as *outré*,[4] this Franco-American dynamic is key to both the Série Noire and the film.

The Série Noire

America's intervention in liberating the country from Nazi occupation and its subsequent political and economic hegemony constitute a key fact of post-war France. Cultural historians[5] have widely documented the peculiar and contradictory nature of the French relationship to America, torn between the seduction of American products and strong political resistance to them, strongly backed by Communist Party polemic. A determined, in some cases state-supported, effort to reassert national identity through culture had to be negotiated with the attraction of popular American artefacts that had permeated France for several decades and were generally associated with modernity. Jazz, for instance, was well established since the 1920s. The cinema, and especially the gangster film, crystallised most spectacularly the full range of responses to American culture, from bitter opposition and vilification to appropriation and syntheses.

Crime movies themselves had a strong basis in a hybrid Franco-American literature. From the time Baudelaire translated Edgar Allan Poe, Anglo-American literature has had a crucial impact on French crime writing.[6] Criminals are a universal phenomenon, and in the early twentieth-century news of French gangs, such as the 'Bande à Bonnot', fascinated the American press – so that when in *Bob*, Roger tells Paulo that it's not Bob who imitated American gangsters but the other way round, he is not just being chauvinistic. A proper archaeology of the dovetailing of French and American traditions in the *policier* genre (which I cannot give here) would also note the early crime series such as the *Zigomar* and *Nick Carter* films and Feuillade's masterpiece *Fantômas*. Yet American dominance began in the 1920s when the American word *gangster* entered French culture and stuck. In the 1930s and 40s 'hard-boiled' writers such as Dashiell Hammett, Raymond Chandler and James M. Cain were translated and began to be adapted to film, along with indigenous writers such as 'Détective' Ashelbé, A. S. Steadman and Léo Malet. Georges Simenon started his long series of atmospheric thrillers, while a strand of populist writers (Francis Carco, Pierre MacOrlan) offered a poetico-erotic exploration of the Parisian underworld which, like Simenon, aimed to expose a human *milieu* rather than crime as such. But crime literature and cinema developed spectacularly after the war, endorsed by a substantial portion of French film-makers, among them, of course, Melville.

The Série Noire – whose name was suggested by the surrealist poet Jacques Prévert – was founded in 1945 by the flamboyant Marcel Duhamel, a translator, occasional actor and former member of the surrealist group. Duhamel actually began with translations of

Peter Cheyney and James Hadley Chase, two British authors of pastiche American crime stories (neither of whom had set foot in the US), before moving on to real American authors such as Horace McCoy, Raymond Chandler and James M. Cain. Yet, such was the Série Noire's 'American' aura that French writers soon began writing 'American' stories under American pseudonymns, such as 'John Silver Lee' and 'Vernon Sullivan' (respectively Thomas Narcejac and Boris Vian). As Claude-Edmonde Magny argues in her influential 1948 study *The Age of the American Novel*,[7] the 'phenomenological' style of American literature, both crime and 'serious' (Faulkner, Hemingway), together with the introduction of working-class and low life, appealed to French intellectuals – from surrealists (like Duhamel) to existentialists – as the antithesis of the refined French literature of introspection by the likes of Gide and Proust. She was echoed by Duhamel who said of the Série Noire books: 'As in all good movies, feelings are expressed by gestures, and readers keen on introspective literature will have to do the work in reverse.'[8] The social slant of American literature – however much it disappeared in French translation – gave political legitimacy to the seduction of all things American, explaining why noir writing has been predominantly considered 'subversive' in France.[9] In its recourse to Anglo-American writers and initial exclusion of French writers, the Série Noire anticipated similar moves by French film critics such as Nino Frank and, most famously, Raymond Borde and Etienne Chaumeton who would define film noir as a purely American phenomenon in their seminal 1954 *Panorama du film noir américain*, ignoring the legacy of French poetic realism.[10] In both cases, 'America' fulfilled a double function: the appeal of attractive modern material goods, and the chance to obliterate the taint of the German occupation.

Soon, though, French authors began to write for the Série Noire under their real names and about French topics. The two key books here are Albert Simonin's *Touchez pas au grisbi* and Auguste Le Breton's *Du rififi chez les hommes*, both published in 1953. Their celebration of a colourful Paris underworld couched in picturesque slang proved irresistible (according to the current Série Noire director, *Grisbi* is still the imprint's best-seller). Like that of jazz, the appeal of the Série Noire was at first confined to an elite social group.[11] In its identity, with its distinctive black and yellow cover, it combined the high-cultural prestige of the House of Gallimard and the lurid appeal of pulp fiction. It only became a mass phenomenon when French authors wrote for it and French cinema adapted it. To the international noir trilogy of violent crime, dark outlook and eroticism, Simonin, Le Breton and their followers added a number of 'French' features: the centrality of Paris, the slang and a more permeable border between criminals and police. Some, Le Breton among them, even boasted first-hand experience of the underworld. Interestingly, crime writing also provided French authors with a forum to deal with the war. A few noir authors wrote exposés of criminals and police mingling with the Gestapo, as in André Héléna's *Les Salauds ont la vie dure* and François Alboni's *Ce bon Monsieur Fred* (both published in 1949).[12] This fusion of gangster crime and war crime is indeed the substance of Melville's own *Un flic*, an unpublished (and unfilmed) script dated from 1956 (his 1972 film, confusingly also called *Un flic*, is a totally different story). In the 1956 *Un flic*, whose plot is reminiscent of Henri-Georges Clouzot's *Manon*, two brothers-in-law, Georges and Robert, crystallise the two sides of the war. Robert is a policeman and former *Résistant*, while Georges becomes involved with the gang of Maurice Zatorre, a big-time gangster and former collaborator, now a king of the black market. Similarly the plot of *Deux hommes dans Manhattan*, as we will see, hinges on the war–crime conjunction. More commonly though, the Série Noire deals with the war in oblique ways: underground activities, plotting, violence, torture, loyalty and betrayal. Many books and films feature a protagonist who, after a period in jail, experiences failure and disappointment; nostalgia for the pre-war is rife. Chronotopes of confinement and stasis can also be related to the war and German occupation, as can the pessimism and violence of the genre, the death-drive of its characters.[13]

The virulent misogyny of the Série Noire should also be understood in relation to this post-war context, as part of the wider 'patriarchal settling of scores' (in Burch and Sellier's terms) that took place at the Liberation to atone for the war's blow to French masculinity. It is evident in a wide range of literature, from popular childhood novels like Hervé Bazin's *Vipère au poing*, to classics of existential literature like Albert Camus' *L'Etranger*. Boris Vian's *J'irai cracher sur vos tombes* (published under the pseudonym of Vernon Sullivan), 'under cover of an American thriller with politically correct anti-racism [...] concocts a revenge story entirely turned against women who are innocent of the crimes they are accused of'.[14] The stereotypical sexuality of the Série Noire – Duhamel talked of love in the Série Noire (from a male point of view) as 'preferably bestial' and Raymond Queneau added 'Brutality and eroticism have replaced scientific deduction'[15] – thus provided a convenient, coded outlet for misogyny at a time when women's emergent emancipation (they had only just been given the vote) also fed this backlash, as illustrated *a contrario* by the hostile reactions to Simone de Beauvoir's 1949 feminist landmark *The Second Sex*.

The post-war French *policier*

The post-war French *policier* closely echoes these developments. Along with continuing traditions of crime *faits divers* among 'ordinary people' (such as the Simenon adaptations or suspenseful films like *Les Diaboliques* [1955]), the post-war *policier*, under the twin impetus of the Série Noire and American films, shifted its emphasis to the professionals of crime: gangsters, police, investigators. Traditionally, this move is viewed as an Americanisation of French cinema and, according to Jill Forbes, it betrays 'the desperation of French filmmakers in the face of American competition'.[16] In my view the picture is more complex. The first wave of post-war *policiers*, whether directly based on the Série Noire or not, like the books went through a parodic phase. Especially noteworthy are the trilogy of films featuring Raymond Rouleau as an investigative journalist: *Mission à Tanger* (1949), *Méfiez-vous des blondes* (1950) and *Massacre en dentelles* (1951). The humorous tone of these films, their accent on action and violence, on high life in luxury exotic locations (such as the French Riviera), the yachts, aeroplanes, night-clubs, villas and large cars offered a deterritorialised and misogynist fantasy. In *Méfiez-vous des blondes*, for instance, a female investigator is kidnapped, beaten up and killed, without her male colleague (Rouleau) seeming particularly upset; the fact that she was a lesbian does not seem accidental. The two 'blondes' of the title, one played by rising star Martine Carol, are at first potentially equally treacherous, although none attains the level of a *femme fatale*. A little later, *La Môme vert-de-gris* (1953) kicked off a highly successful series of Peter Cheyney adaptations starring American actor Eddie Constantine as secret agent Lemmy Caution. Other similar Constantine vehicles such as John Berry's *Je suis un sentimental* (1955) followed. These films, self-evidently, stepped up the 'Americanisation' of the French *policier*.

Their success was not uncontroversial. In the immediate post-war, the thriller – American and French – became embroiled in violent polemics as French cinema defended itself against the American onslaught. The Blum–Byrnes agreements of 1946 and 1948, which guaranteed a quota of exhibition time to French films as part of a wider Franco-American trade agreement, marked the apex of these conflicts. Backed by the Communist Party, press campaigns and street demonstrations took place – at the height of the Cold War – against what was perceived as the American destruction of French film culture.[17] As Patricia Hubert-Lacombe shows, Americans in French films at the time tended to be depicted as rich, vulgar and lacking in culture. Communist critics indicted the American gangster film as 'an agent of youth contamination'[18] and Sadoul attacked such films as *The Asphalt Jungle* (an important reference for *Bob*) as evidence of 'Hollywood decadence'.[19] These polemics hardly dented the enthusiasm of Melville and the future New Wave critics for American cinema, but the communist critics need not have worried unduly: the popularity of American films in France was actually relatively low and national preference ruled.[20] While Westerns were the most rejected genre, police and crime thrillers fared a little better. The rise of the Constantine films, too, corresponded to a decline in anti-American feelings from 1953–4, when issues of decolonisation became more important than the Cold War. The films' humour, the gap between Constantine's athletic 'American' physique and his comically accented French slang also presented a pleasing, cartoon-like vision of American-ness (based, we recall, on already parodic books) which facilitated its reception by French audiences. So far from the *policier* offering 'a pessimistic reflection on the impact of American culture on that of France after the war',[21] it seems more in order to suggest that it reflected a successful cultural hybrid.

The adaptation of French Série Noire writers reterritorialised the genre a step further. Jacques Becker's *Touchez pas au grisbi* in 1954 (based on Simonin), Henri Decoin's *Razzia sur la Chnouf* (1955, based on Le Breton) and Jules Dassin's *Du rififi chez les hommes* in 1955 (based on Le Breton) created a new sub-genre in which Parisian gangsters took centre stage. These, played by veteran stars like Jean Gabin, enjoyed Rouleau and Constantine's high life, but they domesticated the cosmopolitan genre into a familiar, more 'realistic' village-like Paris, creating a highly successful and influential generic matrix which added yet another Franco-American mix to the earlier Série Noire films. My analysis of *Bob* will be conducted with reference to the Série Noire generic matrix, as well as to relevant American films, among them those admired by Melville, such as *The Asphalt Jungle* and *Odds Against Tomorrow*.

Bob, Grisbi, Rififi and *Chnouf*

Bob le flambeur is the story of Bob (Roger Duchesne), an ageing gangster and gambler (*flambeur*), down on his luck but still a 'living legend' in Montmartre. Bob spends his time in cafés and night-clubs with his old friend Roger (André Garet) and young acolyte Paulo (Daniel Cauchy), under the sympathetic gaze of local police inspector Ledru (Guy Decomble). Bob meets Anne (Isabel Corey), a young woman on the make. He turns down her advances, encouraging instead a relationship between her and Paulo. Roger hears of the fabulous holdings in the Deauville casino safe on the eve of the Grand Prix from Jean (Claude Cerval), a croupier. Bob, with Roger, plans to break into the safe as a last job before retiring. The heist is elaborately prepared and rehearsed by a gang assembled for the purpose, but the game is given away by Anne's indiscretion to Marc (Gérard Buhr), a local pimp and informer, and a tip-off from Jean and his wife. Ironically, on the night of the job, Bob at last hits a winning streak and he wins a fortune in the casino. The gang is arrested and Paulo killed. The film ends with Bob and Roger being driven off in Ledru's car, speculating that with a good lawyer Bob will get a light sentence or perhaps even sue for damages.

Bob le flambeur was made on a shoestring budget of about a tenth of the current norm (FF 17.5 million according to most sources),[22] with a small, non-unionised crew including Henri Decae, who had been ostracised by the communist-backed union for filming the Korean war from behind American lines.[23] Practical conditions were difficult: poor lighting, intermittent inability to record sound, makeshift décor – for instance, the interior of the Deauville casino was recreated with blown-up photographs.[24] Melville was shooting for the first time fully in his own studio, but the limited budget partly explains the large amount of location shooting as well as the absence of stars. Bob is played by Roger Duchesne, a minor leading man of the 1930s, surrounded by a host of character actors, the best known being Guy Decomble (Ledru) and Daniel Cauchy (Paulo). Newcomer Isabel Corey plays Anne. Despite being built up by Melville and a few reviewers as an alternative Brigitte Bardot, she faded from film history.

Bob's box-office record was modest, although at 716,920 tickets sold, not catastrophic (results may have been affected by the August release, a bad time in France; posters which emphasised gambling and a semi-naked Corey may have led to disappointment). Given the small budget, however, the film made money.[25] Critical reception was mixed. Melville's credit was still relatively high from *Le Silence de la mer* and *Les Enfants terribles*, but this time his choice of genre disappointed (this, a legacy of the debates mentioned earlier, would be familiar criticism, also levelled at Becker for *Grisbi*). *Bob* was deemed 'amateurish'. Accusations of a clichéd plot, poor script and 'banal' acting (with the exception of Decomble) were made; Duchesne was unfavourably compared to Gabin.[26] Some reviewers, however, saluted Melville's novel look at the city, the film's stylistic charm, the quality of the photography.[27] This was Claude Chabrol's line in his enthusiastic *Cahiers du cinéma* review (under the pseudonym of Jean-Yves Goute). Against the accusation of lack of professionalism, Chabrol praised *Bob*'s 'quality of imperfection',[28] clearly prefiguring his own first films.[29] Truffaut, who had disliked

Melville's work on *Quand tu liras cette lettre* and *Les Enfants terribles* (see Chapter 2), echoed a similar feeling if in a rather patronising way: 'its charm comes from its imperfections and the amateurish side of the undertaking'; he grudgingly conceded that although 'script, mise-en-scène, intentions, all remain vague, [. . .] what is filmed, Pigalle at daybreak, rings truer than usual, and more poetic, too'.[30] Thus the statement by Truffaut biographers de Baecque and Toubiana that '*Bob le flambeur* was much appreciated by Truffaut' is a slight rewriting of history based partly on later appraisals.[31] Indeed when *Bob* was reissued in 1986 the Chabrol line had become the dominant reading. It was hailed as a precursor of the New Wave, 'a masterpiece of cheap *policier*'[32] and a brilliant variation on the genre.[33]

Back in 1956, *Bob* was both helped and hindered by being compared to the highly successful *Grisbi*, *Rififi* and *Chnouf*. Becker's *Grisbi*, released on 17 April 1954, stars Gabin as Max-le-menteur, a well-off ageing gangster about to retire on the proceeds of his last big heist. However, the loot (*grisbi*) is lost because of his bumbling, though much-loved, friend Riton. Success was such that Gabin was promptly cast the following year in *Razzia sur la Chnouf* as Henri le Nantais, head of a drugs squad masquerading as a drugs baron. Based on a novel by Auguste Le Breton (who briefly appears as himself in the film) and directed by Henri Decoin, *Chnouf* was released on 7 April 1955. The next week saw the launch of Jules Dassin's *Du rififi chez les hommes*, also based on Le Breton, lauded for its economical style and tense, silent twenty-minute heist sequence. All three films concern loyalty and betrayal among Parisian gangsters, and feature minimal police presence, slangy dialogue and a high-profile Série Noire writer. This may explain the sense of *déjà vu* expressed by reviewers of *Bob* the following year. Melville, who had been slated to make *Rififi*,[34] was aware of this heritage. A remark in the script of *Bob* (although not in the released film) has a character say about cracking the safe, 'Why don't we do as in *Rififi*?'[35]

Despite similarities, *Bob* significantly diverges from these films. *Grisbi* and *Chnouf* are made by experienced 'quality' French directors (Becker, Decoin), and *Rififi* by acclaimed film noir American émigré director Jules Dassin. They benefit from higher production values, well-known personnel – Alexandre Trauner did the décors of *Rififi*, Jean d'Eaubonne those of *Grisbi* – and stars. By contrast with these classically 'well-made' films, *Bob* exhibits more location shooting than was the norm, but also some blatant disregard for continuity, both in editing ('jump-cuts', bad matches), and in props (cars outside Bob's flat are inconsistent, ash on his suit appears and disappears while he listens to Roger telling him about the casino). Part poverty of means, part inexperience and part aesthetic project, the roughness of *Bob* foregrounds spontaneity and authenticity. Director of photography Henri Decae, who used faster film stock than usual, had, as Chabrol put it, 'a lot to do with the achievements of *Bob*'.[36] As he proved on *Le Silence de la mer*, Decae was happy to use the poor conditions as a spur to innovation, a quality which made him much in demand with the New Wave. As co-producer Silberman put it, 'we had very little light . . . the backgrounds were blurred . . . that's why Malle wanted Decae for *Ascenseur*'.[37] The noir photography of *Bob* makes classic use of light and shadow, as for instance in the Venetian blind motifs of

Ledru's office at night. But there is also extensive use of night-time outdoor photography to depict 'Paris by night'. As in *Silence* too, Melville and Decae deploy darker shadowing than the norm, which at times swallows the features of the actors (in *Grisbi, Rififi* and *Chnouf*, by contrast, they remain visible to play on the importance of the stars).

In narrative structure, *Bob* also departs from these three other films. Most obvious is the full forty-four minutes it takes before getting into the 'action', the preparation of the heist, after lengthy detours following Bob, Roger and Paulo through the streets, cafés and clubs of Montmartre, a race course and the Deauville casino. By contrast, *Rififi* launches into preparations for the robbery very early on and *Chnouf* presses Gabin into his business straight away. Although *Grisbi* is more leisurely and in this respect closer to *Bob*, the rival gang is introduced near the beginning of the film. While *Bob* visits the same topography and deals with the same overt themes and characters as these three films, these are important differences. (Needless to say, early introduction of action is even more in evidence in Hollywood heist films such as *The Asphalt Jungle*. Neil Jordan's *The Good Thief* – the remake of *Bob* – opens on an action-packed night-club scene, which visualises the 'back story' Ledru tells his assistants, about how Bob saved his life in the past.) *Bob* bears striking witness to Godard's point that 'The French don't tell stories; they do something else.'[38] Unravelling what that 'something else' might be is the aim of the following analysis.

The metonymic city of *Bob le flambeur*

Like most French films of the 1950s, *Grisbi* and *Chnouf* are studio-bound, with a few 'airing' location shots. *Rififi* contains more location work than the other two but, until the extraordinary final car ride, locations are functional street views linking locations or places to be 'cased'. By contrast *Bob* foregrounds its Parisian location as a topic in its own right.

The opening sequence: poetic *temps morts*

Bob opens on a quiet dawn scene at the top of Montmartre, with the roofs of Paris in the background. The camera begins panning left and Melville's sonorous voice announces 'Here is, as they will tell it in Montmartre, the strange story of . . .'. The image freezes and the title '*Bob le flambeur*' appears, backed by plaintive trumpet music. After the credits, the camera resumes its left pan over Parisian roofs. We hear church bells and Melville's poetic disquisition about 'the twilight of the morning'. Over a shot of the Sacré Coeur, Melville intones that Montmartre is both 'heaven' and, over a cable car descending (music humorously accentuating its downward movement) . . . 'hell'. The Pigalle metro station appears, accompanied by fairground accordion music. In a more self-conscious form, this is similar to *Grisbi*'s opening: a long pan over the roofs of Paris which slowly settles on a view of Montmartre and Pigalle, with the Sacré Coeur clearly visible at the top, the Moulin Rouge at the bottom. But where *Grisbi* cuts to a well-lit studio scene of a restaurant, and where *Rififi* opens on a card game in a smoke-filled room, *Bob* remains on the streets of Pigalle. As Melville says, Bob is 'a son of Paris'.[39]

The following four-minute sequence details place Pigalle as both centre of sleazy entertainment (strip clubs, neon lights) and 'ordinary' city: apartment blocks, shops, a street-cleaning truck car hosing down the pavement. Melville's voice contrasts 'those who go to work like this cleaning lady who is very late' and 'those who have nothing to do like this young lady very advanced for her age' (a pun on '*en avance*' which means both early and advanced). Although Melville emphasises the random nature of the city ('people are about to pass each other, whose fate will remain separate'), his choice of two women is anything but random. The young woman is Anne, and the cleaning lady alludes to Bob's mother, whose wretched story Bob will later recount. In a typical division of gender, women's presence on the street, unless they are rushing to work, spells sexuality – Anne is picked up by a sailor – and potential danger, as Bob warns her later. Melville's voice now takes us to Bob, via the sign of a gambling den ('Le Grand Jeu') and a mysterious shot of a corner of decaying wall. There we find Bob rolling dice with a few friends, about to leave the empty club. We follow him walking towards Pigalle, the Sacré Coeur on the horizon, accompanied by slow accordion music. A striking overhead shot suddenly shows him as a tiny figure crossing the street. A street-cleaning truck enters the frame, sweeping around the circular place Pigalle. Back at street level, a series of shots shows Bob registering Anne's presence, as she climbs on the back of a motorbike driven by an American sailor. The sequence ends on another overhead shot of the empty square, save for the street-cleaning truck. Its circular, balletic movement, the melancholy music, the misty light and glistening cobblestones,[40] the length of the sequence – all express a poetry of the street above and beyond Bob's story.

Much of this opening sequence constitutes a *temps mort* with little narrative import. Paris is introduced as a place of wandering, the Baudelairian city of the *flâneur*. In the first half of the film especially we will follow Bob, Roger and/or Paulo as at various points they wander the streets. Interestingly, the seemingly slow pace of the film is not created by editing rhythm. *Bob*'s average shot length (8.4 seconds) is actually shorter than *Rififi* (11 seconds) and *Grisbi* (11.1 seconds), as well as *The Asphalt Jungle* (10 seconds). This is partly because of some clusters of very short takes in scenes such as the heist rehearsal and the casino gambling scenes, but also because the decision to shoot apparently 'empty' scenes gives a sense of dilated time. This is an important feature of Melvillian *mise en scène* which we will come across on several occasions.

Montmartre and Pigalle

Bob is set in Montmartre and Pigalle ('heaven and hell'). Although Melville claims to have represented pre-war Montmartre, the intricate street layout and difficult terrain of the area ensured that it changed relatively little. Montmartre on the hill stands for provincial tranquillity. The Sacré Coeur church, regularly seen in the background, together with the sound of its bells, enhances its 'village' identity. Pigalle, at the bottom of the hill, is the centre of sleazy night-life and cosmopolitan tourist haunts, as well as crime. The whole area is clearly demarcated by real street and café names: the Carpeaux, Brasserie Junot, Yvonne's 'Pile ou Face' bar on the rue de Douai. Bob's

Bob le flambeur, the opening sequence: the iconic gangster in his Parisian environment (below and opposite)

CABARET
PIGALLS
PIGALL'S
REVUE FLOOR-SHOW
LES NUS
LES PLUS OSES
DU MONDE
PARIS

Naturistes

studio apartment, on the leafy avenue Junot, unites the two halves of the area. Montmartre (with Pigalle) acts as a metonymic Paris, an enchanted circle which the gangster does not leave with impunity – exactly as Pépé le Moko was symbolically a prisoner in the Casbah (the parallels between Montmartre and the Casbah have often been pointed out).

Pigalle night-clubs are the emblematic location of the 1950s French gangster film, attractively packaging the real-life underpinning of gangsterdom: gambling, drugs and prostitution. While gambling is presented as a harmless pastime,[41] drugs and prostitution are downplayed and linked to the unsympathetic characters – Marc in *Bob*, Angelo in *Grisbi*. Prostitution is euphemistically displaced on to 'dancers' and 'hostesses' (Anne in *Bob*, Lola and Josy in *Grisbi*) and designated as sordid through the pimp, the most despised figure. This leaves the sympathetic gangster hero free to concentrate on the 'clean' technical feat of robbing anonymous banks, jewellery stores and casinos – safe-breakers constituting the aristocracy of hoodlums, in a line from the *gentleman-cambrioleur* figure of early French crime fiction. This flattering picture is given extra glamour with the inclusion of jazz, the traditional accompaniment of illicit pleasures (crime, alcohol and sex). In the late 1950s, jazz also became associated with cinematic novelty in the films of Vadim, Malle and Melville.[42] For Ludovic Tournès, Melville was also a precursor in his use of 'real' French jazz by figures such as Bernard Peiffer in *Lettre*, Christian Chevallier and Martial Solal in *Deux hommes* (Solal was used later by Godard in *À bout de souffle*). The jazz played in *Bob* may not satisfy purists: coolly evocative at times, at others it is mixed with smoother dance rhythms. But, like the ubiquitous African-American players in the clubs, it reveals another kind of American presence, both in life and in films.

The social and geographical anchorage in evidence in *Bob* is more precise than in *Grisbi*, *Rififi* and *Chnouf*. And it is in marked contrast to the anonymous American film noir city. Melville thought *The Asphalt Jungle* the perfect heist movie and for this reason set out to make a different, more light-hearted 'comedy of manners'.[43] Nevertheless, the differences between the two films also express diverging visions of the crime film, predicated on the specificity of Paris as opposed to American cities. The beginning of *Asphalt* introduces its main character Dix (Sterling Hayden) walking hurriedly through a vast city of empty streets and wide vistas.[44] Social historian Louis Chevalier, in his book about the underworld in pre-war Montmartre, points out the spatial difference between Montmartre and Chicago (as two 'capitals of crime'); where in the latter cars are necessary to cover the large distances between key underworld locations, in the former distances are covered on foot, making Bob's huge American car – like Melville's[45] – a statement rather than a vehicle. When Bob drives his car, it is for cruising slowly round Montmartre, not for getting from A to B.

Finally, where the relationship between the hero, the city and the law in *Bob* is one of friendly symbiosis (Ledru stops to greet Bob and give him a lift), in *Asphalt* it is hostile: a police car prowls the city in sinister fashion, and Dix only escapes through complicity at a diner. This difference also affects the depiction of the gangster hero and his 'family'.

'A fine hoodlum face': nostalgia for the classical gangster

Melville introduces Bob as an 'old young man, a legendary figure of a recent past'. The mysterious wall shot over which we hear these words may simply signal Roger's club (though the topography contradicts this), or connote Bob's ageing, as the peeling wall is echoed later in the shot of his mother's house. Inside Roger's club we first see Bob reflected in a window, among a small group of men bathed in a pool of expressionist light in ambiant noir. A tilted close-up shows him throwing dice. Against a striking black-and-white checked wall, Bob, already wearing his trench-coat, puts on his hat. He 'answers' Roger's question ('Are you going to the Carpeaux?') with a silent gesture signalling that he's going to bed. Bob then walks through the night-club, which is empty save for a solitary xylophone player. The musician misses a beat as a 'nod' to Bob as he passes, silhouetted against another geometric background. The 'cool' melancholy tune, played on a single instrument in an empty room, suggests Bob's weariness and essential solitude. Out in the street, the club doorman, a newspaper vendor, Ledru – all call out his name, steadily continuing the build-up of Bob's 'legend'.

Outside the club, Bob stops, looks at himsef in a mirror and says, 'a fine hoodlum face' with a half-smirk as he adjusts his tie. A faint pattern of spots on the mirror accentuates the weathered look. After Ledru has given him a lift, Bob's entrance into the Carpeaux completes his presentation. The camera, from inside the café, shows a frown on his face as he enters, and the music swells dramatically. The next shot tracks forward behind him as he walks to the back of the café. Diffuse light from behind a glass partition (a wonderful example of Decae's ability to make the most of poor conditions) emphasises his black silhouette: the trench-coat tied at the waist, the felt hat, over more elegiac music.

The opening of *Bob* illustrates Melville's dual project. On the one hand, the fashion in which Bob is placed on the streets of Montmartre and Pigalle is almost neo-realist in feel. On the other, the repetition of his name, the excessive musical accompaniment, the reiterated silhouetting, the sardonic narcissism, all point to Melville's self-conscious citation of a Hollywood archetype. Bob is 'a fine hoodlum' on several levels: as the character in this fiction, as a 'quotation' from Hollywood, and incidentally as the actor Roger Duchesne who had, in the 1940s, acquired a minor criminal record.[46] The distance between the naturalistic Parisian environment and the mythical Hollywood gangster is fully claimed by Melville in an act of conscious cinematic nostalgia. *Bob* is far from simply imitating 1950s Hollywood crime films which were then evolving in the direction of organised and boardroom crime (*Executive Suite* [1953], *The Big Heat* [1953]) and violent paranoid noir (*Kiss Me Deadly* [1955], *Invasion of the Body Snatchers* [1956]). And whereas American heist films of the 1950s (*The Asphalt Jungle*; *The Killing* [1956]; *Odds Against Tomorrow*) dress their men in 'ordinary' contemporary garb, Bob's appearance is more evocative of the 1940s iconic gangsters: Bogart in *Casablanca*, Mitchum in *Out of the Past* (1947), Alan Ladd in *This Gun for Hire* (1942) (it is also possible to see Bob, who comes out at night and sleeps through the day, as having faint horror film overtones, as suggested by Melville's reference to him as Dracula[47]). The relative anonymity of Roger Duchesne as opposed to Gabin in *Grisbi* and *Chnouf*, together with his minimalist acting style, emphasises the citation of a type rather than a developed character. Melville here shows his interest in the phenomenology of the criminal rather than his psychology. As in the other French films, he empties his American 'models' of their sociological content. It is noticeable in this respect that only *Rififi*, made by an American director, shows any interest in the origins of criminality. The stage show in *Rififi*, with a silhouetted gangster, shows Dassin equally aware of Hollywood history, but the film has a more serious side, for instance in the inclusion of a young family with a child (as in *The Asphalt Jungle*). In *Bob*, as in *Grisbi*, no such reality intrudes. The Americanness of Bob, like Melville's own Ray-Bans and hats, is a mask, an identity to be adopted or discarded, rather than an essence.

The nostalgia for earlier Hollywood icons, itself filtered by the Série Noire, overlaps with another nostalgia, for pre-war France. References to the past are made throughout the film. Bob's criminal exploits are situated before the war. His age is repeatedly asserted – Ledru: 'He's got wiser with age'; Yvonne: 'You're past the age'; Bob: 'I learnt this before your time'. Although Melville dropped his initial idea of Roger starting the narration in flashback from Deauville,[48] his own voiceover *de facto* puts Bob's story in the past. Melville explicitly depicted the underworld 'with [his] memories of 1935',[49] echoed by Bob's pronouncement to Ledru that 'the underworld is not what it used to be. Now it's all rotten to the core' – a reference to the corrupting influence of the German Occupation. Although Melville's nostalgia has personal dimensions, it is shared by the other French gangsters of the mid-1950s. In the transposition of the American gangster to the French context, instead of the protagonists being turned towards the future, aiming to reach a goal, they are turned towards the past. Their 'tragedy' is no longer the tension between success and failure, as defined by Robert Warshow in the American context,[50] but the melancholy (and doomed) attempt to re-live the past.

The male family of the 1950s *policier*

The nostalgic stance of the Série Noire-inspired French gangster films of the mid-1950s entails a different order of narrative and character. From *Scarface* (1983) and *City Streets* (1938) to *Asphalt Jungle* and *Odds Against Tomorrow*, the American gangster is on the make, desiring financial reward as a means of gaining smarter clothes, bigger cars, more glamorous women, a ranch, and/or of ousting the man at the top and appropriating his ranch, women, etc. Strikingly, the heroes of *Bob*, *Grisbi* and *Chnouf* already enjoy all the perks. Bob, like Max, is already a 'legend'. His status, like Max's, is constantly reiterated by a chorus of faithful male friends and adoring women who understand that 'When Monsieur Bob comes, nothing else matters'. Contrary to the American hero on his Oedipal quest to kill the father, he *is* the father. What's more, his position remains unthreatened. In this respect too the films hark back to *Pépé le Moko* (1937) in which the young Gabin as Pépé was the king of such an entourage. Marc in *Bob*, Angelo in *Grisbi*, the opponents of Henri-le-Nantais in *Chnouf* are annoying obstacles who may do a bit of damage, but they do not fundamentally challenge the hero's position at the head of his male 'family'. Here again *Rififi* emerges as closer to the American model: Tony le Stéphanois is truly washed out at the beginning, humiliated by gambling partners, deserted by his woman, and sick; his aim is to regain his place and potency.

Bob, *Grisbi*, *Chnouf* and to a lesser extent *Rififi* present the convivial world of bourgeois gangsters as a cosy male family. Bob lives in an elegant artist's studio overlooking the Sacré Coeur, and he puts his clothes away on hangers like a neat Parisian bourgeois. In the other films, the gangsters' flats are images of prosperous 1950s modernity. Cafés, bars and night-clubs, all situated close by, extend the close-knit family atmosphere. Most are run by a motherly middle-aged woman whose body is often hidden behind a bar (Yvonne in *Bob*, Madame Bouche and Marinette in *Grisbi*). Other motherly figures are either dead (Bob's mother) or pushed off-screen (his concierge). Young men and women, like Anne and Paulo in *Bob*, are co-opted as symbolic sons and daughters who are counselled, fed and occasionally slapped. Although the misogynist violence is much toned down from the books, the women are marginalised. Thus even though Anne fulfils the traditional role of the betraying female, duplicated by Jean's wife Suzanne, neither attains the status of *femme fatale*. Bob's reaction to Anne's betrayal, apart from a slap, shows that she is only a conductor between men: he is much more annoyed at Paulo's careless talk. Symbolically Paulo will die for his betrayal of the male family.

The male family of *Bob* (like *Grisbi*, etc.), thus defined by its habitat and marginalisation of women, is bound by looks and gestures between the members. There are the discreet but constant 'phatic' contact of pats on the back and on the arm. By contrast with the squalid crimes of Marc the pimp or Angelo the drugs-peddler, *Bob*, *Grisbi* and *Rififi* celebrate the noble skills needed for the planning and/or execution of the heist – *Rififi* here being the ultimate reference. The recourse to medical and military metaphors for Roger cracking the safe and Bob masterminding the operation – however tongue in cheek – celebrate the professionalism involved, the sense of purpose, the sheer pleasure the men take in their teamwork. The urgent music over the safe-cracking rehearsal makes it as exciting as the actual thing (which never takes place). Bob insists on no arms being used for the robbery and when he goes out to the casino in his tuxedo, the camera shows him deliberately leaving his gun inside his handkerchief drawer – a fine image of narcissism and style prevailing over action. These are not violent hoodlums but craftsmen and artists at work. Melville, as he will more explictly in his later gangster films, deploys the heist as a metaphor for film-making, with its planning, timing, almost storyboarding and rehearsing. And, like film-making, robbery is teamwork – with, however, a clear figure at the head.

In the male family of the 1950s *policiers* gangsters are heterosexual, as signalled by their girlfriends, but their main interaction is with each other. This is illustrated by the greater care taken in dressing and lighting the men than their women, who tend to look 'tarty' in comparison with their companions' elegant suits and ties. A key antecedent here is the Jean Gabin figure in *Pépé le Moko*, whose elegance, fetishised by Duvivier's camera, makes him rise above his mundane surroundings.[51] Like *Pépé le Moko* too, noir poetic realist dramas (*La Bête humaine* [1938], *Le Jour se lève* [1939]) had an important romantic component. They included stories of pure love with a woman, against a cor-

The 'real couple' of *Bob le flambeur*: Roger (André Garet), left, and Bob

rupt world. In the post-war gangster films, pure male–female love has disappeared and shifted to pure male friendship. At the end of *Grisbi* the kidnapped Riton is traded for the loot; before letting Riton go, Angelo scrapes the bars to check that they are real gold: this is how much Riton is worth for Max. *Bob* depicts Bob and Roger's friendship in terms that are both more discreet and more extreme. Roger is a subdued presence. Unlike the situation in *Grisbi*, his friendship with Bob is not constantly underlined by the dialogue. Yet, from the first image of Bob who touches him on the sleeve, to the last shot when they are handcuffed together, Roger is the faithful, ever-present friend who discreetly plans everything for Bob, like a wife. Interestingly, the script makes this much more explicit. Roger's voiceover, introducing himself, Bob and Paulo, says of the latter: 'The kid is Paulo. He is like the son Bob and I might have had.'[52] At the end, as they are arrested, the script indicates 'Roger and Bob look at each other. They have never mutually revealed their friendship so much.'[53] In the finished film this is rendered by their amusing conversation about the double-headed coin: 'Roger says: I have known for ten years [that it was fake]; to which Bob replies: I have known for ten years that you knew.'

The script of *Bob* also includes a scene, later deleted, of an encounter between Bob, Roger, Paulo and a transvestite friend, and Roger's mention of visits to a steam bath.[54] If these only amount to a more explicit representation of the bi-sexual world of Pigalle – then the gay centre of Paris – they draw attention to the fact that Bob's closeness to Roger is also paralleled by a lack of interest in women, despite Anne's temptations. *Bob*, in a discreet way, begins the 'homophilic' tradition of Melville's gangster films which, as we will see, is developed explicitly in films like *Ferchaux* and *Un flic*. It is the first of a long line of Melvillian male characters who have withdrawn from sexuality, a playful version of the melancholy characters of the later films (see chapters 5 and 6). Eroticism is sublimated in the companionship of the Pigalle male family, in the heist and in gambling: while luck is Bob's 'old mistress' (in Melville's voiceover), the one-armed bandit in the cupboard is a neat image of a 'secret vice'.

Gambling, fate and authorship

The ending of *Bob* is both witty and cynical. Not only is Bob immensely rich but he, and presumably Roger, will get away with little or no punishment. Nor does the death of Paulo seem to affect them (although it makes 'poetic' sense in relation to his earlier betrayal). With this unusual ending, Melville departs significantly from both his American 'models' and his French 'rivals'. *Asphalt*, *Rififi* and *Chnouf* end on classic retribution and virtue restored: the gangsters either die or are arrested, Henri-le-Nantais dismantles the drugs network. In *Grisbi* Max survives but he loses both his '*grisbi*' and Riton.

With the ending of *Bob*, Melville most explicitly shows his parodic handling of generic codes, substituting hazard and authorial control for fate and retribution. It is thus no surprise that he cites Sacha Guitry's 1936 *Le Roman d'un tricheur* as a key influence.[55] In this film, Guitry's masterpiece, the director/star's famous voice narrates the entire film, in which conventional morality is upturned by gambling: the young hero survives his family on account of his bad behaviour, and as an adult gambles and cheats his way through life; honesty signals his demise. Thus Guitry mocks conventional ideas of good, evil and fate. We first see Bob throwing dice, as if to start the story. Later at Yvonne's bar, whose name, Pile ou Face, alludes to Bob's double-headed coin, he lets dice decide his fate (to go on gambling). Traditional gambling phrases such as '*les jeux sont faits*' and '*rien ne va plus*', heard throughout the final casino scene, take on an added, philosophical meaning. In a light-hearted mode, *Bob* proclaims the arbitrariness of existence and the futility of human endeavour, which will become major themes, in a more sombre mood, in Melville's later thrillers. In this respect Melville's references are not so much the American gangster film – where effort is motivated and hopeful, and failure due to outside intervention – but that of post-war literature, philosophy and theatre of 'the absurd' – the pessimistic vision of a godless and meaningless universe which flourished in the post-war and Occupation climate.

Fate, simultaneously incarnated and mocked in the roll of the dice, is also foregrounded by Melville's all-knowing and controlling voiceover, heard at the beginning and over the last half-hour of the film. At no point essential to narrative comprehension, the voiceover foregrounds authorial control. Like Guitry and Orson Welles, Melville has a deep and rich voice which enhances its authoritative dimension. When Melville's voice is absent, he employs other authorial devices, such as wipes and iris shots, unusual camera angles (high-angle views of Bob in the place Pigalle or in his kitchen, showing the black-and-white tiles which recall the walls in Roger's night-club), and the sometimes overemphatic use of music.

Authorial control, 'imperfect aesthetics', irreverent humour, cinephilia – these are the qualities that precisely endeared Melville to the New Wave critics who were then planning their own films. Two years before *Bob*, François Truffaut published his manifesto article, 'A Certain Tendency of the French Cinema', in which he violently attacked the 'Tradition of Quality', a studio-based cinema of tasteful literary adaptations and polished photography, calling for 'true men of the cinema' to come forward.[56] *Bob* in many respects answered this call to arms. *Bob* was an independent project made outside the mainstream. Its rough aesthetics and use of location shooting in Paris, moreover, the main venue of New Wave cinema, gave it a sense of authenticity, another value Truffaut found lacking in the mainstream cinema. At the same time, the film constantly reminds the viewer of its author. This, too, is coherent with Truffaut's project. Melville's personal implication in *Bob* (director, scriptwriter, studio owner, voiceover) made him a 'man of the cinema' *par excellence*. His cinephilia likewise placed him within the cultural orbit of the New Wave. More precisely, his love of American movies combined with connections with French high culture (for instance, Cocteau, also a New Wave idol) corresponded to the New Wave project of repositioning Hollywood as 'art' – a cultural formation visualised by Bob in his Montmartre studio: a hoodlum in a trench-coat living among fine paintings (the place was apparently modelled on a real artist's studio).[57]

Among the New Wave film-makers, Jean-Luc Godard most explicitly paid tribute to Melville in *À bout de souffle*, where Melville appears as a literary guru interviewed at Orly airport. Melville said he agreed to play Parvulesco 'to please Godard. He had written to me asking me to appear in the film: "Try to talk about women just as you do normally." Which is what I did. I had seen Nabokov in a televised interview, and being, like him, subtle, pretentious, pedantic, a bit cynical, naïve, etc., I based the character on him.'[58] In an anecdotal way, the Melville–Godard connection reveals shared sexual politics, as discussed in Chapter 1. But *À bout de souffle* also shows *Bob*'s legacy textually, in its Parisian location shooting, rough editing and in its hero, Michel Poiccard (Jean-Paul Belmondo). Poiccard asks for a 'Bob Montagné' we never see; like Bob, he is a nonchalant and narcissistic Parisian hoodlum whose 'mirror' is, literally, a still of Humphrey Bogart.

À bout de souffle marks the moment of the two directors' greatest closeness. It would not last. Much later, Godard barely cited Melville in his 1989 *Histoire(s) du cinéma* (a fleeting image of Bob, a brief mention of *Les Enfants terribles*, but more for Cocteau); in Part 3, after some prompting, he recalls Melville (along with Demy and a couple of others) as a 'friend'.[59] But back in 1959–60, by the time Godard made *À bout de souffle*, Melville had moved from *Bob* to *Deux hommes dans Manhattan*, his most 'New Wave' film, yet one which paradoxically heralded his more troubled relationship to the movement.

DEUX HOMMES DANS MANHATTAN: NEW YORK, NEW YORK, IT'S A WONDERFUL TOWN

New York, 23 December. Moreau (Jean-Pierre Melville), a journalist at the French news agency (Agence France Presse – AFP), is asked to trace missing French UN delegate Fèvre-Berthier. He teams up with his photographer friend Delmas (Pierre Grasset), a notorious drunk and cynic. They follow up several leads, interrogating women he has been seen with: stage actress Judith Nelson (Ginger Hall), singer Virginia Graham (Glenda Leigh) and cabaret dancer Bessie (Michèle Bally). They also visit 'Miss Gloria' (Monique Hennessy), a call-girl who specialises in servicing foreign diplomats. All the while they are followed by a mysterious car. In hospital following an attempted suicide, Judith reveals under duress that Fèvre-Berthier, her lover, died of a heart attack at her flat. After stealing her keys, Delmas and Moreau indeed find the body of the diplomat; Delmas re-arranges the body and photographs a salacious death scene, to Moreau's horror. AFP boss Rouvier (Jean Darcante) tells them of Fèvre-Berthier's glorious Resistance record and that the circumstances of his death must be hushed up. He destroys one of Delmas' films which he believes to be the one with the pictures of Fèvre-Berthier. However Delmas, who had kept the right film, visits Fèvre-Berthier's widow to tell her the truth and sell the story to the tabloid press. He is stopped by their daughter Anne (Christiane Eudes), the mysterious follower. Delmas escapes but Moreau and Anne track him down, totally drunk, in an all-night bar. After Moreau punches him and Anne silently begs him, Delmas leaves the bar and throws his films down a drain.

Deux hommes dans Manhattan was shot between November 1958 and April 1959, on a budget of FF 65 million, considerably more than *Bob*, but still a fraction of an average French film at the time. Exteriors were shot in New York, interiors in studios in Paris (see Filmography). Released on 16 October 1959, it was Melville's least successful film at the box office, selling only 308,524 seats (half of *Bob*'s sales). On different occasions, Melville has both named it as one of his most personal films and rejected it as 'unimportant'.[60] Critical reception was very mixed across both the political spectrum and types of publications. But whether negatively or positively, *Deux hommes* was read as part of the New Wave, then in its first high phase. Indeed Jean-Luc Godard thought it should have been part of the 1959 Cannes selection as part of the 'new cinema'.[61] Many reviewers, however, attacked the story as boring and the script as inept. For *L'Aurore*, it was 'only an excuse for a documentary about New York',[62] and in the words of another journalist, was just 'thousands of lights from buildings and the headlights of interminable lines of Cadillacs'.[63] Indicted too was the 'improvised kind of filmmaking of this "New Wave" we're tired of hearing about'.[64] *Le Monde* was equally hard-hitting, asking 'Why the botched script, poor dialogues, insipid scenes? Did Melville think the realism of the décor would authenticate the story?'[65] Undoubtedly the script of *Deux hommes* is not Melville's best, and it is certainly schematic. But the attacks are also evidence of the hostility towards the New Wave, anticipating the more systematic 'paternal punishment' (in Antoine de Baecque's words[66]) which the New Wave would suffer from the autumn of 1960 onwards. More surprising therefore is the harshness of Jean Douchet in *Arts*, given Douchet's and *Arts*' links to the New Wave; Douchet called the film a succession of shots 'strangely made and badly linked together [. . .] Jean-Pierre Melville is too amateurish'.[67]

But *Deux hommes* had its defenders, who invoked the same arguments – the 'amateurishness', the balance of script to documentary – in its defence. *La Croix* saluted Melville as a 'member of the Young Wave long before it had a name'.[68] *Combat* called *Deux hommes* 'a novel and personal film, with a special voice' and, among others, praised

Melville for rendering the atmosphere and 'presence' of the city.[69] Countering the argument of poor script, *France-Observateur* commented that *Deux hommes* was 'an aborted thriller but several successful documentaries'[70] and *Les Lettres françaises* that 'Melville knew how to exploit an insubstantial and predictable script'.[71] In addition virtually all critics – even the negative ones – praised the photography and music, and Pierre Grasset's performance (Melville, on the other hand, did not impress much as an actor). *Cahiers du cinéma*, then in its pro-Melville phase, published a highly complimentary article by Jean Domarchi, who pointed to the modernity of the film as residing in its 'de-dramatisation': 'there is no need for a plot when you know how to speak of the subjects that interest you'.[72] The intimacy with Godard and the *Cahiers du cinéma* group, who chose *Deux hommes* as one of the 'Ten best films of 1959', can actually be seen in the film: 'At one moment in *Deux hommes dans Manhattan* you see a packet of Boyard cigarettes on a bed [in the secretary's flat]. I did that shot for Godard. It was his brand, the only one he smoked. That was when I liked Godard. Since then . . .'.[73] A few appreciative pieces came out in the early 1960s, in the wake of Melville's later successes such as *Léon Morin, prêtre* and *Le Doulos*.[74]

Despite these supportive voices Melville was stung by the hostile reviews and what he perceived as a failure. Later he too related this to the New Wave: '*Deux hommes dans Manhattan* wasn't successful because the time wasn't ripe for a film like that [. . .] this was before the Nouvelle Vague.'[75] But he was plainly wrong since the film was released in October 1959, a few months after the 'explosion' of *Le Beau Serge* (11 February 1959), *Les 400 coups* (3 June 1959) and *Hiroshima, mon amour* (10 June 1959). More pertinently, he points to the release of the film in a major Champs-Elysées first-run cinema, the Marignan – clearly ill-fitted to an intimate, off-beat 'small' film. There must be other reasons why the film failed at a time when the New Wave, precisely, was riding high. Indeed, another intriguing question is why *Deux hommes*, although perceived as a New Wave film at the time, has since dropped out of the New Wave canon. Books and chapters on the movement do not mention it or only marginally (it is included, for instance, by Michel Marie, and in a book of New Wave posters).[76]

Melville's New York: sex and the city

From its first images, *Deux hommes* is a vibrant tribute to the nocturnal beauty of New York, seen through stunning location photography by Michael Shrayer and Melville, not Nicolas Hayer, as mentioned in many reviews (Hayer filmed – no less expertly – the indoor studio scenes). From a moving car, the camera travels through the wide neon-lit Manhattan streets: Times Square, Broadway, 42nd Avenue, 97th Street, and many anonymous ones. Over these images, asymmetrical, modernist blocks carry the credits, accompanied by a triumphant jazz score. Similar street views will punctuate the two investigators' journey throughout the film, emphasising New York's darkness punctured by myriad neon lights. Melville said, 'Except for Times Square, I assure you that in 1958 New York was a dark city. Much more so than Paris [. . .] New York is as dark as it is beautiful.'[77] The vastness and geometric lines of the city are emphasised by lanes of moving traffic, huge cars and expansive roof-top shots, in contrast to the tranquillity, smallness and circularity of

Deux hommes dans Manhattan: Delmas (Pierre Grasset), left, and Moreau in the streets of Manhattan

Paris in *Bob*. When the camera comes down to street level, it mingles in the hurly-burly of Christmas shopping, a long way from the provincial flavour of Montmartre.

Melville conducts the spectator through the New York landmarks: skyscrapers and the UN building, yellow cabs and subway, telephone boxes, newspaper stands, brownstone houses, cinemas, drugstores and Camel adverts with smoke emerging from them, a diner straight out of an Edgar Hopper painting, a bar configured like a saloon (the Pike Slip Inn), evocative names like Greenwich Village and Brooklyn. The high-angle shots, the long vistas, the dawn ending with a bridge in the background recall Dassin's *The Naked City* (1948). The crowded street scenes anticipate John Cassavetes' breakthrough *Shadows* (1960) and Allen Baron's strange and compelling *Blast of Silence* (1961). But the similarity stops there. For despite a reference, early in the film, to ethnic mix – three children, one Italian, one Jewish, one Irish, are picked up by the narrator (Melville) – and despite documentary shots of the UN in session, *Deux hommes* does not, unlike the other New York films, engage with social issues such as crime (*Naked City*) and racism (*Shadows*). Nor does it exude edgy urban anxiety like *Shadows* and *Blast of Silence*. In fact *Deux hommes* pursues *Bob*'s upbeat 'comedy of manners'. Its visual darkness (the whole narrative takes place at night save for the dawn ending) and the chiaroscuro photography in evidence in several indoor scenes (such as in the hospital) do not equate with noir anxiety, fear or horror. Like the Série Noire translations, with *Deux hommes* Melville empties the American referent of its social content and fills it with his own aesthetic and cultural concerns. *Deux hommes* is a personal odyssey which marries cultural pilgrimage with sexual narrative.

Cherchez la femme

Melville has cited *The Woman in Question* (Anthony Asquith, 1950) and *Sapphire* (Basil Dearden, 1958) as reference points for the puzzle-like narrative of *Deux hommes*. In both British films a deceased woman is investigated through friends, lovers and family. *Deux hommes* borrows the sexual investigation but reverses genders: the disappearance of a man is explored, by two men, through five women: his secretary, an actress, a singer, a dancer and a call-girl. The investigation is not conducted by the police (as in the British films) but by a journalist and a photographer for whom Melville cites personal memory as source: '[In 1949–50] I used to spend my evenings at Saint-Germain-des-Prés with two good friends, both journalists, François Nadeau and Jean-François Devay. We were often joined by Georges Dudognon, a photographer, on whom I based the character of Delmas.'[78] Melville may also have been influenced by the two central protagonists – a journalist and a photographer – of the Raymond Rouleau trilogy (*Méfiez-vous des blondes*, etc.), though *Deux hommes* has none of this trilogy's comic-book jocularity. By contrast with the above films, the mystery man remains a cypher (there are no flashbacks) until his body is found and a 'legend' is attached to him. As for the women, each briefly seen and cursorily interviewed, they are never developed as characters. They function, rather, as erotic and cultural signifiers.

Through Judith Nelson at the Mercury Theatre, Melville plays tribute to Orson Welles; through Virginia at the Capitol recording studios to jazz; and through Bessie the dancer at the Ridgewood Tavern strip joint 'in the depths of Brooklyn', to the kind of dive featured in so many American movies (e.g. *The Man With the Golden Arm* [1955]). The three women span a trajectory from high to low culture, and all indirectly reference the cinema. For instance, Bessie's costume evokes Elina Labourdette's in *Les Dames du Bois de Boulogne* and she is shown next to a photograph of Elizabeth Taylor (the dark-skinned Bessie is also, typically, the woman whose body is most prominently displayed, though shots of her topless are cut from the UK video). But more than erotic spectacles *per se*, these women are there to signify their environment. We only get to Nelson after a walk backstage, Virginia Graham is only discovered at the end of a long tracking shot (one minute forty seconds) through the studio, and Bessie appears after Melville has established the banter of her colleagues in the dressing room. We see Nelson again, but the accent is on the hospital décor (dark, gleaming long corridors) and her shockingly brutal treatment by Delmas.

If the women are not erotic spectacle in themselves, they eroticise the city. This point is reinforced by the other two, over-sexualised, women: Françoise, the lesbian secretary (suggestively rubbing her lover's bare back), and Gloria, the comically vulgar call-girl in her so-called 'Franco-Asiatic' boudoir, a rather funny parody of Brigitte Bardot. Night-time, sex, alcohol and jazz conflate, an image of New York which can be traced back to many films and, in France, to Georges Simenon's 1946 novel *Trois chambres à Manhattan*, an earlier, unrealised Melville project.[79] The women also eroticise Melville's love for the city, its cultural landmarks and urban poetry. Jean Domarchi rightly compared the film to a Baudelairian *flânerie*.[80] Although the virulent anti-American feelings of the immediate post-war period had waned, there was a polemic force in claiming the city of

New York as a *cultural* capital. Like his New Wave colleagues, Melville claimed both legitimate and popular American culture as *art*. Only in one striking respect does social reality intrude, but it has nothing to do with New York.

Staging the legacy of the Resistance

Fèvre-Berthier, the missing diplomat, is described as a 'great man', a brilliant person of the 'pre-war class of men', by the head of the UN information office. We do not see Fèvre-Berthier until he emerges, dead, on Judith Nelson's sofa. Delmas moves the body to the bed, makes him look dishevelled and photographs him in that state next to a framed photograph of Nelson. Delmas also takes a pose on the sofa pretending to be the dead man, prompting Moreau's remark, 'Is nothing sacred for you then?' The shocked Moreau forces him to put the body back where it was. Summoned by Moreau, Rouvier, the head of AFP, recalls Fèvre-Berthier's Resistance record, glorious to the point of caricature: London in 1942, hazardous missions, a broken leg, jail, torture, condemnation to death, escape, parachute jump, deportation to a concentration camp, a commendation in Churchill's memoirs as the 'true cement of the Resistance'. The speech, introduced by the first bars of Beethoven's Fifth Symphony (the auditory emblem of the Resistance), is filmed in three long takes of forty-one, forty-two and fifty-seven seconds. Delivered by an experienced theatre actor (Jean Darcante), as against the understated style of Moreau and Delmas, the moment seems extraneous to the rest of the film. Indeed, the few critics who mentioned the scene saw it as forced: 'a dilemma too neatly posed'.[81] For the communist *L'Humanité*, by exonerating the politician, the film also failed adequately to criticise corrupt politicians.[82] But this is missing the point. *Deux hommes* is only superficially about press and politicians' ethics; it is more about the Resistance.

Deux hommes was made during a period of renewal of interest in the Resistance following General de Gaulle's return to power in 1958, but it was a period still essentially respectful of the 'Resistancialist myth' (see Chapter 3). Rouvier's command to hide a sexual peccadillo to protect the glorious past – he decrees they move Fèvre-Berthier's body to his car and pretend the heart attack took place there – translates the ethos of the time. Yet the scene also expresses a fundamental ambiguity. Delmas' salacious *mise en scène* is matched by Rouvier's hypocritical one. Both re-arrange the truth. As later in *L'Armée des ombres*, Melville exposes both respect for the (Gaullist) Resistance and awareness of its constant mythologising.

If *Deux hommes* is seen as a thriller, Fèvre-Berthier is a mere McGuffin; his point is simply to justify a journey through New York. Read across Melville's career, it is a perfect *mise en abyme* of Melville's preoccupations. America, New Wave film-making, jazz, the crime genre are imbricated in its glittering surface – but embedded at the core is the myth of the Resistance.

Deux hommes dans Manhattan, classicism and the New Wave canon

For the viewer *Deux hommes*, like *Bob*, has all the hallmarks of a New Wave film: location shooting, original script, relatively small budget, jazz score and loose, pretext-like narrative. As in *Les 400 coups* and other early New Wave films (and as in contemporary American independent cinema, like *Shadows* and *Blast of Silence*), Melville uses little-known (Pierre Grasset) and non-professional actors, such as himself, Jerry Mengo and Monique Hennessy. The dominant impression is one of authenticity – we are on the streets of New York in winter 1958, when cinemas are showing *Separate Tables* and *Raw Wind in Eden*, of rough-edged spontaneity, and fun. Partly because of their nonchalant performance style (they seem to have a permanent smirk on), Moreau and Delmas appear more like two immature boys than serious investigators. Their immaturity is confirmed by their encounters with women, whom they seem to flee more than pursue (except for the one brutal encounter at the hospital), by Delmas' macabre prank and by his alcoholism – the latter more comically incapacitating than the expression of despair found in *Trois chambres à Manhattan*. Moreau and Delmas are like distant relatives of the characters in *Les Cousins* and *À bout de souffle*, roaming New York instead of Paris. It is on the strength of this set of stylistic features and characterisation that *Deux hommes* is seen as belonging to Melville's 'first manner'.

Yet *Deux hommes*, like *Bob* but even more so, already contains many elements of Melville's later, more classical, style. With all the emphasis on location shooting, a significant amount of the film consists of indoor scenes in which smooth and discreet camera movements, editing and décor both use and refer to the stylistic grammar of classical Hollywood cinema. At the beginning of the film, wide shots of skyscrapers are followed by stunning views of the UN building, roughly juxtaposed in documentary style. Inside, news footage shows a session in progress with a new member being introduced to the Assembly. After Melville's voiceover tells us that Fèvre-Berthier is missing, we are treated to two brief montages of telephones, telex machines and stenographers, a nod to similar scenes in numerous 1930s and 40s Hollywood films. Later a similar effect is achieved with blown-up titles of newspapers (*New York Times*, *Time*, *Life*, *Look*). The next scene takes us into the AFP office whose design seems straight out of the newspaper offices of *Woman of the Year* (1942), with multiple desks, venetian blinds, employees with visors and throbbing telex machines. This scene, separated from the earlier street and UN views by a static shot of the frosted glass door of the AFP, clearly announces that we are moving 'into the story' and into another stylistic space, begining with a discreet *tour-de-force* shot which anticipates the eight-minute eight-second shot of *Le Doulos* (it is worth noting that both were shot by Nicolas Hayer).

The camera starts and ends on telex machines spewing out news items and their clatter, connoting the urgency of international news, will accompany the whole shot (and the scene beyond). In between, the thirty-seven-second take travels 360 degrees around the entire newsroom. Like the *plan-séquence* of *Le Doulos*, the virtuosity of the shot is not necessarily detectable on a first viewing. The movements of the camera (a combination of pan and tracks) are motivated by characters and Melville organises several pauses which in more conventional editing would have corresponded to cuts. We first follow a secretary being handed a document by the head of the office in a glass booth and who then moves away, between desks, towards the middle of the room to hand it to another employee. As she sits down on the edge of a desk in the middle ground of the space the camera pauses. At that point, another secretary, in the foreground, picks up and answers the telephone thus drawing the spectator's attention back to the front

Deux hommes dans Manhattan: Moreau (Melville, centre) in the AFP office

of the frame. A male employee at the back of the room then starts moving to the right, and the camera resumes its pan right until it reaches another male employee in visor cap. The track right continues with this man as he approaches a row of telex machines, pauses by the machine on the left and moves along the row towards the right – all the time accompanied by the camera – until he reaches the one further on the right, which is the one we saw at the beginning of the shot. We have come full circle. The next shot shows, in close-up, a telex moving out of the machine, with the news of Fèvre-Berthier's disappearance. In this elaborately choreographed take Melville conveys a vivid sense of space and movement as well as the bustling atmosphere of the newsroom. Given that he could have shot it in several takes, the *tour-de-force* aspect, as in *Le Doulos*, conveys both his mastery of 'transparent' classical Hollywood cinema and his enjoyment of film form for its own sake. *Deux hommes* is dotted with similarly highly constructed (if shorter) takes, such as the track-and-tilt shot that reveals Delmas in bed in his squalid room, and takes which organise objects and characters in depth (*à la Citizen Kane*). Notable in this respect is a shot of Rouvier, Moreau and Delmas, with a bottle in the foreground, and a shot at the Pike Slip Inn. This self-consciousness is also apparent in the film in the ironic use of 'dramatic' music over shots of Anne's car each time it is shown following Moreau and Delmas. Moreau's entrance, after the long take described above, similarly teases us like so many stars' entrances. We first hear his voice, and only gradually discover him, a discreet dandy in suit and bow-tie, overcoat and hat, a get-up which corresponds to Melville in real life and in the film contrasts with the dishevelled Delmas.

The juxtaposition of self-conscious yet often transparent choreographed indoor studio shooting with documentary-style outdoor cinematography was already present in *Bob*, and will be found in Melville's next film *Léon Morin, prêtre* (see Chapter 3). This hybridity therefore corresponds to a strong stylistic aspect of Melville's 'middle period'. However, in terms of the New Wave, if, as Michel Marie argues, the movement is defined as 'fiction set within real places',[83] then *Deux hommes* represents an uneasy balance. Its fiction is about location, but too many indoor scenes are classically shot in a studio. Marie, one of the few writers to consider (briefly) *Deux hommes* in the context of the New Wave, rightly compares its alternation of staged studio scenes and natural décor with Louis Malle's *Ascenseur pour l'échafaud* (1958). But Malle's film, like *Bob*, can be seen as leading towards the New Wave, and their hybridity was considered an acceptable transition from the mainstream to a new cinema. By contrast, the stylistic hybridity of *Deux hommes*, appearing at a time when studio film-making was proclaimed as totally passé, is more of a problem.

Melville is omnipresent in *Deux hommes* (even more than in *Bob*) – as director, producer, scriptwriter and actor (in fact, we hear his voice twice, as voiceover and as Moreau). Yet this foregrounding of authorship which defined *Bob* as a precursor in 1956 had a different effect in 1959. *Deux hommes* was not a first feature, unlike *Le Beau Serge* and *Les 400 coups*, and at forty-two Melville was not 'young' (nor had he been a rebellious critic). It was thus difficult to integrate him in the New Wave rhetoric of the new and the young – hence perhaps Douchet's patronising tones about Melville's so-called 'amateurism': acceptable for those in their twenties, not those in their forties. Having been called a 'father' of the New Wave, Melville could hardly become one of its favourite sons.

Compared to New Wave films, *Deux hommes* also shows a different relationship between style, contents and moral stance. Jacques Siclier, noting the different reception of *Deux hommes* and *À bout de souffle*, perceptively pointed out:

> In the audience's mind, the 'New Wave' was defined, then, by a particular kind of character and a non-conformist universe, rather than by the way of showing it. *Deux hommes* had the drawback of developing, with great rigour, a moral debate [...] whereas *À bout de souffle* blatantly offered itself as the champion of anti-morality.[84]

If Siclier is too dismissive of 'the way of showing', his main point remains. But here again the predominant issue is not press ethics. *Deux hommes*' head-on confrontation with the Resistance sharply distinguishes it from other New Wave films. Melville, however ambiguously, looks to the past, whereas the New Wave posits a break with it and a move to the future. The one New Wave film that dealt with the war, *Hiroshima, mon amour*, embedded its discourse about the war inside a discourse on the nuclear holocaust and a high modernist form. By comparison, *Deux hommes*' tribute to the Resistance seems naive and passé. Similarly, Melville may have worn his Americanophilia too much on his sleeve. It is one thing to rework the conventions of the Hollywood gangster genre within the Parisian context, as in *Bob* and *À bout de souffle*. It is quite another to worship American culture quite so directly – several shots show Moreau and Delmas looking in from behind window panes, for instance in the theatre and the recording studio. With hindsight, we know how crucial the seductive Parisian context was to the international marketing of New Wave films. *Deux hommes* was too New Wave for its detractors, but not New Wave enough in other respects.

Breaks and continuities

Thematically, as we have seen, *Deux hommes* fits in within Melville's work in several ways: in its Americanophilia primarily, but also in its reference to the war. The film also centres on male friendship and its betrayal, even if this theme is subsumed under the discourse about the city. As the title warns us, this is a 'men's story'. Despite the abundance of female characters, it is not a film about *them*. Rather it is, like *Bob*, an essay on friendship and here specifically the story of a close bond between two men who are on the surface opposite of each other – the neat and pedantic Moreau vs the untidy, pragmatic Delmas – a conflict which comes to a head around the press ethics issue. The script suggests that this dimension was stronger initially since it was Moreau who threw the film in the gutter, a clearer indication of disapproval than in the finished film. In an upbeat fashion *Deux hommes* introduces the notion of the 'crossed friends' with a strong underground bond which will resurface in a much more sombre mood in *Le Doulos*, *L'Ainé des Ferchaux* and *Le Deuxième souffle*. The ending as filmed – Delmas making the final decision by himself and laughing hysterically after he has thrown the films in the gutter – also strongly connotes an 'existentialist' perspective: making a conscious choice but laughing at its absurdity (it is also possible to see Delmas as influenced by Anne's silent gaze, like Jef Costello being touched by Valérie's gaze in *Le Samouraï*). As Melville was himself keen to point out, it is in the end the disreputable Delmas who takes the high moral ground.[85]

Stylistically, the film marks a turning point in Melville's career, between the critically prized but smaller films of the 1940s and 50s and the large-scale genre films of the 1960s. Its 'failure' prompted Melville to move on to bigger budgets and stars, in the Béatrix Beck adaptation of *Léon Morin, prêtre* (Chapter 3) and his first 'stylised' gangster film, the Série Noire adaptation *Le Doulos* (Chapter 5). Thus Melville turned a page with the new decade. However, another film, *L'Ainé des Ferchaux*, needs to be considered next. Although it appeared after *Le Doulos* and is a major film with stars, in colour and CinemaScope, it is closer to *Bob* and *Deux hommes* both in spirit and style, as we shall see.

L'AINÉ DES FERCHAUX: IMAGINED AMERICA

When Michel Maudet (Jean-Paul Belmondo) – freshly released from the army – sees his hopes of becoming a boxing champion dashed, he answers an advertisement for a secretary to businessman Dieudonné Ferchaux (Charles Vanel). A scandal involving Ferchaux's past in Africa and the firm's finances has come to light, which causes Ferchaux to flee Paris immediately for New York with Maudet (who brutally abandons his girlfriend Lina, played by Malvina [Silberberg]), in order to retrieve money he put aside there. Meanwhile his brother, and business partner, Emile (André Certes) commits suicide. Ferchaux is able to retrieve only part of his funds from the New York banks. The two men quickly leave New

York, bound for Venezuela where Ferchaux has more money. En route the two men visit Frank Sinatra's birthplace in Hoboken. As they drive south, followed by the FBI, their relationship sours. Ferchaux becomes increasingly possessive, especially as Maudet briefly picks up a hitch-hiker. When they settle in an isolated house near New Orleans, his health weakens and he quarrels with Maudet, resenting his youth and freedom. Maudet befriends Jeff (Todd Martin), the owner of a local bar where a louche character called Suska (E. F. Medard) hangs out. Maudet leaves Ferchaux with his money and while he is with Lou, a strip-tease dancer (Michèle Mercier), Ferchaux is attacked by Jeff and Suska. Maudet returns, but too late. Before dying Ferchaux gives him the key to his safe in Caracas and the film ends on an ambiguous semi-reconciliation between the two men.

L'Ainé des Ferchaux, released on 2 October 1963, continued the successful run at the box office inaugurated by *Léon Morin, prêtre* and *Le Doulos*. Like the latter film, *Ferchaux* sold an impressive 1.4 million tickets. Although it is one of Melville's least-known and least distributed films today, *Ferchaux* in 1963 was a major production with a quartet of star names: Melville, Simenon (author of the book on which the film is, nominally, based), and the two leads Belmondo and Vanel. The fact that it was Melville's first colour film, shot in wide-screen format Franscope, added appeal. Although in that sense Melville had definitely left behind small-scale projects such as *Deux hommes dans Manhattan*, he was using a blockbuster format to depict an intimate story. This contrast, added to the strangeness of the relationship between the two men who moreover are both unsympathetic characters, goes a long way towards explaining the film's mixed critical reception.

As with *Deux hommes*, most critics focused on the balance between weak script and strong visual spectacle. *Ferchaux* was perceived, negatively, as an excuse for an 'interminable journey through the USA',[86] a long and dull trip only partly mitigated by the beauty of the images and by strong performances.[87] Inconsistencies were picked up (Ferchaux's nose bleeds when Maudet violently jerks the car to a halt, but is miraculously cured in the next shot) and ellipses were felt to make the story at times incomprehensible (why does the brother commit suicide?). In an otherwise generous review, Jean de Baroncelli said in *Le Monde*, 'This intelligent and beautifully-made work, in the end, leaves us rather indifferent.'[88] But, as in the case of *Deux hommes*, the same arguments were upturned by defenders of the film who thought the quality of Henri Decae's images and the performances, especially Vanel's, more than made up for the 'quasi non-story'.[89] As Henry Chapier argued in his enthusiastic review, 'The images of a very "Faulknerian" South will stay in our memory long after the story has faded.'[90]

The other important theme to emerge, again both positively and negatively, from the contemporary reviews is Melville's status as an auteur and his relationship with the New Wave. *Libération* was lukewarm and thought *Ferchaux* 'the hybrid product of a superficial "old wave" American cinema and a deeper literary cinema born of the New Wave'.[91] Jacques Siclier thought 'Melville in regression since *Deux hommes*. Then he influenced the young generation. Now, at the time *Adieu Philippine* comes out, *L'Aîné des Ferchaux* seems already old.'[92] On the whole, though, the consensus was more positive. As Baroncelli put it, 'like all Melville films, *Ferchaux* is an *auteur* film'.[93] For *Les Lettres françaises*, his films 'reveal a vision of the world that is personal to him; this badly constructed, badly narrated film is also, evidently, Melville's most sincere, in which he reveals directly and most completely his tastes and temperament'.[94] The 'tastes' in question were (correctly) identified as America, and the 'temperament' 'a friendship both very virile and too tender', as Claude Mauriac put it in *Le Figaro littéraire*.[95] Melville was thus still seen as within the orbit of the New Wave, as an auteur with a personal vision. But *Ferchaux* also marks a distance from it. Like *Deux hommes* it was evidence of a dual aesthetic. This is the time when, as Jean-Louis Bory put it in *Arts*, 'Jean-Pierre Melville becomes a classic'.[96] This was also the line taken in *Cahiers du cinéma* by Jean Domarchi, who praised Melville's virtuosity and stance vis-à-vis film as spectacle: 'To a modern cinema (Bergman, Antonioni, Resnais) which tries to free itself from American cinema, Melville opposes a return to American classicism.'[97] The two leads also symbolised the New Wave–classicism duality. The young Belmondo connoted a fresh, New Wave masculinity (see the analysis of *Léon Morin* in Chapter 3), while veteran Vanel was a mainstream star. This dual casting practice was common in the early 1960s: see, for instance, Delon and Gabin in *Mélodie en sous-sol* and Gabin and Belmondo in *Un singe en hiver* (both 1962).

From Simenon to Melville

As a version of Georges Simenon's 1945 novel *L'Aîné des Ferchaux*, Melville's film is, to say the least, distant. It is radically different from Melville's other adaptations, noted for their fidelity. Melville says he wrote a first adaptation which had virtually nothing to do with the original, but that 'Fernand Lumbroso, who had paid sixteen million francs for the rights and [. . .] had already signed several contracts with distributors, begged me to go back to an intermediate stage.'[98] Other versions must have been written – one treatment kept in the BIFI archives is, in fact, closer to the novel.[99] This version starts in Manhattan, where Maudet, after being arrested by the police, tells the story in flashback. The first part of the script then follows Simenon: Maudet becomes secretary to Ferchaux and follows him in hiding to a house in Normandy, eventually joined by his girlfriend Lina. When the situation worsens, Ferchaux, Maudet and Lina move to Le Havre (Dunkirk in the novel). As the police get ever closer, the two men flee to America (Panama in the book), this time leaving Lina behind. In the released film, America looms even larger than in this version. Melville removes the whole first part of the story (Normandy, Dunkirk), and the two men fly to America twenty-five minutes into the film (out of a total running time of one hour forty-five minutes) instead of to Panama three-quarters of the way into the novel. As shot by Melville *L'Ainé des Ferchaux* is a road movie taking us from New York to the American South. It could be called 'Two Men in America'. As Melville acknowledged: '*L'Aîné des Ferchaux*, like *Deux hommes dans Manhattan*, is not a *policier*. I made these films because I love America.'[100] Although Maudet in the film wishes to kill Ferchaux, the murder is actually committed by Jeff and Suska (although Jeff's styling as a double of Maudet underlines that Jeff is acting out his, Maudet's, desires). It is true that there is a sordid struggle for Ferchaux's money, but it is nothing like the *grand-guignol* ending of the novel in which Maudet beheads Ferchaux and gives his head to a professional head-shrinker (called Suska) who sells the shrunken heads to tourists as 'Jivaro' curiosities.

So far removed was Melville's film from the book that he wanted to give it a different title, *Un jeune homme honorable*. He proclaimed to all and sundry that his film 'had nothing to do with Simenon's book. I kept the names [title and characters] because my producer had paid a lot of money for the rights.'[101] These drastic changes to the book and Melville's attitude unsurprisingly displeased Simenon fans, among them Claude Gauteur. Gauteur, who has written extensively on Simenon adaptations, judges Melville's *Ferchaux* harshly. He quotes Vanel's disapproval of Melville's script and adds, 'One looks in vain for the slightest similarity with Simenon.'[102] Yet Melville kept more than the title. He retained three important aspects from the book which explain why he would have been attracted to it in the first place: Ferchaux's criminal past coming back to haunt him; the ambiguous, quasi-homoerotic love–hate relationship that develops between the two men (despite his claim that he departed 'absolutely' from the book in this respect);[103] and the confrontation between two Frenchmen and a foreign land (at that point Melville also still wanted to adapt *Trois chambres à Manhattan*, another Simenon novel which is set in the USA). Despite appearences, too, Melville's geographical transposition is 'faithful' to an internal logic. For he replaced a very personal Simenon topography – misty rain-drenched northern landscapes – with a very personal Melville location: America. Both men evoke beloved landscapes imagined from afar: Simenon wrote about Dunkirk and Panama from a small village in the Vendée under the German Occupation; Melville packed his film with nostalgic cinematic references, and shot many 'American' scenes, including outdoor ones, in France. Although this was partly because of contingencies, as explained below, the physical distance parallels the mental one. The change from Simenon's torrid Panama to an American South *à la* Tennessee Williams and Faulkner is a neat transposition, and the removal of Simenon's lurid ending makes the dénouement more believable (a 2001 French television production of the book, starring the older Belmondo in the Vanel part, is much more faithful to the letter of the novel, concluding on Simenon's bizarre and gruesome ending).

A cinematic journey through mythical America

Deux hommes was a nocturnal ode to film noir; *Ferchaux* unfolds as a daytime tribute to corporate America thrillers, the Western and the 'deep South' drama. In this respect, despite surface adjustments to early 1960s America (such as fleeting references to President Kennedy and the Cuban crisis[104]), its points of reference are, as for *Deux hommes*, further back in the past.

Technically *Ferchaux* begins in Paris but symbolically in America, with Michel's last boxing match, a homage to Robert Wise's 1949 *The Set-up* as well as to Belmondo's own earlier boxing career. But where Wise's terse black-and-white drama opens on a straight, medium close-up of the ring and the legs of boxers in action, Melville's film starts with a distant long shot of a ring seen as if through fog, accompanied by modernist music with religious overtones. Belmondo's voiceover introduces himself and tells us his manager will halt his career if 'they don't win tonight', a reference to the French title of *The Set-up*, 'We have won tonight'. With a gong the fight and the credits start, and the music adopts a grander, dramatic tone. Decae's images create a beautiful, dreamy vision bathed in white light, pierced by the reds and blues of the fighters' gowns and shorts. Spatial distance, music and the mist effect both inscribe the scene as already in Michel's past, and establish Melville's fantasmatic relationship to American cinema.

The French journey through cinematic America continues with the sumptuous décors of the Ferchaux conference room and office, which according to Melville is modelled on Robert Wise's 1953 *Executive Suite*. Yet, if the long conference table and dark wood panelling of the office do recall this film, the décor of the Ferchaux headquarters does not have the baroque, religious overtones of Wise's film. When we reach America proper, we are in daytime Manhattan, on the streets among yellow cabs. Corporate America, as in *Executive Suite*, is equated with the might of the skycrapers shown in slow tilts up over a jazz soundtrack. Rather than the dark streets and sleazy jazz and strip-joints of *Deux hommes*, New York now equates with modernist hotel rooms (the Franscope wide format and steely colours used to best advantage) and bank vaults, teasingly shown as if for a robbery sequence. The next scene is the famous visit to Hoboken to see Sinatra's birthplace. Here Maudet, as it were, continues Moreau and Delmas' trip in *Deux hommes*. As his voice describes Sinatra's humble origins in reverential tones, it is tempting to interpret the scene in terms of a double identification of star and director as émigrés: Belmondo's family came to France from Italy, Melville's from central Europe. The latter interpretation is reinforced by the subjective camera looking up at Sinatra's old home, without a reverse angle. The visit, like the whole trip to the South, is shot, in respect of outdoor scenes, from the front of a car. When we see Belmondo and Vanel in the car, the view through the back window is clearly a back-projection. There is an anecdotal reason for this. Vanel wanted to take advantage of the shoot to spend his honeymoon in the USA. To spite him after a quarrel, Melville cancelled the American shoot for the actors. Vanel reports that he and Melville later made up and were prepared to work together before Melville's death intervened.[105] Ironically, although the river scene was actually shot in Provence, Melville reports being congratulated by the American Embassy in France for his representation of the Appalachian mountains 'and in particular the bridge over the river'.[106] Beyond these backstage stories, the use of subjective camera also connotes the closeness Melville feels to the location.

We take to the road. A collage of classic views follows: huge cars and petrol stations, wide open spaces unfolding on both sides of a straight road stretching to infinity, red skies and autumnal leaves. We are in a road movie, with overtones of the Western cued by a harmonica on the soundtrack. Brightly coloured neon signs adorn the road as night falls, diners and motel rooms decorated in primary colours offer a kind of kitsch poetry and evoke, among others, Minnelli's 1950s films – an association reinforced by the fight between Maudet and two GIs in the diner over a Sinatra song on the jukebox.[107] Then comes the deep South: shots of neo-colonial homes and shacks ('residential homes for the whites and residential homes for the blacks'), steamy climate and tropical vegetation in the house in Louisiana. As he enters New Orleans, Belmondo's tongue-in-cheek voiceover states that he wants to see 'its streetcar named Desire'. The cinematic/touristic journey, in long takes and tracking shots, is accompanied by a musical collage: jazz in New York, Sinatra on the jukebox, elegiac cowboy tunes over the wide open landscapes

L'Ainé des Ferchaux: Maudet (Jean-Paul Belmondo) fights with GIs over a Sinatra song

(the scene where Maudet picks up the hitch-hiker strikes a different note, visually because it is shot in Provence, and in its editing; it will be examined in the next section). The final destination, the Louisiana house in a jungle-like garden, is deliberately theatrical. Its setting – distressed walls, venetian blinds, the sound of crickets in the night – obviously evokes the dramas of the deep South, especially *A Streetcar Named Desire* (Elia Kazan, 1951). But it is also a New Orleans twist on the familiar location of many Melville gangsters. Decae here, as he will in *Le Samouraï*, subdues the colour scheme to dreary greys and browns, set off by a few notes of bright colour (the men's yellow suitcases, a bouquet of flowers).

If *Ferchaux* continues the journey through America begun in *Deux hommes*, there is also a sense of deeper involvement. Moreau and Delmas were often distanced from the action (behind windows, for instance) and the 'natives', whom they only interviewed. Here they penetrate the space – the car goes deeper into the South – and they interact with Americans, including physically.

'Homophilia'

Of all Melville's films, *Ferchaux* depicts attraction between two men most explicitly. As he acknowledged: 'Being physically attracted by Maudet, Ferchaux begins to fall in love with him. The fact that he discovers for the first time at the age of 70 that he is capable of homosexuality drives him completely crazy, which is why he behaves like an old woman with his fits of despair and jealousy.'[108] This does not make *Ferchaux* a 'gay film', an impossibility for a mainstream movie of 1963. Apart from Melville's sexist terminology (behaving 'like an old woman' is not meant as a compliment), *Ferchaux* multiplies the signs of the men's heterosexuality: both had female lovers – to Ferchaux's fury Maudet picks up a hitch-hiker (Stefania Sandrelli), and later has a relationship with Michèle Mercier's strip-joint dancer in New Orleans. The star personas of the two leads also militate against a gay reading of their characters.[109] But, as Richard Dyer argues of Jean Gabin in *L'Air de Paris* (1954),[110] it may be that Belmondo and Vanel's heterosexual macho images precisely enabled Melville to depict covertly a homoerotic relationship.

Ferchaux uses narrative motivations such as boxing, swimming and clothes (close-fitting white T-shirts) to display Belmondo's body in a way which can be read as gay, although his athletic physique was part of his heterosexual persona. Indeed several reviewers of *Ferchaux* criticised the frequent displays of his naked torso as cliché. But to be precise, Maudet and Ferchaux's rapport on-screen is neither homosexual nor homoerotic in a modern sense. It may be more appropriate to talk of 'homophilia', a concept which Dyer shows to pertain to the French post-war context. Homophilia, coined by the writer André Baudry, who founded the gay magazine *Arcadie*, refers to a more diffuse and nuanced (and more acceptable at the time) identity than homosexuality.[111] The concept rests on friendship (*amitié*), itself an ambivalent enough category. Reviewers of *Ferchaux* frequently refer to 'friendship', accompanied by adjectives such as 'opaque' or 'uneasy'. Such ambivalence was already present in Simenon's novel; at one point the narrator asks: 'Why did Ferchaux become attached to Michel? Because, from the beginning he felt in him a strength almost equal to that of his own youth. [. . .] Later, some more obscure feelings came into play.'[112] Through visual means, Melville also foregrounds interrogations into the men's identity, with one of his favourite tropes, mirrors. Ferchaux is viewed early on in a series of repeated mirror images (no doubt in homage to Orson Welles too), and Belmondo appears, for instance, in a mirror framed by bottles in Jeff's bar.

At the same time as it may suggest and hint, *Ferchaux* appears to be based on the denial of homophilia. Rather than friendship, dominant emotions are macho competition and humiliation (Ferchaux's categorisation of men as sheep, leopards or jackals). The film builds up a set of parallels and contrasts between the two men which structures their mutual love–hate, attraction–repulsion. Each of them abandons someone: Maudet abandons Lina and his paratrooper cap, Ferchaux his brother and 'goddaughters'. Furthermore, Maudet the has-been unemployed boxer starts at the bottom of the social pile, Ferchaux the arrogant patriarch at the top. One one level *Ferchaux* proposes a classic Oedipal trajectory of the 'son' supplanting his 'father' – and here the casting is inspired since Belmondo does look as if he could be Vanel's son (more than the planned Delon). The psychological reading suggests itself especially as Melville has more or less removed Simenon's social narrative in which Maudet's ambition to climb the social ladder is frequently reiterated; in the film, apart from Maudet's voiceover remark that he pretends not to be impressed by Ferchaux's money on the plane to America (like the children in *Les Enfants terribles* going to the seaside), this dimension has gone. Ferchaux's first 'defeat' in front of Maudet may be social (the bank's refusal to come across with all the money) but others are sexual, beginning with the hitch-hiker episode.

L'Ainé des Ferchaux: suggested homophilia – Ferchaux (Charles Vanel), left, and Maudet

At this point Ferchaux has already witnessed and admired Maudet's physical prowess in the episode with the GIs. The narration, which in the French sequences alternated between the two men, now aligns us with Maudet: unlike Ferchaux we know the FBI is on their trail (in a mysterious car, perhaps a nod to Anne's car in *Deux hommes*). As they drive on, Maudet abruptly stops to pick up the young hitch-hiker, to the chagrin of Ferchaux who hits his nose on the windscreen in the process. Maudet stops the car by a deep valley in a rocky landscape (actually Provence) and goes down to the river with the young woman – for a swim and, it is inferred by shots of the river indicating time passing, sex – while Ferchaux stays in the car. A series of elegiac shots of the landscape with the harmonica tune pursues the Western theme. As the young couple comes back towards the car, there follows an apparently incomprehensible act: Ferchaux empties his suitcase full of money into the wind (although he later reveals he had kept some for himself). A fine image of the futility of effort, as in John Huston's 1948 *The Treasure of the Sierra Madre*, Stanley Kubrick's 1956 *The Killing* and Henri Verneuil's *Mélodie en sous-sol*. As Maudet and the woman scrabble on the mountainside to pick up the notes, an exchange of shots shows Ferchaux looking down at them. As Olivier Bohler says,[113] this can be interpreted as Ferchaux contemplating his distant youth. But the geometry of the shots also suggests Ferchaux asserting his power over Maudet for a last, desperate time. It also inaugurates the theme of the men's suitcases (both a similar yellow) as symbolic of male power and its demise. At the end of the film Maudet's suitcase is mistaken by Jeff and Suska for Ferchaux's (which Maudet has already stolen); while Ferchaux's contains money, Maudet's contains his old boxing gown, symbol of his defeat.

Situated exactly half-way through the film, the river episode is a turning point which, momentarily, seals the two men's 'friendship'. After the woman – who had also tried to steal the money – is unceremoniously dumped, the two men smile and share a cigarette. As the scene preceding the hitch-hiking episode had showed them sharing a motel room, this could signal a return to their 'friendship'. However, after Maudet learns from the FBI that the two cannot leave the USA, their relationship sours. In Louisiana, Maudet (who has now taken up with the strip-tease dancer) becomes ever more attractively virile in tight white T-shirt (shades of Brando in *Streetcar*), while Ferchaux, whose health declines, is at his most neglected in dirty pyjamas. At this point occurs the most explicit reference to homoeroticism. At the climax of a row, Vanel's remark that they are like 'old lovers who no longer love each other' is uttered as Belmondo changes his shirt, the bed positioned between the two. Throughout the last sequences, Melville plays hide and seek with homophilic representation, foregrounding it in dialogue, in excessive 'deep South' emotions and Belmondo's white T-shirts (echoed by Jeff's), yet equally denying it with their abusive dialogue. This ambiguity is encapsulated in the ending. Maudet, having abandoned Ferchaux, returns while Suska and Jeff are attacking Ferchaux, who dies in Maudet's arms. He has just the strength to give him the key to his Caracas safe. To this Maudet replies, 'You and your key can go to hell', yet at the same time he is visibly moved, tears welling in his eyes. This to-and-fro could be a more overt manifestation of the underground attraction of two opposed characters, such as Blot and Gu in *Le Deuxième souffle* (see Chapter 5). It could also be a textual manifestation of the difficulties in representing such a 'homophilic' friendship in a mainstream film of the time, which would explain both the rather unsatisfactory, haltingly slow and repetitive last scenes of the film and the evasive critical commentaries. Rare were the reviews which tackled the topic head-on. One of the few who did was Michel Flacon in *Cinéma 63*, though under the cover of 'respectable' literary references (Oscar Wilde and Balzac).[114]

CONCLUSION: IN AND OUT OF THE NEW WAVE

In 1962, as he was preparing to make *Ferchaux*, Melville was still within the orbit of the New Wave, as shown by his adding the letters 'A.C.I.' after his names on the credits (a reference to the association founded with Truffaut and Godard), and, as we have seen, he was perceived as such by reviews. The unconventional aspect of the narrative of *Ferchaux*, its extensive location shooting and Americanophilia, as in the previous two films examined in this chapter, were still sufficiently close to what the New Wave directors themselves were making. On a personal level, Melville was friendly with Chabrol (acting in *Landru*) and Truffaut, taking the latter's side, for instance, on the very public Jean Aurel–Roger Vadim affair.[115] It was at a dinner party in Melville's home that Truffaut first heard about Ray Bradbury's *Farenheit 451*, and it is to Melville that Truffaut confided his problems with the planning and making of that film.[116] The friendship would come to an end soon after and by 1966 Melville would deplore its demise in *Arts* (see Introduction).

Throughout the 1960s, a more widespread estrangement between the *Cahiers* group and Melville took place. On Melville's side it was concurrent with his greater box-office success and the increased classicism of his work. On the *Cahiers* side it was determined by their changing agenda. Rivette, for instance, criticised Melville's 'imposture' for trying 'artificially to acclimatize to a European context the myths of American cinema'.[117] Meanwhile, the pioneering auteur who had proudly claimed paternity of the New Wave now had few qualms about putting it down with reflections such as 'of course, the New Wave was very disappointing',[118] or 'what they called the New Wave contributed enormously to the deterioration of French cinema'.[119] In 1971 he went so far as to tell Rui Nogueira that 'The New Wave was an inexpensive way of making films. That's all.'[120] By then, of course, he had seen *Cahiers* review *Le Samouraï* and *L'Armée des ombres* in insulting terms (see chapters 1, 3 and 6). The break between Melville and the New Wave was complete.

These critical polemics were not just storms in Parisian tea-cups. Exaggerated and often in bad faith, on both sides, they were also symptomatic of the high economic and cultural stakes the cinema played for in 1960s France. The Melville vs the New Wave drama was played out against a backdrop of dramatically declining audiences (from 354.7 million in 1960 to 184.4 million in 1970). Seen as the white hope of French cinema in 1959–60, the New Wave was soon accused of being the cause of its downfall. Meanwhile Melville by the mid-1960s had become one of the big players in the survival of a quality popular French cinema. From the point of view of an increasingly beleaguered New Wave, subject to vicious French media battering, Melville went from benign godfather to 'the enemy'. But the years from *Bob le flambeur* to *L'Ainé des Ferchaux*, difficult as they were, in retrospect marked a period whose experiments and friendships indelibly marked the course of Melville's career.

NOTES

1. The relationship between the two films is discussed in detail in Ginette Vincendeau, 'Gamblers Anonymous', *Sight and Sound*, vol. 13, no. 3, March 2003, pp. 22–4.
2. Jean-Pierre Melville in Eric Breitbart, 'An Interview with Jean-Pierre Melville', *Film Culture*, no. 35, Winter 1964–5, p. 16.
3. Melville refers to Jules Dassin's *Du rififi chez les hommes* and Decoin's *Razzia sur la Chnouf*. Claude Beylie and Bertrand Tavernier, 'Entretien avec Jean-Pierre Melville', *Cahiers du cinéma*, no. 124, October 1961, p. 14.
4. He thought there was too much slang in it. Rui Nogueira (ed.), *Melville on Melville* (London: Secker and Warburg and BFI, 1971), p. 55.
5. See in particular: Richard Kuisel, *Seducing the French: The Dilemma of Americanization* (Berkeley: University of California Press, 1993); Kristin Ross, *Fast Cars, Clean Bodies, Decolonization and the Reordering of French Culture* (Cambridge, MA: MIT Press, 1995); Patricia Hubert-Lacombe, *Le Cinéma français dans la guerre froide, 1946–1956* (Paris: Éditions L'Harmattan, 1996).
6. For a history of crime literature before the war see Ginette Vincendeau, 'France 1945–65 and Hollywood: The *Policier* as Inter-national Text', *Screen*, vol. 33, no. 1, Spring 1992, pp. 50–80; François Guérif, *Le Cinéma policier français* (Paris: Henri Veyrier, 1981); Jill Forbes, *The Cinema in France After the New Wave* (London: BFI, 1992); special issue of *Les Temps Modernes*, 'Roman noir', no. 595, August–September 1997.
7. Claude-Edmonde Magny, *The Age of the American Novel, The Film Aesthetic of Fiction Between the Two Wars* (New York: Frederick Ungar Publishing Co., 1972) [first published in French as *L'Age du roman américain*, Paris: Éditions du Seuil, 1948]; see also Jean-Paul Schweighaueuser and J.-J. Schleret, 'Roman et film noir', in Claude Mesplède and Jean-Jaques Schleret, *Les Auteurs de la Série Noire, 1945–1995* (Paris: Joseph K, 1996), pp. 501–9.
8. Marcel Duhamel, 'Le manifeste de la Série Noire', <www.gallimard.fr>.
9. See, for example, *Les Temps Modernes*, 'Roman noir', p. 97.
10. See Charles O'Brien, 'Film Noir in France: Before the Liberation', *Iris*, no. 21, Spring 1996, pp. 7–20; Ginette Vincendeau, 'Noir is Also a French Word', in Ian Cameron (ed.), *The Movie Book of Film Noir* (London: Studio Vista, 1992), pp. 49–58.
11. Albert Simonin, *Les Cahiers de la cinémathèque*, no. 25, Spring–Summer 1978, p. 121.
12. José Giovanni (author of *Le Deuxième souffle*) is another such author, though his claim that he was in the Resistance has been later contested; see Robert Deleuse, 'Petite histoire du roman noir français', *Les Temps Modernes*, 'Roman noir', p. 66.
13. Pierre Sorlin, *European Cinemas, European Societies, 1939–1990* (London: Routledge, 1991); Pierre Maillot, *Les Fiancés de Marianne: la société française à travers ses grands acteurs* (Paris: Le Cerf, 1996); Guérif, *Le Cinéma policier français*.
14. Noël Burch and Genèvieve Sellier, *La Drôle de guerre des sexes du cinéma français, 1930–56* (Paris: Nathan, 1996), p. 220.
15. 'Marcel Duhamel, Jean Giono et Raymond Queneau témoignent', Preface to the Série Noire, <www.gallimard.fr>.

16. Jill Forbes, 'Série Noire', in Brian Rigby and Nicholas Hewitt (eds), *France and the Mass Media* (London: Macmillan, 1991) p. 85.
17. On the Blum–Byrnes agreement, see Jean-Pierre Jeancolas, 'From the Blum–Byrnes Agreement to the GATT Affair', in Geoffrey Nowell-Smith and Steven Ricci (eds), *Hollywood & Europe, Economics, Culture, National Identity 1945–95* (London: BFI, 1998), pp. 47–60; Hubert-Lacombe, *Le Cinéma français dans la guerre froide*.
18. Hubert-Lacombe, *Le Cinéma français dans la guerre froide*, p. 177.
19. Georges Sadoul, 'Décadence d'Hollywood', *Les Lettres françaises*, no. 395, 3 January 1952, p. 6.
20. Hubert-Lacombe, *Le Cinéma français dans la guerre froide*, pp. 160–1.
21. Forbes, 'Série Noire', p. 96.
22. See Filmography for more details.
23. Serge Silberman, *Libération*, 20 December 1986.
24. Ibid.
25. Nogueira, *Melville on Melville*, p. 64.
26. R.-M. Arlaud, *Combat*, 3 September 1956.
27. In particular *Franc-Tireur*, 28 August 1956, *Combat*, 3 September 1956.
28. Claude Chabrol, 'Saluer Melville?', *Cahiers du cinéma*, no. 63, October 1956.
29. As Antoine de Baecque points out, the young *Cahiers* critics' reaction to films such as *Bob le flambeur* was a way of talking about their own future work. Antoine de Baecque, *Les Cahiers du cinéma, Histoire d'une revue*, Torne 1 (Paris: *Cahiers du cinéma*, 1991).
30. François Truffaut, in Wheeler Winston Dixon, *The Early Film Criticism of François Truffaut* (Bloomington and Indianapolis: Indiana University Press, 1993), p. 154.
31. Antoine de Baecque and Serge Toubiana, *François Truffaut* (Paris: Éditions Gallimard, 1996), p. 190.
32. *Libération*, 20 December 1986.
33. *Le Figaro*, 20 December 1986.
34. Melville's name and an early budget estimate for *Rififi* are indicated in the *Rififi* production archive (CN0658 B450 [455]f).
35. *Bob le flambeur* – script held at the Bibliothèque du Film (BIFI), Paris. Ref: SCEN0340 B98, p. 75.
36. Chabrol, 'Saluer Melville?', p. 51.
37. Silberman, *Libération*, 20 December 1986.
38. Jean-Luc Godard, in Tom Milne (ed.), *Godard on Godard* (London: Secker and Warburg, 1972), p. 223.
39. Nogueira, *Melville on Melville*, p. 57.
40. Although Melville says he was keen to 'seize that light. [...] We shot for 14 days on place Pigalle to get the continuity of dawn light in the film' (*Les Lettres françaises*, 7 February 1963), continuity is not perfect: one shot shows rain (not just the water from the car), by contrast to the previous and following one.
41. Only Jacques Demy's *La Baie des anges* (1962) pathologises the gambler. It is no accident surely that the gambler there is a woman (Jeanne Moreau).
42. Ludovic Tournès, *New Orleans sur Seine, Histoire du jazz en France* (Paris: Librairie Arthème Fayard, 1999), p. 525.

43. Nogueira, *Melville on Melville*, p. 53.
44. The film is supposed to be situated in a mid-west city but the outdoor scenes were shot in LA.
45. As confirmed by many of his collaborators such as Serge Silberman, co-producer on *Bob*: 'We would eat around 8pm, talk until 10pm and then ride in his big American car (even when broke, Melville drove an American car like Bob le flambeur). Silberman, *Libération*, 20 December 1986.
46. Nogueira, *Melville on Melville*, p. 56.
47. Melville hints at the similarity between Bob and a vampire, who lives only 'from night until dawn'; Nogueira, *Melville on Melville*, p. 57.
48. *Bob le flambeur* – script held at BIFI.
49. Beylie and Tavernier, 'Entretien avec Jean-Pierre Melville', p. 10.
50. Robert Warshow, 'The Gangster as Tragic Hero', in *The Immediate Experience* (New York: Atheneum, 1976), p. 129.
51. See Ginette Vincendeau, *Pépé le Moko* (London: BFI, 1998).
52. *Bob le flambeur* – script held at BIFI, p. 1.
53. Ibid., p. 122.
54. Melville indicates: 'This shot will only be included in the prints for first-run cinemas'. Ibid.
55. Nogueira, *Melville on Melville*, p. 59.
56. François Truffaut, 'A Certain Tendency of the French Cinema', in Bill Nichols (ed.), *Movies and Methods*, vol. I, p. 229; originally published in *Cahiers du cinéma*, no. 31, January 1954 (Berkeley: University of California Press, 1976).
57. Nogueira, *Melville on Melville*, p. 57.
58. Ibid., p. 76.
59. Jean-Luc Godard, *Histoire(s) du cinéma*, episode 3(a).
60. Nogueira, *Melville on Melville*, p. 70.
61. Godard, in Milne, *Godard on Godard*, p. 146.
62. Claude Garson, *L'Aurore*, 10 October 1959.
63. Henry Magnan, *Paris-Jour*, 19 October 1959.
64. Ibid.
65. Jean de Baroncelli, *Le Monde*, 28 October 1959.
66. Antoine de Baecque, *La Nouvelle Vague, Histoire d'une jeunesse* p. 115.
67. Jean Douchet, *Arts*, 21 October 1959.
68. Henry Rabine, *La Croix*, 4 November 1959.
69. Pierre Marcabru, *Combat*, 20 October 1959.
70. Pierre Billard, *France-Observateur*, 22 October 1959.
71. Michel Capdenac, *Les Lettres françaises*, 22 October 1959.
72. Jean Domarchi, 'Plaisir à Melville', *Cahiers du cinéma*, no. 102, December 1959, p. 15.
73. Nogueira, *Melville on Melville*, p. 75.
74. See chapters 3 (*Léon Morin, prêtre*) and 5 (*Le Doulos*) for further details.
75. Nogueira, *Melville on Melville*, p. 70.
76. Michel Marie, *The French New Wave, an Artistic School* (Oxford: Blackwell, 2003); Serge Zreik, *Les Affiches de la Nouvelle Vague; De la Nouvelle Vague au Nouveau Cinéma Français, 1958–1969* (Biarritz: Éditions du PECARI, 1998).

77. Nogueira, *Melville on Melville*, p. 69.
78. Ibid.
79. Melville wanted to shoot it with Jeanne Moreau, but in the end Marcel Carné did, with Annie Girardot, in 1964. There are conflicting accounts of why the Melville/Moreau project did not happen. See Marcel Carné, *Ma vie à belles dents* (Édition définitive, L'Archipel, 1996), pp. 312–13; see also Marcel Ophuls, 'A propos du "Chagrin et la pitié"', *Positif*, no. 469, March 2000, pp. 57–8.
80. Domarchi, 'Plaisir à Melville', p. 16.
81. Marcabru, *Combat*, 20 October 1959.
82. Samuel Lachize, *L'Humanité*, 21 October 1959.
83. Marie, *The French New Wave, an Artistic School*, p. 73.
84. Jacques Siclier, *Nouvelle Vague?* (Paris: Éditions du Cerf, 1961), p. 57.
85. Nogueira, *Melville on Melville*, pp. 70–1.
86. *La Lanterne*, 13 September 1963.
87. *Carrefour*, 9 October 1963; *Télérama*, 13 October 1963.
88. Jean de Baroncelli, *Le Monde*, 6 October 1963.
89. For instance, *Témoignage Chrétien*, 10 October 1963.
90. Henry Chapier, *Combat*, 4 October 1963.
91. Jeander, *Libération*, 6 October 1963.
92. Jacques Siclier, *Télérama*, 13 October 1963.
93. Baroncelli, *Le Monde*, 6 October 1963.
94. Marcel Martin, *Les Lettres françaises*, 10 October 1963.
95. Claude Mauriac, *Le Figaro littéraire*, 10 October 1963.
96. Jean-Louis Bory, *Arts*, 9 October 1963.
97. Jean Domarchi, *Cahiers du cinéma*, no. 149, November 1963, pp. 65–6.
98. Nogueira, *Melville on Melville*, p. 102.
99. *L'Ainé des Ferchaux* – script held at the Bibliothèque du Film (BIFI), Paris. Ref. SCEN0065.
100. François Guérif, *Les Cahiers de la cinémathèque*, no. 25, Spring–Summer 1978, p. 96.
101. Ibid.
102. Claude Gauteur, *D'après Simenon, Simenon & le cinéma* (Carnets, Omnibus, 2001), p. 89.
103. Nogueira, *Melville on Melville*, p. 102.
104. Melville says the sign 'Pray for Peace' was his reference to the Cuban missile crisis. Ibid., p. 107.
105. Charles Vanel, interview with René Prédal, *Cinéma d'Aujourd'hui*, no. 10, November 1976.
106. Nogueira, *Melville on Melville*, p. 105.
107. Melville used a song from Frank Capra's *A Hole in the Head* because he did not need to pay rights. Ibid., pp. 107–8.
108. Nogueira, *Melville on Melville*, p. 106.
109. Although interestingly Vanel had appeared in *Le Salaire de la peur* (1953), in a partnership with Yves Montand which could also be read as homoerotic.

110. Richard Dyer, 'No Place for Homosexuality: Marcel Carné's *L'Air de Paris* (1954)', in Susan Hayward and Ginette Vincendeau (eds), *French Film, Texts and Contexts*, 2nd edition (London and New York: Routledge, 2000), p. 129.
111. Ibid., p. 132.
112. Georges Simenon, *L'Ainé des Ferchaux* (Paris: Gallimard, 1945; Folio Policier edition, 2001), p. 306.
113. Olivier Bohler, 'Jean-Pierre Melville', unpublished thesis, p. 328.
114. Michel Flacon, '*L'Ainé des Ferchaux*', *Cinéma 63*, no. 79, September–October 1963, pp. 119–21.
115. The affair took place because the film's producer had replaced Aurel by Vadim. Judging Vadim a commercial director, Truffaut attacked him in an article, to which Vadim replied, taking Truffaut to court. Media and film personalities took sides, including Melville who was on Truffaut's side (de Baecque, *François Truffaut*, pp. 273–4). The affair itself was a storm in a tea-cup, but it is indicative of allegiances.
116. De Baecque and Toubiana, *François Truffaut*, pp. 279, 334.
117. Jim Hillier (ed.), *Cahiers du cinéma*, Volume 2, *The 1960s New Wave, New Cinema, Re-evaluating Hollywood* (London: Routledge and Kegan Paul, 1986), p. 75.
118. Hillier, *Cahiers du cinéma*, Volume 2, p. 106.
119. *Les Lettres françaises*, 1 November 1967.
120. Nogueira, *Melville on Melville*, p. 77.

5

Série Noire – films noirs: *Le Doulos* (1963) and *Le Deuxième souffle* (1966)

Bob le flambeur and *Deux hommes dans Manhattan*, examined in the preceding chapter, were original thrillers: in their production mode, their large amount of location shooting, their poetic explorations of Paris and New York, and in Melville's playful deployment of generic codes. But also literally they were original screenplays (*L'Ainé des Ferchaux*, based on Simenon, retained very little of the novel). By contrast, the more sombre *Le Doulos* – which Melville considered 'his first real *policier*'[1] – and *Le Deuxième souffle* are faithful adaptions of crime thrillers from Gallimard's famous Série Noire.

Both films were very popular at the box office. Their compelling plotting, generic abstraction and virtuoso yet sober *mise en scène* all drew high praise from contemporary French reviewers. Many of them thought Melville's classicism and professionalism gave a magisterial lesson to the 'anything goes' aesthetics of the New Wave film-makers. Classicism and sobriety: these features are in evidence at times in Melville's previous films, but in *Le Doulos* and *Le Deuxième souffle* they are sustained throughout, while his tendency towards abstraction and self-reflexivity become increasingly prominent. In *Le Doulos* and *Le Deuxième souffle* we are invited to see the gangster genre as offering tales of tragic fate with resonance beyond the criminal underworld.

This chapter explores the narrative and stylistic brilliance of *Le Doulos* and *Le Deuxième souffle*, but it also considers elements which have tended to be neglected: the presence of stars with strong identities (Jean-Paul Belmondo, Lino Ventura), the relationship with the novels on which they are based, and in particular with the Série Noire sub-genre of French thrillers, which in the 1960s was in its heyday.

FRENCH SÉRIE NOIRE CINEMA IN THE 1960S

In the previous chapter we saw how *Bob le flambeur* was a personal take on the Série Noire genre which mobilised commercial appeal through Le Breton's dialogues. With *Le Doulos* and *Le Deuxième souffle* Melville moves fully within the Série Noire orbit. The early 1950s noir matrix – with its combination of light-hearted adaptations of Anglo-American novels and French gangster stories by the likes of Simonin and Le Breton – soon diversified and evolved. Maintaining its spectacular popular momentum, the Série Noire, along with other crime series, generated a vigorous strand of French cinema. Indeed, crime films burgeoned to the extent that 'from the late 1950s to the late 1970s, the *policier* constituted a quarter of French cinema'.[2] There continued to be light-hearted versions of Cheyney featuring Eddie Constantine, as well as mainstream gangster stories based on Simonin, Le Breton and others such as Alphonse Boudard, as well as 'Frenchified' adaptations of American capers such as *Mélodie en sous-sol* (1963). In addition to more Simenon adaptations, a new kind of psychological crime story appeared, located in bourgeois milieux rather than the gangster world, based, for instance, on the Boileau-Narcejac team and Patricia Highsmith (*Plein Soleil*, 1960).

Within this evolving landscape, three other developments are of note. The first was a renewed comic vein. It included comic versions of the *Fantômas* serials (starring Jean Marais and Louis de Funès) and an 'absurdist' mode comprised of films such as *Les Tontons flingueurs* (Georges Lautner, 1963) and *Les Barbouzes* (Georges Lautner, 1964). These films – usually based on French writers – have remained a cult in France although 'inexportable' elsewhere because of their uncompromising slang quotient. The best film in this series, *La Métamorphose des cloportes* (Pierre Granier-Deferre, 1965), exemplifies the appeal of a sub-genre in need of reappraisal. Based on Alphonse Boudard, *Métamorphose* includes a star-studded cast (Lino Ventura, Charles Aznavour, Pierre Brasseur), exquisite noir photography (by Nicolas Hayer, photographer of *Le Doulos*), a jazz score by Jimmy Smith, brilliant slang dialogue by Michel Audiard and parodic characters (for instance, Ventura's philandering small-time crook sports loud check jackets and a fake leopard-skin dressing-gown).

The second development saw several New Wave directors turning to American writers in the Série Noire catalogue for the source of their second or third films: Chabrol made *A double tour* (1959) from Stanley Ellin; Truffaut *Tirez sur le pianiste* (1960) from David Goodis and *La Mariée était en noir* (1967) from William Irish, Godard was 'inspired' by Lionel White's *Obsession* for *Pierrot le fou* (1965). Much has been written about the New Wave directors' attraction to American noir.[3] Here I just want to note that their 'adaptations' of American Série Noire texts, unlike their successful personal and predominantly 'French' films – *Le Beau Serge* for Chabrol, *Les 400 coups* for Truffaut, *À bout de souffle* for Godard – were unsuccessful at the box office (I am not talking of their aesthetic value here). While with Godard it may be a case of excessive self-reflexivity (see the scene in *Une femme est une femme* [1961] where Anna Karina and Jean-Claude Brialy 'talk' through the titles of Série Noire novels), for Chabrol and Truffaut the problem is clearly related to too direct an import, compared to the careful adaptations to the French context of films like *Mélodie en sous-sol*. As Bertrand Tavernier noted, 'The story of *La Mariée était en noir* doesn't work in France and only makes sense in relation to American distances and differences between states.'[4]

The third trend in Série Noire was a growing 'realistic' strand which featured bleaker portrayals of gang life often based on notorious figures of the French underworld. To this strand belong Pierre Lesou and José Giovanni, authors of *Le Doulos* and *Le Deuxième souffle* respectively. Melville accentuated the sombre side of the novels by stripping them of whatever humorous elements they contained. It is significant that, notwithstanding his rejection of realism and his relish for American culture, Melville singled out those particular French writers rather than American ones in the vast Série Noire pool. In December 1962 Truffaut warned Melville that he was misguided to 'imitate American brutality and roughness'.[5] He was referring to *Le Doulos* which was then being completed. The huge success of the film three months later would certainly seem to validate Melville's choice of material. Besides, far from imitating 'American brutality and roughness', *Le Doulos* and *Le Deuxième souffle* are highly stylised reflections on complex literary and filmic Franco-American hybrids. It is time to look at them more closely.

THE TRAGEDY OF AMBIGUITY: *LE DOULOS*

Le Doulos is the story of Maurice Faugel (Serge Reggiani), an ex-convict who, on coming out of jail, settles an old score by killing his friend Gilbert (René Lefevre), a fence, and buries the loot from a high-profile heist. He then plans a robbery with his friend Rémy (Philippe Nahon), with safe-busting equipment lent by another friend, Silien (Jean-Paul Belmondo), a notorious police informer. The robbery goes wrong, Rémy is killed, and Faugel is wounded and later arrested by Inspector Clain (Jean Desailly). Faugel suspects Silien – who meanwhile beats up Faugel's girlfriend Thérèse (Monique Hennessy) – of betrayal. While Faugel is in jail plotting revenge, Silien unearths the money and jewels and kills the two big-time gangsters, Nuttheccio (Michel Piccoli) and Armand (Jacques de Léon) who had masterminded the initial robbery. He also meets up with his former girlfriend Fabienne (Fabienne Dali), currently Nuttheccio's mistress. When Faugel comes out of jail, he (and we) find out that the betrayer is not Silien but Thérèse, whom Silien and Jean (Aimé de March) have disposed of in a staged car crash. Faugel tries to stop the contract killer Kern (Carl Studer) he had paid to kill Silien. On arrival at Silien's house, however, Faugel is mistaken for Silien and killed by Kern. Silien and Kern then kill each other in a shoot-out.

With 1,475,391 tickets sold in France, *Le Doulos* was Melville's second major box-office success after *Léon Morin, prêtre*. The clever plot was a major attraction (publicity urged people not to miss the beginning), as were the performances of Belmondo, the top young male star of the time (see Chapter 3), and Reggiani, who was (rightly) hailed as an actor who had been scandalously ignored by film-makers since *Casque d'or* (1952).[6]

Le Doulos was widely reviewed by the daily and weekly press, where it received flattering comparisons with the three 'gold standards' of *Touchez pas au grisbi*, *Le Trou* (1960) and *Du rififi chez les hommes*. In the cinephile press, Claude Beylie, a Melville fan, wrote an elogious review in *Cahiers du cinéma*,[7] stressing the film's 'moral reflexion' on truth and lies and 'extraordinary craftsman's precision, a high love of style'. References to masterly technique, sobriety, elliptical style and narrative efficiency graced almost every review, summed up by *L'Express* as 'quasi perfection of *Le Doulos*'.[8] An isolated critical note by *Les Nouvelles littéraires* – 'All I see here is a lot of professionalism and a clever use of two remarkable actors, Belmondo and Reggiani'[9] – is worth quoting because the 'all technique and no content' slur will become a leitmotiv of hostile Melville criticism right up till the 1990s. Since 1963, *Le Doulos* has steadily risen to the status of an uncontested 'classic'. It was one of the '100 films' included in a special issue of *Cahiers du cinéma*. For Thierry Jousse (who sees the influence of the film especially on the Coen brothers' *Miller's Crossing* [1990]), '*Le Doulos*, which I long thought an unpleasant and formalist object, has become today a film which I keep going back to, as a whole or in fragments.'[10]

Many reviewers in 1963 praised Melville for reaching out to both popular and cinephile audiences. A few lamented the 'vulgar' genre, although on the whole conceding that Melville had 'transcended' the thriller. Inevitably, references to the 'American-ness' of the film abounded, evidenced by its classicism, and in particular its 'efficiency' and 'sobriety', as well as its noir thematics and visuals. At the same time most reviewers noted that the essential ambiguity and 'tragic' mood of *Le Doulos* endowed it with a strong French and Melvillian streak. If it was formal issues that led to the initial reappraisal of *Le Doulos*, the novel on which it was based has received much less attention. It is here, however, that I intend to begin my analysis.

From Lesou to Melville

Le Doulos was adapted by Melville from the excellent 1957 eponymous novel by Pierre Lesou, a young Série Noire writer noted for his first-hand knowledge of the milieu, taste for stories of male friendship, and self-confessed 'feminophobia'.[11] Melville's references to Lesou's *Doulos* repeatedly emphasise his film's departures from the book, apparently with the writer's approval: 'He [Lesou] even said I should have told him my story before he wrote the book.'[12] Melville claims his characters are more ambiguous than those in the novel – '*Le Doulos* is a very complicated film, very difficult to understand, because I gave a double twist to the situations in the novel' – and that he suppressed the slang in the book. Lesou retorted:

> You only have to read the book and watch the film to see that the shooting was done with 'book in hand'. There is only one exception in the final scene, apart from the shot of Belmondo stroking the horse's neck, Melville's tribute to John Huston's *The Asphalt Jungle*.[13]

If Lesou is exaggerating a little too, the changes are certainly not as significant as Melville suggests. More striking, in fact, apart from the quality of Lesou's writing, are the similarities between his text and Melville's film.[14]

In many scenes, whole passages of dialogue come nearly straight from the novel, the only difference being that Melville did play down the slang. Melville's hoods use a more sober colloquial French, with the exception of Silien who, as in the book, uses 'elegant language'.[15] Yet Melville retained the title of the book, despite the fact that the word 'doulos' (meaning both 'hat' and 'informer') would not have meant much to most viewers – hence the explanation that opens the film, reprised by most reviewers. The gesture was clearly intended to capitalise on the Série Noire's status, as well as to signal the exoticism of the gangsters' world. I also wonder if he liked the poetic alliteration between 'doulos' and 'douleur' (pain), indicating from the start the tragic aspect of the story.

From a structural point of view, Melville's film is remarkably close to the book. Chapters and chronology have been kept.[16] Most characters' names remain – Silien, Faugel, Thérèse, Nuttheccio – though outlandish nicknames have been erased. There is one major narrative alteration, to the ending (plus one or two minor ones, discussed in the course of this chapter). In the film Faugel arrives at the house first and is killed by Kern, who mistakes him for Silien. Silien and Kern then kill each other in a shoot-out, Silien

Le Doulos: the last shot that was discarded. Silien (top left) echoes Faugel (bottom right), with Kern (Carl Studer) in the middle

having just time before he dies to telephone Fabienne to say, 'I won't be coming tonight'. In the book, it is Silien who is first on the scene to be shot down by Kern. When Faugel appears, there is a long gun-battle after which the wounded Faugel phones the police to ask for an ambulance for Mado (Fabienne in the film), who has joined the shoot-out and is also wounded; then both Faugel and Kern die.[17]

What do these differences mean? In the book, since Silien is already dead, Faugel's fight with Kern acts out his guilt for causing Silien's death. On the screen, Melville *causes* Faugel's death by making him visually interchangeable with Silien, two identical dark silhouettes against the sky. Book and film create a nightmarish ending, drenched in stormy rain, which rhymes with the wind and fog of the opening. But Melville's elegantly simplified dénouement, compared to the messy fight in Lesou, enhances the sense of tragedy. Where the book is melodramatic, the film is detached. In the novel, Faugel poignantly almost catches up with Silien before he reaches the house, shouts his name and fires his gun to attract his attention, all in vain against the storm. In the film this is translated as an ironic twist of fate: in his haste Faugel misses the fact that Silien has stopped at a petrol station, overtakes him and reaches the house first, still provoking his and Silien's death. The house is a death-trap in both cases, but where Lesou has the reader share Faugel's desperate point of view, Melville invites the spectator to a deconstruction of tragic inevitability. By switching the order of arrival of the two men, he also, of course, allows the star Belmondo to have the last word, though not image – this is reserved for his *doulos*.

A comparison between book and film also helps us see vividly the sustained process of abstraction to which Melville has subjected the novel in terms of milieu and décor. Melville said: 'I immediately liked [Lesou's book] a lot, not so much in its form, anecdotal and *Montmartroise*, which I did not follow, but in its spirit.'[18] Two processes are at work in Melville's transformation of the book: an abstraction from the picturesque evocation of the underworld (of the kind seen in *Bob*) on the one hand, and a visual and oral hybridisation of the French Série Noire with American gangster films of the 1940s and 50s on the other.

Far from Montmartre: the abstract gangster

In an often repeated quote, Melville said, 'Without the American cinema [of the 1930s], which I loved and still love [...] I would not make films, and I would not have made *Le Doulos*.'[19] Melville goes on to list some items of décor borrowed from American cinema: 'The telephone booth from which Silien calls Salignari', 'the bar [...] which bears no resemblance to a French café, the sash-windows with slatted metal blinds instead of the usual French shutters', 'Clain's office'.[20] I would add the Americanisation of bar names (the 'Sicil' becomes the 'New York', the 'Cockpit' becomes the 'Cotton Club'), the mutation of Citroën into American cars and of Cinzano into whisky, and the ubiquitous jazz soundtrack. Even more obviously, the traditional gangster attire of trench-coat and hat and contrasted black-and-white lighting of *Le Doulos* place it within the iconography of 1940s and 50s American noir. Such visual tropes are embedded within a modified classical American *découpage*, which alternates long *plans-séquences* with rapid cutting (at 640 shots for 103 minutes, and an ASL of nine seconds, *Le Doulos* is fairly average, though this average hides one extraordinary take which lasts eight minutes and eight seconds, examined later). The themes of the story fit both French traditions and Melville's concerns, in particular the foregrounded blurring of the distinction between law and lawlessness which finds its embodiment in the figure of the informer. Moreover, the traditional clarity of action of the American cinema is challenged head-on by *Le Doulos*' complex plotting, ambiguity and withholding of information, right from frame one.

The credits: fate starts ticking away

Le Doulos' credit sequence must stand as one of the most powerfully evocative openings of any thriller. The film begins with the explanation of the word 'doulos' silently unfolding in white letters on a black background:

> In slang, 'Doulos' means 'hat'.
> But in the secret language of policemen and criminals, 'Doulos' is the name given to the person 'who wears one' ...
> The police informer.

As the last sentence appears, the tic-toc of what sounds like a metronome can be faintly heard. The music then starts, picking up the beat with cymbals, while dramatic string chords strike over the names of the producers Carlo Ponti and Georges de Beauregard. The name of the star, Jean-Paul Belmondo, appears next. A man in trench-coat and hat walks steadily from right to left. The metronome beat becomes that of his echoing feet – time is already counted for this man as he grimly walks towards his destiny. From this very first image, Melville blurs his identity. As we see him emerging from the shadows immediately after Belmondo's name, his face invisible, we assume he is Belmondo's character Silien, the 'doulos' – until we see his face a few seconds later and recognise Reggiani (Faugel). Melville repeats this trick several times during the film: when Faugel arrives at Gilbert's, when Silien arrives at Thérèse's, when he unearths the jewels, and at the end. Then, with another loud chord, evoking a gunshot, the title LE DOULOS appears in huge modernist letters (in the French trailer, the letters L.E. D.O.U.L.O.S. appear one by one, each accompanied by a gunshot). For the rest of the credits, over a cool jazz score, Reggiani keeps walking along an elevated walkway bordered by railings, in a dark street crossing under a wide stretch of overhead railway tracks.[21] The camera follows him in a long tracking shot,[22] passing several metallic and wooden pillars. Location and camera movement box him in criss-crossing, harsh vertical and horizontal lines. At one point the camera leaves him to track along the overhead railway tracks and railings, as if to emphasise further his sense of emprisonment. As the name Lesou appears, the music turns more melancholy and wafting fog briefly envelops Reggiani. Another dramatic chord over the name 'Jean-Pierre Melville' brings the credits, the camera and the music to a halt. The camera zooms in on Reggiani's face, against the sound of howling wind. A reverse shot shows a distant Sacré Coeur. A zoom out reveals a dreary landscape of railway tracks and empty streets. Seen from a high angle, Reggiani enters screen left, a tiny figure in this forlorn landscape, lifeless except for passing trains. He ascends the steps to an isolated suburban house. Nicolas Hayer's harsh black-and-white photography is here put to excellent use in the depiction of a grim environment, in contrast to Henri Decae's diffuse and lyrical light in, for example, *Bob le flambeur*.

In starting *Le Doulos* in this urban wasteland, Melville sets out to locate his film in an abstract, generic noir space rather than in the Parisian underworld. As he said, 'With the symbolic zoom at the beginning, I leave Montmartre'[23] (we recall the ubiquity of the Sacré Coeur in *Bob*). The spatial and metaphorical distance from Montmartre and *Bob* is not just that of the half-dozen years separating the two films. It is also a distance from the mainstream French Série Noire. A useful comparison here can be made with *Mélodie en sous-sol*, made and released virtually at the same time as *Le Doulos*, and equally successful. *Mélodie*, directed by Henri Verneuil and starring Jean Gabin and Alain Delon, is based on a Série Noire story by American novelist John Trinian. The credit sequence features Gabin, in a trench-coat, like Faugel emerging from jail and returning home to the suburbs, accompanied by a jazz score. After a long walk through a brutally modernist suburb, Gabin arrives at an isolated small house. But even though Gabin is temporarily unsettled by an alien landscape, the point of the sequence is to focalise, through his eyes, the discovery of the actual suburb of Sarcelles, complete with road sign. Where Verneuil and his scriptwriters – among them Michel Audiard – domesticated an American book to comment on alienating modernisation (before moving on to a light-hearted caper on the Côte d'Azur), Melville *de*-territorialised Lesou, shifting from Montmartre to an abstract and grim landscape.

The credits and opening images of *Le Doulos* thus prepare the viewer for the hybrid world of *Le Doulos*, merging French idioms (language, stars, situations) and American icons into an abstract space. Gone are the book's references to precise locations (Thérèse's flat in Montmartre) and contemporary events (mentions of North Africa on the radio). Likewise Melville destabilises the spectator's identification from the start. Where *Mélodie* repeatedly grounds Gabin's viewpoint (we hear his thoughts in voiceover, and his gaze is directly matched to counter-shots of Sarcelles), Melville obscures the identity of his hero. His refusal to align us with Reggiani's interiority is part of the film's overall system of alienation and confusion, but it is also necessary for the stunning surprise at the end of the next sequence.

Shoot-out at Gilbert's

Le Doulos' first sequence is, in all respects but one, extremely close to Lesou. In book and film, Faugel visits his old friend Gilbert, a fence who has, out of loyalty, been helping him out. Gilbert's concern is genuine and evident in his offers of advice, food, money, shelter and (reluctantly) gun. Their conversation economically fills us in on Faugel's past (jail), present (Thérèse) and future (the heist with Rémy) and on other important characters, in particular Silien and Nuttheccio. In the novel we know that Faugel intends to kill Gilbert for murdering his former girlfriend Arlette. The withholding of this piece of information allows Melville to end the film sequence with a brilliant coup: Faugel turns the gun on Gilbert and shoots. Only later do we learn why he did it. On a first viewing, the surprise is shocking. On repeated viewings, the brilliance remains. But in keeping Faugel's background and mysterious interiority, Melville also builds up what I will call his first abstract gangster, an elaboration on a literary and filmic archetype rather than a rounded portrayal.

Camerawork, décor and lighting construct a hybrid space, part seedy French suburban house with its no-man's-land surroundings,[24] distressed walls and scant furnishings, and part American noir location, with sash windows and expressionist lighting contrasts. Strong shadows mark out Faugel's silhouette as he handles Gilbert's gun, emphasising his duplicity before his shocking act; swinging on its electric cable after Gilbert's collapse, the lamp sweeping the room with light and shadows illustrates dynamically the film's alternation of truth and lies; the violently shaking trees outside the kitchen window express Faugel's inner turmoil. Faugel looks at himself in a *cracked* mirror, a neat commentary on the gangster's narcissism as well as his estranged identity. An African mask incongruously displayed on the entrance hall wall, which Faugel stops to examine briefly, pursues the theme of alienation. But it also alludes to another form of exoticism, that of the mythical American gangster against the background of the French suburban landscape. Faugel's ensemble of trench-coat and hat is shown as 'alien' when we initially see him silhouetted against the doorway, recalling his first appearance in the credits.

Such self-consciousness and anachronism in the use of the gangster dress code has not gone unnoticed. Colin McArthur, Steve Neale and Stella Bruzzi have all, in different ways, commented on this, as have Denitza Bantcheva and Olivier Bohler.[25] The gap between the gangster's 'uniform' and his Parisian surroundings inaugurated in *Bob*

Le Doulos: 'a man in front of a mirror means a stock taking'. Faugel (Serge Reggiani)

Silien (Jean-Paul Belmondo)

is intensified in *Le Doulos* and will be brought to new heights in the Delon trilogy (discussed further in Chapter 6). This gap is particularly evident if we think about it in relation to Gilbert's clothes on the one hand and those worn by Gabin in the title sequence of *Mélodie en sous-sol* on the other. Gilbert's soft corduroy jacket bespeaks his rootedness in the Parisian *banlieue*, Faugel's trench-coat and hat his distance from it. This is why Faugel ignores Gilbert's repeated requests to take them off. Melville's specific use of the mythical outfit also stands out compared with *Mélodie*. There, Gabin is simply Gabin in a trench-coat; his walk, voice, star persona override the significance of the clothes. Faugel on the other hand is subsumed into it, as is Silien. In *Le Doulos*, additionally, the hat is of particular importance. Title, pre-credit text, gestures and dialogue continuously draw attention to it. Faugel tilts his hat back at an insolent angle when Gilbert asks him to remove it but has it removed forcibly by Clain when the latter wants to humiliate him; Silien's hat is given the self-consciously fateful 'No. 13' at the Cotton Club cloakroom; and the last shot of the film, played against three dramatic chords, focuses on it. Sometimes a hat is just a hat, but in *Le Doulos* its significance in terms of the characters' masculinity is hard to miss.

Masculinity, ambiguity and classical cinema

The aspect of *Le Doulos* which has attracted most critical attention is its spectacular narrative twist. Until nearly ninety minutes into the movie, we believe Silien is a nark. His phone call to Salignari, his assault on Thérèse, his appropriation of the jewels, his elaborate *mise en scène* of Nuttheccio and Armand's deaths, all conspire to make the spectator, like Faugel, believe Silien has set him up. When he reveals that Thérèse, not he, was the informer, we are stunned into rereading everything that has gone before. Despite Melville's assertion that he 'gave a double twist to the situations in the novel',[26] *Le Doulos*' structure of deception comes from the book. Although occasionally Lesou gives us access to Faugel's interiority (in Gilbert's scene, in the botched heist in Neuilly, when Faugel wakes up to ponder at length what has happened to him), in all other respects Lesou's reader, like Melville's viewer, is led up the garden path for most of the story. Lesou's Silien is 'a guy who does not exteriorise himself',[27] so that his motivations are always opaque. Clearly the cleverness of Lesou's plotting must have attracted Melville.

As announced by the post-credit quote ('One must choose. To die . . . or to lie?'), each character in *Le Doulos* in turn lies (or may be lying) to someone at some point – Gilbert about Arlette, Faugel about Gilbert, Silien about Faugel, Thérèse about Silien, Clain about the drug squad's threat to Silien, etc. In the trailer, *Le Doulos* is described as both 'A tragedy of lies' and 'Pure mystery'. Even Silien's series of revelations is open to question. As many, including Melville have pointed out, there is no guarantee that he is telling the truth. He is backed up by Jean, but they could be lying together. Melville edits Silien's revelations over dreamy piano music, giving them a distinctly oneiric quality (here I disagree with Colin McArthur's reading of the scene as example of 'cinema of process'[28] – rather than a clinically detailed observation, it is surely an *elliptical* montage of Silien's actions). We also see how skilfully Silien manipulates Fabienne to believe that she 'heard' a gunshot while waiting in the car outside Gilbert's house.

This web of deception means that *Le Doulos* is constantly negotiating issues of truth and lies, appearances and reality – both moral and cinematic. For Zimmer and de Béchade, *Le Doulos* shows that 'the world is but one immense *duperie*, where everyone cheats and steals',[29] while for Bantcheva it 'demonstrates the impossibility of trusting representations of time, space and causality'.[30] For her *Le Doulos* questions the very essence of classical film narration, and 'the greatest liar is without doubt the filmmaker who leads us from one falsehood to another'.[31] From a different perspective, Murray Smith argues that

> the duration and intensity of our aversion towards Silien precludes a simple cognitive revision of our understanding of events and of our moral allegiances. The 'drag' of emotions may make us resist the revision, prompting us to question the reliability of the narration.[32]

These writers thus see *Le Doulos* as a modernist text that deconstructs narration and questions the possibility of stable meaning. Yet the reality effect of images, as opposed to what characters say, in my view problematises these readings. Faugel may swear to Clain that he did not kill Gilbert, but we trust the images that showed him doing it. The camera is not supposed to lie. Which is why, when we *see* the crucial missing information – Thérèse as Salignari's girlfriend, Silien's efforts to get Faugel out of jail, Thérèse's murder – we believe our eyes and retrospectively absolve Silien. Like Kurosawa's *Rashomon* (1950), *Le Doulos* may appear to undermine the essence of classical narration, but ultimately, it reaffirms its power. In this respect, *Le Doulos* is classical rather than modernist – its box-office popularity confirms that a mainstream audience had no problem reading it as a genre film with a clear resolution. The gradual fading of Faugel and his replacement by Silien, the relative weight of the two stars and the film's discourse on masculinity further tilt the weight of *Le Doulos* in favour of Silien as bearer of 'the truth'.

Silien's ascendancy: two women, two heists, two interrogations

Loyalty and betrayal between Faugel and Silien appear to drive the narrative along. Yet Faugel and Silien are only seen together in two scenes, at Thérèse's and at the New York bar. In fact, as Melville says, '*Le Doulos* is about the end of a friendship.'[33] It is also about the difference between two models of masculinity. In the book, Silien is a criminal of legendary status, Faugel one weakened by age and imprisonment. This dichotomy remains in the film, but it is expressed through subtle overlaps and doublings-up, in which Silien overtakes Faugel. Half-way through the film Silien unearthing the jewels that Faugel had buried symbolises this relay between the two characters: the anonymous figure in trench-coat and hat may be Faugel, but is revealed as Silien. Structurally, on both sides of this moment are two sets of parallel scenes which illustrate Silien's ascendancy: scenes at the men's respective girlfriends', and the 'coup' that each of them performs.

The Faugel–Thérèse couple is echoed by Silien–Fabienne. Both women are generically sexy – 'gangsters' molls'. Their apartments are exaggeratedly feminine, as opposed to the masculine exemplar of Silien's house, all modernist luxury, pared-down décor and hard surfaces.[34] But the film also plays on the difference between them. Thérèse's cosy nest with fluffy bedcover and tartan lampshade epitomises a certain loucheness (whisky, jazz on the radio), confirmed by Thérèse's bleached bouffant hair and over-tight, slightly vulgar clothes. Fabienne's grander apartment is filled with exotica, as befits the mistress of A-list Nuttheccio (and Silien). Her Chinese retro-chic couture and dark hair give off a more distinguished aura. Contrast also Silien's savage beating of Thérèse with his softer, if cynical, persuasion of Fabienne. Portrayed as the film's most contemptible character, Thérèse has little of the allure of the American *femme fatale*. Her role is that of alibi rather than object of desire. Meanwhile the violence of her punishment certainly exceeds her crime, especially when compared to the leniency afforded male informers (compare Thérèse's beating and cold-blooded elimination with the gentle treatment of the old man [Charles Bayard] in Neuilly). A 'doulos', without a hat, Thérèse suffers the actual and symbolic indignity of having whisky poured on her head. The excessiveness of her punishment was such that – at a time when reviewers were gender-blind or, like Claude Beylie, positively relished the 'virile philosophy'[35] of the film – a few reviewers picked it up. In particular Patrick Bureau equated Melville and Chabrol's 'ferocious misogyny'.[36] The unusual nature of this criticism for the time is shown by Melville's evasive reply: 'Nothing proves in fact that Thérèse is an informer: this is Belmondo's version.'[37]

But the whisky also connotes Faugel's weakness and lack of control over his woman (his excessive drinking allows Thérèse to betray him to Salignari), whereas Silien only needs to reappear to seduce and manipulate Fabienne. Before he beats up Thérèse, it is also clear that she responds to his flirting. Thus, under the common gangsters' uniform, the contrast between Silien's cool masculinity and Faugel's doomed weakness is underlined by the looks, habitats and narrative fates of their partners.

This difference is also enhanced by the contrast between Faugel's botched heist in Neuilly and Silien's assassination of Nuttheccio and Armand. Faugel's sole 'successful' on-screen job is to kill an unsuspecting, unarmed friend and steal his loot. The only other action we see him attempt is the burglary at Neuilly. But the heist has hardly started before it has to be aborted, and its aftermath is messy. Thus the nobility of shared professionalism which marks the gang's interaction in *Bob* is denied to Faugel. By contrast, Silien's murder of Nuttheccio and Armand is clever and complicated, impeccable in its planning and split-second execution. Silien's accomplished preparing of the 'set' for the murder scene, timing, orchestration and execution with white editor's gloves unmistakably evoke the director, who aligns himself with the more successful gangster and the more glamorous star.

Le Doulos provides a final contrast between the two men: their interrogations by Clain. Though Silien's interrogation comes first, it is more important than Faugel's in terms of both length and intricacy of *mise en scène*. It is worth pausing on this justly celebrated scene.[38]

Clain's interrogation of Silien is a *plan-séquence* of breathtaking virtuosity. Melville claimed that, of all the shots in his film-making career, there were only two he was proud of. One was the German military parade at the beginning of *L'Armée des ombres* (see Chapter 3). The other was 'the nine-minute thirty-eight-second shot in *Le Doulos*'.[39] (Actually in all the versions I have been able to see the scene lasts eight minute and eight seconds, but in the circumstances that's a quibble.[40]) Even if it is not true, as Wagner claims, that 'no reviewer noticed this take',[41] Melville's virtuosity is as impressive as it is understated – far from Ophuls' calligraphy or Welles' bravura. Even though the camera travels around the four sides of the room almost three times in complex patterns, it remains level (with one small exception), and its pan and tracking shots are always motivated by characters' movements and thus 'invisible', at least on a first viewing. On its way, the camera picks up the functional furniture – desks, filing cabinets, bookcase, venetian blinds, lamps, electric fan and typewriter – of an office modelled on 'the office Rouben Mamoulian had built for *City Streets*, and which [he] copied from the New York police headquarters'.[42] There are differences between the two scenes, but disposition and furniture are very similar, and the cinematic American-ness of the office reinforces the generic noir space in which the drama of the two masculine protagonists plays out. Although most of the dialogue between Silien and the inspectors comes straight from the book, Melville removed details that anchor the story in French history, for instance (why?) the fact that Salignari and Silien were friends in the Resistance. Similarly, in Faugel's interrogation, Melville reduced several pages on the criminal's laborious journey from police office to jail, and Clain's reflections on the sociology of criminality.[43]

The contrast between Silien and Faugel's interrogations superficially reinforces the sense of Silien as traitor. His interrogation comes early on, when we still believe him to be a 'doulos'. We have seen him make a phone call to Salignari, and the sequence immediately before the interrogation ends with Faugel saying, 'I must find that bastard Silien.' Towards the end of his long interrogation, Silien agrees to help Clain find Faugel. By contrast, Faugel's interrogation presents him as Silien's victim and makes him repeat that he is not a 'doulos'. The *mise en scène* of the two scenes undercuts Faugel's apparent moral superiority, however. Throughout his interrogation Silien stands immobile in Clain's office, serving as the still centre of the intricate choreography of camera movements as Clain and the other inspectors move in and out of shot. Characters and camera are attracted to him and at one point literally look up to him. By contrast Faugel is seated. A low angle places him in the foreground; venetian blinds (mere background in Silien's case) tower above him, as do Clain and at one point his assistants. Darker lighting and shadows create a menacing atmosphere, where Silien's interrogation is lit in high key. Symbolically, Clain knocks Faugel's hat off and unwittingly reveals his vulnerability by punching his damaged shoulder. Where Silien stands apart (next to portraits of police chiefs), a shot of Faugel from behind Clain's desk materialises his position as criminal. The two men's respective exits finally confirm their unequal status: whereas Silien walks free, leading the policemen through the main exit, Faugel is handcuffed and led up steep stairs, with contrasted lighting, dramatic music and an exaggeratedly high staircase suggesting an ascent to the scaffold.

Star personas

My reading of Silien and Faugel 'against the grain', which ascribes narrative ascendancy and 'truth' to Silien despite the doubt over his character over most of the film, chimes with the status and star personas of the two actors. By the early 1960s Reggiani was a solid character actor rather than a star. While he had starred memorably opposite Simone Signore in Becker's classic *Casque d'or*, his small stature and unconventional looks mostly confined his roles to the doomed or downright villains of *Les Portes de la nuit*, *Manon*, *La Ronde* (1950) and *Marie-Octobre* (1958). In the early 1960s he was at a low ebb in his career, reputed 'to bring bad luck' to a production.[44] The aura of existential doom which suffuses his tragic Manda in *Casque d'or* was, however, the reason Melville insisted on Reggiani for Faugel, seeing the character as 'Manda's grandson'.[45] By contrast, Belmondo in 1963 was in the first flush of his triumphant stardom, riding on the popularity of *À bout de souffle*, *Cartouche* (1962) and Melville's own *Léon Morin, prêtre*. Ten years younger than Reggiani, Belmondo was indelibly associated with both the modernity of the New Wave and the energy of popular cinema (see discussion of *Léon Morin, prêtre* in Chapter 3) by virtue of his insouciant insolence, mobile features, humour and physical energy. Melville admired Belmondo's underplaying, a quality he valued above all others in American actors, and compared him to Robert Ryan and Humphrey Bogart.[46] Reggiani, also understated, is equally brilliant as Faugel, but it was Belmondo who appeared on the poster of *Le Doulos* and who dominated the publicity and reception of the film. His fame, youth, good looks and star persona as a charismatic and sympathetic rebel tips the balance between the two protagonists in his favour. They anchor the reading of the film in his version, a version which reveals Silien as the *deus ex machina* of *Le Doulos*, the figure of the film-maker in the film.

Dénouement in the *banlieue*

While the opening credits and first sequence of *Le Doulos* distil urban alienation and construct the abstract noir space in which the story unfolds, the ending sums up the absurdity of a tragedy which engulfs characters who lie *and* die, contradicting the opening quote with its existential choice.[47] The Chinese screen collapses as in the catastrophic ending of *Les Enfants terribles* (initially 'quoted' in a high-angle shot eventually cut – see still). The mirror reflects the ultimate narcissistic vanity of the fatally wounded hoodlum.

In a more conventional film one could see in this ending a classic 'crime does not pay' message. Silien's palatial new home, paid for with ill-gotten gains, will not be lived in. But this would be to ascribe to the film a moral framework which is alien to it. The incursion into *nouveau riche* suburbia, which rhymes with and yet points to the difference from Gilbert's seedy abode at the beginning, hints at a critique of 1960s embourgeoisement or at least a deliberate departure from it. The reference to *The Asphalt Jungle* points in this direction. Where Sterling Hayden's horse symbolised the dream of a return to rural nostalgia, Belmondo's is a status symbol. A further comparison with *Mélodie* is useful here. Gabin and Delon's heist on the Côte d'Azur shows a congruence between their identity and the new leisure and consumer class. Leaving Sarcelles behind, they want the modern good life. Their demise, following the rules of the genre, depends on bad luck (and censorship). They lose the money (notes spectacularly floating on a swimming pool), but neither of them dies. Silien's new home, by contrast, is an existential deathtrap. Whereas Gabin and Delon are moving with the times, Silien and Faugel are figures from an imaginary cinematic past. Their death is a logical conclusion, signalled from the beginning.

Out of an excellent thriller, Melville fashioned a tragic noir tale, stripped of its sociological depth and conventional moral viewpoint, yet resonant with cinematic art in its purest form. As Bernard Dort put it in *France-Observateur*: 'It is less the crime plot which kept me on the edge of my seat than the *pleasure* Melville takes in making cinema.'[48]

AN AUSTERE MALE EPIC: *LE DEUXIÈME SOUFFLE*

As another French Série Noire adaptation, and for Melville, another film noir,[49] *Le Deuxième souffle* constitutes an obvious pair with *Le Doulos*, which is why I move on to it now, leaving *L'Ainé des Ferchaux*, the film made immediately after *Le Doulos*, to Chapter 4. Some time elapsed between *Le Doulos* and *Ferchaux*, during which a first version of *Le Deuxième souffle*, with a different cast, collapsed. Generally the making of the film was difficult, and '1964 to 1966 were years in the wilderness'[50] for Melville. The result, though, was worth it.

'Public enemy' Gu Minda (Lino Ventura) escapes from jail and returns to Paris to his old flame Manouche (Christine Fabrega) and friend Alban (Michel Constantin). He kills two heavies despatched by gangland rival Jo Ricci (Marcel Bozzufi) to threaten Manouche. This, as well as his escape, is noticed by Inspector Blot (Paul Meurisse) who vows to catch Gu. Manouche and Alban hide Gu and engineer his move to Marseille where, through Orloff (Pierre Zimmer), he hooks up with old friend Paul Ricci (Raymond Pellegrin), Jo's brother. Paul and his acolytes Antoine (Denis Manuel) and Pascal (Pierre Grasset), together with Gu, plan and successfully execute the daring hold-up of a convoy carrying platinum, killing two policemen. Gu goes back into hiding, but is arrested by Blot and his men disguised as gangsters, who trick him into revealing Paul's name. Gu and Paul are brutally interrogated by Inspector Fardiano (Paul Frankeur), although Blot is still on the case. Shamed by the realisation that he has been tricked into talking, Gu tries to commit suicide but is taken to hospital in time. He escapes to clear his name, while Jo, Antoine and Pascal want to punish him for betraying Paul. Gu kidnaps and kills Fardiano, having made him confess on paper how he tricked Gu into betraying Paul and how he used torture. At a final show-down, Gu kills Jo, Antoine and Pascal, but is himself mortally wounded. He dies in the arms of Blot, who passes Fardiano's confession to journalists.

With 1.9 million viewers, *Le Deuxième souffle* turned out to be an even bigger box-office hit than *Le Doulos* and *Léon Morin, prêtre*, confirming Melville as one of French cinema's establishment. The film's reception in the mainstream press was positive to ecstatic. Melville was saluted as both a great entertainer and a great artist, his return after a hiatus of three years saluted as his own 'deuxième souffle' (second wind).[51] Despite a few grumbles about the choice of genre, most writers echoed Claude Mauriac in *Le Figaro littéraire*, for whom 'It is one of the best French films in years.'[52] A lot of attention was devoted to the epic length of the film (two hours twenty minutes), unusual at the time – especially for a thriller – and seen as a sign of audacity.

As in the case of *Le Doulos*, the singularity of *Le Deuxième souffle* was constructed by contrast to other French thrillers, to the New Wave and to American cinema. Melville's professionalism was once again favourably contrasted to the amateurishness of the New Wave and to French comic thrillers, Melville's work appearing superior in its seriousness and 'realism'.[53] Two scenes were pinpointed as exemplary: the opening sequence and the hold-up (both discussed below). Comparisons to tragedy were felt to elevate the gangster film to a noble, transcendental level. Samuel Lachize (*L'Humanité*)[54] typifies this view: 'Honour among thieves, the complicity of cops and murderers, all this is purely symbolic. What is at stake is human dignity, nothing else.' The decision by the Censorship Commission to excise the police interrogation scene where water is poured down Paul's throat with a funnel was picked up by many commentators who thereby placed the film within current debates about police atrocities in the wake of the Ben Barka affair, and general suspicion of the repressive role of the police in the late Gaullist regime. Ventura and Meurisse's performances were universally acclaimed, and several reviewers lauded Melville for making a *different* use of these actors compared to mainstream French thrillers.

Amid this positive, high-profile reception, however, *Le Deuxième souffle* also marked the cinephile establishment's definitive break with Melville. To be sure, cracks had begun to appear with *Léon Morin, prêtre*. This time, though, while Gilles Jacob lavishly (and perceptively) praised the film in *Cinéma 66* and *Positif* gave it a considered if ambivalent review (with reserves over its formalism),[55] *Cahiers du cinéma* weighed into Melville as a 'dishonest' and 'calculating' seeker of acclaim. Supreme insult – Melville was a mere *metteur en scène*, not an auteur.[56] This would remain the *Cahiers* line for the rest of Melville's career, indeed until the reassessment of the late 1990s. Thus the moment when Melville's work, by consensus, reached maturity was also the one when his status as an auteur came under violent attack from the leading specialist film journal.

Like *Le Doulos*, *Le Deuxième souffle* needs to be looked at in relation to the successful Série Noire novel on which it was based. If one reviewer deplored the recourse to 'mass consumption literature',[57] the majority agreed that Giovanni was 'one of the great writers of the Série Noire, of which *Le Deuxième souffle* is a glorious archetype. It is therefore right that this great novel, based on painful personal experience, inspired Melville's masterpiece.'[58]

From Giovanni to Melville

Le Deuxième souffle, published by Gallimard in 1958,[59] is the work of novelist and scriptwriter (later film-maker too) José Giovanni. Like Lesou, Le Breton and some other Série Noire writers, Giovanni flaunted his first-hand knowledge of *le milieu* as a guarantee of authenticity. Despite emphatically rejecting the label of realism for his film, at press screenings Melville, as a journalist noted, 'insisted on drawing attention to the fact that the film's action and characters, borrowed from José Giovanni's novel, were real'.[60] Giovanni was in jail during the German Occupation, and his first novel, *Le Trou*, published in 1957, was based on his own abortive attempt to escape.[61] This novel was turned by Jacques Becker into the film *Le Trou* (1960), a critical benchmark for the French thriller and one of the films Melville admired most. For Gilles Jacob, 'There was *Le Trou*, this jewel in the firmament of the French *policier*. And, a few steps behind, *Classe tous risques* [1960, directed by Claude Sautet also from a Giovanni novel]. Today there is *Le Trou* and *Le Deuxième souffle* and, still behind, Sautet's film.'[62] One can see Giovanni's stamp on all three novels, which concern gangs of criminals tightly united against the law, yet haunted by betrayal and failure. This, of course, is the stuff of many thrillers.

Nevertheless *Le Trou* and especially *Classe tous risques* offer illuminating points of comparison with *Le Deuxième souffle*. While *Le Trou* was an avowed model of stylistic sobriety for Melville, *Classe tous risques*, a tale of a weary middle-aged hoodlum on the run, is obviously close to *Le Deuxième souffle*, a similarity enhanced by the appearance of Ventura as the gangster in both cases. Sautet's elegantly classical film-making also shows by contrast the specificity of Melville's own 'classicism', while Becker's minimalism, partly dictated by the prison setting (like Bresson's 1956 *Un condamné à mort s'est échappé*), throws Melville's own into relief since he deploys it on a much broader canvas.

If in 1966 Melville was happy to relate his film to Giovanni's real gangsters, in 1971 he was telling Nogueira: 'I retained what was Melvillian from the book, and threw everything else out. [...] I pride myself on having made a completely original work.'[63] Predictably, Giovanni took a different view: 'You have read the book, you have seen the film. You can't say there is invention in the situations.'[64] As in the case of *Le Doulos*, the closeness of film to book is striking in terms of events, characters, names and dialogue, including the virtuoso speech by Inspector Blot at the beginning of the film and Gu's lengthy outburst when arrested by Blot's men. Yet Melville did make changes, primarily structural. Giovanni's book moves from Paris in the first two chapters to Marseille for the rest of the story. Melville found these two parts not sufficiently integrated and 'brought Orloff in at the beginning of the film (in the novel he made his first appearance on page 104), so as to dovetail the Marseille story with the Paris story, one within the other'.[65] The first half of the film thus alternates between Paris and Marseille, with intertitles indicating location, date and time to avoid confusion (this explains why once the film has fully moved to Marseille, the intertitles stop even though the rest of the story unfolds over several days). This structural change is not, however, as significant as Melville suggests, as it only actualises what is expressed in the book through verbal references, memories and flashbacks.

Nevertheless, a comparison between book and film, as well as the unpublished script, again illuminates the 'Melvillisation' of the material. This concerns background paring down and the portrayal of the central character. Giovanni surrounds Gu with a host of picturesque details about the Paris and Marseille underworld and police: one of Blot's assistants is a relentless womaniser; Orloff's mother runs a brothel; the Corsican presence in the underworld is more explicitly sketched in;[66] Venture (Paul) has comic interaction with his wife; Gu escapes from the prison hospital with two men rather than on his own, etc. More characters are involved and they are located geographically and ethnically: Italian, Corsican, Greek (only one small trace remains of this in a remark about Gu as a 'wop'). Giovanni's reference to the Algerian origin of the convoy loot is absent from the film. Apart from the necessary simplification typical of all literary adaptations, this stripping bare of the narrative makes the story less socially grounded, more timeless, more tragic and thus more exportable. But the paring down also affects *mise en scène*, right from the opening scene.

After a pre-credit disclaimer and quote (see Filmography for details), *Le Deuxième souffle* opens with three men's escape from jail in the dark. They jump over a wall, one falls (to his death), the other sits atop the wall and helps the last one up (the scrambling

Ventura). The two men flee, cross a wood and board a moving goods train, Ventura again with some difficulty. Giovanni makes this scene a relatively long (eight-page) exposition explaining the death of the third accomplice, Gu's fear as he climbs the wall and his gratitude for his friend's help. The script reduces the scene in length but retains a little dialogue.[67] The film plays the entire scene without dialogue, with only ambiant noises on the soundtrack. Like Bresson in *Un condamné à mort s'est échappé* and Becker in *Le Trou*, Melville puts the accent on the materiality of these noises: bodies scraping against a wall, a dog barking in the distance, running feet, twigs breaking under foot. The absence of dialogue and music underlines Gu's solitude, especially as the escapers run through a desolate wintry forest. The scene is lengthened to allow for the superimposition of the credits, but also to introduce the man-on-the-run theme. The length of the sequence and the silence also make the train more conspicuous. As it chugs along with the breathless Gu clumsily hauling himself on board, it symbolises the story getting under way. Unlike the book, which then has Gu encounter other men and police in a village bar, Melville cuts directly from Gu catching his breath in the dark, empty train wagon to Paul Ricci's luxury night-club. The contrast underlines the distance between the two worlds Gu will try to cross, while a more subtle graphic link is established by the play on cigarettes: we shift from Gu removing a crooked (and unsmoked) cigarette from his mouth to a woman smoking in the club, relayed by female dancers using huge cigarette holders as props. As we shall see, the cigarette thread continues to the end, especially linking Gu and Blot. Melville's simultaneous temporal expansion and paring-down process in evidence in this opening reaches its apotheosis in the hold-up sequence (examined later), and constitutes a key Melvillian stylistic device.

The other significant change to the book relates to Gu. In 1970, Melville told *Télérama* that 'The novel featured a bald 50-year-old man. I had to rewrite the script, the dialogues and the story itself to transform the hero into a solid 40-year-old like Lino Ventura.'[68] If Melville broadly exaggerates the difference with Giovanni's book, the greatest change is the inflection given to the hero's masculinity. Giovanni's Gu is repeatedly described as old and fragile, scarred by life and jail, like Faugel in *Le Doulos*; in this respect the initial casting of Serge Reggiani as Gu made sense. Gu's transformation into a world-weary but more robust individual fits Ventura's physique and star persona, to which I return later. Where Giovanni's protagonist is weak and pathetic, Ventura's Gu is heavy, vulnerable and tragic. A brief example will illustrate this point. Before leaving for Marseille, Gu is driven to Jo Ricci's bar by Alban. His intention is to kill Jo, but at the last minute he 'doesn't feel right' and decides against it. He returns to his hide-out and throws himself on the bed. The scene in the novel is told through Gu's inner thoughts and utterances which clearly reveal first fear and then relief, accompanied by self-disparaging remarks such as 'I'm getting old'.[69] The scene as filmed gives a sense of Gu's anxiety, even despair, but Ventura's powerful physique and concentration in the car, and importantly the virtual absence of dialogue, intimate a difficult but thought-out decision – he 'knows' instinctively what the spectator has been shown, that the police have set a trap. *Mise en scène*, script and Ventura's performance construct a professional who wisely calculates risks rather than, as in the book, a has-been who has lost his nerve. The stripping bare of Giovanni's book also informs Gu's relationship with Manouche and the presence of other women. Though Giovanni uses familiar Série Noire stereotypes – the resigned but loyal gangster moll, the madame, the flighty young things – women are a source of sexual interest and energy, including Manouche for Gu (and later Orloff). This sexual energy is conspicuously absent from male–female relations in the film.

The austere beauty of *Le Deuxième souffle*

The austere black-and-white photography of *Le Deuxième souffle* is an aesthetic statement in itself. In the five years since *Le Doulos*, the proportion of colour films had steadily risen and in 1966 more than two-thirds of French films were in colour, including many on wide screen (as was *L'Ainé des Ferchaux* in 1963). *Le Deuxième souffle* is a large-scale film in which the almost anachronistic use of black and white is not determined, as it is in the contemporary Resistance epic *Paris brûle-t-il?*, by the wish to create a 'historical' look. In contrast to the more systematically expressionistic *Le Doulos*, the harsh greys of *Le Deuxième souffle* and extensive location shooting relate more to television aesthetics (director of photography Marcel Combes, a relative newcomer, also worked in television) than to Hollywood thrillers. Although a few scenes use contrasting noir lighting, notably the interrogation scenes in Fardiano's office, and in outdoor scenes sunshine appears on one or two very brief occasions, the overall mood is that of a bleak, grey, wintry film, yet one on a majestic scale.

Compared to *Bob* and *Deux hommes dans Manhattan*, location shots in *Le Deuxième souffle* are not poetic statements about city streets, nor the realist bustle and clutter of Sautet's *Classe tous risques*, but bleak depictions of Paris and Marseille and unglamorous places in between, as seen when Gu, looking like a nondescript rep, makes his long cross-country journey on a succession of country buses. Even when using locations, Melville subjects them to a process of abstraction. This is true of the mountain setting for the heist (discussed below); contrast also Gu's escapes with those of Abel Davos (Ventura) in *Classe tous risques*. Gu's escapes and lengthy bus ride from Paris to Marseille are solitary, wordless, bleakly shot. Abel's similar adventures take place in busy railway stations, post offices teeming with life and picturesque characters – in several scenes Abel is accompanied by his two young children, and his journey from the South to Paris takes place in an ambulance driven by a young man (Belmondo) whom he befriends. As in *Le Trou* and *Un condamné à mort s'est échappé*, sparse music in *Le Deuxième souffle*, reinforcing the materiality of noises and objects, highlights Gu's solitude and alienation. Even banal situations are imbued with doom-laden significance, such as Gu and Manouche's candle-lit dinner.

Le Deuxième souffle contrasts a bleak French quotidianness with the gangsters' luxury world: big American cars and plush bars and night-clubs off the Champs-Elysées. Paul's night-club fuses French bourgeois taste (crystal wall lights, rococo furniture) with 'American bar', small jazz orchestra and a central dance space occupied by Blue-Bell-style chorus girls. Jo's bar offers a similar combination on a smaller scale, with a jazz score, orientalist prints and hostesses at the American bar (by contrast Sautet's gangsters in *Classe tous risques* meet in ordinary cafés). Thus, although the narrative opposes the two Ricci brothers ('good' Paul and 'bad' Jo), *mise en scène* brings them together. Gu, on the other

Le Deuxième souffle: Gu (Lino Ventura) in anonymous disguise during his flight to Marseille

hand, inhabits another kind of space altogether which is gradually stripped down and in which he is seen in solitary confinement: from the banal Montrouge room to the bare house outside Marseille and finally the shoot-out apartment with sash windows, peeling walls and minimal furnishing – the perfect abstract Melvillian gangster setting for the hero's final scene and death. Alban's ironic remark on taking Gu to the Montrouge hide-out, a laconic 'Your kingdom for a while', turns out to be true of the rest of the film. *Mise en scène* also underlines Manouche's spatial otherness to Gu in contradiction to their overt closeness in the narrative. Although she acts as go-between, ultimately Manouche belongs to the plush night-club and bourgeois salon. This is graphically illustrated by Gu's first arrival in her home: clad in the macho leather jacket and beret of the Resistance fighter, Gu crawls on Manouche's Persian rug next to an antique piece of furniture, emphasising his incongruity in her space. Later, as Gu is hiding after the heist, editing contrasts his space (sparse house, bleak wintry streets) and hers (rococo bed and fur rug). When she leaves the Marseille house, a shot is held to show her empty chair and Gu's loneliness.

These disparate spatial elements are held together by Melville's uncluttered *mise en scène* (even in the luxury night-club) and tight editing which nevertheless makes room for virtuoso camerawork and extended set pieces such as the robbery. Where *Le Doulos* boasts the eight-minute police interrogation, *Le Deuxième souffle* offers Inspector Blot's harangue in Manouche's club after Jacques' killing, shot in a breathtaking *plan-séquence* of just under five minutes. The scene displays Melville's dazzling though *discreet* virtuosity with camera movements, choreographed to serve Paul Meurisse's *tour-de-force* monologue in his characteristically sardonic voice. Other long takes occur in *Le Deuxième souffle*, frequently around Blot/Meurisse in verbal flow (for instance, with Jo Ricci or with his assistants). By contrast, scenes like the bullion robbery and the 'casing' of the Marseille flat are masterpieces of Melvillian economy and sobriety.

A Western in the Marseille hinterland

Melville claimed that 'a passage from the book which lasts two pages – the attack of the convoy – I treated in 20 minutes, and I went in for the description of action in a big way'.[70] In actual fact the six (not two) pages the book devotes to the robbery contain all its basic elements, including the fact that 'the wild and arid landscape evoked the western'.[71] Yet Melville is also right: he turned Giovanni's functional highway robbery into a suspenseful action sequence as well as a *mise en abyme* of the film's most important themes.

Gu, Paul, Antoine and Pascal meet at Paul's house. Tension builds up on the soundtrack with a sparse, low-key jazz beat. Paul, Gu and Pascal exchange a white car for a black Mercedes, while Antoine drives the estate car which will be used to carry the loot back. The men are on their way to ambush a convoy conveying a load of platinum on a desolate road in the arid mountains of the Marseille hinterland – and kill the two-man police motorcycle escort. As Gu, Paul and Pascal climb out of the Mercedes at the top of a hill, their three dark silhouettes, clad in identical hats and overcoats, stand out on the edge of an immense grey and white landscape of clouds, rocky hillside and winding roads. When the heist is completed, the four men, reunited, stand on the edge of a cliff over which the empty van has been toppled. Still in overcoats but now hatless, their black silhouettes again detach themselves against the vast grey landscape. This powerful image was reprised on the film's poster. The sequence lasts twenty minutes overall. Throughout we bite our nails with the four men as they wait for the convoy, execute the policemen, neutralise the guards and an unexpected passer-by (editing becomes very

Le Deuxième souffle: figures in a landscape. The bullion robbery as a 'Western' in the Marseille hinterland (right and opposite)

rapid at this point), load the platinum, stash it away and safely return home. Yet beyond the taut and impeccably timed action, the dominant impression, condensed by the shots of the men on the edge of the abyss, is one of anxiety and solitude.

The heist, as usual, marks both the apotheosis of the gangsters' skills and solidarity, and the beginning of their demise. Antoine kills the first policeman from a distance with his rifle, deliberately removing the telescopic sight as the extreme test of his technique, while Gu guns down the second with a hand-gun from the fast-moving Mercedes. For Melville, this is 'the celebration of a masterpiece executed by two old world craftsmen'.[72] The robbery indeed demonstrates the men's cool control, professional skills and solidarity (Gu to Antoine: 'The two policemen, it was us and nobody else'). The rules of the genre dictate that the heist cannot ultimately be successful, but the failure here is also internally determined. It is Gu's decision to use the same gun (and later show himself in the streets of Marseille) which provokes the downfall and rapid disintegration of the group. As they wait for the convoy to appear, Paul looks down at ants rushing among the stones. There could hardly be a clearer image of the futility of men's action. The camera leaves Paul and tracks along a long metal barrier on the edge of a precipice to the anxious, expectant Gu. At this point the jazz beat rises audibly. The railing and camera movement link the two men but also underline the distance between them, anticipating their imminent separation. The spectacular landscape – as we have noted, a tribute to the Western – dwarfs the men; its barrenness is accentuated further by wind and sparse music. Even with the sea in the background, grey skies and rain eliminate any picturesqueness. While the robbery is the high point of solidarity in the film, every aspect of *mise en scène* dramatises on an epic scale man's essential loneliness.

Casing the joint

Although on occasions Melville delights in virtuoso camerawork to showcase theatrical actors, it is his economy, the unflinching look at the slow process of action in what seems like real time (but of course is not), the suspenseful *temps morts*, that have come to dominate the perception of his style. Writing on *Le Samouraï*, Colin McArthur coins the phrase 'cinema of process', arguing that Melville's film-making goes 'some way to honouring the integrity of actions by allowing them to happen in a way significantly closer to "real" time than was formerly the case in fictive, particularly Hollywood, cinema'.[73] Although I do not entirely adhere to McArthur's reading in terms of 'real time', the attention to detail is, as he says, particularly in evidence in Orloff and Antoine's 'casing' of the room in Marseille. In complete silence, Orloff examines the room in detail and hides a gun on top of a wardrobe, practising how to retrieve it; later Antoine retraces Orloff's steps, finds the gun and removes it. However, when Orloff later confronts Antoine, he suddenly brings another gun out of his coat. Thus, as McArthur says, Melville here 'raises the valency of the process, by locating it within the intensely professional *amour propre* of the characters'.[74] As McArthur also points out, this feature is close to that found in Becker's *Le Trou* and in Dassin's *Rififi*, which both include extended scenes of silent observation of men involved in skilled and concentrated action. In *Le Deuxième souffle*, compared to Giovanni's account, Melville's delight in pure *mise en scène* is even more apparent. In the novel the element of surprise is provided by Orloff simply bringing a partner (Theo). Melville replaces a plausible trick with cerebral empathy (Antoine guesses what Orloff has done; Orloff in turn guesses that Antoine had guessed) and pure *mise en scène*. We see, twice, Antoine and Orloff examining the room in what is ultimately a *temps mort*, since it does not advance the plot (Gu's scene later in the same room is, however, very close to the novel). Orloff, then Antoine, set the stage for Gu's final confrontation in a barren yet culturally charged room. As in Gilbert's house in *Le Doulos* we are in Franco-American territory (old furniture, sash windows), an abstract space in which the men appear as sharp generic silhouettes – Antoine and Orloff in similar coats and hats, Gu in trench-coat. The 'cinema of process' is a formal feature, a delight in cinema for its own sake. But in celebrating the cool, cerebral and 'tragic' masculinity of Melville's heroes, it is also an ideological one.

Gu the 'tragic gangster'

Loyalty and betrayal may be the staple of the gangster genre, but *Le Deuxième souffle* pushes them to extremes. In fact, as Melville says, it is a film about betrayal rather than friendship[75] (as in many ways was *Le Doulos*). The last third of the film, from Gu's arrest, shows him struggling to 'clear his name' from the taint of having betrayed Paul (an accidental betrayal engineered by Blot and relayed through the press by Fardiano). Fury and shame lead him to escape, kill Fardiano and later Pascal, Antoine and Jo, and finally to die himself from Antoine and Blot's assistant's bullets. Strictly in plot terms, it is the fact that he used the same gun twice that sent Blot on his trail and therefore that of his accomplices. Yet this basic professional error which, as Melville says, 'needlessly sacrifices Paul, Antoine and Pascal',[76] is oddly never mentioned by Gu, and it appears to be of no importance compared to the betrayal which everyone knows to be false. This excessive development therefore signals a different symbolic economy to that of the classic breaking of the gangsters' code of honour.

To begin with, in couching the fault in terms of *speaking*, the film pinpoints the gangster's identity as bound up with silence. Gu's reunion with Alban and Manouche at the beginning of the film stresses silence: 'Don't pronounce my name!' His emotional reunion with Paul is also virtually silent. When he meets Jo, Antoine and Pascal in the final scene, his main concern is that they believe *his word*. Ventura's star persona is key here, characterised by a self-contained, physical and silent masculinity. Ventura started out as Gabin's rival Angelo in *Touchez pas au grisbi* and from then on settled into a succession of tough-guy roles, interchangeably policeman or criminal. Ventura's masculinity typically expresses itself as a *potential* (the heavily muscular physique, a legacy of his past as a wrestler, encased in sharp suits) which erupts as with Gabin,[77] his mentor and model, in rare 'explosions' of pent-up verbal and/or physical violence. In *Le Deuxième souffle* these occur when Gu is tricked by Blot and Fardiano; in *Classe tous risques* when he discovers the extent of his former friends' betrayal. These explosions, as for Gabin, underline the silence which normally prevails (a 1972 Ventura vehicle was called *Le Silencieux*).[78] The economy of Ventura's performing style enabled him to embody more or less the same character in comic mode, for instance in *La Métamorphose des cloportes*, or spy adventure, like the film that made him a major star, *Le Gorille vous salue bien* (1958), also based on a Série Noire book. Basically, again as for Gabin, minimalism, silence and popular origins act as a guarantee of authenticity and integrity, channelling spectatorial sympathy towards a character who in *Le Deuxième souffle* as in *Classe tous risques* is a ruthless killer on the run.

In narrative terms, Gu belongs to the world of the gangsters: Alban, Manouche, Paul, Orloff. By the same token, he and Blot are polar opposites. Archetypes of crime and the law, they are embodied by dramatically different actors: silent, physical and 'working-class' Ventura vs eloquent, mannered and 'bourgeois' Meurisse. Gu and Blot are also often filmed differently – talkative Blot in fluid *plan-séquence*, Gu in classic shot counter-shot for exchanges of glances or rapid action editing. Yet, as the most perceptive analyses of *Le Deuxième souffle* (by Gilles Jacob and Olivier Bohler, not to mention Melville himself[79]) have pointed out, there is a strong 'underground' bond between Gu and Blot, visually signalled by the same bent cigarette held by Gu at the beginning of the film and Blot at the end. This point can be taken further. Blot and Gu exist above the rest of their respective clans in which they both have an 'inferior' double: Fardiano for Blot and Paul for Gu. Hence, while Blot arrests Gu through a brilliant Machiavellian device, Fardiano brutally tortures Paul. Blot and Gu emerge as superior, solitary characters, masters of their own fate, figures of the director-in-the-film: Blot as arch-manipulator and Gu as focalising instance. Their symbolic equivalence, signalled by the cigarette, is confirmed by their common (if distant) relationship to Manouche (it is perhaps to preserve this symmetrical structure that Melville deleted the budding Manouche–Orloff relationship from the book). The subterranean Blot–Gu axis explains why the extensive structure of loyalty and support on Gu's side crumbles so rapidly, whether it is Manouche's efforts (ignored), Gu and Antoine's bonding during the heist (instantly forgotten) or Orloff's plan to negotiate on Gu's behalf (knocked on the head).

In this light Gu's death-driven obsession to clear his name can be reread as his unconscious desire to reach Blot, in whose arms he dies. The second pre-credit text tells the viewer: 'At birth, man is given only one right: the choice of his death. But if this choice is dictated by a disgust for life, then his existence will have been pure derision.' *Le Deuxième souffle*, more than any other Melville film at that point in his career, gets close to the notion of 'disgust for life'. Like Faugel, Gu emerges from jail a washed-out character; unlike Bob he is no 'living legend'. His efforts to assert himself end in shame and multiple deaths. Yet his wilful if desperate decision to take charge of his own fate places him within an existentialist perspective: Gu refuses 'bad faith'. He says to Manouche: 'In any case I will not return there [jail]'; 'I played. I lost'. After the heist, he tears off the calendar page for 31 December and stares calmly at the blank page beneath. When he decides to take Orloff's place to deal with Jo, Antoine and Pascal, he shaves off his moustache, which he 'no longer needs', staring at himself in the mirror. When arrested and humiliated by Fardiano, he chooses his own death, trying to slash his wrists by smashing through a window.

But Gu's 'existentialism' is a deeply pessimistic one. He struggles against greater forces – chanelled through Blot, his nemesis as well as alter ego – which annul his efforts, extinguish his 'second wind'. Importantly he also struggles against himself, hence his rage. In *Classe tous risques* Abel is betrayed by his friends; in *Le Deuxième souffle* he betrays himself, a 'fault' which makes him a 'tragic' character. There is a long tradition which sees the gangster as a 'tragic hero', to use Robert Warshow's phrase, a tradition imbued in the French context with a high literary pedigree. André Malraux's 1949 preface to William Faulkner's *Sanctuary* argued that the thriller plot was a mere excuse for 'translating most efficiently an ethical or poetic fact in all its intensity' and that a unique fate was behind all characters, concluding, in a much-quoted phrase, that '*Sanctuary* was the intrusion of Greek tragedy in the thriller novel'.[80] For Warshow the gangster film was 'a consistent and astonishingly complete presentation of the modern sense of tragedy'.[81] Although there were dissenting voices (the Série Noire writer Alphonse Boudard, for instance, railed against 'this mythology of the underworld' and Melville for wanting 'to remake the Atrides among criminals'[82]), many writers, film-makers and critics have since espoused these views, for instance Costa Gavras: 'The policier film is a form of modern tragedy. It is the genre which allows us to say the most about man and his environment.'[83] For Warshow the tragic aspect of the gangster was that he resolved, through his death, the impossible contradiction, inherent in the 'American dream', between success and failure. Despite differences between the American gangster film of the 1930s and 40s that Warshow addresses, Faulkner's *Sanctuary* and Melville's films, impossible contradictions may be seen as informing Gu – between success and failure, solidarity and solitude, life-affirming effort and death-driven stasis – contradictions that are interestingly gendered.

Melville's first melancholy gangster

From the moment Gu laboriously heaves himself onto the train, his vulnerability is emphasised. Although Gu's weakness, compared to Giovanni's book, is significantly modified by Ventura, Gu's trajectory is still a poignant – and doomed – attempt to re-establish his potency. This is achieved on the one hand through the high-risk, 'noble' gestures of the heist, the only moment when Gu bonds with other men. And on the other hand it is achieved through a gradual process of detachment from others to affirm his lack of 'need'. Gu's solitude is constantly underlined by the camera. Unlike in *Bob* there is no warm community in the cafés of Montmartre; compared to *Deux hommes*, *Le Doulos* and *Ferchaux*, there are no close male friendships. The empathy with Blot remains hidden, unlike Bob's friendship with Inspector Ledru. This distance from *Bob* and the 1950s thrillers is evoked by the scene in which Gu eats a solitary meal of paté on New Year's Eve, a tribute to *Touchez pas au grisbi*, in which Jean Gabin and René Dary eat a similar meal, but together. If Gu cuts himself off from male communities, he especially distances himself from women. Manouche's sensible offers of salvation are systematically rejected and femininity relentlessly distanced.

The marginalisation of women in *Le Deuxième souffle* takes obvious narrative forms. The only woman with a speaking part, Manouche, overtly the gangster's mistress, is an idealised, benevolent figure, and Fabrega's clothes and demeanour are smart in a middle-aged, motherly way (the earlier casting of the more mature, more powerful but less conventionally pretty Simone Signoret would have reinforced this point). Like Faugel vis-à-vis Thérèse in *Le Doulos*, Gu cannot bear to depend on Manouche. Her offers of money are contemptuously rejected (as they were, we learn, ten years earlier), her plans for his trip to Marseille discarded and her advice against the heist ignored. When Gu is within her sphere of action he is symbolically emasculated, frequently seen lying in bed in the Montrouge room, or crouching by the fire in the Marseille house. Though a sexual relationship is implied when Manouche comes to dinner in Montrouge, contrary to the book, it has no reviving effect on Gu. The a-sexuality of their relationship is underlined by the way he calls her 'sister', gangster-speak for his woman. Melville claims he kept the form of address to emphasise her ambiguous status, 'because of the *Enfants terribles* part of me – or rather because of [...] *Pierre or the Ambiguities*'.[84] But Gu and Manouche are hardly an ambivalent brother–sister pair like *Les Enfants terribles*, nor an incestuous mother–son pair, as in Herman Melville's *Pierre*. More significant in fact is his systematic distancing from the feminine, echoed by the way *mise en scène* literally and metaphorically 'frames' women.

After Gu's escape from jail, we first encounter women in Paul Ricci's club where, after a brief glimpse of male and female customers smoking, the frame is filled with female dancers in tights and high heels, formal bouffant hairstyles and unusually long cigarette holders. As the camera tracks to follow Paul, the dancers' legs are self-consciously reflected in a series of gilded mirrors which, over the black walls, evoke small cinema screens. Later, as Paul and his informer talk at the bar, women dancers are again reflected in mirrors that line the back of the bar, between them (our first vision of Manouche at home is also in a mirror).

Bob, *Deux hommes*, *Ferchaux* and *Le Doulos* partake of the generic marginalisation of women and in some cases exhibit vicious violence against them. *Le Deuxième souffle* moves into a different register, where the male hero cuts himself off not just from women, but from sexuality, anticipating Melville's later thrillers (see Chapter 6). For Melville, 'the romantic hero, even if he is a gangster, is a solitary rider who has no sexual needs.'[85] Melville's off-the-cuff definition fits within psychoanalytical accounts of melancholy. For Freud, and later Kristeva, melancholy, triggered off by unresolved 'mourning' for the deep unconscious loss of the mother, is characterised, beyond the well-known signs of sadness and withdrawal (and in extreme cases suicidal self-aggression), by a loss of libido.[86]

In *Le Deuxième souffle*, this melancholy withdrawal is not, however, accompanied, as in *Le Doulos* and even more so the Delon trilogy, by the narcissism that is also part of the condition. As Melville said, 'Gu in *Le Deuxième souffle* wore a hat, but I did not show how he put it on'[87] (actually he does, but briefly). Gangsters and policemen are still smart dressers in *Le Deuxième souffle* and Antoine dies against a mirror, his hat rolling onto the floor, as in the end of *Le Doulos*. Blot cuts a bit of a dandy figure and gazes at a men's shirt shop as he comes out of Jo Ricci's. But Gu's first appearance in leather jacket and beret alludes to the Resistance and Ventura's looks construct a rougher figure, more anchored in the French quotidian. And on the whole Paul, Orloff and Blot look more like French bourgeois businessmen in their long overcoats and hats than iconic Hollywood gangsters. *Le Deuxième souffle* in this respect is a transitional film, between the nostalgic vision of 1940s Hollywood gangsters and the narcissistic glamour of Delon in the last trilogy.

Bourgeois gangsters, corrupt police

Despite *Le Deuxième souffle*'s greater realism, to claim it as social commentary would be excessive. Yet in one respect, the depiction of a particularly brutal and corrupt police, it was sufficiently near the bone to attract censorship. On 18 October 1966 the film was screened to the Censorship Commission which awarded it an 18 certificate, 'in view of the excessive violence and pernicious nature of this film, which makes it a particularly dangerous spectacle for young people under 18'. Although Melville claimed later that he was not censored,[88] censorship archives record that the Commission demanded 'the complete excision of the interrogation scene with the funnel; any image of the latter must be removed. This is not normal practice in the French police.' Melville agreed to remove the scene and the film was awarded a general certificate on 28 October and released on 2 November.[89] The 'funnel scene' was widely related in the press to the behaviour of the French police under the German Occupation and the French army in Algeria – as presumably Giovanni intended in 1958 (though ironically doubt has since been cast on his own past during the Occupation).[90] By the time the film came out, it also evoked a

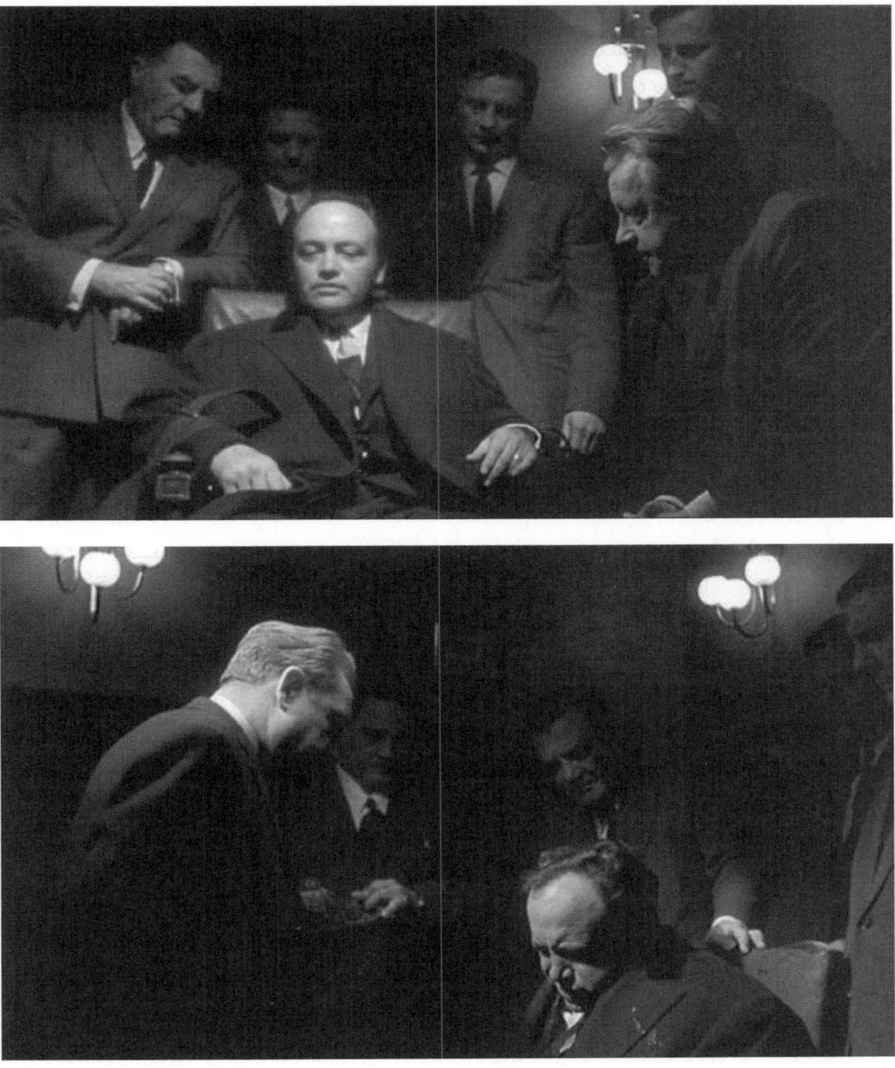

Le Deuxième souffle: Paul Ricci (Raymond Pellegrin) is interrogated by Fardiano (Paul Frankeur) and his men, by having water forced down his throat. The scene missing between these two frames was removed by censorship as evoking interrogating practices too close to the torture method used by the French army during the Algerian war

recent scandal. In late 1965 Mehdi Ben Barka, the Moroccan opposition leader in exile, was arrested, tortured and assassinated by the Moroccan secret police, with complicity from the French police.[91] Samuel Lachize, in *L'Humanité*, summed up ironically: 'Nobody ever gets beaten in French police stations [. . .] Yet this story of gangsters and policemen, complicit in their hatred, seems to us almost pallid compared with what we know was suppressed during the Ben Barka trial.'[92] Claude Mauriac, reviewer for *Le Figaro littéraire*, saw the scene before it was cut and reported that it was 'Terrible. Plausible.'[93] As Michel Duran pointed out in *Le Canard enchaîné*, the removal of the scene meant that Fardiano's forced confession about his interrogation methods made little sense.[94] Enough, however, remains – we see Paul dragged by Fardiano's men, dishevelled and with his clothes soiled – to impart a sense of police brutality. Despite the pre-credit text which informs us that 'The author of this film does not intend to equate Gu Minda's "morals" with Morals', by indicting police viciousness and corruption, Melville slants the film towards Gu. So that when Fardiano berates Gu about the children of the dead policemen, his point has little weight since he is the most discredited character in the film. In this way too, Gu appears as a 'tragic' figure.

TRANSNATIONAL AESTHETICS IN MELVILLE'S SÉRIE NOIRE FILMS

The 1960s in French cinema was a period of crisis, which saw a sharp decline in audiences after the peak of the late 1950s. Melville's films were part of a popular French cinema that was fighting Hollywood (in industry terms, rather than in the ideological terms of the 1950s, as discussed in Chapter 4), yet they were also (and were perceived as) very much within the orbit of American cinema. *Le Doulos* and *Le Deuxième souffle* thus lead us back to our project to locate Melville's work within a transnational history of the cinema.

Several writers, commenting on Melville, have emphasised the difference between French and American thrillers in terms of the greater narrative ambiguity of French films. As *Libération* noted, *Le Doulos* 'was constructed like a very good American thriller. However [. . .] the Americans would never have risked showing us such ambiguous characters. Theirs are always perfectly defined.'[95] 'Ambiguity' here refers to two things. One is a blurring of good and evil, of law and lawlessness. In *Le Doulos* this hinges most prominently around the figure of the informer, Silien. In both *Le Doulos* and *Le Deuxième souffle* closeness is shown or implied between top gangster and top policeman, and both films abundantly display police use of criminal methods (Clain, Blot, Fardiano). This moral blurring means that the French gangsters, unlike their Hollywood equivalent, are not offered a redemptive trajectory. This then explains why both Faugel and Silien must die, and why Gu is fatally shot by both Antoine and the police.

But 'ambiguity' also refers to a more general sense of leaving things implied, unsaid. For instance, in *Le Deuxième souffle* the character of Orloff is barely sketched in, and the relationship between Gu and Manouche, not to mention Blot and Manouche, remains mysterious; an American equivalent would provide a more explicit 'backstory'. This phenomenon is not confined to Melville and can be observed clearly in Hollywood remakes of French films (see Neil Jordan's 'remake' of *Bob* in the previous chapter).

Censorship plays a role in this difference. Despite incurring regular press criticism at least until the late 1960s, in the middle of the decade the *policier* was at the height of its popularity and rarely attracted censorship (the 'funnel scene' of *Le Deuxième souffle*, which 'realistically' targets police and army torture, is an exception, which explains why it was cut). As noted in the previous chapter, the moral blurring of French post-war crime novels and films can be seen both in a long literary history and in relation to the German Occupation, during which members of the underground were recruited by both German and French police. But two further aspects must also be mentioned which place Melville's 1960s films in a wider transnational cultural history.

Even more than in Melville's earlier crime films, *Le Doulos* and *Le Deuxième souffle* adopt the features of American literature's 'behaviourist' approach discussed by Claude-Edmonde Magny, seen in both avant-garde writers such as Faulkner and crime literature, while stripping the stories of most of their social content. Melville's minimalist style, which refrains from explanation or sociological justification, is a perfect match for these formal concerns. *Le Doulos* and *Le Deuxième souffle* also mobilise features of the American cinema of the 1930s and 40s which Melville admired, a cinema which was more classical than the literary experiments celebrated by Magny. At the same time that he was oriented towards the Hollywood past, Melville's increased abstraction in *Le Doulos* and *Le Deuxième souffle* chimes with developments in French high culture. While there appears to be no direct involvement with these art forms, Melville's increasingly pared-down *mise en scène* evokes that of the 'new theatre' (Beckett in particular), while his detached description of characters' behaviour and objects, as well as the attention he draws to the very materiality of his own art form, recalls the Nouveau Roman and new criticism. Like Roland Barthes in *Mythologies* and Georges Perec in *Les Choses*, Melville knew how to combine an avant-garde approach with seductive cultural forms (while commenting on them), including American cinema.

Melville's tribute to American cinema, while it undoubtedly contributed to the popular appeal of his films, was frequently criticised. Director Jean-Pierre Mocky said: 'I am not Melville; I do not watch *Odds Against Tomorrow* hundreds of times; I am not anaesthetised to the point of remaking entire scenes from American movies.'[96] Melville himself contributed to such reductive visions of his work. For instance, he said that the bar in *Le Doulos* 'bears no resemblance to a French café'.[97] What he does not say is that it is typical of the 'American bars' that flourished in areas of Paris such as the Left Bank and Montmartre, where jazz was typically played. Thus, in the first instance, his films bear witness to an international culture in France especially well established in the well-to-do milieux of art, spectacle and crime and the new bourgeoisie.

Second, in *Le Doulos* and *Le Deuxième souffle* Melville adopts several strategies that undermine any crude attempt at separating the 'French' from the 'American'. There *are* quotes, such as Cain's office in *Le Doulos*, from *City Streets* (though close comparison shows differences too). More widespread are spatial juxtapositions, for instance the Anglo-American features (such as sash windows) of Gilbert's house next to the Parisian *zone* in *Le Doulos*, and of the 'shoot-out room' of *Le Deuxième souffle* with the Marseille street. Such juxtapositions emphasise the harmonious contiguity of the spaces as much as their heterogeneity. Another spatial juxtaposition is that of the iconic Hollywood gangster in the 'French' space, as already discussed. More frequently there is hybridisation within the same space, notably in the night-clubs: the Cotton Club in *Le Doulos* and Paul's place in *Le Deuxième souffle*. The internationalism of these spaces acts as a *mise en abyme* of the films in their condensation of international social and cultural factors – jazz, crime, tourism – which, like jazz (and Série Noire literature), helped the post-war new bourgeoisie forge a sense of identity in strong contrast to the old nineteenth-century bourgeois values.[98]

Yet this transnational cinema in the 1960s still retained strong national flavours. For example, in Germany the highly popular (German) Edgar Wallace crime series of that decade mobilised, as Tim Bergfelder shows, a fantasy vision of Britishness located in Britain. By contrast *Le Doulos* and *Le Deuxième souffle* (like the vast majority of French crime production) are located in France. Even though we are no longer in the 'village' Paris of *Bob*, Melville's international fantasy is not 'extraterritorial' as in the Edgar Wallace films. Instead, it is 'reterritorialised', re-appropriated through location, dialogue and stars with strong national identities. Their performance styles suited Melville's increasingly minimalist style, while they reintroduced a human dimension in characters depicted with increasing abstraction and detachment. But one feature shared with the German Edgar Wallace films is the nostalgic aspect of the transnational vision: Edwardian English crime literature there, 1930s and 40s America here. This temporal 'delay', reinforced by the Série Noire, is one reason why Melville was making 'classic' noir gangster stories in the 1960s, at a time when the American genre had moved on to psychological thrillers or Cold War spy stories. It is also explains why Faugel in *Le Doulos* and Gu in *Le Deuxième souffle* are figures from the past, whose exploits are located before the war. Their pre-war heyday is also that of a certain tendency in Hollywood cinema which Melville recreates with his post-war French sensitivity.

Le Deuxième souffle was, in box-office terms, Melville's greatest success to that point. In this film, as well as in *Le Doulos*, he succeeded in channelling a remarkably bleak vision of male 'tragedy' and of the futility of human endeavour through the appealing features of popular cinema and transnational aesthetics. That he could do so was due to the high currency in the mid-1960s of, in equal parts, himself (since *Léon Morin, prêtre*), his stars (Belmondo, Ventura) and the Série Noire. Over these two films, this synergy produced a extraordinary blend of brilliantly economical noir *mise en scène*, pessimistic philosophy and masculinist fantasy which would find its apotheosis in his next thriller, *Le Samouraï*.

NOTES

1. *Les Cahiers de la cinémathèque*, no. 25, Spring–Summer 1978, p. 94.
2. François Guérif and Stéphane Levy-Klein, ibid., p. 75
3. See Michel Marie, *The French New Wave, an Artistic School* (Oxford: Blackwell, 2003); Richard J. Neupert, *A History of the French New Wave* (Madison, WI: University of Wisconsin Press, 2002).
4. Bertrand Tavernier, *Les Cahiers de la cinémathèque*, no. 25, Spring–Summer 1978, p. 104.

5. François Truffaut, *Cahiers du cinéma*, no. 138, December 1962, p. 55.
6. *Paris-Presse*, 14 February 1963.
7. Claude Beylie, *Cahiers du cinéma*, March 1963, pp. 46–9. Beylie also interviewed Melville for the March 1963 *Avant-scène du cinéma* issue on *Le Doulos*.
8. *L'Express*, 14 February 1963.
9. *Les Nouvelles littéraires*, 21 February 1963.
10. *Cahiers du cinéma*, Hors série, 1993, pp. 46–7.
11. Lesou, born in 1930, was twenty-seven when *Le Doulos* was published in 1957. Among many other books, he wrote *Main pleine* (1980), which Melville wanted to adapt but which was eventually directed by Michel Deville as *Lucky Jo* (1964). Details of Lesou's biography from Claude Mesplède and Jean-Jacques Schleret, *Les Auteurs de la Série Noire, 1945–1995* (Paris: Joseph K, 1996), pp. 293–4.
12. Rui Nogueira, *Melville on Melville* (London: Secker and Warburg and BFI, 1971) p. 93.
13. *Les Cahiers de la cinémathèque*, no. 25, Spring–Summer 1978, p. 122.
14. Serge Reggiani seems to be one of the few people to note (retrospectively): 'We shot the adaptation [of *Le Doulos*] which incidentally was very close to the book' (*Le Matin*, 2 November 1983).
15. Pierre V. Lesou, *Le Doulos* (Paris: Éditions Gallimard, 1957) p. 26.
16. (See breakdown in the filmography, pp. 235–7).
17. Melville had planned a different ending, in which Silien phoned the police rather than Fabienne, but in the end, 'Unfortunately, I shot the other version, as used in the film.' Nogueira, *Melville on Melville*, p. 99.
18. Interview with Claude Beylie, *L'Avant-scène du cinéma*, March 1963, p. 6.
19. Ibid., p. 7.
20. Nogueira, *Melville on Melville*, p. 95.
21. This street is rue Watt, near the rue Jenner studios, a street now obliterated by the vast building works around the François Mitterrand Très Grande Bibliothèque.
22. The credits appear to be one continuous take but the screen goes to black on two occasions, so there are probably cuts.
23. Interview with Claude Beylie, *L'Avant-scène du cinéma*, March 1963, p. 6.
24. The 'zone' was the area left unbuilt between the fortifications around Paris, until it was gradually filled up between the wars.
25. Colin McArthur, 'Jean-Pierre Melville', in *Underworld USA* (London: Secker & Warburg, 1972); Stella Bruzzi, 'the Instabilities of the Franco-American Gangster', in *Undressing Cinema, Clothing and Identity in the Movies* (London and New York: Routledge, 1997); Steve Neale, 'Masculinity as Spectacle', in Steven Cohan and Ina Rae Hark (eds), *Screening the Male: Exploring Masculinities in Hollywood Cinema* (London and New York: Routledge 1993); Denitza Bantcheva, *Jean-Pierre Melville: de l'oeuvre à l'homme* (Troyes: Librairie Bleue, 1996); Olivier Bohler, 'Jean-Pierre Melville (unpublished thesis).
26. Nogueira, *Melville on Melville*, pp. 92–3.
27. Lesou, *Le Doulos*, p. 155.

28. Colin McArthur, 'Mise-en-scène degree zero: Jean-Pierre Melville's *Le Samouraï*', in Susan Hayward and Ginette Vincendeau (eds), *French Film, Texts and Contexts*, 2nd edition (London and New York: Routledge, 2000), pp. 189–201.
29. Jacques Zimmer and Chantal de Béchade, *Jean-Pierre Melville* (Paris: Edilig, 1983), p. 74.
30. Bantcheva, *Jean-Pierre Melville*, p. 107.
31. Ibid., p. 52.
32. Murray Smith, *Engaging Characters: Fiction, Emotion and the Cinema* (Oxford: Clarendon Press, 1995), p. 222.
33. *Télérama*, 17 July 1962.
34. The scene was shot in Melville's brother-in-law's house. Photograph held at Bibliothèque du Film (BIFI), Paris.
35. Beylie, *Cahiers du cinéma*, p.49.
36. Patrick Bureau, *Les Lettres françaises*, 14 February 1963.
37. Interview with Claude Beylie, *L'Avant-scène du cinéma*, March 1963, p. 6.
38. See Nogueira, *Melville on Melville*, p. 98, for Melville's account of the preparation and shooting of this scene.
39. Ibid., p. 143.
40. A comparison between two UK broadcasts and a French one yield the same result. As the scene is one continuous take, ending with the men's exit from the room, the only extra footage to make up Melville's stated length would have to be at the beginning of the take.
41. Jean Wagner, *Jean-Pierre Melville* (Paris: Seghers, 1963), p. 69. The *plan-séquence* was actually noticed by *Les Lettres françaises*, 14 February 1963, *France Nouvelle*, 20 February 1963, and *France-Observateur*, 7 February 1963.
42. Nogueira, *Melville on Melville*, p. 95.
43. Lesou, *Le Doulos*, pp. 82–5.
44. Reggiani, interview in *Le Matin*, 2 November 1983.
45. Quoted by Claude-Marie Trémois in *Télérama*, 12 February 1963.
46. Robert Ryan: Jean-Pierre Melville in *Télérama*, 17 July 1962; Humphrey Bogart, *Les Lettres françaises*, 7 February 1963.
47. The original quote by Céline has been truncated. Melville wrote, 'One must choose ... die or lie?' He left out the end of the quote: 'Me, I live!', thereby obviously making the sentence much more pessimistic. Nogueira, *Melville on Melville*, p. 93.
48. Bernard Dort, *France-Observateur*, 7 February 1963.
49. Nogueira, *Melville on Melville*, p. 113.
50. Ibid., p. 112.
51. Various setbacks since *Le Doulos* had delayed the making of *Le Deuxième souffle*. See Chapter 1.
52. Claude Mauriac, *Le Figaro littéraire*, 10 November 1966.
53. For example, Claude-Marie Trémois in *Télérama*, 13 November 1966.
54. Samuel Lachize, *L'Humanité*, 5 November 1966.
55. Gilles Jacob, 'Le Deuxième souffle', *Cinéma 66*, no. 111, 1966, p. 88; Frédéric Vitoux, 'Le Monde des conventions', *Positif*, no. 82, March 1967, pp. 56–8.
56. *Cahiers du cinéma*, no. 186, January 1967, pp. 69–70.

57. *Combat*, 2 November 1966.
58. Pierre Ajame, *Les Nouvelles littéraires*, 6 November 1966.
59. *Les Deuxième souffle* signalled a new turn in Gallimard policy (Guérif); it was the first in the Série Noire to have a new cover design.
60. Marcel Vermeulen, *Le Soir de Bruxelles*, 17 February 1967. See also *L'Aurore* (3 November 1966): 'Giovanni knows perfectly the louche world he describes'; and Jean Rochereau, *La Croix* (5 November 1966): 'The novel which inspired Melville tells a true story in great detail. On screen as in the book the protagonists more or less keep their real names.'
61. Mesplède and Schleret, *Les Auteurs de la Série Noire*, p. 198.
62. Jacob, 'Le Deuxième souffle', p. 88.
63. Nogueira, *Melville on Melville*, p. 113.
64. *Les Cahiers de la cinémathèque*, no. 25, Spring–Summer 1978, p. 89.
65. Nogueira, *Melville on Melville*, p. 111.
66. As José Giovanni said, more generally, 'In France all stories of criminals refer to Corsica although you never see it.' *Arts*, no. 67, 4–10 January 1967.
67. *Les Deuxième souffle* – script held at the Bibliothèque du Film (BIFI), Paris. Ref: SCEN 0836.
68. Alain Dupont, *Télérama*, 4 October 1970.
69. Giovanni, *Le Deuxième souffle*, p. 91.
70. *Les Cahiers de la cinémathèque*, no. 25, Spring–Summer 1978, p. 96; he later put it down to 'a few sentences'. Nogueira, *Melville on Melville*, p. 120.
71. Giovanni, *Le Deuxième souffle*, p. 143.
72. Nogueira, *Melville on Melville*, p. 122.
73. McArthur, 'Mise-en-scène degree zero', in Hayward and Vincendeau (eds), *French Film, Texts and Contexts,* 2nd edition, p. 191.
74. Ibid., p. 193.
75. Nogueira, *Melville on Melville*, p. 116.
76. Ibid., p. 122.
77. Ginette Vincendeau, 'Jean Gabin: From Working-class Hero to Godfather', in *Stars and Stardom in French Cinema* (London and New York: Continuum, 2000), pp. 59–80.
78. Claude Pinoteau, 1972. The film is a spy story in which Ventura is forced by British secret services to betray the Soviet cause he is working for.
79. Jacob, 'Le Deuxième souffle', Bohler, 'Jean-Pierre Melville'; Nogueira, *Melville on Melville*, p. 118.
80. André Malraux, preface to William Faulkner, *Sanctuary* (Paris: Folio Gallimard, 1972), pp. 7–10. Preface originally published in 1949.
81. Robert Warshow, 'The Gangster as Tragic Hero', in *The Immediate Experience* (New York: Antheneum, 1976), p. 129.
82. *Les Cahiers de la cinémathèque*, no. 25, Spring–Summer 1978, p. 109.
83. Ibid., p. 79.
84. Nogueira, *Melville on Melville*, p. 120.
85. Melville, quoted in Zimmer and de Béchade, *Jean-Pierre Melville*, p. 33.
86. See Sigmund Freud, 'Mourning and Melancholy' and Julia Kristeva, 'Black Sun: Depression and Melancholy', in Jennifer Radden (ed.), *The Nature of Melancholy* (Oxford: Oxford University Press, 2000), pp. 283–94, 336–43.

87. *Les Cahiers de la cinémathèque*, no 25, Spring–Summer 1978, p. 95.
88. Nogueira, *Melville on Melville*, p. 123.
89. Centre de la Cinématographie, Paris, censorship file for *Le Deuxième souffle*.
90. Robert Deleuse, 'Petite histoire du roman noir français', *Les Temps Modernes*, 'Roman noir', no. 595, August–September 1997, p. 66.
91. The Ben Barka affair was seen by some historians as contributing to the May 1968 events (the affair was later fictionalised in Yves Boisset's 1972 *L'Attentat*).
92. Lachize, *L'Humanité*, 5 November 1966.
93. Mauriac, *Le Figaro littéraire*, 10 November 1966.
94. Michel Duran, *Le Canard enchaîné*, 9 November 1966.
95. *Libération*, 17 February 1963.
96. Jean-Pierre Mocky, *Les Cahiers de la cinémathèque*, no. 25, Spring–Summer 1978, p. 99.
97. Nogueira, *Melville on Melville*, p. 95.
98. Ludovic Tournès, *New Orleans sur seine, Histoire du jazz en France* (Paris: Librairie Arthème Fayard, 1999), p. 341.

6

The Delon Trilogy: *Le Samouraï* (1967), *Le Cercle rouge* (1970), *Un flic* (1972)

With his last three gangster films, *Le Samouraï*, *Le Cercle rouge* and *Un flic*, Melville reached the apogee of his career as a popular film-maker. His Resistance epic *L'Armée des ombres*, made in 1969 between *Le Samouraï* and *Le Cercle rouge*, is stylistically part of his 'late manner'. However, thematically it belongs to his war films and is thus analysed in Chapter 3.

Le Samouraï is, for many, Melville's masterpiece, the culmination of his artistic achievements as well as a film of exquisite beauty. For Jacques Doniol-Valcroze, writing shortly after Melville's death, *Le Samouraï* was his 'most achieved [. . .] most perfect, film'.[1] *Le Cercle rouge* turned out to be Melville's greatest hit and, on account of its quartet of stars and absorbing heist sequence, one of his best loved. *Un flic* elicited violently hostile responses, but it did well at the box office and it contains two sequences of breathtaking virtuosity – the opening sequence and the train robbery – if not more. Its bleak and strange beauty is a fitting if 'flawed' epitaph to a career cut short by Melville's untimely death in 1973. *Le Samouraï*, *Le Cercle rouge* and *Un flic* are examined here together as the 'Delon trilogy' for obvious reasons, since Delon features in all three, but also to draw attention to the centrality of the star, who was then at the height of his power (not to mention beauty), in constructing the archetype of 'Melvillian masculinity'. Delon's character and performance in these three films also concentrates the set of larger paradoxes that pertain to the three films as a whole: they were Melville's most austere stylistically and most extreme in their depiction of masculinity, yet they were also his most popular at the box office; they were simultaneously his most avant-garde and his most mainstream, his best loved by the audience, and most savagely pilloried by critics.

One question these films pose, therefore, is of their attraction for a wide, 'family' audience, given their bleak vision of masculinity and, concurrently, erasure of femininity. While pursuing a stylistic and generic analysis of these films (their relation to their American 'models', for instance), I will address the question of the appeal of each film in turn, and return to the question at the end of the chapter, in an attempt to place these films in a historical context despite their evident stylisation and apparent lack of realism and historicity.

LE SAMOURAÏ: MELVILLE'S MASTERPIECE

Melville's most famous film has been described as both a 'remake' of Frank Tuttle's *This Gun for Hire* (1942) and as based on a novel by Joan MacLeod called *The Ronin*.[2] Melville alludes to the Graham Greene novel on which *This Gun for Hire* is based and Robert

Bresson's *Pickpocket* (1958) as inspirations. The film's title and the post-credit quote 'from the book of Bushido' (actually by Melville) evidently refer to the Japanese tradition of the samurai (and ronin), as this chapter will discuss. Technically though, it appears, despite this plethora of sources, that *Le Samouraï* was, as Melville says, 'an original story',[3] although two different scripts have survived, one of them bearing the mysterious mention 'based on Jean-Pierre Melville's novel'.[4]

Melville had wanted to make *Le Samouraï* for some time (he said he had written it in 1963), just as he had also wanted Alain Delon for an earlier project, Pierre Lesou's *Main pleine* (later filmed by Michel Deville as *Lucky Jo* [1964], with Eddie Constantine). Following several other setbacks, Melville sent Delon the story of *Le Samouraï*, which he had written 'with him in mind'.[5] What happened next, as recounted by Melville and confirmed by Delon's biographers, has become legend:

> The reading took place at his apartment. [. . .] Alain listened without moving until suddenly, looking up to glance at his watch, he stopped me: "You've been reading the script for seven and a half minutes now and there hasn't been a word of dialogue. That's good enough for me. I'll do the film. What's the title?" "Le Samouraï", I told him. Without a word he signed to me to follow him. He led me to his bedroom: all it contained was a leather couch and a samurai's lance, sword and dagger.[6]

Le Samouraï is the story of Jef Costello (Delon), a contract killer. Jef steals a car and constructs an alibi with his girlfriend Jane (Nathalie Delon) and a group of poker players before killing Martey, the owner of a night-club. Although he is seen by the club's pianist (Caty Rosier), she and the barman deny having seen him to the Inspector in charge of the enquiry (François Périer). Jef's alibi holds and the police release him, although the Inspector believes him, and Jane, guilty. Jef collects his money for the killing but is shot and wounded by a henchmen sent by his double-crossing, as yet unknown, employer. While Jef returns to Martey's night-club, the police bug his flat (he later disables the device). He sleeps with the pianist, asking her (in vain) who the boss is. Jef is given another 2 million francs to execute another contract and he finally finds out the identity of the boss, Olivier Rey (Jean-Pierre Posier). The police put in place a complex trail to follow Jef in the métro but lose him. He steals another car, and, after killing Rey, returns to Martey's, ostensibly to kill the pianist, his new contract. However, he had emptied the magazine of his gun and, as he pretends to shoot her, he is shot in the back by the police (see Filmography for a more detailed synopsis).

Le Samouraï: bad press

With almost two million viewers in France, *Le Samouraï* (which came out on 25 October 1967) was a hit. However, in contrast to its current elevated status, its critical reception in 1967 was tempestuous. The following opinions give a flavour of the debate. While Michel Cournot in *Le Nouvel Observateur* judged *Le Samouraï* to be 'a very banal gangster story, nothing more. [...] Delon's vacant face looks like that of a bloated Henry Fonda, listless and witless',[7] Jacques Zimmer in *Image et son* made the lofty claim that

'*Le Samouraï* is like a Picasso: three bold strokes of breathtaking simplicity, fifty years of work, a hundred sketches . . . and the talent of the master.'[8] The two camps were roughly of equal weight, with the mainstream press tending towards the positive, and the specialist journals towards the negative. Insults in one camp matched the extravagant praise of the other. On the positive side, there was talk of 'perfection',[9] of 'lacework on celluloid'[10] and 'dazzling technique',[11] but also of a 'hieratic' representation of the gangster world, of 'a great tragedy of solitude'.[12] Melville was compared to Bresson. Detractors invoked formulaism, pretentiousness and vacuity. *Le Canard enchaîné* thought that 'Melville takes himself for an *auteur* [. . .] this is an empty film'.[13] In *L'Aurore*,[14] but also in *Cahiers du cinéma*,[15] critics indicted the banality of 'yet another' gangster story, while *Positif* saw only 'lots of walking and métro riding, Delon's face is rigidly fixed, as boring as a piece of wood'.[16] *Le Samouraï* was even, bizarrely in view of their singular inefficiency in the film, accused of being a 'eulogy to the methods and spirit of the French police in 1967'.[17] Even a single publication could be split down the middle: in *Le Nouvel Observateur* Cournot (already cited) talked of Melville as 'a remarkable technician who has strictly nothing to say', while a few weeks later Michel Mardore, comparing *Le Samouraï* to Jacques Tati's *Playtime* (1967), described it as 'Melville's most personal, and also most perfect, film'.[18]

As alluded to in Chapter 1, the problem was that Melville had made his most extravagantly stylised work to date at a time when the French critical agenda was becoming most politicised. This explains how in 1969 Melville could be seen in *Cahiers* as reactionary, and how in 1970 Serge Daney and Jean-Pierre Oudart could talk of his late gangster films as 'pseudo-films', inspired by, but actually inferior to, the aesthetics of advertising. For Daney and Oudart, memorably, Claude Lelouch should be 'singing the praises of a brand of denims' and Melville doing the same for 'a style in raincoats'.[19] Although these polemics have died down, *Le Samouraï* has continued to attract extreme views. For Bertrand Tavernier (an earlier supporter of Melville, but writing this in 1978), with *Le Samouraï*, 'You are in a cinema which copies or reproduces another cinema, without the slightest relationship with French society',[20] while in 1996 the film-maker John Woo wrote: 'Melville is a God for me. [. . .] *Le Samouraï* is one of the foreign films which had the most influence on Hong Kong cinema, especially that of the young generation.'[21] One can see why Tavernier, who has made naturalistic *policiers* such as *L'Horloger de Saint Paul* (1974) and *L627* (1992), would find *Le Samouraï* too detached from French society, and conversely how this detachment would precisely help the film 'travel' well. With very few exceptions (such as the ones quoted above), Delon's performance was one aspect of the film which generated a consensus. His Jef Costello was a defining moment in both his and Melville's career.

Alain Delon and *Le Samouraï*: perfect fit

Melville's determination to cast Delon stemmed from his admiration for the star and belief that '[in France] we only have two models: Delon, Belmondo'.[22] Without going along with this *reductio ad absurdum*, Belmondo and Delon indeed were among the top stars in late-1960s France. Delon in 1967–8 was named one of the ten 'most admired men in France'.[23] Both he and Belmondo brought a new masculinity to French cinema, predicated on a combination of youth and handsome physique, modernity and crime.[24] Belmondo has been discussed in chapters 3, 4 and 5 for his performances in *Léon Morin, prêtre*, *L'Ainé des Ferchaux* and *Le Doulos*. Here I want to consider the convergence of Delon's star persona with Jef Costello in *Le Samouraï*.

Delon's exceptional good looks and the controlled virility of his performance merged the taciturn toughness of Clint Eastwood with the more 'ordinary' minimalism of Jean Gabin.[25] This vision of masculinity, as we have seen, informs earlier Melville gangsters, such as those played by Belmondo and Ventura. But Belmondo, despite Melville's attempt to tone down his exuberance, could not help infusing his characters with a certain kinetic liveliness, while Ventura brought a more sociologically grounded world-weariness to Gu in *Le Deuxième souffle* and Gerbier in *L'Armée des ombres*. Delon pushed the Melvillian hero towards an extreme of androgynous beauty, and a cool, almost cruelly smooth surface. These qualities had already been celebrated by, among others, Visconti in *Rocco and His Brothers* (1960) and *The Leopard* (1963), and René Clément in *Plein Soleil* and *Les Félins* (1964). Through the Clément films, and thrillers like *Mélodie en sous-sol*, Delon also built up a criminal persona. Indeed, as I develop elsewhere,[26] his beauty, in its 'excess', was always foregrounded (shots of Delon in mirrors and doorways) by the films as a cruel weapon in itself. The specular aspect of Delon's performance meshed with Melville's concern with the identity of the gangster as *image*. Delon as both object of the gaze and narrative agent embodied the *homme fatal*, the *femme fatale* and the male protagonist of film noir rolled into one. This is, to me, the significance of the short scene towards the beginning of *Le Samouraï*, where Delon, in his car, is watched admiringly by a pretty woman. Minimalist body language signals that he has noticed her gaze, but having flashed a blank look at her, he turns away, not even gratifying her with a smile. *Le Samouraï* refers explicitly to Delon's stardom in other ways, emphasising androgyny by juxtaposing him with his (then) wife Nathalie Delon, noted for her startling resemblance to him,[27] and through the 'clothes parade' at the police station. In order to test a witness's statement, the Inspector puts Jef among rows of men and makes them exchange their clothes, so that they end up as a crowd of 'gangsters' in various shades of coats and hats. Set among anonymous and less good-looking actors, Delon's charismatic looks leap out at the spectator as 'star', just as they do, as 'character', at the witness who has no trouble singling out Jef (partly out of sexual jealousy).

Melville cast Delon allegedly also because 'there was something Japanese about him',[28] and he matched the film's blue-grey colour scheme to the star's eyes. He mobilised Delon's elegant, slim body and graceful movements in several sequences where Jef is walking through the city. Finally, Delon's understated minimalist performance is highlighted by the contrast with François Périer's more 'actory' and talkative embodiment of the Inspector, similar to the Gu–Blot pair in *Le Deuxième souffle*. Thus Delon's star image, looks and performance style contributed significantly to the construction of Jef as character, in a perfect example of Richard Dyer's concept of the 'fit' between star and character.[29] But the influence cut both ways. *Le Samouraï* lastingly inflected Delon's persona in the direction of a greater seriousness and instrospection, and a durable association with the underworld. Delon's highly public real-life involvement with the *milieu* in 1968 (discussed later) retrospectively strengthened this association, but it is anachronistic to read it into *Le Samouraï*, as people often do. Superseding *Rocco* and *Plein Soleil*, *Le Samouraï* became the *locus classicus* of Delon's stardom. This affinity, by all accounts duplicating friendship between director and star (until, that is, the aftermath of *Un flic*),[30] resulted in a partnership reflected in Melville's last *policier* trilogy, and, for Delon, an impressive string of gangster and *flic* roles which ensured his popularity through the 1970s and beyond.

Franco-American detachment: 'remaking' *This Gun for Hire*

As we have seen, Melville's previous gangster films featured 'families' or groups of men among whom loyalty and betrayal emphasised interdependence. *Le Samouraï* by contrast showcases the solitude of a male hero whose only close companion is a caged bullfinch.[31] Jef is a gangster without a gang. In this sense *Le Samouraï* is both archetypal and exceptional for Melville, who will return to actual gangs in *Le Cercle rouge* and *Un flic*. Like Bob, Faugel and Silien, however, Jef has been perceived as a walking 'quote' – with his name, occupation, trench-coat and felt hat – of the classic American noir gangster. In its iconography, *Le Samouraï*, like *Le Doulos*, multiplies Hollywood citations: the line-up at the police station, 'lifted' from *The Asphalt Jungle*, with Jef, like Dix (Sterling Hayden) staring down at police and witnesses, the police station offices, the black-and-white views of American fire escapes through Jef's (sash) windows. These, however, are not examples of 'copying' or 'reproduction', as Tavernier and others would have it, but formal elements that are self-consciously reworked in Melville's original design. This design also includes French icons of modernity, in particular the Citroën DS, a mythical car for a mythical hero, and the space-age design of Martey's night-club, evocative of André Courrèges. These in turn contrast with the bleak run-down look of Jef's room and the suburban garage (continuing a dichotomy noted in *Le Doulos* and *Le Deuxième souffle*). Melville's Franco-American hybrid is, as ever, tongue in cheek: as Jef approaches the poker players in order to construct his alibi, the soundtrack begins with accordion music and ends with American radio. It is thus with some justification that Melville said, 'I make gangster films, inspired by the gangster novels, but I don't make American films, even though I like the American *films noirs* better than anything.'[32]

To appreciate the singularity of *Le Samouraï*, then, it is useful to compare it with its supposed 'model', *This Gun for Hire*, especially since the latter, as James Naremore reminds us, was a key film in the French definition of the film noir canon by Raymond Borde and Etienne Chaumeton.[33] The narratives of the two films are close. Alan Ladd plays Philip Raven, a contract killer who successfully executes a killing but is double-crossed by his employer. He goes in search of the man to avenge himself, helped by a cabaret singer, Ellen Graham (Veronica Lake), who happens to be the girlfriend of the policeman on his trail. Raven tracks down his crooked employer and the latter's corrupt boss and kills him in a complicated finale in which the old man dies of a heart attack and Raven is also mortally wounded.

Both films start with the hero in his bedroom, showing some affection for a pet: Jef for his bird (he strokes the cage with torn bank notes), Raven for a kitten. In both cases the hero puts on a trench-coat and hat before leaving to go on 'a job'. Yet the two scenes concentrate the aesthetic and ideological differences between Melville and the classical Hollywood tradition he reworks, in terms of the hero, his environment and the relationship between the two. Raven's dingy room is teeming with naturalistic detail: unmade bed, papers, a wash-basin. An open window lets in jaunty honky-tonk piano music. Raven is first seen lying on the bed, but he sits up immediately and moves briskly, filling the space; low-angle shots show him towering above the room even as he sits on the bed. *Le Samouraï*, by contrast, opens on a dark, bare room. The sound of cars swishing by and the darkness suggest winter and rain. It takes some time to discern Jef lying on the bed (most first-time viewers become aware of him through his cigarette smoke).[34] His position suggests spatial confinement, even death. The 'American' fire-escape vista (possibly homage to Dix's room in *The Asphalt Jungle*) immediately posits a non-naturalistic space. The distorted calligraphy of the credits hints at mental disorder and anticipates the distortion of space (halting zoom/track) that occurs immediately after. A feeling of otherworldliness is further enhanced by the music, a bleak tune with religious overtones. As Jef gets up, the camera reveals more of the room, whose walls and minimal furniture are a dominant 'distressed' grey. Raven's room is that of a down-at-heel small-time hitman, notwithstanding his 'angelic killer'[35] face; Jef's gives the impression of a literal and metaphorical cell – windows look out on an unreal 'America', an empty frame above the fireplace remains where a mirror presumably was. Where *This Gun for Hire* immediately introduces rapid-fire noir dialogue, *Le Samouraï* emphasises glacial silence. The two men put on similar clothes, but where Raven's are briskly functional (albeit generic), Jef's give rise to a slow ritual in front of a mirror. Raven, going out, blends with his environment; Jef's clothes will, throughout, signal his difference from his surroundings. Both men share a silhouette, but they are sharply distinguished as soon as they move.

Where the ending of *This Gun for Hire* offers moral redemption to Raven (the double legacy of Graham Greene and the Production Code), that of *Le Samouraï* provides no such comfort. It is a Brechtian, distanced suicide. While Raven dies tenderly, attended by Ellen, saying 'Did I do all right for you?' (to which she nods assent), Jef collapses at the feet of the raised stage on which the pianist remains, the end theatrically marked by a musician lightly striking drums and cymbals before the final freeze-frame.

This comparison is not meant to apportion a greater artistic value to either film, but it helps elucidate Melville's strategies in reworking classical Hollywood cinema. As Göran Hermerén discusses in the context of art history, 'influence' includes a range of possibilities, from copy to allusion, via borrowings, citations, tributes and paraphrases.[36] Hermerén's discussion of Picasso's 'paraphrase' of Velasquez's *Las Meninas* gets close to Melville's reworking of blocks of narrative into a totally different visual design in which the 'original' is detached from its social and historical background. So, for instance, while *This Gun for Hire* makes clear references to the impact of World War II on the characters, Melville is at pains to remove Jef from 1967 Paris. As discussed in earlier chapters, it is possible to read Melville's tribute to the Hollywood noir gangster as a homology of his nostalgia for pre-war France, and thus as an acknowledgment of the traumatic break of the war (as do McArthur and Bohler[37]); but the textual evidence in this film is oblique at best. On the other hand *Le Samourai* offers ample comment on the gender dimension of its main character. In this respect, it is instructive to compare the role of women in *Le Samouraï* and *This Gun for Hire*.

Melancholy masculinity

Tragically useless women

In *This Gun for Hire*, a shrill and luridly made-up maid enters the room and immediately chases the kitten away. In response, Raven grabs her, tears off one shoulder of her dress and violently slaps her in the face. This is designed to show Raven's brutality (which typically Borde and Chaumeton approve of as 'Baudelairian'[38]), but also his mobility. Delon by contrast is alone and immobile. The American film also crucially shows a woman entering the hero's space. Not only is Jef alone, but emphatically no woman will cross his threshold. *Le Samouraï* splits the Ellen character in two, the girlfriend and the pianist, but the comparison confirms both the marginality of women in the Melvillian universe and the importance of solitude to Jef's masculinity. Lake and Ladd became a star couple out of this film, but *Le Samouraï* confirms the gender imbalance in French stardom (neither Nathalie Delon nor Rosier had much of a career).

For Jef, sex with Jane is, literally, an *alibi*, and the pianist's function is to connect Jef with Rey. The pianist's identity as both helper and betrayer (in each case on Rey's instruction) is echoed in set design: her place, as Jef discovers later, is also Rey's. In any case, neither woman has any impact on Jef's fate: the decision to end his life is his. In the evocative words of a critic, women in *Le Samouraï* are beautiful but 'tragically useless'.[39]

Le Samouraï: Jef Costello and his shadow seen by the pianist (Caty Rosier)

This marginality is visualised in their confinement to enclosed 'feminine' spaces – bedroom, bed, stage – while Jef wanders the city's streets, corridors and underground. In this respect we may note that the last person he flees in the métro chase is a pretty young woman. He leaps over the moving walkway barrier and runs, a neat image of his flight from femininity. With Jef, Melville pushes his concept of masculinity to an extreme that is so self-enclosed that it becomes 'autistic', a concept refracted through a series of metaphors.

Animal, warrior, dandy, professional

Le Samouraï's opening 'quote' from the 'Book of Bushido' links Jef to a tiger in the jungle, and we next see him with his caged bird. Rey describes him as a lone (and wounded) wolf (we may note that both Jef and Raven are wounded in the arm). What are we to make of these animal metaphors, beyond the obvious *mise en abyme* of the caged bird? The tiger connects to Delon's star persona: his graceful gestures were frequently described as 'feline', while the quote is a deft allusion to the (asphalt) jungle. Tiger and wolf are beautiful, powerful and dangerous but also hunted animals, like Jef. They are, in this sense, masculine metaphors. At the same time, they, like the bird, connote a natural empathy: Jef 'senses' he is being followed in the métro, where rationally he could not possibly know, in the same way as the bird 'warns' him that his space has been invaded. The bird, like Raven's kitten, signals a potential for affection and therefore vulnerability which is not otherwise displayed. So, paradoxically, the animal metaphors 'humanise' Jef, they elicit empathy.

The title and opening quote also explicitly introduce the notion of Jef as samurai, and implicitly as part of a larger paradigm of warriors, from contemporary wars to Hollywood cinema. Of Jef's clothes in *Le Samouraï* Melville said: 'It's a man's get-up, an echo both of the Western and of military uniform. And there are the guns too, it all springs from the barrack-room. Men *are* soldiers.'[40]

Although Jef is more akin to the 'ronin' (the wandering, lordless warrior), he is a 'samurai' in that he abides by a code of conduct inspired by the Bushido. As David Desser explains, samurai films emerge from a culture in which there is approval of suicide[41] and self-sacrifice, and celebration of the 'nobility of failure',[42] elements which find a clear equivalent in *Le Samouraï*. Desser and other writers on Japanese cinema show that the myth of the samurai/ronin has a social function in Japan: to resolve – through death – conflicts that arise from the contradictory pulls between overbearing duty and personal inclination or feeling.[43] As with his appropriation of American cinema, Melville's take on the samurai/ronin tradition largely empties it of this historic/social context – for instance, one cannot easily identify 'feelings' or 'emotions' in Jef Costello – but retains its bleak underpinning. It is possible to see the samurai within Melville's nihilistic, 'existentialist' approach to a meaningless post-war world. The interest in the samurai and Japanese culture and cinema in general also denotes a fascination with the exotic, as witnessed by Melville's extensive use of orientalism in his décors (see Rey's apartment), a fascination which permeated French culture in the 1960s, culminating in Roland Barthes' book, *L'Empire des signes* (1970). The narrative similarity between the samurai narrative and *Le Samouraï* is clear from Mitsuhiro Yoshimoto's account of an early script of *The Seven Samurai* (1954) as 'One day of a samurai's life: he gets up in the morning, goes to work at a castle, makes some mistake on the job, and goes home to commit *seppuku*, or ritual suicide.'[44] But recourse to the samurai must also be seen as the appropriation of a narrative structure and ethical framework whose origins confer credibility and prestige on an excessively masculine, death-driven form.

Samurai, like soldiers and gangsters, are defined by dress. One of the most discussed moments in *Le Samouraï* occurs when Jef leaves his room and puts on his trench-coat and hat. The camera (taking the place of the mirror) pauses as Jef studies himself and runs two fingers along the brim of his hat. Melville confirmed: 'To see him get dressed was in a way to witness a [significant] act.'[45] Clothes historian Farid Chenoune explains how hoodlum fashion in the 1920s and 30s 'added up to an identifiable school of stylishness that, far from operating as camouflage, ultimately functioned like warrior dress',[46] a notion eminently applicable to Jef.

Countering Laura Mulvey and Steve Neale's argument that the male body cannot be a 'legitimate' erotic object of the gaze, Stella Bruzzi in *Undressing Cinema* discusses the 'overt narcissism'[47] of the gangster film genre, displayed in the characters' investment in clothes. She points to Melville's greater self-consciousness in *Le Samouraï*, compared to the Hollywood movies. Although Bruzzi's observations are generally acute, I want to modify her conclusion about a 'critical dissolution of Jef's sartorial image, moments of crisis in *Le Samouraï* being marked by the gradual, painful fragmentation of the initial Trilby, suit and trenchcoat "ideal"'.[48] Although Jef's wound, which signals his betrayal, is traumatic, it also allows for another kind of narcissistic display as he tends it (the muscles revealed by the clinging white T-shirt, similar to Belmondo in *L'Aîné des Ferchaux*). More fundamentally, Jef's trajectory cannot be read unproblematically as

Le Samouraï: Jef Costello (Alain Delon) and his archetypal narcissistic gesture

downward. His two visits to the club after the wounding are conducted with great aplomb and in full 'warrior dress', his armour now reconfigured as black coat over his suit, and hat. Within both an 'existentialist' reading, and the samurai code of conduct, Jef's death is fully claimed, predicted from the start of the film, and carefully signposted: it is announced by the theft of a black Citroën car (as opposed to the grey-green one of the beginning), by the garage mechanic's 'It's the last time' (to which Jef answers 'OK'), by Jef's 'I'm going' to Rey, and by the fact that, unlike in the first killing, for the last he switches the car off and leaves his hat with the cloakroom assistant.

Jef should also be seen in the light of the dandy. Linked to historical figures such as Beau Brummel, Byron and Oscar Wilde, the dandy has been defined in ways which match Jef's behaviour. The dandy is a narcissistic, usually aristocratic figure excessively concerned with clothes and display, as 'signifying a certain ritual of life [. . .] but detached from everyday life'.[49] As important to the dandy's 'signifying practice' as his clothes is his *impassibility*.[50] Jean-Paul Sartre, perhaps predictably, considered the dandy 'sterile' and 'absurd'.[51] But if all writers agree on his arrogant detachment, psychoanalyst Françoise Dolto pointed out that this detachment meant that the dandy 'would accept no authority, not even that of love',[52] echoing Klaus Theweleit's observation that 'for soldiers, "women" and any kind of "love relationship" were no longer significant issues'.[53] Merging the characteristics of the warrior and the dandy, Jef is thus an extreme manifestation of Melville's earlier gangsters, in flight from women and the domestic, either to a 'homophilic' world (*Bob le flambeur*, *L'Ainé des Ferchaux*) or an increasingly 'autistic' one (*Le Doulos*, *Le Deuxième souffle*). Can it be pure chance that Jef, on being released by the police, escapes through a building situated on rue Lord Byron?

Melancholia, rituals and 'cool'

Melville's thrillers, like most French thrillers (until that time anyway), eschew violent action such as car chases and expansive physical violence. Action and movement instead materialise in the carefully planned and professionally executed gestures, either the heist (see *Le Deuxième souffle*, *Le Cercle rouge* and *Un flic*), or, in Jef's case, the contract killing. Melville endows these moments with a particularly ritualistic aspect.

Jef executes two actual killings, those of Martey and Rey. Both are preceded by ritual dressing and examination in the mirror and both are filmed in exactly the same way: Jef puts on the white editing gloves which, since *Le Doulos*, signify the meticulousness of the Melvillian gangster. He then confronts the enemy, removing both hands from his pockets as he does so. There follows a shot of the adversary taking out his gun, followed by a close-up of Jef's gun and then a wider shot of the action. By showing the action in this way, Melville emphasises the icon of the gun and the white gloves, and shows the shots, in effect, as 'impossible', since Jef's hands are out of his pockets as his adversary draws his gun; yet he still fires first. Of course such bravura is also a quote, especially from the Western. While it emphasises Jef's mythic invulnerability, it de-naturalises the killings and insists on their ritualistic aspect (the exact same gestures, the exact same sequence of shots).

The killings, the sartorial routine, Jef's lengthy walks through corridors, his obsessive returns to the night-club, to the same type of car and same garage, his lines of Evian bottles and packets of Gitanes, all continue the theme of his ritualistic behaviour. I am grateful to Olivier Bohler for pointing out the work of scientist Hubertus Tellenbach, who, in clinical studies of patients suffering from acute melancholia, observed their obsessional performance of ritualistic tasks and the uneconomical, slow, excessive minutia of their behaviour.[54] The conflation of ritualistic behaviour and melancholia is particularly appropriate for Jef. Melancholia of course has also a distinguished psychoanalytical history. Freud and later Kristeva convincingly link it to loss and mourning (actual or symbolic). But its ancient association with the artistic temperament also underlines the status of Jef – and Melville – as artists. Kristeva describes melancholia as entailing a loss of libido, a withdrawal from eros,[55] which compounds the explanation for Jef's flight from women. This, to me, refutes the common assertion that Jef has 'fallen in love' with the pianist. If her gaze is crucial to Jef's trajectory (and to the plot), I would argue in the light of the above discussion that the sadness of Jef's gaze at her at the end of the film is an expression of mourning at his ability to be in love, rather than his love for her (while he may also express sadness at her betrayal).

Melville in *Le Samouraï* pushed the figure of the gangster to the limits of its archetype, or rather, to use Olivier Bohler's evocative phrase of a 'telotype', the end of the line of the archetype. As Bruzzi also suggests, the simultaneous apotheosis and death of the gangster in Jef recalls Melville's pronouncement as 'Parvulesco' in *À bout de souffle*, that he would like 'to become eternal and then die'.[56] How can we understand the popular success of a character of such hermeticism and melancholia, not to mention rejection of the feminine? The film enlists empathy with Jef in narrative terms, against the faceless boss. When we finally see Rey, his ultra-modern flat, which resembles an art gallery, spells wealth and decadence, against Jef's bleak apartment. As the other hitman says, 'we are not in their league'. Jef's double-crossing by Rey and by the pianist thus present him as a 'tragic' figure heroically fighting greater forces. As Melville, echoing both Malraux and Warshow (see Chapter 5) put it shortly after the release of *Le Samouraï*, 'The world of criminals is the last bastion where the forces of good and evil confront each other. It is the refuge of modern tragedy.'[57] He was also at pains to stress his valorisation of 'tragedy' and dismissal of 'melodrama'.[58] Although he does not say so, the cultural gendering of both forms is clear. But Delon's charisma, looks and star persona also play a part. His limpid blue eyes, especially shot through the rain-swept windscreen of his first DS, evoke tears and become the sign of vulnerability under the steely armour. They are again prominent at the end, as he gazes at the pianist shortly before his death. Detached from women, Jef concentrates 'feminine' sensitivity and masculine 'cool', a virtually autistic disengagement from and denial of emotion.[59] While the former explains the affect produced by the character, the latter goes towards explaining its exportability and influence over the work of film-makers such as Walter Hill (*The Driver*), the Coen brothers (*Miller's Crossing*), Quentin Tarantino (*Reservoir Dogs*, 1992), John Woo (*The Killer*, 1989) and Luc Besson (*Léon*, 1994). These film-makers' admiration for *Le Samouraï*, however, is not uniquely linked to character construction. It has also to do with the aesthetics of the film.

Baroque minimalism

Le Samouraï, a colour film, paradoxically inhabits an even sparser and more melancholy universe than *Le Doulos* and *Le Deuxième souffle*. Famously Melville talked of making a 'black and white film in colour' and substituted xeroxes of bank notes in the opening scene to mute the colour further.[60] The narrow blue-grey palette of the film matches not only Jef's blue eyes, but his grey and black outfits and his two Citroën DS cars, his room in shades of grey only relieved by the pink and blue of the Evian bottles and packets of Gitanes. But what makes *Le Samouraï* special is the combination of this colour range with other features of *mise en scène* such as composition and editing. For comparison, Costa-Gavras' *L'Aveu* (1969) uses minimalist décor and a similar colour scheme in its lengthy prison scenes. Yet Costa-Gavras infuses these scenes with the 'busyness' of naturalistic detail and sound, as opposed to Melville's stillness.

Le Samouraï eschews spectacular violence but creates tension and suspense through editing, for example in the killing scenes described earlier. Or in the two appearances of the other hitman. On the first occasion on the railway bridge, his back startlingly appears in a counter-shot, where the preceding shot had suggested an empty landscape. The dramatic change of scale between the two shots contributes to the effect (anticipating similar techniques in 'cinéma du look' films such as *Diva* [1981] and *Nikita* [1990]). In the man's irruption in Delon's room, surprise is achieved within the frame by using the opaque glass partition to the kitchen as 'edit'. The quietness of the opening scene is echoed throughout the film by the slow, systematic, pace of Delon's tread, seen at length in various examples of McArthur's 'cinema of process'. As mentioned in earlier chap-

Le Samouraï and the 'cinema of process': Jef Costello (Alain Delon) steals a car (right and opposite)

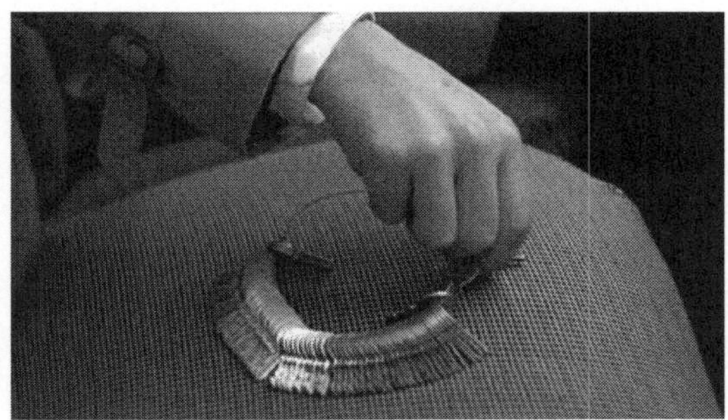

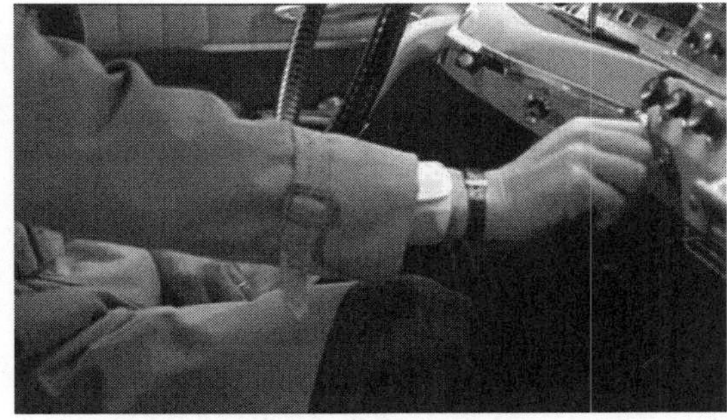

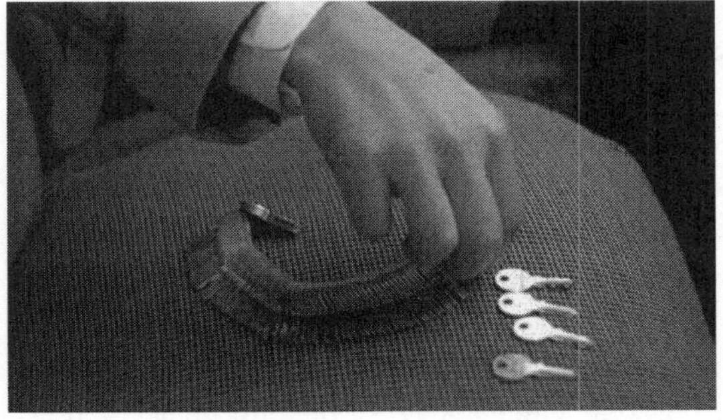

ters, McArthur defines the 'cinema of process' as the way Melville respects the 'integrity of action', a respect for duration, closer to 'real' time.[61] McArthur's notion is seductive and accurately describes the *feeling* of watching these scenes, such as the celebrated theft of the first car, in which Jef systematically tries four keys in the ignition until the fifth one fits. McArthur argues that a Hollywood movie would have dealt with the incident more quickly. Actually, Melville's scene consists of four shots of thirty seconds in total (fifteen seconds of which are taken by the first shot, when Jef gets into the car). The shot in which Delon tries three of the keys lasts only nine seconds, which does seem short especially as he cannot look at what he is doing. Rather than duration, the distinguishing feature is the simplicity and minimalism of the composition – the camera remains on Delon's face as he tries the keys – and the choice of event (as McArthur suggests, an American Jef might have quickly jump-started the car, thus importing movement into the frame). Stillness, minimalist sound and simplicity of composition are in evidence in two other examples of 'cinema of process': the changing of the car number plates (which occurs twice) and the métro chase. The first changing of the plates is mesmerising in its duration, especially as the two men remain completely silent. The soundtrack includes noises which, in addition to those of the mechanic, emphasise the silence and forlorn nature of the place: a dog barking, a train in the distance. Yet the scene is under two minutes long and it contains thirteen shots, so its ASL, under ten seconds, is lower than that of the film as a whole (eleven seconds). The famous métro sequence, similarly, is eight minutes long, but 'feels' much longer. Tension is created by a contrast between relatively lengthy takes of Jef waiting or walking slowly, and clusters of rapid editing (for instance, between over and underground), as a result of which the ASL is very low, just above six seconds.

The cinema of process is a clear echo of the much admired behaviourism of American cinema. But where this is allied in Hollywood cinema with clarity of exposition and verbalisation (see the comparison with *This Gun for Hire*), *Le Samouraï*, if in an extreme way, exemplifies the Melvillian withholding of information, which contributes to the attention to *mise en scène*, forcing the spectator to concentrate on the 'mystery' on-screen. We are given absolutely no information on the past of the characters, including Jef. Information instead is relayed by *mise en scène*: Jef's room and the garage street in their bleakness speak of his melancholia. By contrast, the metal, plastic and glass décor at Martey's, where he stands out as utterly different, speaks of a harsh and sterile bourgeois world. Noises, but also music, fill the void left by narrative opacity. As composer François de Roubaix said,

> The first reel of 'Samouraï' contains exactly three words, on the other hand there is a lot of music whose role is to prepare the spectator and define the character. The fatality which attaches to Jef Costello must be perceived on the level of music.[62]

As the split critical reactions discussed earlier testify, the formal beauty and rigour of *Le Samouraï* have been either revered as pure cinematic art or denounced as 'vacuous' triumph of style over content. One helpful way of sidestepping this dichotomy is to think of Melville's last three thrillers as 'mannerist'. Mannerism refers originally to painting, designating the privileging of form over content, but also an 'ideal of artistic refinement'. The search for effect, which can include baroque distortion of forms,[63] is thus part of an aesthetic plan, not a covering for 'emptiness'. In the cinema, mannerism is usually associated with more baroque film-makers, and in the French context, with the film-makers of the 'cinéma du look'. Melville of course appears as the opposite of baroque in his minimalism and sobriety. Yet *Le Samouraï* resorts to expressionistic excess in décor, as discussed, and its sobriety does not preclude highly virtuoso sequences such as the métro chase. I would thus like to venture that Melville's cinema, during this late period, is, in its mannerism, one of 'baroque minimalism', a notion I will return to in relation to *Le Cercle rouge* and *Un flic* and in the conclusion to this book.

LE CERCLE ROUGE: 'FRENCH, POPULAR, AND PRESTIGIOUS'

Le Cercle rouge opens with the image of a laughing jade Buddha and another Melvillian 'quote'. Here, the text, supposedly by Rama Krishna, warns of impending death: 'When men are meant to meet again, even if they don't know it, anything may happen to each of them and they may follow diverging paths. On the appointed day, inevitably they will meet again in the red circle.' As with *Le Samouraï* the orientalist reference is a little hazy (mixing Buddhist and Hindu references), but the contrast between the laughing figure which starts rotating and the morbid text is chilling, foreseeing the catastrophic ending and the dichotomy between the spectacular surface and the underlying 'tragic' message of the film.

Le Cercle rouge is the story of four men from disparate backgrounds who eventually meet in the 'red circle'. The film starts in Marseille, where Inspector Mattei (Bourvil) is escorting prisoner Vogel (Gian-Maria Volonté) to Paris on the night train. At dawn, Vogel succeeds in slipping his handcuffs and jumping through the window. Also in Marseille, Corey (Alain Delon) is released from jail after having been alerted to a possible heist by a bent prison guard. He visits Rico (André Ekyan), a one-time friend who now lives with his former mistress (Ana Douking). Corey removes money and a gun from Rico's safe and later, at a pool room, sees off two hoodlums sent by Rico to retrieve the cash. He buys an ostentatious American car and sets off for Paris, on the way (unknowingly)

Le Cercle rouge: Mattei (Bourvil), right, handcuffed to Vogel (Gian-Maria Volonté)

picking up the fleeing Vogel who hides in the boot. The two men join forces to kill two gangsters sent after Corey by Rico and become friends. In Paris, Mattei does the rounds of his informers, including night-club owner Santi (François Périer), an acquaintance of Vogel's. Corey and Vogel decide to do the jewellery job indicated by the prison guard, with the help of the fourth main character, ace marksman Jansen (Yves Montand), an alcoholic ex-policeman. Mattei arrests Santi. Corey, Vogel and Jansen successfully carry out the daring heist. Their fence, however, primed by Rico who is still seeking revenge, refuses the loot. Mattei turns up the pressure on Santi by arresting his son for drug dealing. Corey meets a new 'fence', none other than the persistent Mattei in disguise. The latter lures him and Jansen to his isolated country house. Despite Vogel coming to the rescue, all three men are shot dead by the police. The film ends on Mattei removing some jewels from his own hand, while the cynical boss of Internal Affairs intones his eternal refrain, 'all guilty'.

Le Cercle rouge came out on 21 October 1971 and was a huge hit – Melville's biggest – with over four million tickets sold in France. Its critical reception was as split, though not as heated, as that of *Le Samouraï*. Some reviewers deplored the continued fashion for the *policier*, Melville's 'imitation' of American cinema, and the fact that he was repeating himself: *Le Cercle rouge* was not as original as *Le Samouraï*, it was 'another Melville';[64] Melville was 'running on the spot'.[65] In much harsher tones, *Cahiers du cinéma* and *Positif* continued their anti-Melville crusade. Jacques Aumont in *Cahiers* thought that this 'harmful' film, 'over two sinister hours, only regurgitated the earlier Melvilles',[66] and Albert Bolduc in *Positif* declared that its characters were 'monotonous puppets'.[67] Most reviewers, however, applauded *Le Cercle rouge* as the culmination of Melvillian themes (solitude, male friendship, betrayal, death); for Jean Wagner, 'Under so-called commercial films, [Melville makes] the most personal works one can see in France.'[68] There was a veritable chorus of praise for the 'remarkable', the sumptuous yet classical *mise en scène*, the perfection of *Le Cercle rouge* as a 'lesson in cinema'. Melville fan Henry Chapier eulogised that 'The art of Melville is that of cinema itself, which is the art of the look and not that of the word.'[69]

In the post-May 1968 climate, some reactions are more revealing about the period's critical agenda, especially in political terms, than about the film itself. Already *L'Armée des ombres*, released in September 1969, had had a highly politicised reception (see Chapter 3). So, while Noël Simsolo indicted Melville as right-wing (Gaullist) and deplored the way *Le Cercle rouge* 'agrees with the aesthetic and political ideology of the government under which it was made',[70] and Aumont in *Cahiers* thought the film supported the Government's repressive policies,[71] some left-wing publications saw the emphasis on surveillance (in the heist sequence) as a critique of the police state.[72] At the same time, the presence of Yves Montand and Gian-Maria Volonté prompted comparisons (of various shades) with the currently popular political thriller. *Le Cercle rouge* was also (usually favourably) contrasted to the rise of sexually explicit cinema. In this respect the extreme male focus and marginalisation of women was ascribed not to misogyny but to a refreshing refusal of 'vulgarity'. Unsurprisingly, the Catholic *La Croix* approved: *Le*

Cercle rouge 'is a comfort against many things, and first of all the aphrodisiac civilisation'.[73] More pervasively, the sense of 'tragedy', the pessimism of the film were deemed to be rightfully men's preserve: *Le Journal du dimanche*, for instance, thought the film 'not misogynistic but alien to the feminine universe'.[74]

L'Express ran a cover story by Pierre Billard which offered a perceptive analysis in film industry terms. With its budget of FF 9.75 million,[75] *Le Cercle rouge* was the epitome of the new blockbuster, designed to counter the 'crisis' of French cinema. This type of production corresponded to changing cinemagoing habits: at a time of declining audiences and waning of regular, 'Saturday night' cinemagoing, spectators could only be lured into the cinema by a small number of genre films displaying cinema's attractions on a massive scale, in terms of colour, landscapes and stars. Billard was right. In late-1960s/early 1970s French cinema, this meant 'family' comedies – a week after *Le Cercle rouge*, for instance, Louis de Funès's hit *Le Gendarme en ballade* and the Annie Girardot–Brigitte Bardot comedy *Les Novices* were released – or *policiers*. Unlike the critically despised comedies, however, Melville's films also had serious credentials, especially after *Le Samouraï* and *L'Armée des ombres*, so *Le Cercle rouge* combined massive popular appeal with cultural legitimacy. It is therefore not surprising that it was chosen to open a new series of television broadcasts of French films on the A2 channel in 1975, under the title 'French, popular, and prestigious'. Thus, while much critical discourse on Melville has focused on his 'American-ness', from an industry point of view he was making the kind of French film that was helping combat Hollywood.

The triumph of *Le Cercle rouge*, of course, owed a great deal to its quartet of stars. Delon was on familiar generic territory after *Le Samouraï*, but also *Le Clan des Siciliens* (Henri Verneuil, 1969) and *Borsalino* (Jacques Deray, 1970). He and Melville slightly altered his look, among other things to signal difference from these recent films: here Delon sports an unfamiliar moustache and darkened hair.[76] Since *Le Samouraï*, Delon had also been in the news. In 1968, the suspicious (and still unresolved) assassination of his Yugoslav friend-secretary Stefan Markovic publicised the presence of members of the French and Yugoslav underworlds among his entourage. The 'Markovic affair', a heady mixture of gangland and sexual scandal, added an extra-cinematic layer to his image that would endure. Montand was also familiar to *policier* viewers, as either gangster or cop, especially after Costa-Gavras' *Compartiment tueurs* (1965) rekindled his film career. At the time of *Le Cercle rouge*, both he and the Italian Gian-Maria Volonté had acquired a specific image in political thrillers such as *Z* (1969, Montand) and *Indagine su un cittadino al di sopra di ogni sospetto* (1970, Volonté). But it was the unexpected presence of comic Bourvil as the sombre Inspector Mattei that stole the show. Bourvil, much-loved since the 1950s for his 'simpleton' persona, and the star of two massive comedy hits of the 1960s, *Le Corniaud* (1965) and *La Grande vadrouille* (1966), both co-starring de Funès, here accomplished every comic's dream of playing a tragic character. As Mattei is reprimanded for letting Vogel escape, his boss ponders how strange it is that a Corsican[77] should be blond with blue eyes, thereby pointing out not just the opacity of the character but the star's famous Normandy origins. Bourvil's performance as the solitary policeman who goes home to a cold flat populated only by three cats (recalling Jef Costello and his bird) was all the more poignant because he was then very ill. *Le Cercle rouge* was to be his penultimate film and he died a few days before its release. *Le Cercle rouge*, of all Melville's films, is perhaps the one that corresponds most to his '*mille-feuilles*' theory (see Chapter 1) of layering 'serious' themes with entertaining spectacle. *Le Cercle rouge* mobilises the pleasures of the 'cinema of attractions' on a grand scale while offering a totally bleak vision. While Melville protests,

> I wanted to write a robbery script long before I saw *The Asphalt Jungle*, before I'd even heard of it, and well before things like *Du Rififi chez les hommes*. It's also a sort of digest of all the thriller-type films I have made previously[78]

Le Cercle rouge is both a consummate distillation of the heist genre and a totally original take on it.

Le Cercle rouge as heist movie: 'remaking' *Asphalt Jungle* and *Rififi*

The reviewers who criticised *Le Cercle rouge* for its 'banal plot' were obviously missing a point. As Melville said, 'I forced myself to make a film with situations that were absolutely and totally conventional, from beginning to end. And everybody liked the film.'[79] *Le Cercle rouge* follows the familiar heist (or caper) film pattern: a group of disparate men come together, successfully perform a daring burglary, but fail in the aftermath because of a technical hitch or betrayal. *Le Cercle rouge* makes those conventions deliberately visible. It is replete with overdetermined moments (Corey and Vogel's meeting, the ending), coincidences (the guilt of Santi's son), 'unbelievable' events (how does Vogel get out of Corey's boot? Why don't they disable the very visible videotape mechanism?) and excess: for instance, the betrayal by the fence, under pressure from Corey's relentless pursuer, Rico, is doubled up by Santi's – implied – betrayal under equivalent pressure from Mattei. *Le Cercle rouge* is also highly referential. As Pierre Lesou put it, '*The Asphalt Jungle* is, again, evoked in *Le Cercle rouge*, with its jewellery scene, and the photo-electric cells which force the burglars to perform acrobatics.'[80] He could equally have mentioned *Rififi*: the heist set on place Vendôme, Montand casing the joint dressed like Dassin, the long burglary performed in total silence. Melville, as usual, also cast the net of influences wider. His film's stillness and attention to detail, the importance of sound, its 'cinema of process' but also some plot details evoke *Le Trou*. His script

> is an original in the sense that it was written by me and by me alone, but it won't take you long to realize it's a transposed Western, with the action taking place in Paris instead of the West, in our time rather than after the Civil War, and with cars replacing the horse.[81]

He could also have mentioned war and spy films, for instance John Huston's *The Kremlin Letter* (1969), which he particularly admired, and which, in its scale, colour scheme and bleak view of masculinity, is another relevant source.

The heist movie as self-conscious cinema of attractions

Le Cercle rouge starts in spectacular fashion: in a short pre-credit sequence, a car full of men looking like gangsters (though all but one are policemen) tears up to a station where two of them board a train. The massive night-train slowly moving out of the station, with the credits superimposed, tells us this blockbuster is getting under way, its plush interiors that we are in for a pleasurable visual experience. The next scene, depicting Mattei and Vogel settling down in their Pullman car, is a model of Melvillian *mise en scène*. It is conducted in silence, motion suggested by the slight shaking of the train. Tension arises from the calmly observed gestures, even before Vogel starts bending a pin to pick the lock of the handcuff that now attaches him to his bunk. The contradictory bond between the two men sharing such a small space adds to the tension, until the climactic moment when Vogel crashes through the window and escapes. As Jean-Louis Bory put it, in *Le Cercle rouge*, 'violence is rare and almost immediately extreme'.[82]

As Corey gets out of jail, parallel editing, similar framing and sound 'bridges' establish Vogel's affinities with him, while Delon's unflappability asserts his domination over Rico and his steely control in the billiard scene recalls *Le Samouraï*. Silently slipping its owner a note to keep the hall open, Corey begins playing on his own among the rows of deserted billiard tables, an expanse of green baize and low lights. Then Melville cuts to an overhead shot which shows Corey's skilful play, the white and red balls and cue standing out against the brilliant green surface. We are taken by surprise as another cue enters the frame, before the camera returns to a level position and we see the two heavies sent by Rico, whom Corey,

Le Cercle rouge: Corey (Alain Delon) celebrates his new freedom with a billiard game

however, quickly puts in their place. The geometric simplicity of the game belies the skill required, a good image of *Le Cercle rouge* and Melville's cinema as a whole.

In *Le Cercle rouge* Melville had both a large budget and total control but he put these to the service of a particularly sober and classical *mise en scène*: less 'baroquely' minimalist than *Le Samouraï* and with fewer flourishes than, say, *Le Doulos*; for example, although the film's rhythm is relatively slow, with a number of long takes (around twenty seconds, and a *plan-séquence* of forty-nine seconds when Mattei visits one of his informers), there are no extreme long takes. However, Melville's understated virtuosity is still in evidence, in some high-angle shots (the billiard scene, in the jeweller's staircase), in his use of off-screen space – the surprise intrusion over the billiard scene, duplicated by Mattei's hand proffering a lighter when he meets Corey at Santi's. Melville's virtuosity is particularly sustained, together with narrative economy, in the three scenes set at Santi's night-club, as they concentrate gangsters and police presence in particularly subtle ways. Each contains female dancers on a central stage who are almost always visible in the foreground or background, or even faintly reflected in the plate-glass door. In the first scene, a complex twenty-second take tracks Santi coming out of his office, greeting customers and meeting Mattei at the bar. In the second scene, as Jansen and Corey are sitting down, the camera follows their conversation in a medium shot and then tracks over their heads to show Santi being arrested by Mattei's men. In this thirty-two-second take two spatial planes and two strands of action are combined in an apparently effortless, yet technically dazzling fashion.

As Kim Newman points out, the heist/caper film is akin to the musical and the war film in containing big set pieces which stop the flow of the narrative.[83] Yet interestingly, *The Asphalt Jungle*, widely acknowledged as a model of this sub-genre, spends relatively little time on its heist (ten minutes). The length (twenty-five minutes) and lack of dialogue of the sequence in *Le Cercle rouge* pay more direct homage to *Rififi*. Both length and silence are, however, self-consciously pointed out. As he watches the tape the next day, Mattei ironically remarks 'they're not talkative'. Like Dassin in *Rififi*, but also Becker in *Le Trou*, Melville 'forces us to listen to silence', as Jean-Louis Bory puts it.[84] Even compared to *Rififi* Melville elongates the scene, not in overall duration, but in the type of activities filmed. Where *Rififi* concentrates more on physical action (drilling through the ceiling, moving the safe), *Le Cercle rouge* shows Corey and Vogel walking through a labyrinth of corridors and courtyards, accompanied by an evocative aural montage (steps, silent courtyards, distant parties, printworks) for *six minutes* before they arrive outside the guard's window and 'proper' action begins – a good example of 'cinema of process'. Compared to *Rififi*, Melville also enhances the set, using colour and lighting – the theatricality of the interiors at the jeweller's is stressed by turning lights on and off – and by spreading out the jewels in glass cases, throughout the whole splendid room, where in *Rififi*, as in *Asphalt*, they were in a safe. A beautiful shot shows Corey and Vogel on the roof-tops, with the Eiffel Tower and the top of Napoleon's column silhouetted against dark blue sky, and a pan reveals the empty place Vendôme, like an extended set, while the rising, though subdued, beat of the music creates muted suspense.

The heist in *Asphalt* and *Rififi* takes place in less impressive surroundings, using a *bricolage* of familiar objects (a carpet, a hammer, an umbrella, dynamite as 'soup'). In *Le Cercle rouge*, by contrast, the space is both grander and more anonymous, as are the gangsters themselves under their masks. In the corresponding sequences in *Asphalt* and *Rififi* the men's faces are visible, and their individuality exploited, while they work towards the common effort. Their reactions, triumphs and fears are reflected on their faces and are crucial to the meaning of the scene. But Jansen, Corey and Vogel perform the whole burglary wearing elegant black silk masks and white gloves. Corey and Vogel wear identical jackets, trousers, shoes, cloth caps and masks, and on first viewing are almost impossible to tell apart, except when a close-up shows Delon's blue eyes.

As in *Rififi* and *Asphalt*, the men work against the clock, literally here the guard's loudly ticking clock, heard whenever we cut to his bound and gagged figure. His raising of the alarm just as the band escapes adds to the tension but does not bring the police, whereas in *Asphalt* and *Rififi* their presence was visible (in fact, in *Le Cercle rouge*, as in *Le Samouraï*, the police are either absent or excessively present). Where time in *Asphalt* was measured by Dix looking out and commenting on what he saw, and in *Rififi* Jo measured events against his little book, in *Le Cercle rouge* things are recorded on a videotape which Corey and Vogel could easily have destroyed; its presence therefore is deliberate. Throughout the film, instruments of representation are alluded to, including the reference to Nicéphore Niepce, the French inventor of photography, and, as Olivier Bohler points out,[85] Jansen's name evokes Janssen, the inventor of a pre-cinematic photographic recording tool.[86] The newspaper headline the day after, screaming 'Sensational affair', draws our attention to the way the film has just pulled off a sensational coup. As the cherry on the cake, Melville carefully shows us that the brass lock hit by Jansen's shot to disable the alarm bears the letters 'JPM'. Thus, while preserving traditional suspense and respecting the rules of the genre, Melville uses the burglary in a highly self-reflexive way, the meticulously planned and brilliantly executed heist standing for the precision of his film-making.

Masculinity and professional gestures

As he and Corey set about planning the burglary, Vogel claims to be a 'dilettante'. He is depicted as a 'wild card', signalled by his unruly hair (compared to the smoothness of Delon and Montand's) – Melville also reportedly asked the Italian Volonté to tone down his 'gesticulations'.[87] Yet of course he will turn out to be utterly professional. The heist in *Le Cercle rouge* as in its illustrious predecessors – *Asphalt* and *Rififi* but also *Le Deuxième souffle* – beyond its spectacular function is also the stage for the display of masculinity in motion. Its emphasis on action, movement and skills, control and discipline places it within a traditional sphere, where, to quote Pat Kirkham and Janet Thumim, 'competence and prowess are important markers [. . .] of masculinity'.[88] The professionalism of the heist confers nobility on men, to which women have no access.

The heist's vision of professionalism is a perverse one. We admire the men for their skills and the satisfaction of a 'job well done', so much that we forget they deploy them in the service of crime. This is partly because, as Kirkham and Thumim say, 'prowess is such a significant marker that it does not always matter how it is manifested',[89] and partly because the heist mobilises, within the criminal world, the most noble kind of work, that of the craftsman. See, for instance, Jansen's concocting of the metal alloy, depicted in a series of shots linked by wipes to indicate concentration and passing of time. Professional skills are a core element of male bonding because they stand for trust. For instance, Corey and Vogel, from inside the jewellers, have no way of knowing that Jansen is outside when they open the door at the agreed time to let him in. They look at their watches, at each other, open the door. Jansen is there.

Jansen vividly illustrates how professional skills are used as a *cure* for ailing masculinity. We are brutally introduced to him in the throes of *delirium tremens*, rendered expressionistically with rats, lizards, scorpions, snakes and huge spiders crawling over his bed (Melville's indication in the script is of a 'Faulknerian alcoholism delirium'[90]). Some reviewers criticised the scene as out of character. Yet it makes perfect sense. Although we are given little information about his past, it emerges that Jansen, an ex-policeman and ace marksman, is in this parlous state because he is *out of work*. A surreal framed picture of a gun on the wall of his dingy room taunts the unshaven, sweaty and uncoordinated figure who pants and shouts as the telephone rings. Corey and Vogel's request for him to join them for the heist provides a miraculous cure, whose steps we follow. Jansen first meets Corey at Santi's and indicates his vulnerability by refusing a drink. Later, as he 'cases the joint', smartly dressed, his hand shakes slightly as he opens the door to the jeweller's. Jansen continues his rehabilitation with target practice and casts special bullets with rigorous scientific precision. He carries his rifle in a violin case which economically connotes art and skill. As he arrives at the scene he opens his case in which rifle and tripod are neatly encased in blue velvet and he proceeds calmly to lay them down on the table, like medical instruments. At the climax of the burglary he performs the virtuoso shot which disables the alarm system, taking the rifle off the tripod and shooting 'by hand' (like Pascal in *Le Deuxième souffle*). He then takes out a silver flask and just sniffs it.[91] His now complete, cool and co-ordinated masculine figure is confirmed by his ability to look at himself in the mirror again. As reflected in his increasing elegance, it also finally accords with Yves Montand's urbane star persona.

However, as in *Le Samouraï*, the masculine ideal attained in *Le Cercle rouge* is one of introspection and loneliness. Jansen's triumphant return to form will not lead to a 'normal' social life, but to a different kind of solitude, similar to that of Mattei who, as a policeman with a shady past, is a reverse version of himself. What these two solitudes share, as well as with the Corey–Vogel couple, is the absence of women.

Goodbye to women

Le Cercle rouge features the smallest feminine presence in the whole Melvillian oeuvre. Melville justified it as a reaction against the rising tide of eroticism ('I did it quite unconsciously, with no purpose in mind, simply in reaction against everything I have had to see over the last three years at the Commission de Censure'[92]) and because of his 'old Testament side'.[93] The erasure of women is both an extreme distillation of the genre and a logical conclusion of Melville's own work. As we might expect, in *Le Cercle rouge* it is also highly self-conscious (so much for an 'unconscious' reaction).

In *Le Cercle rouge*, women appear as spectacle in a literal sense in the cabaret scenes, in three separate rather tacky, trance-like female song-and-dance routines. As in Melville's previous thrillers, style and elegance are projected on the men, while women look motherly or caricaturally sexy. Melville's own practice reflected this priority. Discussing the 'capital' importance of male clothes, he said: 'Most of the time my assistants deal with dressing actresses. This interests me less [than dressing male actors].'[94] The three scenes at Santi's dramatise this feature. In the first show the dancers are dressed as prostitutes (short slit skirts, fish-net tights, swinging bags), in the second as flappers dancing the Charleston (to the tune of 'Chicago'), and in the third as 'savages' to a heavy drum beat. The stage is situated in the middle of the club and in each case the camera shows the gangsters in front of or beyond the stage. Melville thus points out the generic status of *all* his characters: men in gangster uniform meet while women act out feminine myths (the prostitute, the flapper, the savage). In those scenes, equally spectacular representations of masculinity and femininity are juxtaposed without interacting. These self-conscious 'gangsters' are, however, also narrative agents, whereas the women never leave the stage. The one who does, the Playboy Bunny who gives Corey a red rose on the third and last occasion, by violating this spatial division, spells trouble. These scenes show Melville, as Laura Mulvey has argued about Godard,[95] both analytical of and complicit in sexist representations of women. Analytical because of the self-consciousness, complicit because the scenes lock women in these sexist representations. As in *Le Samouraï*, the stage displays and confines women.

The 'uselessness' of women in *Le Cercle rouge*, to take up the expression used in relation to *Le Samouraï*, is graphically demonstrated in another key scene which, on the surface appears as a *temps mort*, with little narrative importance and yet which gives crucial information. Corey on leaving jail is handed three photographs of a woman which he ostensibly tries to leave behind. He then places one of them, clearly of his former mistress (now Rico's), in the latter's safe after he has helped himself to the money and the gun. The self-conscious play with the exchange value of female sexuality could hardly be clearer. The woman's pose on the photograph exactly duplicates the (nameless) woman herself, as she is glimpsed in bed and then behind the door.[96] This is expanded on in a later scene when Corey enters his flat for the first time since he has come out of jail, and carefully goes round the space with a torch. The use of the torch is not strictly necessary, but the fact that the flat is dusty and covered with cobwebs as well as the curtains blowing in front of the open windows (suggesting the woman's abandon) are better picked out by the 'expressionist' lighting this affords. Corey uses the torch to illuminate a series of erotic prints on the wall, ingeniously signalling his dormant sexuality. The camera then pans to a bedside table where the same framed photograph stands. Corey picks it up and throws it in the bin as Vogel stands silently next to him. Not only are women redundant, but heterosexual sexuality is renounced too (in the script, Melville stresses that although Corey looks at a pretty waitress in a café, on his release from jail, he visits a billiard hall rather than a brothel as in *Le Clan des Siciliens*). Corey finally discarding the last image of his mistress in the waste-paper basket, with Vogel moving in, can be read as suggesting homosexuality, particularly as we see them getting dressed together the next morning, Vogel wearing Corey's pyjamas (with a monogrammed 'C'), but this remains a suggestion; Vogel is shown to sleep on the sofa. Vogel wearing Corey's pyjamas may also be a distant homage to Riton wearing Max's pyjamas in *Touchez pas au grisbi*. Later, however, as Corey goes to meet the fence, Vogel picks up the red rose given to him by the waitress, while looking at Corey getting into his car. Nevertheless, as in *L'Ainé des Ferchaux*, the representation of the two men is more accurately described as *homophilic*. Sexuality in *Le Cercle rouge* is entirely sublimated – in the persona of stars, professional skills, narcissistic dress and an abundance of phallic imagery: the usual cars and guns, but also long instruments, billiard cues and the column of the place Vendôme.

As in Melville's earlier films, the *modus vivendi* is that of the solitary male or the male couple itself suggested as sterile by *mise en scène*: Corey and Vogel's moment of intense bonding is set in vast, frozen fields bathed in the dominant cold blue-grey colour scheme. The wide-open horizon proposes a mythical, Western-like dimension, but landscape and colour scheme speak of essential solitude, represented further by Jansen and Mattei. The picture of a wife and child on the latter's desk hints at a past family, but like Corey's woman, it is in the past, framed, and brutally knocked down (by Santi). In the Melvillian system, the family, not just women, brings vulnerability – as demonstrated by Santi and his son, echoing Mathilde and her daughter in *L'Armée des ombres*. Although I accept the generic nature of this marginalisation, its historicity also needs to be discussed, as I will do at the end of this chapter.

The red circle: 'all guilty'

The extreme bleakness of Melville's vision in *Le Cercle rouge* rests on two paradoxes: men must leave women and family behind, but only to achieve loneliness and death, in the same way as the heist celebrates superior virile skills but dramatises ultimately its futility.

Jansen gives up his share of the money, making his participation pure *acte gratuit* – as (Melville points out) when Jo in *Le Trou* says to Manu, 'I will dig the hole with you but I will not leave.'[97] As in *Rififi*, it is made clear that the jewels will be unusable – they are 'too big' for the gang, such disproportion giving part of its poetic force to the act in the first place. But more fundamentally, Melville's protagonists, like Jef, have no use for worldly goods. They mostly live in small, sometimes sordid surroundings. Jansen's room is covered with wallpaper which evokes the bars of a jail, and it is only furnished with incongruous large trunks. As Melville points out in the script, Corey's flat *has been* beautiful. Even devoid of some of its dust, it is only briefly shown in daylight here. Despite the carefully chosen modern furniture, objects and paintings, it appears functional; each scene shows Corey leaving it. Mattei's flat is equally carefully furnished but again it is cold and functional, a place for cats rather than humans.

In *Asphalt* the robbery is accomplished by each member of the group for a stated purpose: the money will help a struggling family, permit an escape to exotic places, enable the purchase of a dream home. When they fail, the viewer feels compassion and pathos, culminating in the final lyrical drive by the dying Dix with Doll (Jean Hagen) at his side. In *Rififi* Dassin both follows and departs from the American 'model': the men excitedly discuss what they will do with the money, but Tony, the head of the gang, only shrugs and says, 'Oh, me . . .'. So Dassin introduces a more sombre note, hinting at Tony's existential despair and the futility of the heist. His final car ride shows a similar duality. The badly wounded Tony driving his little godson home is a clear echo of *Asphalt*, a source of both suspense and pathos for the spectator. At the same time the child, firing a toy gun and wearing a cowboy costume, signals a self-conscious distance from the 'original'.

The end of *Le Cercle rouge* is pure generic commentary – all the emotions of *Asphalt* and *Rififi* have been spent. The gangsters do not die because crime must not pay but because their demise follows the rules of the genre, foretold by the opening quote. Pathos is replaced with cerebral inevitability, and the rather heavily reiterated leitmotiv of 'all guilty'. From the opening images of Mattei and Vogel handcuffed together, the boundaries between criminals and police are blurred. As the director says later ironically to Mattei, 'travelling together in a wagon-lit creates links'. Policemen are disguised as gangsters (Mattei), gangsters are former policemen (Jansen). Policemen use blackmail as 'routine', but by doing so uncover the guilt of supposedly 'innocent' people (Santi's son). Mattei startingly steals some of the jewels from the heist, and in an act of potential career suicide (like Blot at the end of *Le Deuxième souffle*) hands them over to a colleague in full view of the director. The presumption of guilt is all the more powerful in that we know virtually nothing about the past of the characters. As in *Le Samouraï*, these beautiful but cold settings echo the anonymity of the characters. Corey's possessions enumerated by the prison staff pretty much sum up his 'baggage' as a character: 'a wallet, FF 30,000, three photographs, a driving licence, an *expired* passport, a watch, a set of keys and *that's it*'. We do not know what Corey and Vogel had done to be in jail, why Jansen left the police or what is in the Mattei dossier. Even the décor of the director's office suggests his own guilt, with its sombre antique decoration and, as suggested by Melville in the script, 'carefully balanced' chiaroscuro.[98] Indeed *his* guilt is locked into the same red circle: Jansen tells Corey that he learnt about the special alloy from . . . the same director of Internal Affairs.

It is not surprising then, as we saw earlier, that commentators trying to link the film to the post-1968 context ended up with confused and contradictory views. Despite a few references to contemporary events – Claude Tenne (mentioned by Mattei) was a member of the OAS sent to jail but who escaped,[99] the passing of Les Halles is bemoaned, the lines of policemen evoke the massed CRS of May 1968 – the universe of *Le Cercle rouge* alternates 'hyper-realist' décors such as the place Vendôme, a railway crossing house or a roadside cafeteria, with oneiric moments, such as the hunt for Vogel in the forest,[100] and places. The house in Louveciennes, the setting of the final 'red circle', is presented as a fairy-tale castle in its architecture and the misty lighting that surrounds it. Generically it is a transposition of the location outside Paris in which trouble always occurs in the *policier* (as in *Touchez pas au grisbi*, *Bob le flambeur* and *Rififi*, for instance). But it is also the confirmation of Melville's removal of his film from the present. As he was at pains to reiterate, 'I know the underworld I describe is not the real underworld [. . .] My films are dreamed films.'[101] Crime and punishment in *Le Cercle rouge* are not moral or ideological, but mystical (the orientalist 'red circle') and aesthetic.

For Melville, one suspects, the red circle is ultimately purely aesthetic. His script annotation for Corey's red chalk on the billiard cue is that it is 'the first object in a warm colour since the beginning of the film'.[102] In fact, it has been preceded by the red circle on the post-credit text, the red light that the police car goes through on the way to the station, and indeed the film is punctuated with red: lights, chalk, roses, bloodstains which stand out again the dark/cold dominant colours. One is reminded of Godard's famous pronouncement: 'this is not blood, this is red.'[103] As Corey and Vogel escape from the death-trap house and, together with Jansen, are killed, the camera hardly lingers on their bodies or faces, but swiftly moves on to Mattei and the director. If the end of *Le Samouraï* was distanced theatrically, with a musical flourish and freeze-frame, the end of *Le Cercle rouge* is distanced cinematically, emphasising aesthetic experience over compassion or pathos. As *Cinémonde* applauded, 'What makes Melville a true creator is that everything is false,'[104] a notion eminently applicable to *Un flic*, to which I now turn.

UN FLIC: MELVILLE'S TROUBLED SWANSONG

Un flic opens with a quote from François-Eugène Vidocq (1775–1857), an escaped convict who became Chief of Police and published his memoirs in 1828. An inspiration for Balzac's Vautrin and a great influence on the French *policier*, Vidocq remains emblematic of the porous border between crime and the law. The quote, 'The only feelings man could ever inspire in the policeman are ambiguity and derision', thus strikes a keynote: *Un flic* will be a meditation on ambiguity (legal, moral or sexual) and derision. This is the meaning of the parallel editing in the opening sequence: four gangsters dressed like bank managers rob a bank, while Alain Delon, the gangster of *Le Samouraï* and *Le Cercle rouge* now plays Edouard Coleman, a police inspector who maintains highly ambivalent ties with the chief villain, Simon.

On a stormy, deserted Atlantic beach in winter, four gangsters – Simon (Richard Crenna), Marc (André Pousse), Paul (Riccardo Cucciolla) and Louis (Michael Conrad) – rob a bank. An employee shoots Marc and is killed. The four men escape, bury the loot and take the badly wounded Marc to a clinic. Meanwhile in Paris Inspector Coleman (Delon), with his assistant Morand (Paul Crauchet), investigates a murdered woman and a theft by a young gay male prostitute, meets a transvestite prostitute (Valérie Wilson) who is one of his informers, and interrogates three pickpockets. He visits Cathy (Catherine Deneuve) at the night-club owned by Simon, his friend. Cathy, dressed as a nurse, kills Marc with a lethal injection to prevent him from talking. She and Coleman meet in a hotel room. Simon, Louis and Paul plan their next big heist, the theft of a suitcase full of drugs on the Paris–Lisbon train. Coleman finds out about the job from the transvestite informer and decides to let the border police intercept the drugs. But Simon and his gang get to it first in their daring heist, in which Simon is dropped onto the moving train by helicopter and later picked up in the same way. A furious Coleman takes it out on the transvestite. Coleman arrests Louis who reveals Simon's involvement. Coleman warns Simon who in turn warns Paul. Paul commits suicide as Coleman is about to arrest him. As Simon tries to escape with Cathy, Coleman shoots him in self-defence, although it transpires that Simon had no weapon and has in effect 'committed suicide'. Coleman returns to his routine.

Killing by the press

Although *Un flic* – released 25 October 1972 – did not achieve the stratospheric results of *Le Cercle rouge*, its box-office takings (2.8 million tickets) were excellent, higher than those of *Le Samouraï* for instance (even more impressive given that in the intervening five years overall French box office had dropped by about 30 million cinemagoers a year). Yet the reputation of Melville's last film is that of a failure, on account of the severe thrashing it received from the French press. Review after review talked of boredom, emptiness, excessive mannerism and incoherence – Louis Chauvet in *Le Figaro* even reproduced the press book's summary as evidence that the film was incomprehensible.[105] There were too many improbabilities: among others, the fact that Coleman warns Simon without arresting him straight away, that he shuts the door on Paul's suicide rather than preventing it, and that, as a Parisian *flic*, he drives a huge American car and works in hyper-modernist offices. The use of models for the train and helicopter was singled out as particularly unacceptable. Melville's impeccable technique was recognised in two sequences, namely the opening bank robbery and the train heist, but the overwhelming feeling was that this was simply not enough. Robert Chazal in *France-Soir* spoke of 'gratuitous virtuosity'[106] and *Le Canard enchaîné* compared Melville to 'those who speak brilliantly to say nothing'.[107] Most damagingly Melville's staunch fans, Baroncelli, Chapier and Beylie now turned against him – as summed up by Baroncelli: 'One would like to write that *Un flic* is the quintessence of Melvillian cinema. Unfortunately it is only its caricature,'[108] while Chapier thought the whole thing was 'infinitely embarrassing for those who always loved him'.[109] There were some small pockets of praise, for the heist sequences, and for the performances, although many thought Delon was miscast. But even the most positive responses, such as by Albert Cervoni in *France nouvelle*,[110] were lukewarm. Cervoni talked of Melville having 'once more, made a very good film [but] the same very good film'. And Jean Rochereau in *La Croix* issued 'a gentle warning'.[111] Only Claude Mauriac in *L'Express* wrote a truly enthusiastic (and perceptive) review.[112] But these were tiny islands in a tide of hostility and by all accounts Melville was extremely hurt by this devastating and sometimes abusive response (*Positif*, for instance, demanded, 'it is about time "Inspector" Melville was made redundant').[113]

Were the critics right? Melville's last film *is* strange and, if not incoherent, certainly uneven, investing more in set pieces than tight plotting. There is a problem with Delon, although not so much miscasting as the fact that his role is eclipsed by Simon, especially in the middle section of the film when he disappears for half an hour (Melville offered Delon either part but the star chose to play the *flic* partly to break with his gangster image – a shrewd move in the long run, but clearly not at the time).[114] Still, given, at the very least, two breathtaking sequences, why so much hatred? In the ferocious and highly volatile French critical milieu of the time, Melville suffered a backlash after the triumph of *Le Cercle rouge*. But evidently the surfacing of the normally hidden sexual ambivalence of the 'virile' gangster was 'too much'. *Un flic* is both opaque and obvious in its portrayal of 'homophilia' and the critics' responses at the time are an interesting mixture of denial (mostly) and abuse (sometimes). This coalesced round the figure of the transvestite, either ignored or referred to as 'detestable',[115] a 'dramatically useless and purely sensational detail'.[116] Only Edmond Gilles in *L'Humanité*[117] noted, 'not without ambiguity, [Coleman] plays with the passion that a transvestite has for him'. Similarly, the relationship between Coleman and Simon appeared as a caricature of Melville's 'virile friendships', while Deneuve was a parody of the marginal Melvillian women. There is undeniably truth in these views, even though they do not exhaust the meaning of the film. Claude Mauriac was one of the few who noted at the time: 'A woman between two men? Rather two men opaquely facing each other and trying to reach each other through a transparent woman.'[118] In total contrast, Serge Daney, who in the late 1960s had vilified Melville, wrote in 1988 of how 'beautiful' *Un flic* was, concluding: 'Like all great filmmakers, [Melville] is content with filming what, that is to say, whom, he loves.'[119] In July 2002 Louis Skorecki wrote two brief but extravagant pieces in *Libération* on the occasion of a television broadcast of the film. On 8 July he called *Un flic* 'a subdued pastel-coloured masterpiece with gay overtones (not outrageously queeny, a real gay film: glorious, massive, amorous) [...] We love you Melville.' Three days later, on 11 July, he extolled Melville's representation of 'sublimely queer gangsters' and harangued critics who 'in a rush to praise his worst films (*Le Samouraï*), ignored his masterpieces and buried his most beautiful, his last, *Un flic*'. While Skorecki somewhat overstates textual evidence, the discrepancy of these readings, beyond wildly different critical climates, is ample testimony to the textual ambivalence built into *Un flic*.

Mannerism, spectacle and the *policier*: the two heists

It seems that in the hostile climate of its 1972 reception, *Un flic* could not do anything right. Misunderstood by reviewers such as René Prédal, as attempting a 'slice of life' of 'routine' police work,[120] and shown to real cops for their opinion, the film could only fail. On the other hand even those prepared to see it in stylistic terms disliked what they considered to be its 'excessive mannerism'.[121] Seen more dispassionately today, *Un flic* certainly makes no claim to conventional realism. Although Skorecki's claim that it is Melville's most beautiful film is far-fetched, the two heist sequences at the very least are magisterial demonstrations of Melvillian *mise en scène* and genre distillation.

A 'Western' on a family beach in the Vendée

Un flic opens on a foggy view of high-rise buildings and cranes. We are by the sea and soon, over the opening credits, the camera reveals views of a totally empty beach, lined with an immense cliff of brutally modern blocks of flats, running continuously along the beach. Some of the soulless blocks have balconies which in their design evoke waves, echoing the real waves opposite, and anticipating the police headquarters later on.

A huge American car (a black Plymouth, similar to Corey's in *Le Cercle rouge*) stealthily advances along the deserted seafront and stops in view of a street corner bank, a branch of the Banque Nationale de Paris (BNP). The car's windscreen mists up, rain falls like melancholy tears. In the car are four gangsters, one wearing a trench-coat, the others dark coats and all wearing hats. With a discreet 'bing' on the soundtrack, the lights on the promenade come on. Parallel editing now takes us to Edouard Coleman (Delon) in an equally large black American car, driving down the pre-Christmas Champs-Elysées. Here too lights come on, as the music becomes more lyrical. An obvious parallel between the gangsters and Coleman is established, as is the theatricality of the scene (despite location shooting in both cases), with the stress on the lights being 'switched on'. Melville frequently invokes the Western as a source; here the similarity with a bank in a small Far West town is evident.

Reviewing the film in *Le Figaro*[12] Louis Chauvet ironically dubbed this sequence the 'slowest and most languid hold-up of the century'. Unwittingly he had a point. The whole sequence lasts sixteen minutes (eleven minutes until the get-away), an inordinate length in view of the hold-up action which only takes a few minutes. What Melville shows us is the lengthy run-up: one by one, three of the gangsters come out of the car and walk to the bank, battling against the violent wind and rain, holding on to their hats, while huge waves crash against a jetty (Louis, the driver, remains in the car). Melville elongates the sequence no doubt because of the extraordinary setting, the empty modern blocks facing the immemorial sea, which eloquently conveys his discourse on the 'modern world', as will be discussed later. But the gangsters' separate progress to the BNP has another purpose. As they fight the hostile elements, they are also 'in their element', like a concrete *mise en abyme* of Melvillian gangsterdom: fighting a hostile world to perform an act that can only lead to ruin and death. The third man, Paul, hesitates a fraction too long before leaving the car under Louis' stern gaze, a weakness which will accompany him throughout the film. Paul has a wife, ignorant of his criminal activities and yet who is presented as a silent reproach. Like Mathilde in *L'Armée des ombres* and Santi in *Le Cercle rouge*, Paul's familial connection makes him the weakest link, and he commits suicide as the police arrest him.

As we move into the bank just before closing time, a few pan shots reveal the space, criss-crossed by vertical bars which imprison both the bank teller and, in the reverse point of view, the gangsters themselves. Paul and Marc's dark coats make them look like bank managers – we learn later that Paul *is* a bank manager who has been made redundant (conversely, the two innocent customers who are caught in the hold-up are middle-aged men in overcoats who could be gangsters). Simon, Marc and Paul wear hats that distinguish them from the staff and 'ordinary' customers. All three in unison put on identical dark glasses as the music swells, cuing the action. An employee lowers the iron curtain outside, effectively completing the theatrical setting. The action 'proper' can now begin. Yet this is conducted quietly – Simon murmurs 'two steps backward' to the cashier – even when Marc produces a machine gun and the cashier fires back at him and hits the alarm. The shrill sound does not produce any visible panic or hurry. Silence prevails, with absolutely minimal dialogue. It is as if both employees and gangsters were playing their part in a ghostly ritual. As they make their get-away in the car with the wounded Marc, Simon's order to 'keep your hats on until the station' is practical (they must be recognised as they pretend to take the train, so that they can make their real get-away with their other car waiting at the station) and self-conscious: keep your image intact.

Un flic: gangsters fighting the elements, gangsters in their element – the opening bank robbery

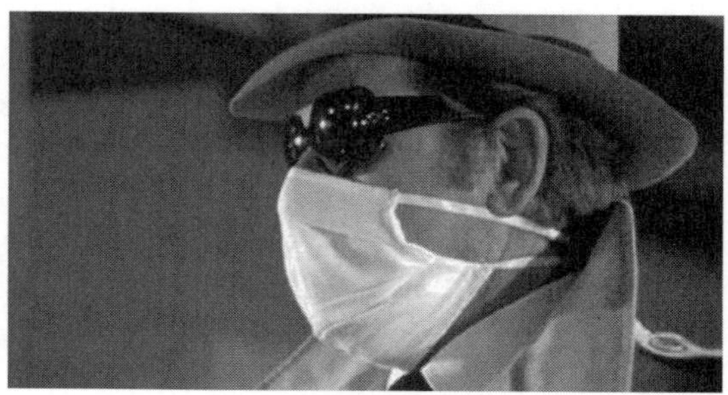

Real-time heist

After the gangsters leave Marc at the clinic, they next meet at the Louvre where Simon is shown in a shot counter-shot exchange, looking at a self-portrait of Van Gogh, both wearing a hat and framed in similar positions. The idea of the criminal as artist is not new, but here the choice of painting is not innocent, connoting anguish as well as male artistic genius, in anticipation of Simon's planning and execution of the train heist. The ridicule poured on the use of models for this sequence is partly justified: train and helicopter do look like toys, even if they are, arguably, used with ironic self-consciousness – is Melville not acknowledging this when he cuts, at the end of the sequence, to a real helicopter dropping the men back at their starting point? Whatever the pros and cons of the models, the sequence on the train is of such fantastic precision and suspense that one forgives the defect. One is not surprised to hear that Melville may have spent 'eight months editing the film'.[123]

The plan is simple, as outlined by the gang in their hide-out (which contains one great virtuoso shot, one minute long, circling around the men before zooming in on the map): Simon is dropped on the roof of the moving Paris–Lisbon train, as it enters a 50km straight stretch south of Bordeaux, at lower speed because of electrical work on the track. He must retrieve the two suitcases full of drugs from Mathieu la valise (Léon Minisini), sleeping in one of the carriages, and be lifted, with the cases, onto the helicopter. They have twenty minutes to do the job, which is exactly how long the sequence lasts. The fine-tuning is reiterated in the sequence, when Paul in the helicopter looks at his watch and says, 'He's got ten minutes left', exactly ten minutes of screen time before the end of the sequence. Thus Melville in this sequence perhaps more than in any other in his work (with the possible exception of the eight-minute eight-second *plan-séquence* of *Le Doulos*) plays with the notion of real time. One take in particular exemplifies this extreme version of 'cinema of process' in action. Simon enters the train, wearing a zipped flying suit. Entering the toilet, he proceeds to wash his face, meticulously comb his hair, remove his shoes and the suit, to reveal a beautiful dressing-gown, and stow all these clothes in a small locker to which he has the key. All this is shot in one extraordinary, three-minute *plan-séquence*. The combination of cramped space, which forces the camera to fly up and down Crenna's body, the movement and noise of the train and the stretched sense of time produce agonising suspense, heightened by Simon's calm. Not only does he smoothe his hair twice, he even bothers to make a proper parting. The *plan-séquence*, obviously conducted in silence, is an episode of pure behaviourist cinema. The encounter with another passenger creates an added tension as Simon smokes a cigarette to let the man return to his room. He then unlocks the door to Mathieu's cabin, knocks him out, gags him and takes the cases. A reverse (though shorter) forty-second take in which Simon puts the flying suit on again matches the opening shot. He is lifted to safety just in time for the helicopter to avoid a church tower.

Narrative trouble

In between the brilliantly conducted heist sequences discussed above, the narrative of *Un flic* moves awkwardly along, violating a number of mainstream cinema 'rules'. Its progression is uneven, especially compared to the tight structure and unity of *Le Samouraï* and *Le Cercle rouge*. Almost half of the film is occupied by the two heists, in two uneven blocks of sixteen and twenty-eight minutes (including the run-up to it in the latter case), while between the two we move through a series of disparate spaces – club, clinic, museum, hotels, offices – sometimes shown in a particularly dislocated fashion. For instance, in the hotel scene with Cathy and Coleman, the camera immediately moves up to a mirrored ceiling and later adopts a position from that ceiling, a disorienting sense of space which duplicates the opacity of their relationship. In the strange, futuristic office of the police headquarters, whose 'wavy' surface evokes a delirious vision, at the same time as it recalls the balconies on the beach, Coleman's office sports two huge maps, one of New York and one of Paris. Simon's club is also a confusing space. The first characters seen in it are Coleman and Cathy – Simon's own entrance at the end of the scene shown as an intrusion (on a first viewing one may miss the fact that it's called 'Simon's' and be even more confused). Another perplexing moment, especially on first viewing, is the scene at Bordeaux station when Coleman and his men watch the drugs consignment being put onto the train. Why they don't arrest the traffickers there and then? To add to the confusion the line of four gangsters on the platform echoes exactly Coleman and his men a few yards away. One of the gangsters (Jacques Leroy), briefly seen, even resembles Crenna.

The use of stars seems similarly perverse. Catherine Deneuve, one of the biggest female stars of the time, is reduced to a bit player; her lines would fit on half a page. However, her few appearances serve, in typically self-conscious Melvillian fashion, as a

Un flic: stars rather than characters: Coleman (Alain Delon) and Cathy (Catherine Deneuve)

commentary on stardom. We first see her as Coleman doodles on the piano in Simon's club. Deneuve appears out of the backroom, as if lured by his music. She remains in the doorway, barely moving, smiling, not speaking. Her pose in a frame within a frame, her glamorous make-up and jewellery, her silence and immobility, and the shot counter-shot editing between her and Delon playing the piano, evoke more a 'summit meeting' between two stars than an encounter between characters. She is next seen as an 'angel of death' when she administers the lethal injection to Marc, the reverse of Mathilde in *L'Armée des ombres* (where the latter looked like the 'black spider' to save a life, Deneuve is in pristine white to kill). Her role in *Un flic* aligns with that part of her star image which emphasised the 'perverse' nature of her beauty, in particular in *Belle de jour* (1967), *La Sirène du Mississipi* (1969) and *Tristana* (1970).[124] The 'Belle de jour' image is referenced again when she appears in the suspiciously luxurious, bordello-like hotel room with Coleman, and they engage in an erotic pretence of arrest. Finally, in another brief appearance, she is the 'woman in the middle', locked in an exchange of gazes between Simon and Coleman. Her presence in the film is, as can be seen, actually quite rich at the level of a comment on stardom, but as a character she is almost completely empty. As also, strangely, is Delon, since Coleman's part ends up relatively marginal compared with the little-known Crenna, who is given prime screen time in the two best sequences of the film. Melville's cinephilic gesture of casting an American 'B' actor here backfired (Crenna's dubbing, though technically accomplished, does not help matters).

All these features clearly contributed to the critical unease and bafflement at the time. In a wild speculation, Jean Rochereau, one of the few sympathetic reviewers, argued that Coleman may have been an accomplice of Simon's in the drugs business. For him that was the only explanation: 'If you cannot hang on to the hypothesis of a Coleman–gangsters complicity, the film is a failure.'[125] There is no textual evidence that Coleman is a crook, even though he wants to delay the release of Marc Albouis' identity and warns

Simon of his impending arrest. Melville also inserts a deliberate ambiguity: when Cathy, referring to Paul, Louis and Simon as partners in the forthcoming heist, asks, 'all three of you know?', Simon replies, 'no, all four of us'. Is the fourth accomplice her, as seems most likely – or could it just be Coleman?

Yet more convincing is the argument that the ambiguity is personal and sexual. After all, Coleman does arrest the gang. Cathy is sexually shared by the two men and about half-way into the film, a silent play on their reciprocal gazes at the bar stresses the ambiguity of their desires. Although a dance number is taking place in the background, the more ponderous film music takes over the strident jazz of the number, thus marking the moment out as 'serious'. Editing cuts between medium two-shots and close-ups of the characters' eyes, denying a firm anchorage. Each character could be addressing his/her amused and desiring gazes to either of the other two. But the possibility that the significant pair is Simon and Coleman is as strong as the other combinations (Cathy–Simon, whom we have just seen kiss, and Cathy–Coleman, whom we have seen in the hotel; in addition Coleman has just been seen gesturing to one of the female dancers).

Is Cathy the object of desire of both men, or is she performing the role of heterosexual alibi for a homosexual love story? Is *Un flic*, as Daney and Skorecki argue, a gay film? Not explicitly. Even homophilia, as in *Bob le flambeur*, *L'Ainé des Ferchaux* and *Le Cercle rouge*, is implied, but never shown, which of course it could not be. The marginalisation of women and the glamorisation of men (Simon striking a dandy figure at the Louvre and on the train) are all generic. However *Un flic*, in addition to the ambiguous relationship between Coleman and Simon via Cathy, also multiplies figures of gay iconography. There is the young gay thief and the older 'gentleman' (Jean Desailly, surrounded by antiques, if not an antique dealer); there is the butch look of Mathieu la valise, whom Melville describes in the script as 'handsome [...] his hair is a little too blond. He is a "muscle man", but his face has something strange, artificial, non virile about it.'[126] And there is the transvestite, whose amorous glances at Coleman are undisguised. His attitude, however, is more ambiguous. If their looks are equally desiring when they first meet in the car, later Coleman turns nasty,[127] slapping and humiliatingly telling her to 'dress as a man'. As she leaves the police building, the suddenly lyrical music seems to underline her genuine pain, yet Coleman's attitude remains one of cold contempt.[128]

Are the overtly gay characters there to deflect attention from a central vision of homosexuality which must 'remain in the closet' (in a classic strategy discussed by Richard Dyer in relation to *L'Air de Paris*[129])? Or is their presence a symptom of homophobic stereotyping: for instance, the transvestite as an extreme view of the informer, whose inferior status is traditionally given the derogatory *feminine* slang name of *donneuse*, as Denitza Bantcheva points out,[130] or the pathetic old 'invert' robbed by a cynical young male lover – all foils for the successful, virile, gangster and flic? Either way, homophilia and possibly repressed homosexuality are pushed here to an extreme. The friendships that characterised the Bob–Roger, Faugel–Silien and Corey–Vogel pairs, as well as the hidden affinities of Gu–Blot and Mattei–Vogel, here become more explicit and problematic. The currents and counter-currents of opacity and repression emerge symptomatically, as in the second part of *L'Ainé des Ferchaux*, as spatial and narrative dislocations. Literally, they create narrative trouble. Given Melville's mastery of narrative economy, amply demonstrated in his earlier 1960s gangster films, the notion of a return of the repressed causing ambiguity and even incoherence is certainly more plausible than the charge of ineptitude. It is a great pity that Melville's sudden death robbed him of the possibility to counter or further elucidate this 'mystery'.

MELVILLE'S LAST THREE GANGSTER FILMS: FLIGHT FROM MODERNITY, FLIGHT FROM FEMININITY

In the course of this chapter, as in chapters 4 and 5, we have looked at Melville's representation of gangsters in terms of *mise en scène* and generic features, American and Japanese antecedents, investment in the narcissism of dress, homophilia, and their configuration as 'tragic', the latter an important component of the films' cultural prestige. As Christine Gledhill put it, 'It is this – the inevitability and mode of the gangster's death – which permits critics' frequent appeal to tragedy as a justification for taking the genre seriously.'[131] Apart from the specific 'problem' of *Un flic* at the time, Melville's last three films *have* been taken seriously. They have also been very popular at the box office. The question thus remains, posed at the beginning of this chapter, of the appeal of the Melvillian universe, dominated by ritual, violence, futility and death. Granted the not negligible aesthetic appeal, did the films 'speak' to their audience about concrete social issues? Their male focus invites a gender reading. Feminist readings of the gangsters' macho posture have sometimes seen it as evidence of weakness, of 'masculinity in crisis'. As Kirkham and Thumim put it, 'We are invited to understand that the tough or cynical exterior masks – it is *only* a mask – vulnerability which lies beneath/within.'[132] I am personally suspicious of the notion of 'masculinity in crisis' as applied to such dominant and popular forms, yet it might be helpful to bear it in mind.

In order to achieve their death-driven goal, the heroes in *Le Samouraï*, *Le Cercle rouge* and *Un flic* must be free of ties. The elimination of women means that relationships – with lovers and wives, family and children, in short with life – are effectively absent as they spell weakness, and perversely threaten to distract the hero from his deathly trajectory into the 'normal world'. For instance, Weber's wife in *Un flic* believes that his trips to carry out the robberies are motivated by his search for a job. The concealment of his criminal life preserves his masculine ego while driving him surely to death. Even if, compared to Simon's public and spectacular suicide at the end, his death is ignominious (hidden away in the bathroom), basically removing yourself is preferable to facing 'normal life' and women. How can we make sense of this morbidity and its attraction for a 'family' audience?

Melville's films may be nostalgically steeped in the aura of the American gangster film of the 1930s and in that of the Japanese samurai, but they also spoke to, and about, 1960s France – despite Melville's numerous denials. The last three films inhabit the affluent quartiers of the Champs-Elysées where the moneyed bourgeoisie meets big-time criminality and high-class prostitution. These separate worlds intersect in luxury night-clubs and bars with ostentatious modernist décor – Martey's, Santi's, Simon's – and they no longer host the cosy 'families' of Montmartre hoodlums of *Bob le flambeur*. The gangsters mingle with the new cadres who rose to prominence through the 1950s and 60s. In *Le Samouraï*, Jef gets rid of his (damaged) trench-coat and dons a dark coat and hat to perform his ultimate contract, his own suicide. In *Le Cercle rouge*, Jansen blends perfectly with the rich customers at the jeweller's. The opening robbery in *Un flic* shows Paul, Marc and Louis dressed as businessmen (Farid Chenoune has shown how the gangster attire from the 1930s duplicated that of the businessman[133]). The sharp suits, dark glasses, slicked hair, hats and streamlined briefcases thus connote both gangsterism and the new capitalism lording it over France in the last decade of its post-war economic boom – their sharp lines now also contrast with the 'soft' clothes and hairstyles of the hippie era.

The 1960s saw the climax of France's state-led modernisation, reflected in deep political, economic and psychological changes, including the rise of what Roland Barthes called 'structural man'.[134] As Kristin Ross put it, in the new era, 'subjectivity, consciousness, and agency – what passed for *l'homme*, in short, under the now obsolete terms of bourgeois humanism – are effaced to the profit of rules, codes, and structures'.[135] One fascinating aspect of this shift is the flight from the political into structuralism. I would like to suggest a homology, with Melville, of a flight from the historical into aesthetic mannerism (which I do not mean as a derogatory but a descriptive term). To be sure, this was coherent with Melville's aesthetic programme from early on, but it became particularly extreme in the late 1960s.

In this context, Melville's gangsters are complex figures. In their morbidity and penchant for *actes gratuits* they are typical of the modernist sensitivity – arising from existentialism and evoking tropes from the new novel and absurdist theatre. Theirs is not a triumphant rule, but a melancholy one, an important reason why Delon was the perfect star for these late films. But their behaviour is contradictory. On the one hand their professionalism aligns them with the highly skilled technocrat, the lynchpin of the new establishment. Jef's cool precision, the spectacular heists of *Le Cercle rouge* and *Un flic* show the gangsters' mastery of new technology.

Pared-down *mise en scène* showcases an increasingly cold, linear, modernist world in washed-out greys, blues and greens. Sometimes it is a fantasy amalgam of French and American locations – Parisian rooms open up on a New York vista (Jef's room in *Le Samouraï*), police maps show the streets of New York as well as Paris (*Un flic*). But location shooting as well as set designs (for instance, the cabaret scenes) also show us a brutally real modernist Paris. Like Godard in *Alphaville* (1965) and Tati in *Playtime*, Melville creates an aesthetically pleasing and yet disturbing universe, both futuristic and contemporary: the night-clubs with space-age décor of white walls, plexiglass bubbles and steel tubes, the distorted walls of the modern police headquarters in *Un flic*, the cold modern apartments, the 'ruined' St-Jean de Monts beach with its ugly apartment blocks stretching to infinity, the price of the new leisure society. The simultaneous display and suspicion of modernity is also evident in the fact that the most spectacular modern flats, richly decorated with modern art, are those of the arch villains: Olivier Rey in *Le Samouraï*, Rico in *Le Cercle rouge*.

Concomitant with the process of modernisation was the rise of a technologically advanced domesticity. Thompkins sees the Western's male universe as a rejection of the domestic femininity of nineteenth-century religious and literary culture, as well as a reaction to twentieth-century female emancipation.[136] Similarly, the maleness of Melville's movies can be read as a flight from both the rising domesticity and increased female emancipation of the 1960s. The 'autistic' Melville hero responds to a crisis in 'human' identity, but in a gendered way. Technology can be harnessed by men – the cars, the guns, the trains and helicopters, the alarm technology – but the feminine-oriented technologies, those which contribute to the 'colonisation of everyday life',[137] must be suppressed. It is telling in this respect that the few shots in kitchens are occupied by men who are definitely not cooking: Jef dressing his wound, Jansen casting his bullets. Similarly, in *Un flic*, the window displays of the department stores are associated with the encounters with the 'feminine' transvestite.

The refuge of these men then is the cinematic past and an 'old' environment. They are deeply nostalgic creatures who are prone to holing up in shabby, old-fashioned suburban environments (Jef's and Jansen's lodgings, the house where the gangsters meet in *Un flic*), and they do not partake of the riches they may win. Significantly they are middle-aged. In *Le Cercle rouge*, the group includes no young man, unlike *Asphalt* and *Rififi*. This explains also the decision to give Delon a moustache. As Melville said, 'If I give Delon a moustache, that's it, he's a man, not just a nice young man, but a man.'[138] The late Melvillian gangsters are the end of the line of generic refinement, their distance from the 'model' of pre-war Hollywood increasingly stretched and unreal.

Thus Melville's extreme construction of masculinity in the last three gangster films both celebrates and critiques the shift towards a cool, hard, technocratic society. Whatever the weight one wishes to ascribe to the expression or repression of homophilia, the films show the gangsters as controlling patriarchal figures who relegate women to marginal and circumscribed spaces, in order to enjoy the thrill of death-defying and death-seeking acts. As Jane Thompkins says, the prestige of facing death is the ultimate test of strength in the Western: 'In an atheist world, facing death is an exploit *per se*.'[139] These gangsters are largely cinematic constructions with a high aesthetic pedigree which this chapter, and book, salutes. However, at the same time, their mobilisation of a pre-war cinematic universe, their refusal of modernity, also directs a nostalgic glance at a world before female emancipation.

NOTES

1. Jacques Doniol-Valcroze, 'La marque Melville', *L'Express*, 13 August 1973.
2. I have been unable to trace this novel.
3. Patrick Bureau, 'Chroniques Melvilliennes – I', *Cinéma 68*, no. 128, August–September 1968, p. 42.
4. *Le Samouraï* – script held at the Bibliothèque du Film (BIFI), Paris. Ref: SCEN 2417 B731.
5. Rui Nogueira and François Truchaud, 'A Samurai in Paris', *Sight and Sound*, vol. 37, no. 3, Summer 1968, p. 121.
6. Rui Nogueira, *Melville on Melville* (London: Secker and Warburg and BFI, 1971), pp. 128–9. For Delon biography, see Bernard Violet, *Les Mystères Delon* (Paris: Flammarion, 2000).

7. Michel Cournot, *Le Nouvel Observateur*, 1 November 1967.
8. Jacques Zimmer, 'le Samouraï', *Image et son*, no. 211, December 1967, pp. 127–8.
9. *Réforme*, 4 November 1967.
10. Samuel Lachize, *L'Humanité*, 28 October 1967.
11. *La Croix*, 6 November 1967.
12. Robert Chazal, *France-Soir*, 26 October 1967.
13. *Le Canard enchaîné*, 1 November 1967.
14. *L'Aurore*, 26 October 1967.
15. J. N., *Cahiers du cinéma*, no. 196, December 1967, p. 72.
16. Paul-Louis Thirard, *Positif*, no. 94, April 1968, p. 70.
17. Cournot, *Le Nouvel Observateur*, 1 November 1967.
18. Michel Mardore, *Le Nouvel Observateur*, 20 December 1967.
19. Serge Daney and Jean-Pierre Oudart, 'Work, Reading, Pleasure', *Cahiers du cinéma*, no. 222, July 1970, in Nick Browne (ed.), *Cahiers du Cinéma 1969–1972, The Politics of Representation* (London: Routledge/BFI, 1990), p. 117.
20. Bertrand Tavernier, in *Les Cahiers de la cinémathèque*, no. 25, Spring–Summer 1978, p. 105.
21. John Woo, 'Le style Melville, propos de John Woo', *Cahiers du cinéma*, no. 507, November 1996.
22. *Les Cahiers de la cinémathèque*, no. 25, Spring–Summer 1978, p. 97.
23. Violet, *Les Mystères Delon*, p. 221.
24. For a connection between male stars and crime in the post-War period, see Pierre Maillot, *Les Fiancés de Marianne: la société française à travers ses grands acteurs* (Paris: Le Cerf, 1996), and Ginette Vincendeau, *Stars and Stardom in French Cinema* (London and New York: Continuum, 2000).
25. See Ginette Vincendeau, 'From Proletarian Hero to Godfather: Jean Gabin and "Paradigmatic" French Masculinity', in Pat Kirkham and Janet Thumim (eds), *Me Jane, Masculinity, Movies and Women* (London: Lawrence & Wishart, 1995), pp. 249–62.
26. Vincendeau, *Stars and Stardom in French Cinema*, pp. 158–95.
27 Delon and Nathalie Delon were about to separate at that point.
28. Melville, interviewed in a television documentary on Delon: 'Profession: Star; Nationality: Française', directed by Jean Quaratino (1999).
29. Richard Dyer, *Stars*, new edition (London: BFI, 1998), p. 29.
30. See Violet, *Les Mystères Delon*, pp. 307–8.
31. One possible antecedent of Jef's bird may be the character of Tony le Stéphanois in Auguste Le Breton's *Du Rififi chez les hommes* (Paris: Gallimard, 1953), who also lives alone with a bird.
32. Nogueira and Truchaud, 'A Samurai in Paris', p. 119.
33. James Naremore, *More Than Night* (Berkeley, CA: University of California Press, 1998), pp. 73–4.
34. Although the DVD image is infinitely clearer than any of the video releases.
35. Raymond Borde and Etienne Chaumeton, quoted by Naremore, *More Than Night*, p. 73.
36. Göran Hermerén, *Influence in Art and Literature* (Princeton, NJ: Princeton University Press, 1975).

37. Colin McArthur, 'Mise-en-scène degree zero: Jean-Pierre Melville's *Le Samouraï*' in Susan Hayward and Ginette Vincendeau (eds), *French Film, Texts and Contexts, 2nd edition* (London and New York: Routledge, 2000), p. 199. Olivier Bohler makes a similar argument through 'Jean-Pierre Melville', unpublished thesis.
38. Naremore, *More Than Night*, pp. 73–4.
39. Guy Daussois, '*Le Samouraï*, du grand cinéma spectaculaire', *Le Populaire*, 14 November 1967.
40. Nogueira and Truchaud, 'A Samurai in Paris', p.121.
41. David Desser, *The Samurai Films of Akira Kurosawa* (Epping: Bowker, 1983), p. 145.
42. Ibid., 147.
43. J. L. Anderson, 'Japanese Swordfighters and American Gunfighters', *Cinema Journal*, vol. 12, no. 2, Spring 1973, p. 3.
44. Mitsuhiro Yoshimoto, *Kurosawa* (Durham, NC: Duke University Press, 2000), p. 204.
45. Jean-Pierre Melville, in *Les Cahiers de la cinémathèque*, no. 25, Spring–Summer 1978, p. 95.
46. Farid Chenoune, *A History of Men's Fashion* (Paris: Flammanion, 1993) p. 196.
47. Stella Bruzzi, *Undressing Cinema* (London: Routledge, 1997), p. 69.
48. Ibid., p. 80.
49. Emilien Carassus, *Le Mythe du dandy* (Paris: Librairie Armand Colin, 1971), p. 100.
50. Ibid., p. 135.
51. Ibid., p. 298.
52. Ibid., p. 310.
53. Klaus Theweleit, *Male Fantasies* (Cambridge: Polity Press, vol. 2: 1989), p. 171.
54. Bohler, 'Jean-Pierre Melville', p. 178.
55. Julia Kristeva, 'Black Sun: Depression and Melancholy', in Jennifer Radden (ed.), *The Nature of Melancholy* (Oxford: Oxford University Press, 2000), pp. 336–43.
56. Bruzzi, *Undressing Cinema*, p. 82.
57. Jean-Pierre Melville, interview with Claude-Marie Trémois, *Télérama*, 12 November 1967.
58. Patrick Bureau, 'Chroniques Melvilliennes – II', *Cinéma 68*, no. 129, October 1968, p. 90.
59. Autism, according to the Collins dictionary, means an 'abnormal self-absorption', a 'limited ability to communicate' and 'difficulties with language'.
60. Nogueira, *Melville on Melville*, p. 130.
61. McArthur, 'Mise-en-scène degree zero', in Hayward and Vincendeau (eds), *French Film, Texts and Contexts, 2nd edition*, p. 191.
62. François de Roubaix, *Image et son*, no. 215, March 1968, pp. 110–12.
63. Jacques Aumont and Michel Marie, *Dictionnaire théorique et critique du cinéma* (Paris: Nathan, 2001), p. 121.
64. Albert Cervoni, *France nouvelle*, 28 October 1970.
65. Gaston Haustrate, *Témoignage chrétien*, 3 November 1970.
66. Jacques Aumont, *Cahiers du cinéma*, no. 225, November–December 1970, p. 61.
67. Albert Bolduc, *Positif*, no. 124, February 1971.
68. Jean Wagner, *Téléciné*, no. 166, October–November 1970.
69. Henry Chapier, *Combat*, 22 October 1970.
70. Noël Simsolo, *La Saison cinématographique*, 1971, pp. 38–40.

71. 'Une conception pour le moins marcellinienne de la police' – a reference to Raymond Marcellin, Georges Pompidou's Minister for the Interior. Aumont, *Cahiers du cinéma*, no. 225, November–December 1970, p. 62.
72. Jean Duflot, *Politique-Hebdo*, 22 October 1970; Samuel Lachize, *L'Humanité-Dimanche*, 25 October 1970.
73. *La Croix*, 2 November 1970.
74. *Le Journal du dimanche*, 1 November 1970.
75. Centre National de la Cinématographie, Censorship Commission file on *Le Cercle rouge*.
76. Violet, *Les Mystères Delon*, p. 299.
77. Mattei is a Corsican name.
78. Nogueira, *Melville on Melville*, p. 154.
79. *Les Cahiers de la cinémathèque*, no. 25, Spring–Summer 1978, p. 95.
80. Ibid., p. 122.
81. Nogueira, *Melville on Melville*, p. 155.
82. Jean-Louis Bory, *Le Nouvel Observateur*, 2 November 1970.
83. Kim Newman, 'The Caper Film', in Phil Hardy (ed.), *The BFI Companion to Crime* (London: Cassell/BFI, 1997), p. 82.
84. Bory, *Le Nouvel Observateur*, 2 November 1970.
85. Bohler, 'Jean-Pierre Melville', p. 419.
86. Janssen invented the 'astronomical revolver', designed to record Venus' passage in front of the sun in 1874, the inspiration for Marey's 'photographic gun', one of the inventions that led to the cinematograph.
87. Nogueira, *Melville on Melville*, p. 164.
88. Pat Kirkham and Janet Thumim, 'Me Jane', in Pat Kirkham and Janet Thumim (eds), *Me Jane, Masculinity, Movies and Women* (London: Lawrence & Wishart, 1995), p. 26.
89. Ibid.
90. *Le Cercle rouge* – script held at the Bibliothèque du Film (BIFI), Paris. Ref: SCEN0501 B148.
91. This is rendered more minimally than in the script which had Jansen 'pull a quarter-litre flask out of the inside pocket of his jacket, and conscientiously empty it down his throat', ibid., p. 115.
92. Nogueira, *Melville on Melville*, p. 63.
93. Ibid.
94. Bureau, 'Chroniques Melvilliennes – II', p. 80.
95. L'aura Mulvey and Colin MacCabe, 'Images of Women, Images of Sexuality', in Colin MacCabe, *Godard: Images, Sounds, Politics* (London: BFI/Macmillan, 1980), pp. 79–105.
96. Glimpsed is the word in the British FilmFour broadcast, which cuts the shot of the naked woman getting out of bed.
97. Melville, interview with Gérard Langlois, *Les Lettres françaises*, 28 October 1970.
98. *Le Cercle rouge* – script held at BIFI, pp. 50–1.
99. Nogueira, *Melville on Melville*, p. 157.
100. Several writers have rightly pointed out echoes of the hunt in Jean Renoir's *La Règle du jeu* (1939).

101. Jean-Pierre Melville in *Le Monde*, 22 October 1970.
102. *Le Cercle rouge* – script held at BIFI, p. 26.
103. Jean-Luc Godard, in Tom Milne (ed.), *Godard on Godard* (London: Secker and Warburg, 1972), p. 217.
104. Jean-Jacques Simon, *Cinémonde*, November 1970.
105. Louis Chauvet, *Le Figaro*, 27 October 1972.
106. Robert Chazal, *France-Soir*, 1 November 1972.
107. *Le Canard enchaîné*, 1 November 1972.
108. Jean de Baroncelli, *Le Monde*, 31 October 1972.
109. Henry Chapier, *Combat*, 28 October 1972; Claude Beylie, *Écran*, no. 10, December 1972, p. 72.
110. Albert Cervoni, *France nouvelle*, 24 October 1972.
111. Jean Rochereau, *La Croix*, 6 November 1972.
112. Claude Mauriac, *L'Express*, 30 October 1972.
113. 'G. L.', *Positif*, no. 147, February 1973.
114. *France-Soir*, 31 October 1972; see also Violet, *Les Mystères Delon*, p. 307. Violet also indicates that Delon deliberately put on 5kg to play the part of Coleman according to Melville's wishes (ibid.).
115. Jean-Louis Tallenay, *Télérama*, 5 November 1972.
116. René Prédal, *Jeune Cinéma*, December–January 1972–3, p. 48.
117. Edmond Gilles, *L'Humanité*, 15 November 1972.
118. Claude Mauriac, *L'Express*, 30 October 1972.
119. Serge Daney, 'Un flic dans le petit écrin', *Devant la recrudescence des vols de sacs à main* (Lyon: Aleas Editeur, 1991), p. 25.
120. Prédal, *Jeune Cinéma*, December–January 1972–3.
121. Among others: Chapier, *Combat*, 28 October 1972; Jean de Baroncelli, *Le Monde*, 31 October 1972.
122. Chauvet, *Le Figaro*, 27 October 1972.
123. Michel Marmin, *Valeurs actuelles*, 6 November 1972.
124. For a further discussion of Deneuve, see Vincendeau, *Stars and Stardom in French Cinema*, pp. 196–214.
125. Rochereau, *La Croix*, 6 November 1972.
126. *Un flic* – script held at the Bibliothèque du film (BIFI), Paris. Ref: SCEN2733 B835.
127. The character, referred to as 'Gaby' in many filmographies (but not in the film or the credits), is played by a woman, Valérie Wilson.
128. Here I disagree with Bohler's view of the scene as a 'love declaration' (Bohler, 'Jean-Pierre Melville', p. 437).
129. Richard Dyer, 'No Place for Homosexuality: Marcel Carné's *L'Air de Paris* (1954)', in Hayward and Vincendeau, *French Film, Texts and Contexts*, p. 131.
130. Denitza Bantcheva, *Jean-Pierre Melville: de l'oeuvre à l'homme* (Troyes: Librairie Bleue, 1996), p. 83.
131. Christine Gledhill, 'The Gangster/Crime Film', in Pam Cook (ed.), *The Cinema Book* (London: BFI, 1986), p. 89.

132. Kirkham and Thumim, 'Me Jane', pp. 30–1.
133. Chenoune, *A History of Men's Fashion*.
134. Kristin Ross, *Fast Cars, Clean Bodies, Decolonization and the Reordering of French Culture* (Cambridge, MA, and London: MIT Press, 1995), p. 160.
135. Ibid., p. 161.
136. Jane Thompkins, *West of Everything, The Inner Life of Westerns* (New York and Oxford: Oxford University Press, 1992).
137. Ross, *Fast Cars, Clean Bodies, Decolonization and the Reordering of French Culture*, p. 77.
138. Nogueira, *Melville on Melville*, p. 163.
139. Thompkins, *West of Everything, The Inner Life of Westerns*, p. 31.

Conclusion: Neither American nor French, but Melvillian[1]

This book has examined the contribution Jean-Pierre Melville made to post-war French cinema through an analysis of his thirteen features (and one short film). As the sub-title, 'An American in Paris', indicates, I have been concerned with tracing the influence of American cinema on Melville's work, but equally I have been keen to embed it in the French context from which it arose and to which it was primarily addressed. Ultimately, I hope to have shown that Melville's films were equally indebted to both national traditions and distanced from them.

In the course of my analysis, like other Melville scholars and fans, I have been attracted to the thematic and stylistic features that make Melville's cinema so distinctive, and which he has himself signposted. To keep the geographical metaphor, the Melvillian map may be summarised as comprising the following 'regions':

- the rebel film-maker of the early years, *Résistant* in war, in career and films;
- the independent film-maker and studio owner;
- the adaptor of canonical authors (Vercors, Cocteau, Kessel) as well as Série Noire *policiers*;
- the Parisian intellectual proudly parading ostentatious Americana (the Ray-Bans, the Pontiac Firebird, the Stetson hats, the list of sixty-four American directors);
- the 1950s father/godfather/uncle of the New Wave;
- the successful mainstream film-maker of 1960s popular films with major stars, at loggerheads with the French critical establishment;
- the maker of increasingly bleak gangster/'samurai' films, culminating in *Le Samouraï* and *Le Cercle rouge*, and the equally sombre war film *L'Armée des ombres*, couched in minimalist, 'mannerist' style;
- the poet of male solitude and melancholy, of impossible love, of loyalty and betrayal, of an obsession with death, reflected in the (sometimes invented) epigrams and proverbs which adorn his film credits from *Le Doulos* onwards.

Cutting across these areas, I isolate three thematic clusters which emerge as 'fault lines' in the Melvillian landscape: the war and the Resistance; transnational generic codes; sexuality and gender. Interestingly, these three clusters correspond to three areas of mystery or at least ambiguity in Melville's own life, which emerged in Chapter 1.

Melville's participation in the Resistance was both unarguable (his joining of the Free French army in 1943–4) and hazy (his presence in London). This may be because his presence as a relatively humble *Résistant* was not recorded,[2] or because he somewhat exaggerated his London episode, or a bit of both. Whatever, ambiguity surfaces as one of the fundamental structuring devices of his three war films – *Le Silence de la mer*, *Léon Morin, prêtre*, *L'Armée des ombres*. In each case having been incredibly persistent in obtaining the rights and/or waiting for the correct conditions to adapt the books, Melville then systematically stripped them of their historical and social content (especially *Léon Morin, prêtre* and *L'Armée des ombres*, whereas *Le Silence de la mer*, the most faithful adaptation, is also the most poetic and stylised of the three novels). Instead of the banalities, triumphs and tragedies of everyday struggle, the films are pervaded by rituals, *actes gratuits* and the futility of action (at its strongest in *L'Armée des ombres* but already present in *Silence*, in von Ebrennac's gesture in volunteering for the Eastern front). The three war novels – which incidentally are three of, if not *the*, greatest French Resistance stories – function as both mask and display. They enable Melville – and his audience – to be projected back into French history, while indirectly reflecting on the contemporary. Their increasing ambivalence is a result of a growing mismatch between the hope of renewal they originally contained and the disillusion that followed, provoking nostalgia for a romanticised pre-war existence. That ambivalence may have been a deeply personal one, but its textual and historical evidence has given Melville's films a symbolic national resonance – indeed, it is a powerful reason for the films' popular success.

A second cluster of ambivalent meanings is attached to the choice of the gangster genre. Melville may or may not have had personal acquaintances in the underworld – the 'reality' hardly matters. His fascination for the underworld was emphatically not for the minutia of their lives or the sociological dilemmas of crime and law enforcement. From *Bob le flambeur* to *Un flic*, Melville's gangsters are increasingly detached from any realistic context, and they anachronistically 'quote' or 'paraphrase' the 1930s to 40s Hollywood hoodlum, crossed with the figure of the samurai (there are also echoes of some Japanese crime films, notably Kurosawa's *Stray Dog* (1949) and *High and Low* (1963), but they themselves were in symbiosis with Hollywood). That Melville's increasingly abstract, ghostly male figures – epitomised by Alain Delon's Jef Costello in *Le Samouraï* – 'speak' his discourse on 'tragic' masculinity is not in doubt. They also offer a sophisticated comment on transnational generic codes and their skilful appropriation by Melville, which, drawing on the work of art historian Göran Hermerén,[3] I would qualify as neither 'translation' (like *Mélodie en sous-sol*) nor 'tribute' (like *Tirez sur le pianiste*), but a recoding, or 'paraphrase' – a careful transposition from one aesthetic universe to another. No wonder Melville felt irritated when told he was making 'American films': 'Nothing could be less true. [...] My cinema is specifically French. [...] The best proof of the fact that they are not American is that the Americans don't want them. They don't understand my films, the motivations of my characters.'[4] As the comparisons in this book should make clear, Melville's 'emptying out' of traditional characterisation, withdrawal of information, simultaneous dilation and slowing down of action violate many 'rules' of classical Hollywood cinema.

America enabled Melville to orient himself on the French cultural map, in a typical French post-war gesture, also illustrated, though differently, by Jean-Luc Godard.

Anticipating New Wave film-makers, Melville was a firm believer in the equal artistic worth of French modernist literature (Proust, Gide, Cocteau) with, say, *Gone With the Wind*, Frank Lloyd's *Cavalcade* and Frank Sinatra. On the other hand, unlike Godard he did not treat Hollywood, in Peter Wollen's words, as 'a kind of conceptual property store from which he could serendipitously loot ideas for scenes, shots and moods'.[5] Melville's stylistic appropriation was more traditional, in that he endorsed Hollywood's mandate of entertainment as opposed to Godard's counter-cinema, yet at the same time it was more more controlled and systematic, unlike Godardian improvisation. Also, his point of reference was an increasingly nostalgic view of the formal classicism of Hollywood. In this respect the extremely broad church of his 'sixty-four American directors' (see Appendix 3) anticipates the influential definition of 'classical Hollywood cinema' by David Bordwell, Kristin Thompson and Janet Staiger across a wide sample of 'random' films twenty-five years later.[6] Melville's trajectory during the 1960s, in its divergence from Godard's, also points to its own historicity. During the 1960s Godard left his Americanist period behind and moved towards an increased politicisation, while Melville merged the 'cinema of attractions' of the heist blockbuster with mannerism. Here too he emerges as Janus-faced, on the cusp of modernist and post-modernist cinema, both offering 'old-fashioned entertainment' and prefiguring Martin Scorsese's view of a post-classical cinema as inevitably 'condemned, like the artists who followed the High Renaissance, to echo and embellish the great unselfconscious works of the past'.[7]

The third cluster of Melvillian ambiguities relates to sexuality and gender. Innuendos concerning Melville's own sexuality recur in reviews and commentaries, never substantiated, yet persistent enough that they can't be ignored, especially as they are linked to the films' characters. Melville's films offer a consistent discourse on masculinity as lonely, melancholy and death-driven, which has generally be taken as evidence of tragic profundity. Male bonding has been understood as simply generic, but in some cases its inherent sexual ambivalence has surfaced as 'narrative trouble', particularly in *L'Aîné des Ferchaux* and *Un flic*. Discussing the end of *Ferchaux*, in which Maudet (Jean-Paul Belmondo) abuses the dying Ferchaux (Charles Vanel) but is also moved to tears, Melville commented: 'The expression in Maudet's eyes belies the words he speaks. Don't forget that Maudet is a Melvillian hero.'[8] Melville's sociologically detached cinema through the 1960s and early 70s struck a note of dissent with three dominant modes of French cinema: the political (especially in this case the 'political thriller'), the comic and the sexual. But if Melville turned his back on the rising tide of sexual images, he did not turn his back on misogyny. Working in the crime genre offered a convenient vehicle through which to channel women's distantiation, oblivion or victimisation.

Gathering these three sets of ambiguities enables us to define Melville's nostalgic gaze towards pre-war Hollywood as a double flight, from the social and from women, and an ambivalent take on modernity. At this point, however, I must complete my analysis by turning to an essential, fourth, element: the images and sounds of Melville's cinema, which are no less complex. Melville professed a dislike for realism yet filled his films with hyper-realist detail. His stretching of time, his behaviourist observation of action coupled with minimalist sets and performances, the heightened quality of sound and silence, the stark black-and-white or cool colour schemes deliver a de-familiarisation of ordinary gestures and generic patterns. But whereas the minimalism of his *mise en scène* normally detaches it from its context, a final ambivalence returns us to 1960s France.

Melville's minimalist *mise en scène* simultaneously celebrates and critiques the hard lines and bare surfaces of modernist architecture and décor: the night-club of *Le Samouraï*, the roadside cafeteria of *Le Cercle rouge*, the desolate beach at the beginning of *Un flic*, spaces from which the gangsters take refuge, in grim, archaic, anonymous suburban rooms. In Chapter 6 I argue that the Melville gangsters' flight from women is a flight from modernity, a nostalgic desire for a time before women's entry in the public sphere and a hardening against the 'feminisation' of everyday life. Yet, at the same time as they evinced a nostalgic gaze towards classicism, Melville's films, in their stylistic mannerism and erasure of the social, also corresponded to the most modern developments in 1950s and 60s French culture: the rise of a technocratic world, the victory of structuralism over history; of language and 'communication' for its own sake. This dual vision is, of course, another reason why the films appealed to a wide audience, but also why, after the critical oblivion of the 1970s and 80s, he has again become so relevant, and exportable.

Just as he appropriated the transnational codes and iconic patterns of the gangster genre, primarily from Hollywood, American (and Hong Kong) film-makers have borrowed from, alluded and paid tribute to Melville. And, as Melville reconfigured Hollywood codes to his own purposes, so they have bent his work to suit their own agenda. The films of the directors most associated with Melville – Walter Hill, John Woo, Quentin Tarantino, the Coen brothers, Luc Besson – have inevitably stepped up the violence, which in some cases may be 'stylised' but is much more graphic. As Kristin Thompson and David Bord-well argue, 'Woo invoked Jean-Pierre Melville's films in celebrating an underworld code of trust and honour, but his characters are far more boyish and narcissistic than their French counterparts';[9] Tarantino's on the other hand are verbose and comic (*Pulp Fiction*) where Melville's are taciturn and tragic. The *cinéma du look* of Luc Besson uses some formal features (abstraction, stylisation) that are Melvillian, but characterisation is, as in Woo and Tarantino, different (Léon is more boyish and more comic) and importantly, the point of reference has changed, from classical Hollywood cinema to contemporary Holly-wood film and television, and advertising. In turn this reflects the different audiences addressed by these films. Within the fragmented turn-of-the-twenty-first-century audience, Woo, Tarantino, Besson *et al*. address a predominantly young, male audience. Melville by comparison addressed an audience that was still a 'family audience'. It is not the least remarkable aspect of his work that he was able to explore the sets of deep stylistic, historical and ideological ambiguities that he did in a mainstream popular format. Towards the end of his career he declared, 'You do not put people in a cinema to teach them something, but to amuse them, to tell them a story as best you can, and deliver the kind of music-hall that, in the end, cinema is.'[10] By going back to pre-cinema entertainment, Melville was also going back to his own pre-cinema, as it were, the circus which he celebrates in his short film *24 heures de la vie d'un clown*. By (perhaps too modestly) playing down the seriousness of his own work, he is also pointing out a primordial aspect of it, the reason we keep going back to his films, the pleasure of the text.

Bob le flambeur: Bob (Roger Duchesne)

NOTES

1. This phrase is taken from Jacques Doniol-Valcroze's obituary of Melville in *L'Express*, 13 August 1973.
2. This was confirmed by Pierre Gauthier, historiographer of the Free French division, interviewed by Véronique Bourdis-Gispalou, 2 July 2002, in conversation with the author.
3. Göran Hermerén, *Influence in Art and Literature* (Princeton, NJ: Princeton University Press, 1975).
4. François Guérif, 'Jean-Pierre Melville', *Les Cahiers de la cinémathèque*, no. 25, Spring–Summer 1978, p. 96.
5. Peter Wollen, 'JLG', in *Paris Hollywood: Writings on Film* (London and New York: Verso, 2002), p. 76.
6. David Bordwell, Kristin Thompson and Janet Staiger, *The Classical Hollywood Cinema: Film Style and Mode of Production to 1960* (New York: Columbia University Press, 1985).
7. Martin Scorsese, quoted in Ian Christie, 'Passion and Restraint, Ian Christie talks with Martin Scorsese', in Ginette Vincendeau (ed.), *Film/Literature/Heritage, A Sight and Sound Reader* (London: BFI, 2001), p. 66.
8. Rui Nogueira (ed.), *Melville on Melville* (London: Secker and Warburg and BFI, 1971), p. 110.
9. Kristin Thompson and David Bordwell, *Film History, An Introduction* (New York: McGraw-Hill, Inc., 1994), p. 778.
10. Patrick Bureau, 'Chroniques Melvilliennes – II', *Cinéma 68*, no. 129, October 1968, p. 85.

Filmography

1946: *24 HEURES DE LA VIE D'UN CLOWN*
Director: Jean-Pierre Melville
Producers: Jean-Pierre Melville and Pierre Braunberger
Script: Jean-Pierre Melville
Voiceover: Jean-Pierre Melville
Directors of photography: Gustave Raulet, André Villard
Editor: Monique Bonnot
Music: Henri Cassel

Cast: The clowns Béby and Maïss, Mrs Béby, staff at the Médrano circus, passers-by.

Black and white
Running time: 17 minutes

Notes

Little information is available on this film. Although the credits only mention Melville as producer, other sources indicate Pierre Braunberger as co-producer. Braunberger claims, 'I worked on *24 heures de la vie d'un clown* with Melville, a short and charming film.'[1]

The film begins with a still picture of Béby with some text and a signature at the bottom, unfortunately illegible on the only video recording available to view this film.

Synopsis

In Montmartre (Pigalle), a man looks at his watch: it is 11.50pm. In the Médrano circus, Béby's act with his partner, Maïss, is coming to an end. The two men take off their make-up in their dressing room. We follow Béby home, see him eat a meal prepared by his wife (spaghetti, which he complains about). Béby shows us round his room, full of photographs and books relating to his career, goes to bed and says his prayers, accompanied by his dog. In the morning he goes to the public baths to take a bath. He admires a beautiful young woman in the street, for which he is reprimanded by his wife. He goes to his local café where he shows customers a few tricks with his hat. He meets Maïss at a café terrace, where they observe real-life incidents as an inspiration for their act. They go to Médrano, apply their make-up and go on stage. We see part of their act, which reworks some of the afternoon's incidents. The film ends with the same man in the street looking at his watch, just before midnight.

1947–9: *LE SILENCE DE LA MER*

Director: Jean-Pierre Melville
Production company: Melville-Productions
Production director: Edmond Vaxelaire
Assistant producer: Marcel Cartier
Distributor: Pierre Braunberger[2]
Assistant directors: Jacques Guymont, Michel Drach
Script: Jean-Pierre Melville
Based on the novel by Vercors (1942)
Director of photography: Henri Decae
Editing: Jean-Pierre Melville and Henri Decae[3]
Music: Edgar Bischoff
Orchestra conductor: Paul Bonneau (Grand Orchestre des Concerts Colonne)
Sound engineer: Carrère
Chief electrician: Magot
Costumes: Traonquez
Still photography: Agis

Cast: Howard Vernon (Werner von Ebrennac); Nicole Stéphane (the niece); Jean-Marie Robain (the uncle; also voiceover); Ami Aaröe (von Ebrennac's fiancée); Georges Patrix (the orderly); Denis Sadier (von Ebrennac's SS friend); Rudelle, Fromm, Vernier, Max Hermann, Schniedel (German officers); Henri Cavalier; Dietrich Kandler.

Black and white
Running time: 86 minutes
First released Paris: 22 April 1949

Post-credit text: Ce film n'a pas la prétention d'apporter une solution au problème des relations entre la France et l'Allemagne, problème qui se posera aussi longtemps que les crimes de la Barbarie Nazie, perpétrés avec la complicité du peuple allemand, resteront dans la mémoire des hommes . . .

This film does not claim to solve the problem of relations between France and Germany, a problem which will exist for as long as the barbarous Nazi crimes, perpetrated with the complicity of the German people, remain in people's memory . . .

Notes

The scenes showing von Ebrennac in Paris were shot on location, including those at the Kommandantur, for which Melville used 'the office which had actually served the purpose, so as to have the view of the Opéra from the window'.[4] The bulk of the film was shot at Vercors' home in Villiers-sur-Morin in the Seine-et-Marne département, east of Paris. Shooting took place over several months during 1947 and 1948 – 11 August 1947 to December 1947 according to Melville, 5 September 1947 to 18 May 1948 according to CNC files, and 'over a year, a couple of days here and then, whenever Melville found the money', according to Vernon.[5]

Details about production costs are equally contradictory. According to Melville, 'The film cost 30,000 F for the rights, 30,000 to record the score with 120 musicians, 60,000 for everything else – a hundred and twenty thousand in all. At that time a film like Jean Delannoy's *La Symphonie pastorale* cost one million francs.'[6] Distributor Pierre Braunberger, however, while recognising the film was cheap, puts the cost at 'about FF 20m'.[7] Braunberger's role in the film is itself contested. Melville claims that 'Braunberger [. . .] came to see me and managed to persuade me to give him the film. I made a silly mistake there!',[8] and his widow Florence Welsh confirms, 'We were robbed by Braunberger, the film's distrubutor.'[9] Braunberger for his part claims that

> At the Liberation I read in *L'Intransigeant* that someone named Grumbach was about to shoot *Le Silence de la mer*. [. . .] 'He had met Nicole Stéphane, who was to act in the film, and who had already invested FF5m. With this money, Melville had shot a few takes and recorded the credit music, with 40 musicians. He had no money left [. . .] I then offered to help him finish the film, or more accurately produce it. We quickly came to an agreement. I discovered that he did not have the rights. [. . .] We took the risk. [. . .] The film did good business as it was quite successful.'[10]

Synopsis

A prologue shows two men exchanging a suitcase containing underground newspapers and a copy of Vercors' book *Le Silence de la mer*.

In a small French village, an old man (Jean-Marie Robain) recalls how he and his niece (Nicole Stéphane) decide to respond to the billeting of German officer Werner von Ebrennaç (Howard Vernon) by maintaining silence. Every evening a uniformed von Ebrennac comes into the library where they sit by the fireside, and politely says good night. After a month, he changes into civilian clothes, warms himself by the fire and launches into a series of long monologues about his love for France and French culture. One day he and the niece meet while she is walking her dog; neither speaks. The German officer's monologues now include discussions of fairy tales such as Beauty and the Beast, hinting at his love for the niece. He plays Bach on the harmonium and enthuses about his discovery of France as a soldier. A flashback shows him firing from a tank in view of Chartres cathedral. Another flashback evokes an episode with his German fiancée in which her cruelty to a bug prompts him to break his engagement with her. In the spring he appears in tennis clothes and announces his forthcoming leave in Paris. We see him in front of Parisian monuments. After his return he does not visit the uncle and niece for a week, though the uncle sees him accidentally at the local Kommandantur. Three days later von Ebrennac (in uniform) tells them about his shocking discovery of the camps and of the Nazi plan to crush France. He has decided to volunteer for the Eastern front; the niece says 'adieu', her first and only word to him. In the morning the uncle prominently displays a quotation saying 'It is a noble thing for a soldier to disobey a criminal order', but Ebrennac leaves. We see the last lines of Vercors' book and an inscription about its underground publication.

1950: *LES ENFANTS TERRIBLES*

Assistant production manager: J. Boussard
Director: Jean-Pierre Melville
Production company: O.G.C.
Producer: Jean-Pierre Melville
Production directors: Jean-Pierre Melville, Jacques Braley
Production manager: P. Schwob
Assistant directors: Claude Pinoteau, Jacques Guymont, Michel Drach
Script: Jean-Pierre Melville, Jean Cocteau
Based on *Les Enfants terribles*, novel by Jean Cocteau (1929)
Dialogues: Jean Cocteau
Voiceover: Jean Cocteau
Director of photography: Henri Decae
Camera operator: Jean Thibaudier
Editor: Monique Bonnot
Assistant editors: C. Charbonneau, C. Durand
Set decorator: Emile Mathys
Music: Vivaldi's Concerto in D Minor for orchestra and strings; Bach's Concerto in D Minor for four pianos, based on Vivaldi's Concerto Grosso
Piano players: Jacqueline Bonneau, Andrée Collard, Geneviève Joy, Elaine Richepin
Song 'Were You Smiling At Me' by Melvyn Martin
Musical director: Paul Bonneau
Sound: Jacques Gallois, Jacques Carrère (sound mixing); R. Durand (sound recording)
Dresses by Christian Dior
Make-up: Arakelian
Still photography: A. Dino

Cast: Nicole Stéphane (Elisabeth); Edouard Dermithe (Paul) [also spelt Dermit, Dhermitt]; Jacques Bernard (Gérard); Renée Cosima (Dargelos/Agathe); Adeline Aucoc (Mariette); Maurice Revel (the doctor); Roger Gaillard (Gérard's uncle); Melvyn Martin (Michael); Jean-Marie Robain (the school bursar); Emile Mathys (The *censeur* [deputy head]); Annabel Buffet (Dior model); Maria Cyliakus (the mother); Rachel Devirys.

Uncredited: Hélène Rémy; Etienne Aubray; Jean-Pierre Melville and Jean Cocteau (in train dining room).

Black and white
Running time: 107 minutes
First released Paris: 29 March 1950

Notes

Shot on location in Paris (Société Nationale des Entreprises de Presse for 'gallery' scenes, Théâtre Pigalle), Montmorency ('seaside' shoplifting scene) and Ermenonville (Michael's car accident), and at the rue Jenner studios, November 1949–January 1950. The shoplifting scene was directed by Cocteau, as Melville was ill that day, a fact that has been widely reported, though Melville claims Cocteau followed his instructions to the letter.[11]

Synopsis

Paul (Edouard Dermithe), a pupil at the Lycée Condercet in Paris, falls ill when hit by a snowball containing a stone thrown by fellow pupil Dargelos (Renée Cosima), with whom he is infatuated (and who is later expelled). Paul begins a reclusive existence with his sister Elisabeth (Nicole Stéphane) and their sick mother in their flat in rue du Rocher. Paul and Elisabeth turn their cluttered bedroom into a 'theatre' where they live a close, incestuous relationship and play ritualistic games witnessed by their friend Gérard (Jacques Bernard) (who secretly loves Paul, then Elisabeth). When the mother dies, the maid, Mariette, looks after the children, paid for by the kindly doctor. Gérard's wealthy uncle takes them to the seaside, where they mischievously steal from shops and frighten small children. Back in Paris Elisabeth finds a job as a couture model. There she meets Agathe (Renée Cosima), who is introduced into the circle and makes a strong impression on Paul because of her uncanny resemblance to Dargelos. To Paul's annoyance, Elisabeth marries a rich American, Michael, who dies in a car crash immediately after the wedding. Elisabeth, Paul, Agathe and Gérard move into Michael's huge town house, where Paul recreates his old room in a gallery. When Agathe and Paul separately confess their love for each other to Elisabeth, she lies and schemes to separate them, convincing Agathe to marry Gérard instead. Paul's illness gets worse after the newlyweds leave. Gérard and Agathe later come to visit, bringing a (black) ball of a poisonous substance sent by Dargelos whom they meet by chance. Elisabeth dreams that Paul is dead. One night Agathe comes back to say Paul had written to say he was going to kill himself. They arrive in his bedroom too late. As Paul dies, Elisabeth shoots herself.

1953: *QUAND TU LIRAS CETTE LETTRE*

Director: Jean-Pierre Melville
Production company: Jad Films/S. G. C. (Paris)/Titanus-Dauria (Rome)
Producer: Louis Dubois
Production director: Paul Temps
Production manager: Caubrelier
Assistant directors: Pierre Blondy, Yannick Andrei
Trainee assistant director: Martine Sachot
Script and dialogues: Jacques Deval
Adaptation: Jean-Pierre Melville
Director of photography: Henri Alekan

Camera operator: Henri Tiquet
Assistant cameramen: Wladimir Yvanoff, Menvielle
Editor: Marinette Cadix
Assistant editor: Yo Maurette
Art directors: Raymond Cabutti, Robert Gys
Assistant decorator: Daniel Guéret
Assistant set designer: Christides
Music: Bernard Peiffer
Sound: Julien Coutelier
Sound editing: Jacques Carrère
Sound assistants: Gerardot, Bessières
Juliette Gréco and Irène Galter's dresses: Marian de Kers
Philippe Lemaire and Daniel Cauchy's uniforms: La Belle Jardinière
Make-up: Janine Jarreau
Make-up assistant: Nora Stern
Drawings: Neveu
Still photography: Carvel
Continuity: Dagmar Bolin

Cast: Juliette Gréco (Thérèse); Philippe Lemaire (Max); Daniel Cauchy (Biquet); Irène Galter (Denise); Yvonne Sanson (Irène); Jacques Deval (the judge); Jean-Marie Robain (the lawyer); Robert Dalban (the barman); Fernand Sardou (the garage mechanic); Philippe Richard (the butcher); Suzanne Hédouin (the buffet manageress); Léon Larive (the judge's clerk); Marcel Delaître (the grandfather); Jane Morlet (the grandmother); Suzy Willy (Mme Gobert); Roland Lesaffre (Roland); Robert Hébert (the doctor); Louis Pérault (the porter); Colette Régis (the mother superior); Yvonne de Bray (old woman in train); Claude Borelli (Lola); Mel Martin (dancer); Marjorie, Shouky, Céline and Marie-Thérèse (dancers from La Nouvelle Ève); Claude Hennessy; Adeline Aucoc; Alain Nobis; Marcel Arnal; Louise Nova; Colette Fleury.

Black and white
Running time: 104 minutes
First released Paris: 11 November 1953

Notes

Italian co-production (alternative title: *Lèvres interdites*) filmed on location in Cannes and around Paris (Enghein, La Varenne, Chennevières), and at the Boulogne-Billancourt studios, 23 February–21 March 1953.

The film had to be presented twice to the Censorship Commission (22 June and 8 July 1953) but was eventually awarded a general certificate.

Some sources indicate a guitar solo by Sacha Distel, as well as the following actors in the cast: Françoise Alban, Paul Temps, Lucienne Juillet and Hélène Dana (as 'the naked girl'), though they do not appear on the film's credits.

Synopsis

The story is set in Cannes. On the sudden death of her parents, novice Thérèse (Juliette Gréco) reluctantly leaves her convent to run the family's stationery shop and support her younger sister Denise (Irène Galter). Meanwhile Max (Philippe Lemaire), a young mechanic and boxer at the Riviera Dancing club, seduces a rich older woman, Irène (Yvonne Sanson), with the help of Carlton Hotel groom Biquet (Daniel Cauchy). Max chats up Denise in the street but when he visits the shop, a suspicious Thérèse sends him packing. Max becomes Irène's lover and chauffeur. When Denise delivers stationery to Irène at the Carlton she finds Max, who rapes her. Distraught, she tries to commit suicide by jumping off a boat, leaving a letter for her sister. She is rescued in time. In order to stop Biquet blackmailing him, Max doctors Irène's car, which Biquet is supposed to borrow that evening. However, Irène takes the car and is seriously injured when it crashes. Max is cleared by the judge, although Irène's jewels have disappeared (in fact stolen by Biquet). Thérèse waits for Max outside the courtroom and, literally at gunpoint, forces him to marry Denise to atone for the rape. Max, however, falls in love with Thérèse. He steals the dowry money Denise is given by her grandparents in order to join Biquet in Tangiers. Hoping Thérèse will join him, he asks her to meet him the following day in Marseille. Thérèse, meanwhile, dispatches Denise to the grandparents' farm and decides to return to the convent. Max, who believes she is joining him, waits for her at a railway station, but accidentally falls under the train that probably carries her towards the convent.

1956: *BOB LE FLAMBEUR*

Director: Jean-Pierre Melville
Production company: Organisation Générale Cinématographique/La Cyme/Play Art
Producers: Jean-Pierre Melville, Serge Silberman
Production director: Florence Melville
Production manager: Philippe Schwob
Assistant directors: François Gir, Yves-André Hubert, Léo Fortel
Script: Jean-Pierre Melville
Adaptation: Jean-Pierre Melville and Auguste Le Breton
Dialogues: Auguste Le Breton
Voiceover: Jean-Pierre Melville
Director of photography: Henri Decae
Camera operator: Maurice Blettery
Editor: Monique Bonnot
Assistant editors: Jeanne-Marie Favier, Yolande Palamanghi
Continuity: Jacqueline Parey
Music: Eddie Barclay, Jo Boyer
Orchestration: Didier Bollan, Jimmy Walther (piano)
Décor: Claude Bouxin, with Martine Sachot, Raymond Aupée
Sound: Pierre Philippenko, Jacques Carrère
Costumes: Ted Lapidus

Cast: Roger Duchesne (Bob Montagné); Daniel Cauchy (Paulo); Guy Decomble (Inspector Ledru); Isabel Corey (Anne); André Garet (Roger); Claude Cerval (Jean); Colette Fleury (Suzanne); Gérard Buhr (Marc); Simone Paris (Yvonne); Howard Vernon (McKimmie); Germaine Licht (the concierge, not on film credits but widely credited in various sources); Jean-Marie Rivière (P'tit Louis); Henri Allaume, Albert Cuvellier, Chris Kersen (gangsters); René Havard (Inspector Morin); Annick Bertrand (first woman in the bar); Yannick Arvel (second woman in bar); Yvette Amirante (Anne's friend); François André (himself, as director of Deauville casino); Tételman (croupier, not on film credits but widely credited in various sources); Germaine Amiel; Dominique Antoine; Duilio Carmine; Roland Charbaux; Pierre Durrieu; Jean-Marie Robain; Evelyne Rey.

Black and white
Running time: 102 minutes
First released Paris: 24 August 1956

Notes

Shot on location in Paris and Deauville; interiors at the rue Jenner studio, from May to September 1955, though some sources indicate a longer period.[12] According to the Nogueira interview, it cost FF 17.5 million – compared with the average feature budget at that time of FF 180 million (although CNC censorship files indicate an estimate of FF 32 million).

Synopsis

Bob le flambeur is the story of Bob (Roger Duchesne), an ageing gangster and gambler (*flambeur*) down on his luck but still a 'living legend' in Montmartre. Bob spends his time in cafés and night-clubs with his old friend Roger (André Garet) and young protégé Paulo (Daniel Cauchy), under the benign gaze of local police inspector Ledru (Guy Decomble). Bob rebuffs a request for money by local pimp and informer Marc, whom he despises. Bob meets Anne (Isabel Corey), a young woman on the make whom he decides to take under his wing. Despite her advances, he encourages her instead to take up with Paulo. Having won some money at the races, he goes to Deauville with Roger to play the casino. He loses everything. Roger hears of the fabulous deposits in the casino safe on the eve of the Grand Prix from Jean, a former criminal who is now a croupier. Bob, with Roger, plans to crack the safe as a last job before retiring. The heist is elaborately prepared and rehearsed by a gang assembled for the purpose. However, Paulo boasts about the job to Anne, who in turn tells Marc, with whom she is also sleeping. Meanwhile Jean is pressurised by his wife Suzanne to demand more money for his part in the job, but as they cannot find Bob they decide to go to the police to stop the heist. On the night of the robbery, Bob gambles to pass the time. His winning streak returns and he wins so much that he forgets about the heist. The gang is arrested by Ledru's men before entering the casino and Paulo is killed. Bob and Roger are driven away in Ledru's car, with Bob's winnings in the boot. They joke that with the good lawyer he can now afford Bob may get off with a light sentence or perhaps even sue for damages.

1959: *DEUX HOMMES DANS MANHATTAN*

Director: Jean-Pierre Melville
Production Company: O. G. C./Alter Films
Producer: Jean-Pierre Melville
Production managers: Florence Melville, Alain Terouanne[13]
Assistant directors: Yannick Andreï, Charles Bitsch
Script, adaptation, dialogues: Jean-Pierre Melville
Directors of photography: Michael Shrayer and Jean-Pierre Melville (in New York), Nicolas Hayer (interior studio scenes shot in Paris)
Camera operators: Jacques Lang, Charles Bitsch, Claude Beaugé[14]
Editor: Monique Bonnot
Assistant editor: Françoise Bonnot
Art director: Daniel Guéret
Assistant art director: Martine Sachot
Furniture: Roger Bar
Set builder: Raymond Aupée
Props: George Balland
Music: Christian Chevallier, Martial Solal
Musical director: Paul Bonneau
Music recorded by Gaby Jarret (trumpet: Bernard Hulin; harmonica: Albert Raisner)
Sound: Jacques Gallois, Jacques Carrère (sound editing)
Sound assistants: Corvaisier, Loiseau
Script girl: Ghislaine du Sire
Photographer: Guy André

Cast: Pierre Grasset (Delmas); Jean-Pierre Melville (Moreau; also voiceover); Christiane Eudes (Anne Fèvre-Berthier); Ginger Hall (Judith Nelson); Monique Hennessy (Gloria); Jean Darcante (Rouvier); Jerry Mengo (McKimmie); Colette Fleury (Françoise, Fèvre-Berthier's secretary); Glenda Leigh (Virginia, the singer); Jean Lara (Aubert); Michèle Bailly (Bessie); Paula Dehelly (Mme Fèvre-Berthier); Carl Studer (policeman); Gloria Kayser; Hyman Yanovitz (doorman at Mercury Theatre); Billy Beck; Tételman; Art Simmons; Nancy Delorme; Carole Sands; Barbara Hall; Monica Ford; Deya Kent, William Kearne.

Uncredited: Jean-Pierre Darras (the drunk); Bernard Hulin (trumpeter).

Black and white
Running time: 84 minutes
First released Paris: 16 October 1959

Notes

After several aborted projects with Pierre Grasset (see Chapter 1), the initial idea for this film was called *L'A.F.P. nous communique*, the story about the President of the French cabinet who dies of a heart atack in his mistress's flat.[15] Melville abandoned the project because of De Gaulle's coming to power. ('*L'A.F.P. nous communique* died with the Fourth Republic.'[16]

The film was shot on location in New York (November 1958), and at the Boulogne-Billancourt studios (February–April 1959), as the rue Jenner studios were rented out.

Synopsis

In New York just before Christmas, the absence of French delegate Fèvre-Berthier is noticed from a UN session. The French news agency AFP is informed and journalist Moreau (Jean-Pierre Melville) asked to investigate. Against the advice of his boss, Moreau decides to team with his disreputable photographer pal Delmas (Pierre Grasset), a notorious drunk and cynic. On the way to join Delmas he consults the head of the UN Press Office McKimmie (Jerry Mengo), who directs him to Fèvre-Berthier secretary (Colette Fleury). She tells Moreau to '*chercher la femme*'. Delmas produces photos of Fèvre-Berthier with three women: the actress Judith Nelson (Ginger Hall), the singer Virginia Graham (Glenda Leigh) and the dancer Bessie (Michèle Bally). The two men decide to track down each in turn, respectively at the Mercury Theatre, the Capitol recording studio and the Ridgewood Tavern, a strip-joint in Brooklyn. They also visit 'Miss Gloria' (Monique Hennessy), a call-girl who specialises in foreign diplomats. All the women deny any knowledge of Fèvre-Berthier's whereabouts. As they drive around he city, they are tailed by a mysterious car. Stopping at a diner, they hear on the radio of Judith Nelson's attempted suicide and trace her to the Roosevelt hospital. There Delmas unscrupulously extracts from her the information that Fèvre-Berthier has died of a heart attack in her apartment and steals her key. They find the body dead on Judith Nelson's sofa. To Moreau's horror, Delmas engineers and photographs a gruesome *mise en scène* to suggest Fèvre-Berthier died in salacious circumstances. The head of AFP arrives and lectures the two men on Fèvre-Berthier's glorious Resistance record, justifying concealment of the circumstances of his death. He orders Delmas to hand over his negatives and destroys them (or so he thinks) before carrying Fèvre-Berthier's body to his car. Delmas visits Fèvre-Berthier's widow with the reluctant Moreau. He wants to tell what they have discovered and sell the story to the scandal press. Her daughter Anne (Christiane Eudes) intervenes and begs them to say nothing. It turns out she was the driver of the mysterious car, following them to find out the truth and protect her mother. Delmas, who had actually held on to the films containing the compromising pictures, flees from the flat. In hot pursuit, Moreau and Anne eventually find him totally drunk at a late-night bar. Moreau punches him but Anne's imploring expression convinces him to do the honourable thing. He throws the rolls of film in the gutter and laughs, as dawn rises over New York.

1961: *LÉON MORIN, PRÊTRE*

Director: Jean-Pierre Melville

Production company: Compagnie Cinématographique de France/Compana Cinematografica Champion (Rome)

Producers: Carlo Ponti, Georges de Beauregard

Production managers: Marcel Georges, Edith Tertza, Bruna Drigo
Assistant directors: Volker Schloendorff, Jacqueline Parey, Luc Andrieux
Script: Jean-Pierre Melville
Based on the novel by Béatrix[17] Beck
Dialogues: Jean-Pierre Melville
Director of photography: Henri Decae
Camera operators: Jean Rabier, Jean-Paul Schwartz, Claude Amiot
Editors:[18] Jacqueline Meppiel, Nadine Marquand, Marie-Josephe Yoyotte
Art direction: Daniel Guéret, Donald Cardwell
Assistant art director: Robert Christides
Music: Martial Solal, Albert Raisner (harmonica)
Sound: Guy Villette, Jacques Maumont, Robert Cambourakis, Jean Gaudelet
Dresser: Paulette Breil
Make-up: Christine Fornelli
Props: Jean Brunet, Robert Testand
Photographer: Raymond Gauchetier
Credits: Jean Fouchet

Cast: Jean-Paul Belmondo (Léon Morin); Emmanuele[19] Riva (Barny); Irène Tunc (Christine); Nicole Mirel (Sabine); Marielle, Chantal and Patricia Gozzi[20] (France); Gisèle Grimm (Lucienne); Marco Béhar (Edelman); Monique Bertho (Marion); Marc Heyraud; Nina Grégoire; Monique Hennessy[21] (Arlette); Edith Loria (Danielle); Micheline Schererrer; Renée Liques; Simone Vannier, Lucienne Marchand, Nelly Pitorre (secretaries); Ernest Varial (director); Cedric Grant, George Lambert (GIs); Gérard Buhr (German soldier); Howard Vernon (German officer).

Uncredited: Madeleine Ganne (Betty); Adeline Aucoc (old lady in church); Saint-Eve (priest); Volker Schloendorff (German sentry).

Black and white
Running time: 111 minutes on pre-recorded VHS,[22] cut from an original 193 minutes
First released Paris: 22 September 1961
Prizes: Grand Prix de la ville de Venice, 1961

Notes

The interiors were shot in Melville's rue Jenner studio, outdoor locations in Montfort L'Amaury (near Paris) and Grenoble.

The Censorship Commission delivered a 'tous publics' (general) certificate on 20 September 1961.

The budget quoted in the CNC files is FF 2,143,600.

Synopsis

A small town in the French Alps during World War II under Italian and German occupation. Barny (Emmanuele Riva) has been relocated there with the correspondence school she works for. Her daughter France is looked after by nearby farmers. From a distance she 'loves' Sabine, the director's secretary. Barny and her friends Lucienne and Jenny organise the baptism of their children who are half-Jewish. A staunch atheist (though baptised), she decides on a whim to provoke a priest chosen at random by telling him that 'religion is the opium of the masses'. To her surprise Léon Morin (Jean-Paul Belmondo) reacts sympathetically.

Barny and Morin meet regularly and discuss the theological books he lends her. Off-screen, Italian and German soldiers fight and deportations start. Barny and her colleagues argue about racism. A Jewish philosophy teacher goes into hiding. Barny slaps her colleague Christine (Irène Tunc) but they make up. Morin supports the Resistance and hides Jews against the instructions of the Bishop. France, who is now in the care of two old ladies, tells Barny she believes in God. She befriends a German soldier who gives her a bracelet. Barny and Morin have increasingly intimate discussions. Morin also sees Christine and other women from the town. Sabine's brother is deported. Barny re-converts to Catholicism. She argues with Christine about the latter's collaborationism and anti-Semitism. Morin says he let Resistance fighters hide in his church.

When the town is liberated, Barny and her colleagues discuss reprisals against collaborators and women accused of sleeping with the enemy. An American GI harasses Barny but she escapes. France returns to live with her so Morin now visits them at home. Barny has an erotic dream about Morin. Later she asks him if he would marry her were he a Protestant. He leaves abruptly without reply. On his next visit, she tries to seduce him. He recoils and reprimands her, ordering her to confess. Morin tells her he has been allocated to a country parish. Barny leaves his now bare rooms for the last time, in tears.

1963: *LE DOULOS*

Director: Jean-Pierre Melville
Production company: Rome-Paris Films, C. C. Champion (Rome)
Distribution: Lux-Films, CCF
Producers: Georges de Beauregard (Production director), Carlo Ponti
Assistant directors: Charles Bitsch, Volker Schloendorff
Script: Jean-Pierre Melville
Based on the novel by Pierre V. Lesou (1957)
Adaptation and dialogues: Jean-Pierre Melville
Director of photography: Nicolas Hayer
Camera operator: Henri Tiquet
Editor: Monique Bonnot, with Michèle Boehm
Art director: Daniel Guéret, with Donald Cardwell
Assistant art director: Pierre Charron
Jewels: René Longuet
Music: Paul Misraki, with Jacques Loussier (piano-bar)
Orchestra conducted by Jacques Metehem
Sound: Julien Coutellier, with Revelli and Gaudelet
Continuity: Elisabeth Rappeneau

Production managers: Jean Pieuchot, Roger Scipion
Production stills: Raymond Voinquel
Assistants: André Dubreuil, Etienne Rosenfeld
Publicity: Bertrand Tavernier

Cast: Jean-Paul Belmondo (Silien); Serge Reggiani (Maurice Faugel); Jean Desailly (Inspector Clain); René Lefevre (Gilbert); Marcel Cuvelier (first detective); Aimé de March (Jean); Fabienne Dali (Fabienne); Monique Hennessy (Thérèse); Carl Studer (Kern); Christian Lude (the doctor); Jacques de Léon (Armand); Jack Léonard (second detective); Paulette Breil (Anita); Philippe Nahon (Rémy); Charles Bayard (old man); Daniel Crohem (Inspector Salignari); Charles Bouillaud (barman); Michel Piccoli (Nuttheccio).

Uncredited: Georges Sellier (barman); Andrès (maître d'hôtel).

Black and white
Running time: 108 minutes.[23]
First released Paris: 8 February 1963

Pre-credit text: En argot, 'Doulos' veut dire 'chapeau'.
Mais, dans le langage secret des policiers et des hors-la-loi, 'Doulos' est le nom que l'on donne à celui 'qui en porte un' . . .
L'indicateur de police.

In slang, 'Doulos' means 'hat'.
But in the secret language of policemen and criminals, 'Doulos' is the name given to the person 'who wears one' . . .
The police informer.

Post-credit text: Il faut choisir.
Mourir . . . ou mentir?

One must choose.
To die . . . or to lie?

Notes

Le Doulos was shot at the rue Jenner studio, Paris, April–June 1962, with some location shooting in Paris and the suburbs. The CNC files indicate an estimated budget of FF 2,113,000. The Censorship Commission classified the film as forbidden to minors below the age of thirteen, 'in view of the violent climate which may shock children' (this classification was confirmed in 1978 but revoked in 1983 when the film was passed for all audiences).

Melville shot *Le Doulos* allegedly to help Georges de Beauregard out of a fix.

'You're going to make *L'Ainé des Ferchaux* with Belmondo next August,' he said, 'but

I know he'd be willing to make another film with you immediately. Now don't tell me that in the whole Série Noire there isn't one book you would like to film right now [. . .]' And in fact there was a book by Pierre Lesou which I particularly liked: *Le Doulos*. I therefore agreed, but on one condition *sine qua non*: that Reggiani play the role of Maurice Faugel. [. . .] I was determined to have Belmondo as Silien. I thought it would be amusing to have him go from priest to stool-pigeon.[24]

According to Belmondo biographers Jérôme Strazzulla and Stéphane Leduc, the star was less keen, having clashed with Melville on the shooting of *Léon Morin, prêtre* over working methods (Melville finding Belmondo too 'relaxed'), and during the shooting of *Le Doulos* the relationship between the two was tense.[25]

Synopsis

In view of the complex nature of the plot, and the discussion of its relationship with the book in Chapter 5, the synopsis is laid out below in sequences, with cross-references to the book's chapters.

Credits

Maurice Faugel (Serge Reggiani) walks purposefully along a dingy street under railway tracks.

Sequence 1: Gilbert (Chapter I)

On his release from jail, Faugel shoots Gilbert Varnove (René Lefevre), a former friend, because he had killed Faugel's girlfriend Arlette. Gilbert, a fence, was examining jewels from a robbery committed by Nuttheccio (Michel Piccoli) and Armand, whose visit he was expecting. As the two men arrive, Faugel escapes unseen; he buries the money and jewels, as well as the murder weapon.

Sequence 2: Thérèse and Silien (Chapters II–IV)

(i) At Thérèse's flat (Chapter II). Faugel is at home at his new girlfriend Thérèse and receives visits from his friends Jean and Silien (Jean-Paul Belmondo), a notorious police informer and friend of Inspector Salignari. Silien brings the safe-busting equipment Faugel needs to rob a mansion in Neuilly with his friend Rémy.

(ii) Silien phones Salignari from a public telephone (Chapter III).

(iii) Faugel and Rémy take the métro for Neuilly. Meanwhile, Silien returns to Thérèse's flat, beats her up and ties her to the radiator (Chapter IV).

Sequence 3: The robbery (Chapter V)

The burglary has barely started when Faugel spies police cars. In the attempt to escape, Salignari shoots Rémy dead and is in turn killed by Faugel, who is himself wounded. Faugel is mysteriously rescued by a car.

Sequence 4: At Jean's (Chapter VI)

Faugel wakes up at Jean's house with Jean's woman, Anita, and a doctor tending his wound. Despite the doctor's order not to move for twenty-four hours, he angrily leaves in search of Silien whom he believes has betrayed him.

Sequence 5: Clain and Silien (Chapter VII)

Silien is picked up by Inspector Clain who asks him to finger Rémy's accomplice (not knowing it is Faugel) and also interrogates him about Gilbert's death. Believing Faugel is involved in the latter, he forces Silien to phone various bars to find Faugel.

Sequence 6: Faugel's arrest (Chapters VIII–XI)

(i) Faugel is arrested in a bar (Chapter VIII).
(ii) Faugel is interrogated by Clain (Chapter IX).
(iii) Silien unearths the jewels (Chapter X).
(iv) Faugel is in jail, where he meets Kern (Chapter XI).

Sequence 7: The Cotton Club (Chapters XII–XIII)

(i) Silien visits Nuttheccio's night-club, The Cotton Club, where he talks to his former girlfriend Fabienne (now with Nuttheccio) (Chapter XII).
(ii) In bed, Silien convinces Fabienne that she had heard a gunshot while waiting for Nuttheccio and Armand outside Gilbert's house (Chapter XIII).

Sequence 8: Nuttheccio's office (Chapter XIV)

Silien kills Nuttheccio and Armand in Nuttheccio's office, and engineers their deaths to look like a row over the jewels which he leaves in the safe.

Sequence 9: The New York bar: revelation (Chapter XV)

Faugel is released from jail. At the New York bar, he learns from Jean and Silien, in a flashback, how he had been misled and how Silien had arranged his release by staging the deaths of Nuttheccio and Armand; and how Thérèse, not Silien, was the informer, and how consequently Silien and Jean have killed her and disposed of her body.

Silien leaves for his house in Ponthierry to meet a mysterious German, Kern, contracted in jail by Faugel to kill him for the supposed betrayal.

Sequence 10: Shoot-out at Ponthierry (Chapter XVI)

Faugel reaches the house first, but is mistaken for Silien by Kern and killed. When Silien arrives, a shoot-out follows, in which both Kern and Silien also die.

1963: *L'AINÉ DES FERCHAUX*[26]

Director: Jean-Pierre Melville, A.C.I.
Production company: Spectacles Lumbroso (Paris), Ultra Film (Rome)[27]
Producer: Fernand Lumbroso
Production managers: Jerôme Sutter, Jean Darvey
Script, adaptation and dialogues: Jean-Pierre Melville

Based on the novel by Georges Simenon (*L'Aîné des Ferchaux*, 1945)
Director of photography: Henri Decae
Camera operator: Alain Douarinot
Second unit cinematographer: Michael Shrayer
Assistant cameramen: François Lauliac, Alain Derobe
Editors: Monique Bonnot, Claude Durand
Assistant editors: Annie Baronnet, Nicole Taroni
Art director: Daniel Guéret
Sets: Georges Fontenelle, Louis Seuret
Props: Louis Charpeau
Assistant decorators: Donald Cardwell, Jean-Jacques Fabre
Music: Georges Delerue (harmonica: Albert Raisner)
Sound: Jean-Claude Marchetti, Julien Coutelier
Sound assistants: Victor Rinelli, Jean Gaudelet
Continuity: Elisabeth Rappeneau
General manager: Paule Pastier
Production secretary: Antoinette Delarue
Assistant directors: Yves Boisset, Georges Pellegrin
Trainee: Alain Bonnot
Stills photography: Raymond Voinquel

Cast: Jean-Paul Belmondo (Michel Maudet); Charles Vanel (Dieudonné Ferchaux); Stefania Sandrelli (Angie, the hitch-hiker); Michèle Mercier (Lou); Andrex (Monsieur Andrei); Malvina [Silberberg] (Lina); Ginger Hall (the nurse); Delia Kent (the prostitute); Barbara Sommers (Lou's friend); André Certes (Emile Ferchaux); Jerry Mengo (a banker); Todd Martin (Jeff); E. F. Medard (Suska); Andrès (the butler); Dominique Zardi (the boxing speaker); Hugues Wanner, Paul Sorrèze, Charles Bayard, Pierre Leproux, Zeller (board members); Simone Darot; Maurice Auzel; Eddie Somers.

Kodak Eastmancolour
Wide-screen (Franscope)
Running time: 104 minutes
First released Paris: 2 October 1963

Notes

L'Ainé des Ferchaux was shot in the rue Jenner studios from 27 August to 5 October 1962 and on location in France and the USA in October–November 1962 (CNC file). The estimated budget registered at the CNC was FF 2,650,000. The original title was *Un jeune homme honorable*.

Alain Delon, under contract with producer Lumbroso, was initially contracted to be the lead in an adaptation of *L'Ainé des Ferchaux* with a different director. The contract was annulled and the film offered to Belmondo, who asked for Melville. For the older man, Melville says he wanted Spencer Tracy (who was too ill) and Charles Boyer (too good looking),[28] so he went to Vanel 'because I thought he was a great actor'.[29] For a discussion of the adaption, see Chapter 4.

A new version was made for French television in 2001, co-produced by Jean-Paul Belmondo, allegedly blocking French distribution of Melville's film on French territory.[30]

Synopsis

Michel Maudet (Jean-Paul Belmondo) – freshly released from the army – sees his hopes of a boxing career dashed when he loses a match. He answers an advertisement for a secretary to businessman Dieudonné Ferchaux (Charles Vanel). A scandal involving Ferchaux's past in Africa (where he killed 'three niggers') and the firm's finances has come to light; Ferchaux flees Paris for New York, where he has hidden funds, accompanied by Maudet who brutally abandons his girlfriend Lina. As they take the plane to New York, Ferchaux's brother and business partner Emile commits suicide. Ferchaux is able to withdraw only part of his fortune from the New York banks. The two men quickly leave New York, bound for Venezuela where Ferchaux has more money. En route the two men visit Frank Sinatra's birthplace in Hoboken. As they drive south, followed by the FBI, their relationship sours. Ferchaux becomes increasingly possessive, especially when Maudet picks up an attractive young woman hitch-hiker with whom he has sex but who he later drops as she tries to steal the money. The FBI tell Maudet that they won't extradite Ferchaux but that neither will he be allowed to leave the USA, a piece of information he does not pass on to Ferchaux. The two men rent an isolated house near New Orleans, where Ferchaux's health declines and he frequently quarrels with Maudet, resenting his youth and freedom. Maudet befriends Jeff, the owner of a local bar where a louche character called Suska hangs out. He also meets Lou, a striptease dancer in New Orleans (Michèle Mercier). Maudet leaves Ferchaux, taking his money. While he is with Lou, Ferchaux is attacked by Jeff and Suska. Maudet comes back, but too late. Before dying Ferchaux gives him the key to his safe in Caracas, and the film ends on an ambiguous semi-reconciliation between the two men.

1966: *LE DEUXIÈME SOUFFLE*

Director: Jean-Pierre Melville
Production company: Les Productions Montaigne/Charles Lumbroso
Producers: Charles Lumbroso, André Labay
Director of production: Alain Quéffélean
Assistant directors: Jean-François Adam, Georges Pellegrin
Second assistant: Ole Michelsen
Script: Jean-Pierre Melville
Based on the novel *Le Deuxième souffle* by José Giovanni (1958)
Dialogues: José Giovanni, Jean-Pierre Melville
Director of photography: Marcel Combes
Camera operator: Jean Charvein
Camera assistants: Jacques Nibert, Jean-Claude Boussard
Editors: Monique Bonnot, Michèle Boehm

Assistant editors: Catherine Moulin, Ziva Postee
Assistant art director: Guy Maugin
Set decorator: Jean-Jacques Fabre
Furniture: Claude Thery
Props: Jean Dardeau, Daniel Villeroy
Music: Bernard Gérard
Sound: Alex Pront
Sound recording: Jacques Gallois
Costumes: Michel Tellin (clothes); Max (furs); Paulette Laurie (jewels)
Continuity: Suzanne Durrenberger
Production manager (Paris): Robert Porte
Production manager (Marseille): Marcel Correnson
General production manager: Francis Pettier
Production manager (location): Louis Seuret
Other collaborators: Henri Tiquet, François Dupont-Midy, Claude Veriat, Roger Cosson

Cast: Lino Ventura (Gustave [Gu] Minda); Paul Meurisse (Inspector Blot); Raymond Pellegrin (Paul Ricci); Christine Fabrega (Manouche); Marcel Bozzufi (Jo Ricci); Paul Frankeur (Inspector Fardiano); Denis Manuel (Antoine Ripa); Jean Négroni (a policeman); Michel Constantin (Alban); Pierre Zimmer (Orloff); Pierre Grasset (Pascal Léonetti); Raymond Loyer (Jacques le Notaire); Albert Dagnant (Jeannot Franchi); Jean-Claude Bercq; Régis Outin; Jack Léonard; Albert Michel; Nina Michaelsen; Betty Anglade; A. Layle; Louis Bugetti; Sylvain; Roger Fradet; Roger Perrinoz; Jean de Beaumont; Marcel Berrier; J. Dubos; Pierre Gualdi; R. Pequignot.

Black and white
Running time: 140 minutes
First released Paris: 2 November 1966

Pre-credit text: L'Auteur de ce film n'entend pas assimiler la 'morale' de GUSTAVE MINDA à la Morale. Il tient à preciser que les circonstances, les situations et les personnages de cette histoire n'ont aucune base réelle et que, par conséquent il ne peut être question de porter un jugement sur les méthodes d'enquête à partir de cette oeuvre d'imagination inspirée par un roman.

A sa naissance il n'est donné à l'homme qu'un seul droit: le choix de sa mort. Mais si ce choix est commandé par le dégoût de sa vie, alors son existence n'aura été que pure derision . . .

The author of this film does not intend to equate Gu Minda's 'morals' with Morals. He wishes to specify that the circumstances, situations and characters of this story have no real basis and that, consequently, there is no question of judging the methods of investigation [depicted in the film] on the basis of this work of imagination based on a novel.

At birth, man is given only one right: the choice of his death. But if this choice is dictated by a disgust for life, then his existence will have been pure derision . . .

Notes

Le Deuxième souffle was filmed on location in Paris, Marseille and the Marseille region, and at the rue Jenner studios, over two periods: February–March and June–August 1966.

From the start the production was problematic. Melville started planning the film in 1963, but 'Jose Giovanni [the book's author] who had sold me the rights to his novel, sold them to a production company in May 1964, believing he was free of commitment with me.'[31] It appears that Denys de la Patellière was interested in the project, planning to cast Jean Gabin and Lino Ventura as Minda and Blot.[32] To regain the rights, Melville went through 'a series of court cases for two years, during which [he] refused to make any other film, until the start of the shoot in early 1966'.[33]

Problems did not stop there. Melville says he 'started shooting on 21 February 1966, and on 17 February nothing had been decided. This explains why I used Marcel Combes as lighting cameraman.' In response to Nogueira who points out that the camerawork is excellent, Melville counters 'That's true, but I had to do everything myself [. . .]. We continued working until 14 March in extremely difficult conditions and then had to stop for three months. When we started again on 7 June, it seemed like a miracle. 1964 to 1966 were years in the wilderness for me.'[34] One of the difficulties was over casting. Melville's original cast, which included Serge Reggiani as Gu Minda, fell through. Melville is vague on why this was so,[35] but Reggiani claims Melville unilaterally redrew his contract, prompting him to pull out.[36] Melville's relationship with Reggiani's replacement, Lino Ventura (a much bigger star),[37] was tense. The following anecdote recounted by Melville gives a clue as to why:

> During a shoot, directing actors is what I love most, but they must do what I say. It is not always easy with 'characters' like Lino Ventura. You have to be hypocritical: in *Le Deuxième souffle*, Lino climbs on to a moving train. He normally gets a stuntman for this kind of scene. During rehearsals I played his understudy myself and leapt into the train which was going at 18km/h. Lino thus felt obliged to do the scene himself, but when he started moving, I increased the train's speed to 32 km/h. He was furious but the scene was a success.[38]

Le Deuxième souffle also encountered censorship difficulties, especially for the scene in which Paul Ricci (Pellegrin) is interrogated by the police, using a funnel to pour water down his throat. In February 1964, the Censorship Commission wrote a negative report on the script, threatening a 13 certificate, 'because of the numerous scenes of violence and murder. Additionally, the tortures perpetrated by the police call for the highest reservations.' On 18 October 1966 the film was screened to the Commission, which awarded an 18 certificate, 'in view of the excessive violence and the pernicious nature of this film, which makes it a particularly dangerous spectacle for young people under 18'. The Commission demanded 'the complete excision of the interrogation scene with the funnel; any image of the latter must be removed. This is not normal practice in the French police.' Melville agreed to remove the scene and the film was awarded a general certificate on 28 October.[39]

Synopsis

The synopsis is laid out with the chronological markers as indicated in the film (they stop after 28 December although the action takes place over several days after that).

20 November, 5.58am: Gu Minda (Lino Ventura) and two other men escape from jail. One dies in the attempt. Gu and the other man run (the credits appear over their running) and jump on to a moving goods train. Soon the other man jumps out; Minda remains on the train.

Marseille, 20 November, 11pm: In his night-club, gangster Paul Ricci (Raymond Pellegrin) is informed that a convoy carrying platinum will leave on 28 December. Against his advice, his friend Jeannot goes to Paris to kill rival gangster Jacques le Notaire.

Paris, 21 November: At Manouche's night-club Jeannot kills Jacques and is wounded. Inspector Blot (Paul Meurisse) arrives on the scene but makes no arrests. Gu's escape is announced.

Marseille, 22 November: Paul Ricci is informed that Jacques is in a coma. He goes to Paris.

Paris, 23 November, 12.25am: Two hoodlums threaten Manouche and Alban. Gu arrives and disarms them. He finds out that gangster Jo Ricci (Paul's brother [Marcel Bozzufi]) had sent them to blackmail Manouche (Christine Fabrega). He shoots them dead. Alban and Manouche take Gu to a hide-out in the suburbs (Montrouge).

Paul Ricci visits the dying Jeannot and his brother Jo. Back in Marseille he suggests to his friends Antoine and Pascal that Orloff replace Jeannot for the heist. Orloff is non-committal.

24 November: Blot connects the hoodlums' deaths to Gu's escape. He grants Manouche permission to leave Paris. She has dinner with Gu in his hide-out.

Blot visits Jo Ricci and tells him Gu is looking for him.

Gu sets out to take revenge on Jo Ricci but pulls out at the last minute.

26 November: Manouche travels to Marseille to ask her friend Theo for help in finding a house, obtaining false identity papers and securing a boat for Gu to escape.

27 November: Gu receives escape plans from Manouche. Alban gives him his favourite gun.

7 December: Gu travels to Marseille using local buses and coaches.

8 December: In Marseille, Theo tells Orloff about Gu. Out of friendship, Orloff offers to obtain the papers. He also asks Theo to tell Gu about the heist.

10 December: Gu arrives in Marseille. Despite Manouche's opposition he agrees to do the job for the money. Paul Ricci, an old friend, is keen to have him in the team, despite the reservations of Antoine and Pascal.

Night of 27–8 December: Gu and Manouche have dinner by a Christmas tree. She leaves for Paris.

The same night, 11.58pm: Paul Ricci learns that the convoy is due to leave at 2pm the next day.

28 December:

Gu, Paul, Antoine and Pascal successfully ambush the convoy, killing two guards and tying up several witnesses, and steal the bullion.
The police discover the theft and killings. Blot is brought in from Paris, to the fury of local Inspector Fardiano.

Gu, still in hiding, walks the streets of Marseille. He is given his share of the loot.
On 1 January Gu is arrested by police disguised as gangsters, who trick him into revealing Paul's name. Paul is arrested and both are brutally interrogated by Fardiano. Distraught at the idea of being thought an informer, Gu tries to kill himself. Jo Ricci comes to Marseille to help his brother.
Manouche comes back to Marseille. Orloff offers to help by intervening with Pascal, Antoine and Jo who want to take revenge against Gu. Orloff tells them he'll kill Gu if he has proof that Gu betrayed Paul.
Gu escapes from the prison hospital. He kidnaps Fardiano, forces him to confess (on paper) that he had lied about Gu's betrayal and used torture, and then kills him.
Gu knocks Orloff out to confront Antoine, Pascal and Jo himself. He kills all three of them but is shot by Antoine and a policeman. He dies in Blot's arms, handing him Fardiano's confession which Blot makes sure is picked up by a journalist.

1967: *LE SAMOURAÏ*

Director: Jean-Pierre Melville
Production company: Filmel-Eugène Lépicier–C.I.C.C. (Paris); FIDA Cinematografica (Rome)
Head of production: Georges Casati
Production manager: Jean Pieuchot
Assistant director: Georges Pellegrin
Script and dialogues: Jean-Pierre Melville
Director of photography: Henri Decae
Camera operator: Jean Charvein (studio), Henri Decae (location)
Camera assistants: François Lauliac, Jean-Paul Cornu
Editor: Monique Bonnot, with Yo Maurette
Assistant editors: Madeleine Bagiau, Geneviève Letellier, Madeleine Guérin, Geneviève Adam
Continuity: Betty Elvira
Art director: François de Lamothe, with Théobald Meurisse
Furniture: Robert Christides
Assistant furniture: André Boumedil
Props: Angelo Rizzi
Props assistant: Philippe Turlure
Paintings from the Blumenthal-Mommaton gallery
Music: François de Roubaix
Sound design: Alex Pront

Sound mixing: Robert Pouret
Sound engineer: René Longuet
Sound assistant: Pierre Davoust
Fur coats: Robert Beaulieu

Cast: Alain Delon (Jef Costello); François Périer (the Inspector); Nathalie Delon (Jane Lagrange); Caty Rosier (Valérie, the pianist); Michel Boisrond (Wiener); Jacques Leroy (the man on the bridge); Robert Favart (barman); Jean-Pierre Posier (Olivier Rey); Catherine Jourdan (cloakroom assistant); Roger Fradet, Carlo Nell, Robert Rondo (first, second and third assistant inspectors); André Salgues (Garet) (the garage man); André Thorent (policeman-taxi driver); Jacques Deschamps (speaker policeman); Georges Casati (Damolini); Jack Léonard (Garcia); Pierre Vaudier, Maurice Magalon (first and second policemen on night raid); Gaston Meunier (butler); Jean Gold (first night-club patron); Georges Billy (second night-club patron); Ari Aricardi, Bonnafoux (poker players); Catalano (a policeman); Carl Lechner (Jef's look-alike); Maria Maneva (the young woman with the chewing-gum).

Kodak Eastmancolour
Running length: 100 minutes
First released Paris: 25 October 1967

Post-credit text: Il n'y a pas de plus profonde solitude que celle du samouraï si ce n'est celle d'un tigre dans la jungle ... peut-être ... Le Bushido (Le livre des samouraï).

There is no more profound solitude than the samurai's, except that of the tiger ... in the jungle ... maybe ... The Bushido (The book of the samurai).

The UK video sub-titles translate the text as 'There is no deeper solitude than the samurai's ... unless perhaps it be that of the tiger in the jungle'. I prefer the word 'profound' to 'deeper', as closer to the original if less elegant, and adopt Melville's phrasing, as it retains the emphasis on 'maybe' (see Chapter 6).

Notes

The credits indicate 'shot in the rue Jenner studio'. In fact, Melville's studio burnt down half-way through the shooting of the film. The film was part-shot in the St Maurice studios near Paris, and on location in Paris and the suburbs, June to August 1967.

There is some uncertainty about the origin of the script. No mention except Melville is made on the credits (or in Melville's interviews), though various written sources indicate a novel called *The Ronin* by Joan (or Goan) McLeod, which I have been unable to trace. See Chapter 6 for a discussion of the 'origins' of *Le Samouraï*.

Spellings vary between credits and other written mentions. I have adopted the credits spelling for Jef and Jane (instead of the more common Jeff and Jeanne). The actor who plays the garage assistant is credited as André Salgues, but as André Garret in

Melville's interview with Nogueira, and on the credits of *Bob le flambeur*, where he plays Roger. Jane Lagrange is played by Nathalie Delon, then married to Alain Delon (and mother of their son Anthony Delon); according to Melville, the film marked their separation.[40]

Synopsis

Jef Costello (Alain Delon), a hitman, steals a car and constructs an alibi with his girlfriend Jane (Nathalie Delon) and a group of poker players before successfully executing a contract to kill Martey, the director of a night-club. He is, however, seen by the club's pianist (Caty Rosier). He disposes of his gun and rejoins the poker players, but is arrested as part of a police raid. The pianist and the barman deny having seen him to the inspector in charge of the inquiry (François Périer). Jane's other lover Wiener (Michel Boisrond) remembers that he saw Jef come out of her building. The police have to release him, although the inspector believes him, and Jane, guilty. They lose his trail in the métro. Jef collects his money for the killing but is shot and wounded by henchmen sent by his double-crossing, as yet unknown, employer. Back home, he tends his wound. His employer and his accomplices discuss getting rid of him, as his arrest is a potential danger. While Jef returns to the club in full view of everyone, the police bug his flat. He waits for the pianist outside Martey's and goes back to her place, asking her (in vain) who the boss is. The police brutally threaten Jane in her flat, but she won't talk. Back in his flat, Jef finds the bug and disables it. He goes out to phone the pianist. Back in his room, he is surprised by the man who had previously wounded him. He is paid a further FF 2 million to execute another contract. Jef forces the man to reveal the identity of their employer, Olivier Rey. The police put in place a complex trail to follow Jef in the métro but lose him again. He steals another car, visits Jane to say goodbye and kills Olivier Rey in the latter's flat. He then goes to Martey's, ostensibly to kill the pianist, who turns out to be the new contract. But he has emptied the gun and as he pretends to aim he is shot in the back by the police and dies.

1969: *L'ARMÉE DES OMBRES*

Director: Jean-Pierre Melville
Production company: Corona (Paris)/Fono Roma (Rome)
Producer: Jacques Dorfmann [some sources also indicate Robert Dorfmann]
Production manager: Alain Quéffélean
General manager: J. P. Spiri-Mercanton
Assistant directors: Jean-François Adam, Georges Pellegrin, J. C. Ventura
Script and dialogues: Jean-Pierre Melville
Based on the novel by Joseph Kessel (1943)
Adviser on foreign dialogue: Howard Vernon
Director of photography: Pierre Lhomme
Camera operator: Philippe Brun
Assistant camera operators: Pierre Li, Jacques Renard
Aerial photography: Walter Wottitz
Editor: Françoise Bonnot

Sound editing: Robert Pouret
Continuity: Betty Elvira
Art director: Théobald Meurisse
Assistant art director: Roger Volper
Assistant decorators: Enriqué Sonnois, Marc Desages
Music: Eric de Marsan
Piano-bar: Bob Vatel
Sound: Jacques Carrère, Alex Pront, Jean Neni
Sound operator: Victor Revelli
Costumes: Colette Baudot
Make-up: Maud Begon
Still photography: Raymond Voinquel
Credits and special effects: Eurocitel

Cast: Lino Ventura (Philippe Gerbier); Paul Meurisse (Luc Jardie); Jean-Pierre Cassel (Jean-François Jardie); Simone Signoret (Mathilde); Claude Mann (Le Masque); Paul Crauchet (Félix); Christian Barbier (Le Bison); Serge Reggiani (barber); André Dewavrin, aka 'Colonel Passy' (himself); Alain Decok (Legrain); Alain Mottet (head of camp); Alain Libolt (Paul Dounat, the traitor); Jean-Marie Robain (Baron de Ferté-Talloire); Albert Michel (gendarme); Denis Sadier (Gestapo doctor); Georges Sellier (Colonel Jarret du Plessis); Marco Perrin (Octove Bonnafous); Hubert de Lapparent (Aubert); Colin Mann ('dispatcher'); Anthony Stuart (RAF major); Michel Fretault (anonymous patriot); Adrien Cayla-Legrand (Général de Gaulle); Gérard Huart (prisoner); Percival Russell (German soldier); Michel Dacquin (condemned prisoner); Jeanne Pérez (Marie); Jacques Marbeuf (German officer); Pierre Vaudier; Franz Sauer.

Uncredited: Nathalie Delon (Jean-François' girlfriend); Gaston Meunier (luggage controller); Marcel Bernier (customs officer).

Kodak Eastmancolour
Running time: 140 minutes
First released Paris: 12 September 1969

Pre-credit text: Mauvais souvenirs, soyez pourtant les bienvenus ... vous êtes ma jeunesse lointaine ... (Courteline)

Bad memories, you are welcome ... you are my distant youth ... (Courteline)

Notes

Filmed on location in Paris, France and London and at the Boulogne-Billancourt studios, January–March 1969. The opening sequence of German soldiers marching down the Champs-Elysées was originally placed at the end of the film, but moved on Melville's request by letter dated 16 September, a few days after the release of the film (12 September).[41]

Synopsis

Resistance agent Philippe Gerbier (Lino Ventura) is interned in a Vichy camp. Before he can escape as planned he is transferred to the Hôtel Majestic in Paris from which he escapes by killing a German guard and hiding in a barber's shop. He joins his comrades Félix (Paul Crauchet) and Le Bison (Christian Barbier) in Marseille and, together with Le Masque (Claude Mann), executes the young traitor who had denounced him.

A new recruit, Jean-François Jardie (Jean-Pierre Cassel), delivers a radio transmitter to Mathilde (Simone Signoret) in Paris and visits his older brother Luc (Paul Meurisse), who, unbeknown to him, is the head of the whole network. Gerbier uses a Lyon theatre agency as a front. On the Mediterranean coast, they help conceal British and Canadian pilots. He and Luc Jardie board a submarine bound for London. In London Gerbier and Luc Jardie meet General de Gaulle who decorates Jardie. Félix is arrested in Lyon. Gerbier is parachuted back into France taking temporary refuge in a chateau. Mathilde devises a plan in which she, Le Masque and Le Bison in German disguise will rescue Félix from the Gestapo hospital; the plan goes without a hitch but to their dismay Félix is too badly tortured to be moved. Jean-François gets himself arrested to reach Félix but it is too late. He is tortured.

Gerbier is arrested in a Lyon restaurant. Mathilde helps him escape under fire from a Gestapo shooting gallery. Wounded, he hides in an isolated safe house. Mathilde is arrested. Fearing the Germans will use her daughter (of whom she has kept a photograph) to make her talk, Jardie and Gerbier decide she must die. They gun her down near the Arc de Triomphe in Paris. The film ends on a text which records that Gerbier, Le Masque, Le Bison and Jardie all later die in action or under torture.

1970: *LE CERCLE ROUGE*

Director: Jean-Pierre Melville
Production companies: Corona (Paris), Selenia (Rome)
Producer: Robert Dorfmann
Production manager: A. Quéffélean
Production supervisor: G. Crosnier
Assistant directors: Bernard Stora, Pierre Tati, Bernard Girardot
Trainee assistant director: Michel Léonard
Script and dialogues: Jean-Pierre Melville
Director of photography: Henri Decae
Camera operator: Charles-Henri Montel
Assistant camera operators: François Lauliac, Jean-Paul Cornu
Editor: Marie-Sophie Dubus
Assistant editors: Elizabeth Sarradieu, G. Grenet
Trainee editor: Claudine Kaufmann
Art director: Théo Meurisse
Set designer: Pierre Charron
Assistant set designer: Marc Desages
Props: René Albouze

Music: Eric de Marsan
Sound: Jean Nény
Sound engineer: Jacques Carrère
Sound assistant: Guy Chichignoud
Perchman: Victor Revelli
Costumes: Colette Baudot
Jewels: René Longuet
Continuity: J. Parey

Cast: Alain Delon (Corey); André Bourvil (Inspector Mattei); Gian-Maria Volonté (Vogel); Yves Montand (Jansen); François Périer (Santi); André Ekyan (Rico); Pierre Collet (Prison Warden); Paul Amiot (Director IGS [Internal Affairs]); Paul Crauchet (the fence); Jean-Pierre Posier (Mattei's assistant); Jean-Marc Boris (Santi's son); Ana Douking (Rico's mistress); Yves Arcanel (investigating judge); René Berthier (Mattei's boss); Jean Champion (railway crossing guard); Robert Favart (jewellery sales assistant); Pierre Lecomte (assistant to Director IGS); Yvan Chiffre, Roger Fradet, Jacques Léonard, Jacques Leroy, Robert Rondo (policemen).

Kodak Eastmancolour
Running time: 134 minutes
First released Paris: 21 October 1970

Pre-credit text: Cakyamuni le Solitaire, dit Sidarta Gautama le Sage, dit le Bouddah, se saisit d'un morceau de craie rouge, traca un cercle et dit: Quand des hommes, même s'ils l'ignorent, doivent se retrouver un jour, tout peut arriver à chacun d'entre eux et ils peuvent suivre des chemins divergents. Au jour dit, inéluctablement, ils seront réunis dans le cercle rouge.
Rama Krishna

Cakyamuni the Loner, also known as Sidarta Gautama the Wise, also known as the Buddha, took a piece of red chalk, drew a circle and said: When men are meant to meet again, even if they don't know it, anything may happen to each of them and they may follow diverging paths. On the appointed day, inevitably they will meet again in the red circle.
Rama Krishna

Notes

Le Cercle rouge was shot in the Boulogne-Billancourt studios, and on location in and around Paris, in Marseille and Châlon-sur-Saône, January–April 1970. The recorded estimated budget is FF 9,750,000.[42]

Melville reported a difficult shoot ('instead of completing it in forty-five to fifty days, which would have been normal, it took me sixty-six days'), and fiercely criticised most of his collaborators, except Pierre Charron, the set designer.[43]

Synopsis

The action begins in Marseille, where Inspector Mattei (Bourvil) is escorting Vogel (Gian-Maria Volonté), a notorious criminal, to Paris on the night train. During the night, Vogel frees himself from his handcuffs and leaps from the train. At the same time, Corey (Alain Delon) is being released from jail in Marseille. Courtesy of a bent prison guard, he is in possession of inside information about the alarm system at a high-class jeweller's on the place Vendôme in Paris. Corey looks up Rico (André Ekyan), a former friend who has betrayed him and taken up with his former mistress (Ana Douking). Corey takes money and a gun from Rico's safe and later, at a deserted billiard hall, sees off two of Rico's pursuing heavies. He buys a large American car and sets off for Paris. Meanwhile, Vogel eludes a massive police search and at a roadside café slips into the unlocked boot of Corey's car. After bluffing his way through a police check, Corey draws up in a deserted field and tells Vogel to come out. The two men's friendship is cemented when they kill two more of Rico's gang out to take revenge. In Paris, Mattei is reprimanded by his ultimate boss, the Director of Internal Affairs, for allowing Vogel to escape. 'All men are guilty,' the director tells him and later looks up his file. Mattei does the rounds of his informers, including night-club owner Santi (François Périer), an acquaintance of Vogel. Corey and Vogel decide to do the place Vendôme jewellery job with the help of ace marksman Jansen (Yves Montand), an ex-policeman and alcoholic. Corey and Jansen meet at Santi's club while the latter is arrested. While Jansen cases the jeweller's, does some target practice and casts special bullets with which to immobilise the alarm system, Corey recruits a fence (Paul Crauchet). Rico, still seeking revenge, finds out about the robbery from the prison guard. Corey, Vogel and Jansen successfully carry out the heist and escape just as the guard sounds the alarm. Their fence, however, primed by Rico, refuses the loot. Mattei puts more pressure on Santi by arresting his son for drug dealing. Corey gets the name of a new fence. However, presumably through Santi (although he has also received an anonymous letter), Mattei discovers his identity and takes his place. He lures Corey and Jansen with the jewels to his isolated country house. Despite Vogel's aid, all three men are shot dead by the police. The film ends with Mattei removing some of the jewels while the Director of Internal Affairs repeats that 'all men are guilty'.

1972: *UN FLIC*

Director: Jean-Pierre Melville

Production companies: Films Corona (Paris), Oceania Prodzioni Internazionali Cinematografiche Euro International Films (Italy)

Producer: Robert Dorfmann

Production director: Pierre Saint-Blancat

Production managers: Jean Drouin, Phillip Kenny

Assistant directors: Marc Grunebaum, Jean-François Delon, Pierre Tati

Trainee assistant directors: Bernard Girardot, Philippe Martin

Script and dialogues: Jean-Pierre Melville

Director of photography: Walter Wottitz

Camera operator: André Domage
First camera assistant: Valéry Ivanov
Editor: Patricia Nény
Assistant editors: Marie-José Audiard, Sophie Tati
Art director: Théo Meurisse
Set designer: Pierre Charron
Assistant set designer: Enrique Sondis
Props: René Albouze
Music: Michel Colombier
Song: Charles Aznavour (lyrics), Isabelle Aubret (vocals)
Sound: André Hervée
Sound editor: Maurice Laumain
Costumes: Colette Baudot
Fur coats: Jeanne Nataf
Catherine Deneuve's black dress: Yves Saint-Laurent
Make-up: Michel Deruelle
Continuity: Florence Moncorgé

Cast: Alain Delon (Edouard Coleman); Richard Crenna (Simon); Catherine Deneuve (Cathy); Riccardo Cucciolla (Paul Weber); Michael Conrad (Louis Costa); André Pousse (Marc Albouis); Paul Crauchet (Morand); Valérie Wilson (transvestite); Simone Valère (Paul's wife); Léon Minisini (Mathieu la valise); Jean Desailly (man who has been robbed); Henri Marteau (fire range inspector); Catherine Rethi (clinic receptionist); Stan Dylik; Roger Fradet; Jacques Leroy; Nicole Témine; Pierre Vaudier; Louis Grandidier; Philippe Gasté; Dominique Zentar; Jako Mica; Jo Tafenelli; Georges Florian; Jacques Galland; Jean-Pierre Posier; Michel Frétault; Gene Moyle.

Kodak Eastmancolour
Running time: 94 minutes
First released Paris: 25 October 1972

Pre-credit text: Les seuls sentiments que l'homme ait jamais été capable d'inspirer au policier sont l'ambiguité et la dérision. François-Eugène Vidocq

The only feelings man could ever inspire in the policeman are ambiguity and derision. François-Eugène Vidocq

End-credit song:

> Chacun de nous est seul sur l'autre rive
> Du fleuve trouble des passions
> Pour voir partir à la dérive
> Ses illusions

Adieu ce qui fut nous
Vive que vive
Le destin a tiré un trait
C'est ainsi que les choses arrivent
Arrivent
Voici venir le temps des regrets

Each of us is alone on the other side
Of the murky river of passions
Watching our illusions being cast adrift
Goodbye to what we were
Let it be
Fate has drawn the line
This is the way things are
Now comes the time of regrets

Notes

First title: Nuit sur la cité
Shot in the Boulogne-Billancourt studios and on location in Paris and the Vendée coast.
Estimated budget: FF 10,910.000 (CNC file).

Synopsis

On a stormy, deserted Atlantic beach in winter, a gang – Simon (Richard Crenna), Marc (André Pousse), Paul (Riccardo Cucciolla) and Louis (Michael Conrad) – robs a bank. A teller sounds the alarm, shoots Marc and is killed. The men escape, bury the loot and take Marc to a clinic. Meanwhile in Paris, Inspector Coleman (Delon), accompanied by his assistant Morand (Paul Crauchet), goes about his routine assignments, investigating the murder of a woman and a theft by a young gay male prostitute, meeting a transvestite informer (Valérie Wilson) and interrogating three pickpockets. Paul pretends to his wife that he is looking for work. Coleman visits Cathy (Catherine Deneuve) at the nightclub owned by Simon, his friend. The gangsters meet to confer at the Louvre. To prevent him talking, Simon, Louis and Paul send Cathy, dressed as a nurse, to kill Marc by giving him a lethal injection. Marc's (unidentified) body is examined by Coleman in the morgue. He and Cathy meet in a hotel room. Simon, Louis and Paul plan their next big heist (which the first one only served to finance), the theft of drugs to be convoyed by Mathieu (Léon Minisini) on the Paris–Lisbon train. Coleman finds out about the drugs haul from the transvestite and decides to let the border police intercept it. But Simon and his gang get there first with a daring heist in which Simon is dropped onto the moving train by helicopter and later picked up in the same way. A furious Coleman violently rounds on the transvestite, telling 'her' to dress as a man. Marc's identity is revealed and Coleman arrests Louis who confesses that Simon is involved. Coleman warns Simon who in turn warns Paul. Paul shoots himself rather than be arrested. Simon hides in a hotel and, as he tries to escape with Cathy, is stopped by Coleman who had tapped their telephone. Coleman shoots Simon in what seems like self-defence, although it transpires that Simon had no weapon and had in effect 'committed suicide'. Coleman returns to his routine work, driving around the streets of Paris with Morand, waiting for the next call.

NOTES

1. Pierre Braunberger, *Cinémamémoire* (Paris: Éditions du Centre Pompidou and Centre National de la Cinématographie, 1987), p. 141.
2. Florence Welsh (Melville's widow) claims that 'at the time of *Le Silence de la mer*, we were robbed by Braunberger, the film's distributor', in Denitza Bantcheva, *Jean-Pierre Melville: de l'oeuvre à l'homme* (Troyes: Librairie Bleue, 1996), p. 175.
3. Editors are not mentioned on the credits but indicated in *La Cinématographie Française*, 7 March 1949.
4. Rui Nogueira (ed.), *Melville on Melville* (London: Secker and Warburg and BFI, 1971), p. 30.
5. Howard Vernon, *Le Quotidien de Paris*, 5 November 1987.
6. Nogueira, *Melville on Melville*, p. 37.
7. Braunberger, *Cinémamémoire*, p. 141.
8. Nogueira, *Melville on Melville*, p. 36.
9. Bantcheva, *Jean-Pierre Melville*, p. 175.
10. Braunberger, *Cinémamémoire*, p. 141.
11. Nogueira, *Melville on Melville*, p. 40.
12. Nogueira (ibid., p. 57) indicates May–September, Daniel Cauchy (Criterion DVD interview) indicates an extended (eighteen-month) period of filming.
13. Nogueira, *Melville on Melville*, p.170, also gives Raymond Blondy as a production manager.
14. Nogueira also gives François Reichenbach. Ibid.
15. Ibid.
16. Ibid.
17. Spelt Béatrice on credits.
18. Denise de Casabianca and Agnès Guillemot also worked as editors on the film, but there was a row with Melville who said: 'I didn't list them all on the credits because Casabianca and Guillemot worked very little on the film. But I listed the other three in order of preference. They then all banded together to sue Georges de Beauregard. I went along to plead my own case and obtained a decision from the court which is now law in France, whereby it is the director who establishes the credits. And the title-card on which they were listed in order of preference remained in the film. Nogueira, *Melville on Melville*, p. 87.
19. Frequently spelt Emmanuelle.
20. Melville claims four Gozzi sisters were used to play Barny's daughter France, although only three are credited (Patricia, Marielle, Chantal). There is a continuity error (apparently deliberate) in the scene where France tells her mother that she has been going to catechism, and where two shots of France show two different sisters.
21. Monique Hennessy was Melville's secretary. She also appears in *Deux hommes dans Manhattan* and in *Le Doulos*.

22. Pre-recorded sleeve gives 120 minutes; Nogueira, *Melville on Melville*, gives 128 minutes.
23. UK and French TV broadcast tapes have a running length of 104 minutes.
24. Nogueira, *Melville on Melville*, pp. 91–2.
25. Jérôme Strazzulla and Stéphane Leduc, *Belmondo, L'Histoire d'une vie* (Paris: Éditions Ramsay, 1996), p. 91.
26. Although the word 'aîné' is spelt with a circumflex on the 'i', the film titles are written without.
27. Lumbroso and Ultra Film figure on the credits. According to the CNC files, two other companies, UFA Comacico and Sicilia Cinematografica were involved.
28. *France-Soir*, 17 September 2001.
29. Nogueira, *Melville on Melville*, p. 102.
30. *France-Soir*, 17 September 2001.
31. Melville, interview with Alain Dupont, *Télérama*, 4 October 1970.
32. M. Aubriant in *Candide*, 7 November 1966.
33. Melville, interview with Alain Dupont, *Télérama*, 4 October 1970.
34. Nogueira, *Melville on Melville*, p. 112.
35. Ibid.
36. Serge Reggiani, *Le Matin*, 2 November 1983.
37. Gilles Durieux, *Lino Ventura* (Paris: Flammarion, 2001), p. 227.
38. Melville, interview with Alain Dupont, *Télérama*, 4 October 1970.
39. Centre National de la Cinématographie, Censorship Commission file on *Le Deuxième souffle*.
40. Nogueira, *Melville on Melville*, p. 134.
41. The letter dated 16 September and signed by producer Jacques Dorfmann asked for the displacement of the scene from end to beginning of the film, and the shortening of the taking off and landing of aeroplanes at the Baron's home; Mathilde and Gerbier walking in the park; the Lyon restaurant scene at the end; and departure from the cells' corridor, shortening the whole film from 3,984m to 3,922m. Permission was granted. The initial placement of the scene at the end of the film is confirmed by the script. *L'Armée des ombres* – script held at the Bibliothèque du film (BIFI), Paris. Ref: SCEN0169 B49.
42. Centre National de la Cinématographie, Censorship Commission file on *Le Cercle rouge*.
43. Nogueira, *Melville on Melville*, pp. 152–3.

Bibliography

References are primarily in French and in English, although a few references in Italian are indicated.

PUBLISHED SOURCE NOVELS

Beck, Béatrix, *Léon Morin, prêtre* (Paris: Éditions Gallimard, 1952).
Cocteau, Jean, *Les Enfants terribles* (Paris: Éditions Grasset, 1929).
Giovanni, José, *Le Deuxième souffle* (Paris: Éditions Gallimard, 1958).
Kessel, Joseph, *L'Armée des ombres* (Alger: Éditions Edmond Charlot, 1943).
Lesou, Pierre V., *Le Doulos* (Paris: Éditions Gallimard, 1957).
Simenon, Georges, *L'Aîné des Ferchaux* (Paris: Éditions Gallimard, 1945).
Vercors, *Le Silence de la mer* (Paris: Les Éditions de Minuit, 1942).

PUBLISHED SCRIPTS

Léon Morin, prêtre, *L'Avant-scène du cinéma*, no. 10, December 1961.
Le Doulos, *L'Avant-scène du cinéma*, no. 24, March 1963.

UNPUBLISHED SCRIPTS HELD AT THE BIBLIOTHÈQUE DU FILM (BIFI), PARIS – IN CHRONOLOGICAL ORDER

Le Silence de la mer – CJ1360 B176
Les Enfants terribles – PINOTEAU07 B3
Quand tu liras cette lettre – SCEN2251 B676
Un flic (1956) [unrealised] – SCEN2733 B835
Bob le flambeur – SCEN0340 B98
Deux hommes dans Manhattan – SCEN0827 B250
Le Doulos – SCEN0886 B269
Léon Morin, prêtre – SCEN1526 B450
L'Aîné des Ferchaux – SCEN0065 B19
Le Deuxième souffle – SCEN0836 B253
L'Armée des ombres – SCEN0169 B49
Le Samouraï – SCEN2417 B731
Le Cercle rouge – SCEN0501 B148
Un flic (1972) – SCEN2733 B835

BOOKS ON MELVILLE

Bantcheva, Denitza, *Jean-Pierre Melville: de l'oeuvre à l'homme* (Troyes: Librairie Bleue, 1996).

Barat, François, *L'Entretien avec Jean-Pierre Melville* (Paris: Seguier, 1999).
Gaeta, Pino, *Jean-Pierre Melville* (Rome: Il Castoro Cinema, 1996).
Nogueira, Rui (ed.), *Melville on Melville* (London: Secker and Warburg and BFI, 1971).
French editions: Rui Nogueira, *Le Cinéma selon Melville* (Paris: Seghers, 1973), reprinted as *Le Cinéma selon Jean-Pierre Melville: entretiens avec Rui Nogueira* (Paris: Cahiers du cinéma, 1996), with postface by Philippe Labro.
Vialle, Gabriel, 'Jean-Pierre Melville 1917–1973', *Anthologie du cinéma* (Paris: L'Avant-scène du cinéma, 1974).
Wagner, Jean, *Jean-Pierre Melville* (Paris: Seghers, 1963).
Zimmer, Jacques, and de Béchade, Chantal, *Jean-Pierre Melville* (Paris: Edilig, 1983).

CHAPTERS IN BOOKS

Armes, Roy, 'Jean-Pierre Melville', in Peter Cowie (ed.), *International Film Guide* (London: Tantivy Press, 1971).
—, 'Jean-Pierre Melville: Appearance and Identity', in *The Ambiguous Image, Narrative Style in Modern European Cinema* (London: Secker and Warburg, 1976).
Leguèbe, Eric, 'Jean-Pierre Melville', in *Confessions, Un siècle de cinéma français par ceux qui l'ont fait* (Paris: Ifrane Editions, 1995).
McArthur, Colin, 'Jean-Pierre Melville', in *Underworld USA* (London: Secker and Warburg, 1972).
Milne, Tom, 'Jean-Pierre Melville', in Richard Roud (ed.), *Cinema, A Critical Dictionary* (London: Secker and Warburg, 1980).
Renaud, Tristan, 'Jean-Pierre Melville', in Jean-Louis Bory and Claude-Michel Cluny, *Dossiers du cinéma: cinéastes I* (Paris: Casterman, 1971).
Siclier, Jacques, 'Jean-Pierre Melville', in *Nouvelle Vague?* (Paris: Éditions du Cerf, 1961).

ARTICLES (IN CHRONOLOGICAL ORDER)

Main articles on Melville (and occasionally by Melville), as well as articles on specific films when they make references to Melville's work in general (film titles are indicated in brackets when not explicit in the heading). All other reviews or articles on single films are referenced in the chapter endnotes.

1949

Melville, Jean-Pierre, 'Il n'y a plus à chercher, il faut oser', *L'Écran français*, no. 201, 3 May 1949, p. 3.

1957

Bitsch, Charles, Chabrol, Claude, Doniol-Valcroze, Jacques, de Givray, Claude, Godard, Jean-Luc, Lachenay, Robert, Marcorelles, Louis and Moullet, Luc, 'Soixante metteurs-en-scène français', *Cahiers du cinéma*, no. 71, May 1957, p. 60.

1959

Beylie, Claude, 'Melville le flambeur', *Cinéma 59*, no. 40, October 1959, pp. 77–80.

Domarchi, Jean, 'Plaisir à Melville', *Cahiers du cinéma*, no. 102, December 1959, pp. 8–16.

1960

Ledieu, Christian, 'Étude 6: Jean-Pierre Melville', *Études Cinématographiques*, no. 6–7, Winter 1960, pp. 438–46.

'Jean-Pierre Melville, inventeur de la nouvelle vague: entretien avec Bertrand Tavernier', *Cinéma 60*, no. 46, May 1960, pp. 23–6.

Melville, Jean Pierre, 'Le plus grand film français' [*Le Trou*], *Cahiers du cinéma*, no. 107, May 1960, pp. 7–12.

1961

Beylie, Claude, and Tavernier, Bertrand, 'Entretien avec Jean-Pierre Melville', *Cahiers du cinéma*, no. 124, October 1961, pp. 1–22.

—, 'Le point de vue du réalisateur' [*Léon Morin, prêtre*], *Télérama*, no. 612, 8 October 1961, pp. 29–30.

Collet, Jean, 'Une cathédrale tout en verre', *Télérama*, no. 612, 8 October 1961, pp. 4–5.

Anon., 'Belmondo and Melville' [*Léon Morin, prêtre*], *Film* (BFFS), no. 30, Winter 1961, p. 2.

Sautet, Claude, 'L'envers d'un coup de poing' [*Léon Morin, prêtre*], *L'Avant-scène du cinéma*, no. 10, December 1961, p. 7.

1962

Collet, Jean, 'Entretien avec Jean-Pierre Melville', *Télérama*, no. 670, 18 November 1962, pp. 57–8.

Melville, Jean-Pierre, 'La nouvelle Vague? Je l'ai inventée en 1937', *Arts*, no. 866, 25 April 1962.

Melville, Jean-Pierre, 'Finding the Truth Without Faith', *Films and Filming*, vol. 8, March 1962, p. 9.

Culier, Dan A., and Lobet, Marc, 'Plan fixe sur Jean-Pierre Melville', *Script*, no. 3, February 1962, pp. 2–16.

Anon., 'Cent soixante-deux nouveaux cinéastes français', *Cahiers du cinéma*, no. 138, December 1962, pp. 60–84.

G. L., 'Melville, Jean-Pierre', *Positif*, no. 46, June 1962, pp. 31–2.

1963

Beylie, Claude, 'Pour saluer Jean-Pierre Melville', *Cinématexte*, no. 7, January 1963, p. 2.

Porcile, François, 'Jean-Pierre Melville ou l'amour du cinéma', *Cinématexte*, no. 7, January 1963, pp. 3–8.

Melville, Jean-Pierre (montage of interviews by Bertrand Tavernier, Claude Beylie, Michel Dancourt and Jean Collet), 'Propos de Jean-Pierre Melville', *Cinématexte*, no. 7, January 1963, pp. 9–13.

Melville, Jean-Pierre, 'Le cinémois de Jean-Pierre Melville', *Cinéma 63*, no. 75, April 1963, pp. 4–11.

1964

Melville, Jean-Pierre, 'Le Trou', *Cinéma 64*, no. 88, July–August 1964, pp. 61–2.

Breitbart, Eric, 'An Interview with Jean-Pierre Melville', *Film Culture*, no. 35, Winter 1964–5, pp. 15–19.

1965

Milne, Tom, review of Jean Wagner's book on Melville, *Cinema Studies*, vol. 2, no. 1, June 1965, p. 14.

Melville, Jean-Pierre, 'Qui? Pourquoi? Comment?' Jean-Pierre Melville answers 'Sept questions aux cinéastes', *Cahiers du cinéma*, no. 161–2, January 1965, pp. 14 and 49.

1966

Melville, Jean-Pierre, 'Le cas Truffaut', *Arts Loisirs*, no. 64, 14–20 December 1966, pp. 46–7.

1967

Trémois, Claude-Marie, Interview with Jean-Pierre Melville, *Télérama*, 12 November 1967.

Pennec, Claude, 'Le réalisateur', *Art et Essai*, no. 34, 16 November 1967, p. 29.

1968

Nogueira, Rui, and Truchaud, François, 'A Samuraï in Paris', *Sight and Sound*, vol. 37, no. 3, Summer 1968, pp. 119–23.

Bureau, Patrick, 'Chroniques Melvilliennes – I', *Cinéma 68*, no. 128, August–September 1968, pp. 32–43.

—, 'Chroniques Melvilliennes – II', *Cinéma 68*, no. 129, October 1968, pp. 74–91.

1969

Beylie, Claude, 'L'Armée des ombres: haute fidélité', *Cinéma 69*, no. 140, November 1969, pp. 123–6.

1970

Milne, Tom, *Focus on Film* [*Le Samouraï*], no. 4, September–October 1970, p. 6.

1971

Melville, Jean-Pierre, 'C'est le plus grand film de l'année (a propos de *Catch 22*)', *Nouveau Cinémonde*, no. 1850, March 1971, pp. 26–8.

Chitarin, Attilio, 'Il cerchio et le ombre', *Cinema Sessanta*, no. 81–2, January–April 1971, pp. 34–42.

Nogueira, Rui, 'Jean-Pierre Melville talks to Rui Nogueira about *Le Chagrin et la pitié*', *Sight and Sound*, vol. 40, no. 4, Autumn 1971, pp. 181–2, 207.

1973

Doniol-Valcroze, Jacques, 'La marque Melville', *L'Express*, 13 August 1973.

Renaud, Tristan, 'Il fut quand même Melville', *Cinéma 72*, no. 180, September–October 1973, pp. 14–15.

Beylie, Claude, 'Quand tu liras cette lettre . . .', *Écran*, no. 18, September–October 1973, pp. 18–19.

Angelot, Daniel, 'Mort d'un cinéaste: J-P Melville', *Cinématographe*, no. 4, October 1973, p. 44.

1974

Favra, Claudio G., 'Jean-Pierre Melville o il gusto magico dell'avventura', *Rivista del Cinematografo*, no. 5, May 1974, pp. 19–26.

1978

Guérif, François, 'Jean-Pierre Melville', *Les Cahiers de la cinémathèque*, no. 25, Spring–Summer 1978, pp. 94–7 [NB: part of dossier on French crime film].

Petit, Chris, 'Withdrawal Symptoms', *Time Out*, no. 418, 7 April 1978, p. 13.

1980

Fieschi, Jacques, 'Un héros de la forme', *Cinématographe*, no. 63, December 1980, pp. 40–2.

1983

Thompson, David, 'Out of the Shadows', *City Limits*, no. 75, 11 March 1983, pp. 10–12.

Schloendorff, Volker, 'Hommage to a Master', *Time Out*, no. 654, 4 March 1983, pp. 27–8.

Peachment, Chris, 'Jean-Pierre Melville in Context', National Film Theatre, March 1983, pp. 2–8.

1985

Ciment, Michel, 'Entretien avec Serge Silberman', *Positif*, no. 296, October 1985, pp. 53–9.

1987

Beylie, Claude, 'Jean-Pierre Melville, lucidité et classicisme', *Cinéma*, no. 416, 18 November 1987, pp. 13–14.

1989

Anon., 'Jean-Pierre Melville', *Film Dope*, no. 42, October 1989, pp. 15–16.

1990

'Jean-Pierre Melville, un artisan du cinéma', *Ciné-Revue*, no. 15, 12 April 1990, pp. 32–3.

1992

Nevers, Camille, 'Rencontre avec Quentin Tarantino', *Cahiers du cinéma*, no. 457, June 1992, p. 49.

1993

Hoberman, J., 'Father and Sons', *Premiere* [US], September 1993, pp. 43–4.

1994

Magny, Joel, 'Melville ou l'imitation du cinéma', *Cahiers du cinéma*, no. 478, April 1994, p. 8.

B, J.-P., 'Florence', *Le Film Français*, no. 2526, 30 September 1994, pp. 23–4.

1995

Royer, Philippe, 'Le petit théâtre de Jean-Pierre Melville, sur *Le Doulos*, *Le Deuxième souffle* et *Le Samouraï*', *Positif*, no. 418, December 1995, pp. 100–3 [NB: part of dossier 'Le film criminel français (2)'].

Thoret, Jean-Baptiste, 'The Killer', *L'Écran fantastique*, no. 142, May–June 1995, pp. 48–52.

1996

Hogue, Peter, 'Melville, the Elective Affinities', *Film Comment*, vol. 32, no. 6, November–December 1996, pp. 17–22.

Cahiers du cinéma, no. 507, November 1996 – includes:

Jousse, Thierry, and Toubiana, Serge, 'Le Deuxième souffle de Melville', pp. 62–3.

Burdeau, Emmanuel, 'Le revolver et la culture', pp. 64–7.

Frodon, Jean-Marie, '*L'Armée des ombres*, le monument piégé d'un résistant', pp. 69–71.

Rauger, Jean-François, 'L'attente hypnotique', pp. 72–3.

Chabrol, Claude, 'L'homme au Stetson', pp. 74–5.

Grasset, Pierre, 'Melville par Pierre Grasset', pp. 76–7.

Saada, Nicolas, 'Melville et ses disciples', pp. 78–9.

Woo, John, 'Le style Melville, propos de John Woo', pp. 80–1.

Busca, Jean-Pierre, 'Jean-Pierre Melville, 'Portrait en 9 poses', *Le Film Français*, no. 2617, 21 June 1996, p. 32.

Rehm, Jean-Pierre, 'Douleur du *Doulos*', *Trafic*, no. 20, Autumn–Winter 1996, pp. 66–73.

Tiberghien, Gilles A., 'Melville: le dernier cercle', *Trafic*, no. 20, Autumn–Winter 1996, pp. 58–65.

Rauger, Jean-François, 'Jean-Pierre Melville, ancêtres et héritiers', *Cinémathèque Française*, November–December 1996, pp. 26–33.

1997

'Interview with Philippe Labro', *Télérama*, no. 2474, 11 June 1997, p. 124.

Millet, Raphaël, 'Les statues meurent aussi, fantômes melvilliens', *Cinémathèque*, no. 12, Autumn 1997, pp. 78–87.

Aubron, Hervé, 'Résistance à l'histoire: à propos de *L'Armée des ombres*', *Vertigo*, no. 16, 1997, pp. 147–51.

2000

Orr, John, 'Jean-Pierre Melville', *Film West*, no. 41, Autumn 2000, pp. 44–5.

Melville, Jean-Pierre, 'A propos du *Chagrin et de la pitié*', *Positif*, no. 481, March 2000, pp. 57–60. Translation of interview with Rui Nogueira published in *Sight and Sound*, vol. 40, no. 4, Autumn 1971, pp. 181–2 and 207.

2001

Crèvecoeur, Dominique, 'Entretien avec Dominique Crèvecoeur', in Françoise Puaux (ed.), 'Le machisme à l'écran', *CinémAction*, no. 99, *2e trimestre* 2001, pp. 153–7.

Appendix 1: Melville's Films at the French Box Office (Admissions)

Release Date	Title	Admissions (All France)	Admissions (Paris only)	Total Annual Admissions (Millions)
1946	*24 heures de la vie d'un clown* (short)	[figures not available]		
22 April 1949	*Le Silence de la mer*	1,371,687	464,032	400.0
29 March 1950	*Les Enfants terribles*	719,844	255,224	370.7
11 November 1953	*Quand tu liras cette lettre*	1,160,986	255,746	370.6
24 August 1956	*Bob le flambeur*	716,920	221,659	398.9
16 October 1959	*Deux hommes dans Manhattan*	308,524	96,490	353.7
22 September 1961	*Léon Morin, prêtre*	1,702,860	328,651	328.4
8 February 1963	*Le Doulos*	1,475,391	485,186	292.1
2 October 1963	*L'Ainé des Ferchaux*	1,484,948	337,934	292.1
2 November 1966	*Le Deuxième souffle*	1,912,749	647,857	234.7
25 October 1967	*Le Samouraï*	1,932,372	508,017	211.4
12 September 1969	*L'Armée des ombres*	1,401,822	338,535	182.1
21 October 1970	*Le Cercle rouge*	4,339,821	911,338	184.4
25 October 1972	*Un flic*	2,832,912	677,411	177.0

Source: Individual box-office statistics available in *Ciné-Passions, 7e art et Industrie de 1945 à 2000* (Éditions Dixit/CNC, 2000). Yearly total of tickets sold is indicated for comparative purposes, given the substantial decline in overall audience within the span of Melville's career.

Appendix 2: Melville's Films as Actor

1948
Les Drames du Bois de Boulogne (short; director: Jacques Loew)

1949
Orphée (director: Jean Cocteau)

1951
Quatre sans millions! [alternative titles: *Cri du coeur*; *Si ça vous chante*; director: Jacques Loew)

1957
Un amour de poche (director: Pierre Kast)
Mimi Pinson (director: Robert Darène)

1959
Deux hommes dans Manhattan (director: Jean-Pierre Melville)

1960
À bout de souffle (director: Jean-Luc Godard)

1962
Landru (director: Claude Chabrol)

Appendix 3: Melville's Pantheon of Sixty-four Pre-war American Directors

1. Lloyd BACON
2. Busby BERKELEY
3. Richard BOLESLAVSKI
4. Frank BORZAGE
5. Clarence BROWN
6. Harold S. BUCQUET
7. Frank CAPRA
8. Jack CONWAY
9. Merian C. COOPER
10. John CROMWELL
11. James CRUZE
12. George CUKOR
13. Michael CURTIZ
14. Cecil B. DEMILLE
15. William DIETERLE
16. Allan DWAN
17. Ray ENRIGHT
18. George FITZMAURICE
19. Robert FLAHERTY
20. Victor FLEMING
21. John FORD
22. Sidney FRANKLIN
23. Tay GARNETT
24. Edmund GOULDING
25. Alfred GREEN
26. Edward GRIFFITH
27. Henry HATHAWAY
28. Howard HAWKS
29. Ben HECHT
30. Garson KANIN
31. William KEIGHLEY
32. Henry KING
33. Henry KOSTER
34. Gregory LA CAVA

35. Sidney LANFIELD
36. Fritz LANG
37. Mitchell LEISEN
38. Robert Z. LEONARD
39. Mervyn LE ROY
40. Frank LLOYD
41. Ernst LUBITSCH
42. Rouben MAMOULIAN
43. Archie MAYO
44. Leo McCAREY
45. Norman Z. McLEOD
46. Lewis MILESTONE
47. Elliot NUGENT
48. Henry C. POTTER
49. Gregory RATOFF
50. Roy DEL RUTH
51. Mark SANDRICH
52. Alfred SANTELL
53. Ernest SCHOEDSACK
54. John M. STAHL
55. Josef von STERNBERG
56. George STEVENS
57. Norman TAUROG
58. Richard THORPE
59. W. S. VAN DYKE
60. King VIDOR
61. William WELLMAN
62. James WHALE
63. Sam WOOD
64. William WYLER

Source: *Cahiers du cinéma*, no. 124, October 1961, p. 63.

NB: This list, for some reason entitled 'Jean-Pierre Melville's 63' in its first appearance in *Cahiers du cinéma*, has been since referred to as such, including by Melville. However, there were sixty-four names in it, as above.

Index

Films indexed by title are by JPM unless otherwise stated
Page numbers in *italic* indicate illustrations; those in **bold** indicate detailed analysis
The Filmography is indexed only for background information in the notes, not (for reasons of space) for cast/crew credits
n = endnote